MW00838154

50% OFF Online PCCN Prep Co

Dear Customer,

We consider it an honor and a privilege that you chose our PCCN Study Guide. As a way of showing our appreciation and to help us better serve you, we have partnered with Mometrix Test Preparation to offer you **50% off their online PCCN Prep Course.** Many PCCN courses are needlessly expensive and don't deliver enough value. With their course, you get access to the best PCCN prep material, and **you only pay half price**.

Mometrix has structured their online course to perfectly complement your printed study guide. The PCCN Prep Course contains **in-depth lessons** that cover all the most important topics, **90+ video reviews** that explain difficult concepts, over **500 practice questions** to ensure you feel prepared, and more than **900 digital flashcards**, so you can study while you're on the go.

Online PCCN Prep Course

Topics Covered:

- Clinical Judgement
  - Cardiovascular
  - Pulmonary
  - Endocrine
  - Hematology/Immunology/Oncology
  - Neurological
  - Gastrointestinal
  - Renal
  - Musculoskeletal
  - And more
- Professional Caring and Ethical Practice
  - Systems Thinking
  - Ethics
  - Patient Rights
  - Therapeutic Relationships
  - Grief and Loss
  - Principles of Education
  - And more

Course Features:

- PCCN Study Guide
  - Get content that complements our best-selling study guide.
- 4 Full-Length Practice Tests
  - With over 500 practice questions, you can test yourself again and again.
- Mobile Friendly
  - If you need to study on the go, the course is easily accessible from your mobile device.
- PCCN Flashcards
  - Their course includes a flashcard mode consisting of over 900 content cards to help you study.

To receive this discount, visit their website: mometrix.com/university/pccn/ or simply scan this QR code with your smartphone. At the checkout page, enter the discount code: **TPBPCCN50**

If you have any questions or concerns, please don't hesitate to contact Mometrix at support@mometrix.com.

SCAN HERE

FREE Test Taking Tips Video/DVD Offer

To better serve you, we created videos covering test taking tips that we want to give you for FREE. **These videos cover world-class tips that will help you succeed on your test.**

We just ask that you send us feedback about this product. Please let us know what you thought about it—whether good, bad, or indifferent.

To get your **FREE videos**, you can use the QR code below or email freevideos@studyguideteam.com with "Free Videos" in the subject line and the following information in the body of the email:

a. The title of your product

b. Your product rating on a scale of 1-5, with 5 being the highest

c. Your feedback about the product

If you have any questions or concerns, please don't hesitate to contact us at info@studyguideteam.com.

Thank you!

SCAN HERE

PCCN Study Guide

3 Practice Tests and Exam Prep Review Book for the Progressive Care Nursing Certification (400+ Questions)
[2nd Edition]

Joshua Rueda

Written and edited by TPB Publishing.

ISBN 13: 9781637753200
ISBN 10: 1637753209

Table of Contents

Welcome

Dear Reader,

Welcome to your new Test Prep Books study guide! We are pleased that you chose us to help you prepare for your exam. There are many study options to choose from, and we appreciate you choosing us. Studying can be a daunting task, but we have designed a smart, effective study guide to help prepare you for what lies ahead.

Whether you're a parent helping your child learn and grow, a high school student working hard to get into your dream college, or a nursing student studying for a complex exam, we want to help give you the tools you need to succeed. We hope this study guide gives you the skills and the confidence to thrive, and we can't thank you enough for allowing us to be part of your journey.

In an effort to continue to improve our products, we welcome feedback from our customers. We look forward to hearing from you. Suggestions, success stories, and criticisms can all be communicated by emailing us at info@studyguideteam.com.

Sincerely,
Test Prep Books Team

FREE Videos/DVD OFFER

Doing well on your exam requires both knowing the test content and understanding how to use that knowledge to do well on the test. We offer completely FREE test taking tip videos. **These videos cover world-class tips that you can use to succeed on your test.**

To get your **FREE videos**, you can use the QR code below or email freevideos@studyguideteam.com with "Free Videos" in the subject line and the following information in the body of the email:

a. The title of your product
b. Your product rating on a scale of 1-5, with 5 being the highest
c. Your feedback about the product

If you have any questions or concerns, please don't hesitate to contact us at info@studyguideteam.com.

SCAN HERE

Quick Overview

As you draw closer to taking your exam, effective preparation becomes more and more important. Thankfully, you have this study guide to help you get ready. Use this guide to help keep your studying on track and refer to it often.

This study guide contains several key sections that will help you be successful on your exam. The guide contains tips for what you should do the night before and the day of the test. Also included are test-taking tips. Knowing the right information is not always enough. Many well-prepared test takers struggle with exams. These tips will help equip you to accurately read, assess, and answer test questions.

A large part of the guide is devoted to showing you what content to expect on the exam and to helping you better understand that content. In this guide are practice test questions so that you can see how well you have grasped the content. Then, answer explanations are provided so that you can understand why you missed certain questions.

Don't try to cram the night before you take your exam. This is not a wise strategy for a few reasons. First, your retention of the information will be low. Your time would be better used by reviewing information you already know rather than trying to learn a lot of new information. Second, you will likely become stressed as you try to gain a large amount of knowledge in a short amount of time. Third, you will be depriving yourself of sleep. So be sure to go to bed at a reasonable time the night before. Being well-rested helps you focus and remain calm.

Be sure to eat a substantial breakfast the morning of the exam. If you are taking the exam in the afternoon, be sure to have a good lunch as well. Being hungry is distracting and can make it difficult to focus. You have hopefully spent lots of time preparing for the exam. Don't let an empty stomach get in the way of success!

When travelling to the testing center, leave earlier than needed. That way, you have a buffer in case you experience any delays. This will help you remain calm and will keep you from missing your appointment time at the testing center.

Be sure to pace yourself during the exam. Don't try to rush through the exam. There is no need to risk performing poorly on the exam just so you can leave the testing center early. Allow yourself to use all of the allotted time if needed.

Remain positive while taking the exam even if you feel like you are performing poorly. Thinking about the content you should have mastered will not help you perform better on the exam.

Once the exam is complete, take some time to relax. Even if you feel that you need to take the exam again, you will be well served by some down time before you begin studying again. It's often easier to convince yourself to study if you know that it will come with a reward!

Test-Taking Strategies

1. Predicting the Answer

When you feel confident in your preparation for a multiple-choice test, try predicting the answer before reading the answer choices. This is especially useful on questions that test objective factual knowledge. By predicting the answer before reading the available choices, you eliminate the possibility that you will be distracted or led astray by an incorrect answer choice. You will feel more confident in your selection if you read the question, predict the answer, and then find your prediction among the answer choices. After using this strategy, be sure to still read all of the answer choices carefully and completely. If you feel unprepared, you should not attempt to predict the answers. This would be a waste of time and an opportunity for your mind to wander in the wrong direction.

2. Reading the Whole Question

Too often, test takers scan a multiple-choice question, recognize a few familiar words, and immediately jump to the answer choices. Test authors are aware of this common impatience, and they will sometimes prey upon it. For instance, a test author might subtly turn the question into a negative, or he or she might redirect the focus of the question right at the end. The only way to avoid falling into these traps is to read the entirety of the question carefully before reading the answer choices.

3. Looking for Wrong Answers

Long and complicated multiple-choice questions can be intimidating. One way to simplify a difficult multiple-choice question is to eliminate all of the answer choices that are clearly wrong. In most sets of answers, there will be at least one selection that can be dismissed right away. If the test is administered on paper, the test taker could draw a line through it to indicate that it may be ignored; otherwise, the test taker will have to perform this operation mentally or on scratch paper. In either case, once the obviously incorrect answers have been eliminated, the remaining choices may be considered. Sometimes identifying the clearly wrong answers will give the test taker some information about the correct answer. For instance, if one of the remaining answer choices is a direct opposite of one of the eliminated answer choices, it may well be the correct answer. The opposite of obviously wrong is obviously right! Of course, this is not always the case. Some answers are obviously incorrect simply because they are irrelevant to the question being asked. Still, identifying and eliminating some incorrect answer choices is a good way to simplify a multiple-choice question.

4. Don't Overanalyze

Anxious test takers often overanalyze questions. When you are nervous, your brain will often run wild, causing you to make associations and discover clues that don't actually exist. If you feel that this may be a problem for you, do whatever you can to slow down during the test. Try taking a deep breath or counting to ten. As you read and consider the question, restrict yourself to the particular words used by the author. Avoid thought tangents about what the author *really* meant, or what he or she was *trying* to say. The only things that matter on a multiple-choice test are the words that are actually in the question. You must avoid reading too much into a multiple-choice question, or supposing that the writer meant something other than what he or she wrote.

5. No Need for Panic

It is wise to learn as many strategies as possible before taking a multiple-choice test, but it is likely that you will come across a few questions for which you simply don't know the answer. In this situation, avoid panicking. Because most multiple-choice tests include dozens of questions, the relative value of a single wrong answer is small. As much as possible, you should compartmentalize each question on a multiple-choice test. In other words, you should not allow your feelings about one question to affect your success on the others. When you find a question that you either don't understand or don't know how to answer, just take a deep breath and do your best. Read the entire question slowly and carefully. Try rephrasing the question a couple of different ways. Then, read all of the answer choices carefully. After eliminating obviously wrong answers, make a selection and move on to the next question.

6. Confusing Answer Choices

When working on a difficult multiple-choice question, there may be a tendency to focus on the answer choices that are the easiest to understand. Many people, whether consciously or not, gravitate to the answer choices that require the least concentration, knowledge, and memory. This is a mistake. When you come across an answer choice that is confusing, you should give it extra attention. A question might be confusing because you do not know the subject matter to which it refers. If this is the case, don't eliminate the answer before you have affirmatively settled on another. When you come across an answer choice of this type, set it aside as you look at the remaining choices. If you can confidently assert that one of the other choices is correct, you can leave the confusing answer aside. Otherwise, you will need to take a moment to try to better understand the confusing answer choice. Rephrasing is one way to tease out the sense of a confusing answer choice.

7. Your First Instinct

Many people struggle with multiple-choice tests because they overthink the questions. If you have studied sufficiently for the test, you should be prepared to trust your first instinct once you have carefully and completely read the question and all of the answer choices. There is a great deal of research suggesting that the mind can come to the correct conclusion very quickly once it has obtained all of the relevant information. At times, it may seem to you as if your intuition is working faster even than your reasoning mind. This may in fact be true. The knowledge you obtain while studying may be retrieved from your subconscious before you have a chance to work out the associations that support it. Verify your instinct by working out the reasons that it should be trusted.

8. Key Words

Many test takers struggle with multiple-choice questions because they have poor reading comprehension skills. Quickly reading and understanding a multiple-choice question requires a mixture of skill and experience. To help with this, try jotting down a few key words and phrases on a piece of scrap paper. Doing this concentrates the process of reading and forces the mind to weigh the relative importance of the question's parts. In selecting words and phrases to write down, the test taker thinks about the question more deeply and carefully. This is especially true for multiple-choice questions that are preceded by a long prompt.

9. Subtle Negatives

One of the oldest tricks in the multiple-choice test writer's book is to subtly reverse the meaning of a question with a word like *not* or *except*. If you are not paying attention to each word in the question, you can easily be led astray by this trick. For instance, a common question format is, "Which of the following is...?" Obviously, if the question instead is, "Which of the following is not...?," then the answer will be quite different. Even worse, the test makers are aware of the potential for this mistake and will include one answer choice that would be correct if the question were not negated or reversed. A test taker who misses the reversal will find what he or she believes to be a correct answer and will be so confident that he or she will fail to reread the question and discover the original error. The only way to avoid this is to practice a wide variety of multiple-choice questions and to pay close attention to each and every word.

10. Reading Every Answer Choice

It may seem obvious, but you should always read every one of the answer choices! Too many test takers fall into the habit of scanning the question and assuming that they understand the question because they recognize a few key words. From there, they pick the first answer choice that answers the question they believe they have read. Test takers who read all of the answer choices might discover that one of the latter answer choices is actually *more* correct. Moreover, reading all of the answer choices can remind you of facts related to the question that can help you arrive at the correct answer. Sometimes, a misstatement or incorrect detail in one of the latter answer choices will trigger your memory of the subject and will enable you to find the right answer. Failing to read all of the answer choices is like not reading all of the items on a restaurant menu: you might miss out on the perfect choice.

11. Spot the Hedges

One of the keys to success on multiple-choice tests is paying close attention to every word. This is never truer than with words like almost, most, some, and sometimes. These words are called "hedges" because they indicate that a statement is not totally true or not true in every place and time. An absolute statement will contain no hedges, but in many subjects, the answers are not always straightforward or absolute. There are always exceptions to the rules in these subjects. For this reason, you should favor those multiple-choice questions that contain hedging language. The presence of qualifying words indicates that the author is taking special care with their words, which is certainly important when composing the right answer. After all, there are many ways to be wrong, but there is only one way to be right! For this reason, it is wise to avoid answers that are absolute when taking a multiple-choice test. An absolute answer is one that says things are either all one way or all another. They often include words like *every*, *always*, *best*, and *never*. If you are taking a multiple-choice test in a subject that doesn't lend itself to absolute answers, be on your guard if you see any of these words.

12. Long Answers

In many subject areas, the answers are not simple. As already mentioned, the right answer often requires hedges. Another common feature of the answers to a complex or subjective question are qualifying clauses, which are groups of words that subtly modify the meaning of the sentence. If the question or answer choice describes a rule to which there are exceptions or the subject matter is complicated, ambiguous, or confusing, the correct answer will require many words in order to be expressed clearly and accurately. In essence, you should not be deterred by answer choices that seem excessively long. Oftentimes, the author of the text will not be able to write the correct answer without offering some qualifications and modifications. Your job is to read the answer choices thoroughly and completely and to select the one that most accurately and precisely answers the question.

13. Restating to Understand

Sometimes, a question on a multiple-choice test is difficult not because of what it asks but because of how it is written. If this is the case, restate the question or answer choice in different words. This process serves a couple of important purposes. First, it forces you to concentrate on the core of the question. In order to rephrase the question accurately, you have to understand it well. Rephrasing the question will concentrate your mind on the key words and ideas. Second, it will present the information to your mind in a fresh way. This process may trigger your memory and render some useful scrap of information picked up while studying.

14. True Statements

Sometimes an answer choice will be true in itself, but it does not answer the question. This is one of the main reasons why it is essential to read the question carefully and completely before proceeding to the answer choices. Too often, test takers skip ahead to the answer choices and look for true statements. Having found one of these, they are content to select it without reference to the question above. Obviously, this provides an easy way for test makers to play tricks. The savvy test taker will always read the entire question before turning to the answer choices. Then, having settled on a correct answer choice, he or she will refer to the original question and ensure that the selected answer is relevant. The mistake of choosing a correct-but-irrelevant answer choice is especially common on questions related to specific pieces of objective knowledge. A prepared test taker will have a wealth of factual knowledge at their disposal, and should not be careless in its application.

15. No Patterns

One of the more dangerous ideas that circulates about multiple-choice tests is that the correct answers tend to fall into patterns. These erroneous ideas range from a belief that B and C are the most common right answers, to the idea that an unprepared test-taker should answer "A-B-A-C-A-D-A-B-A." It cannot be emphasized enough that pattern-seeking of this type is exactly the WRONG way to approach a multiple-choice test. To begin with, it is highly unlikely that the test maker will plot the correct answers according to some predetermined pattern. The questions are scrambled and delivered in a random order. Furthermore, even if the test maker was following a pattern in the assignation of correct answers, there is no reason why the test taker would know which pattern he or she was using. Any attempt to discern a pattern in the answer choices is a waste of time and a distraction from the real work of taking the test. A test taker would be much better served by extra preparation before the test than by reliance on a pattern in the answers.

Bonus Content

We host multiple bonus items online, including all 3 practice tests in digital format. Scan the QR code or go to this link to access this content:

testprepbooks.com/bonus/pccn

SCAN ME

The first time you access the tests, you will need to register as a "new user" and verify your email address.

If you have any issues, please email support@testprepbooks.com.

Introduction to the PCCN Exam

Function of the Exam

The Progressive Care Certified Nurse (PCCN®) exam is required to obtain the PCCN® specialty certification, which is one of several specialty certifications offered to nurses by the AACN Certification Corporation. The PCCN® certification is designed for progressive care nurses who provide nursing care for adult patients who are acutely ill. Although most of the patients progressive care nurses will provide care for are moderately stable, the patients are at an elevated risk of becoming unstable. Accordingly, progressive care nurses, who typically work in progressive care units, need to deliver high-intensity, specialized care to their patients with a high degree of vigilance. Care may be focused on a specific system, such as renal, cardiac, or pulmonary, or it may be more generalized, geared toward multisystem, systemic issues.

Progressive care nurses who are seeking PCCN® certification typically work in progressive care settings and may be involved in immediate and emergency care, step-down care, direct observation, telemetry, and transitional care units.

The PCCN® exam is designed based on a job analysis, which examines the practice and skills of registered nurses (RNs) or advanced practice registered nurses (APRNs) who provide direct care to adult patients who are acutely ill. This process occurs at least every five years and helps determine and validate the abilities, skills, and knowledge needed to work with this patient population. An expert PCCN® panel then works to ensure the exam is designed to reflect the findings of the job analysis and clinical practice.

Exam candidates must have a current, unencumbered RN or APRN license. Additionally, one of the following two clinical practice requirements must be met prior to sitting for the exam:

- At least 1,750 hours providing direct care to acutely ill adult patients over the previous two years as an RN or APRN, with at least 875 of those hours obtained in the most recent year
- At least 2,000 hours providing direct care to acutely ill adult patients over the previous five years as an RN or APRN, with at least 144 of those hours obtained in the most recent year

It should be noted that orientation hours do not count towards minimum hour requirements unless the candidate was the assigned nurse who was providing direct care to adult patients with acute illnesses during those hours.

Test Administration

Candidates can register online or via a paper application for the exam. After receiving an approval-to-test email, they can schedule their exam administration. The exam is offered twice daily, Monday through Friday, and some Saturdays, at more than 300 PSI/AMP testing locations around the United States. The exam is offered in computer and paper-and-pencil format. Scores are provided immediately after submitting the computer-based version, and are received three to four weeks after sitting for the paper version. The exam may be retaken, but a fee will be incurred.

Test Format

The PCCN® exam contains 125 multiple-choice questions, of which, 100 are scored. The remaining 25, which are randomly scattered throughout the exam, are used to gauge their worth for inclusion in future versions. Test takers are given 150 minutes to complete the exam. Clinical Judgment comprises 80% of the questions while Professional Caring and Ethical Practice topics contribute 20% of the questions. The following table provides the domains of the exam and the breakdown of their percentage contributions to the total:

Domain	Percentage of Exam
Clinical Judgement	80%
Cardiovascular	33%
Pulmonary	14%
Endocrine/Hematology/Neurology/Gastrointestinal/Renal	18%
Musculoskeletal/Multisystem/Psychosocial	15%
Professional Caring and Ethical Practice	20%

Scoring

A panel of subject matter and exam experts establish the passing score of the PCCN®. The passing score is established via the modified Angoff, a criterion-referenced process for setting standards. Each test taker's PCCN® performance is compared to the predetermined standard to determine their passing status. The difficulty rating of each question also impacts the value of answering a question correctly. The passing score is said to be established to identify those candidates who possess an acceptable level of knowledge and skill in providing care to acutely ill adult patients. Candidates who successfully pass the exam receive a certificate denoting their specialty certification within three to four weeks after passing the test.

Study Prep Plan for the PCCN Exam

1 **Schedule** - Use one of our study schedules below or come up with one of your own.

2 **Relax** - Test anxiety can hurt even the best students. There are many ways to reduce stress. Find the one that works best for you.

3 **Execute** - Once you have a good plan in place, be sure to stick to it.

One Week Study Schedule

Day 1	Clinical Judgment
Day 2	Pulmonary
Day 3	Endocrine/Hematology/Neurology/ Gastrointestinal/Renal
Day 4	Musculoskeletal/Multisystem/Psychosocial
Day 5	Practice Test #1
Day 6	Practice Tests #2 & #3
Day 7	Take Your Exam!

Two Week Study Schedule

Day 1	Clinical Judgment	Day 8	Musculoskeletal/ Multisystem/Psychosocial
Day 2	Dysrhythmias	Day 9	Behavioral/Psychosocial
Day 3	Hypertensive Crisis	Day 10	Professional Caring and Ethical Practice
Day 4	Pulmonary	Day 11	Practice Test #1
Day 5	Respiratory Depression	Day 12	Practice Test #2
Day 6	Endocrine/Hematology/ Neurology/ Gastrointestinal/Renal	Day 13	Practice Test #3
Day 7	Gastrointestinal	Day 14	Take Your Exam!

One Month Study Schedule

Day 1	Clinical Judgment	Day 11	Respiratory Depression	Day 21	Response to Diversity
Day 2	Acute Inflammatory Disease	Day 12	Thoracic Surgery	Day 22	Facilitation of Learning
Day 3	Cardiac Surgery	Day 13	Endocrine/Hematology/ Neurology/ Gastrointestinal/Renal	Day 23	Collaboration
Day 4	Dysrhythmias	Day 14	Hematology/ Immunology/Oncology	Day 24	Practice Test #1
Day 5	Genetic Cardiac Disease	Day 15	Neurology	Day 25	Answer Explanations #1
Day 6	Hypertensive Crisis	Day 16	Gastrointestinal	Day 26	Practice Test #2
Day 7	Septal Defects	Day 17	Renal	Day 27	Answer Explanations #2
Day 8	Pulmonary	Day 18	Musculoskeletal/ Multisystem/ Psychosocial	Day 28	Practice Test #3
Day 9	COPD Exacerbation	Day 19	Behavioral/Psychosocial	Day 29	Answer Explanations #3
Day 10	Pulmonary Embolism	Day 20	Professional Caring and Ethical Practice	Day 30	Take Your Exam!

Build your own prep plan by visiting:
testprepbooks.com/prep

As you study for your test, we'd like to take the opportunity to remind you that you are capable of great things! With the right tools and dedication, you truly can do anything you set your mind to. The fact that you are holding this book right now shows how committed you are. In case no one has told you lately, you've got this! Our intention behind including this coloring page is to give you the chance to take some time to engage your creative side when you need a little brain-break from studying. As a company, we want to encourage people like you to achieve their dreams by providing good quality study materials for the tests and certifications that improve careers and change lives. As individuals, many of us have taken such tests in our careers, and we know how challenging this process can be. While we can't come alongside you and cheer you on personally, we can offer you the space to recall your purpose, reconnect with your passion, and refresh your brain through an artistic practice. We wish you every success, and happy studying!

Cardiovascular

Cardiovascular issues can be life threatening. Any condition that impedes circulation has the potential to damage the **myocardium**, or heart muscle. A damaged myocardium may be unable to meet the oxygen demands of the body. It is important to quickly identify any patient exhibiting symptoms indicative of such emergencies so that they can receive prompt treatment to prevent further cardiovascular injury or death. Every patient presenting with possible cardiovascular symptoms should immediately be given a focused assessment followed by a history and physical. Simultaneously, an intravenous (IV) line should be established and an electrocardiogram (ECG) and laboratory and radiographic studies should be performed. The triage, assessment, diagnostics, and treatment of such patients must be prioritized to preserve cardiac function and, ultimately, life.

Upon completion of a health history with regard to the cardiovascular system, the nurse should examine the patient for signs and symptoms of cardiovascular compromise, including chest pain, palpitations, paresthesia, cold extremities, and edema. In general, the nurse should note overall appearance, including skin color, posture, and gait to uncover potential issues, and examine skin tone to determine whether it is pink, pallor, red, or cyanotic, and assess nail beds and capillary refill. The nurse should examine the skin for the presence of hair, rashes, and lesions, and assess pain, including what exacerbates and diminishes it. If edema is noted, the nurse should use the assessment scale for pitting edema to note specifics, which ranges from 1+ for slight pitting to 4+ for very deep pits lasting 2-5 minutes.

The nurse should assess carotid pulses in the neck and neck range of motion. Using a pulse scale rated from 0—4+, with 0 meaning absent and 4+ meaning strong and bounding, the nurse should assess the following pulse points: temporal, apical, brachial, radial, ulnar, femoral, popliteal, posterior tibial, and dorsal pedis. The nurse should auscultate the **aortic area**, which is found at the second right intercostal space and right sternal border, the **pulmonic area**, which is found second to the left intercostal space and left sternal border, the **tricuspid area**, which is located at the fourth left intercostal space and the left sternal border, and finally, the **mitral area**, which spans the fifth left intercostal space and the midclavicular line.

The **electrocardiogram** (ECG) captures a graphic record of the depolarization and repolarization of the atria and ventricles to understand the direction and magnitude of the electrical activity and determine a diagnosis. Before engaging in ECG lead placement, there are some basic considerations for the nurse to understand. First, the nurse should count the intercostal spaces starting right below the clavicle and working down to the nipple, or just below the breast for patients with large breasts. Second, the nurse should ensure a clean working space; this means the skin should be prepped to be dry, hair-free, and oil free to ensure a strong read. Third, the nurse should obtain a baseline understanding of the patient's status, including vital signs and oxygenation, before obtaining an ECG reading. Once the patient is ready, the nurse should assist them to a supine or semi-Fowler's position with arms relaxed by their side if tolerated.

The nurse should ensure that the patient's shoulders are relaxed if possible and that their legs are uncrossed, while quietly resting in a still position. Additionally, the nurse should ensure that mobile devices are removed, as they can interfere with the reading by producing artifact. Placement of the electrodes is key to receiving an accurate read, so the nurse should take great care in applying fresh pads with moist gels over the sites ensuring to avoid bones and areas of greatest muscle movement.

The majority of patients with simple cardiac concerns are placed on **telemetry monitoring**, which involves five leads (1 precordial lead, along with 4 extremity leads: RL, RA, LL, LA). This intervention provides continuous information regarding the patient's cardiac rhythm by offering views of much of the electrical activity. However, the 5-lead system is inferior to the 12-lead system and the rarely used 15-lead system that both offer details regarding ST information. When the information gathered from five leads is deemed insufficient because a critical event is suspected, the care team should opt to increase the views by applying additional electrodes. If cardiac ischemia is suspected, a 12-lead ECG should be performed.

The results will help to reveal if the patient has experienced a **STEMI** (ST elevation myocardial infarction), also known as a **heart attack**. When working with a 12-lead cardiac monitoring system, the nurse should review changes to determine the affected area of the heart. If changes are noted in leads I, aVL, V5, and V6, the patient is suffering from lateral wall ischemia, injury, or infarction. If changes are noted in leads II, III, and aVF, the patient is suffering from inferior wall ischemia, injury, or infarction. If changes are noted in leads V1 and V2, the patient is suffering from septal wall ischemia, injury, or infarction. Finally, if changes are noted in leads V3 and V4, the patient is suffering from anterior wall ischemia, injury, or infarction.

Electrocardiograph electrode placement sites:

- V1: Fourth intercostal space, right of sternum
- V2: Fourth intercostal space, left of sternum
- V3: Between V2 and V4, midway
- V4: Fifth intercostal space, midclavicular line
- V5: Fifth intercostal space, anterior axillary line
- V6: Fifth intercostal space, midaxillary line
- RL (green): Right leg, between right ankle and torso
- RA (white): Right arm, between right shoulder and wrist
- LL (red): Left leg, between left ankle and torso
- LA (black): Left arm, between left shoulder and wrist
- aVR: Right shoulder
- aVL: Left shoulder
- aVF: Umbilicus

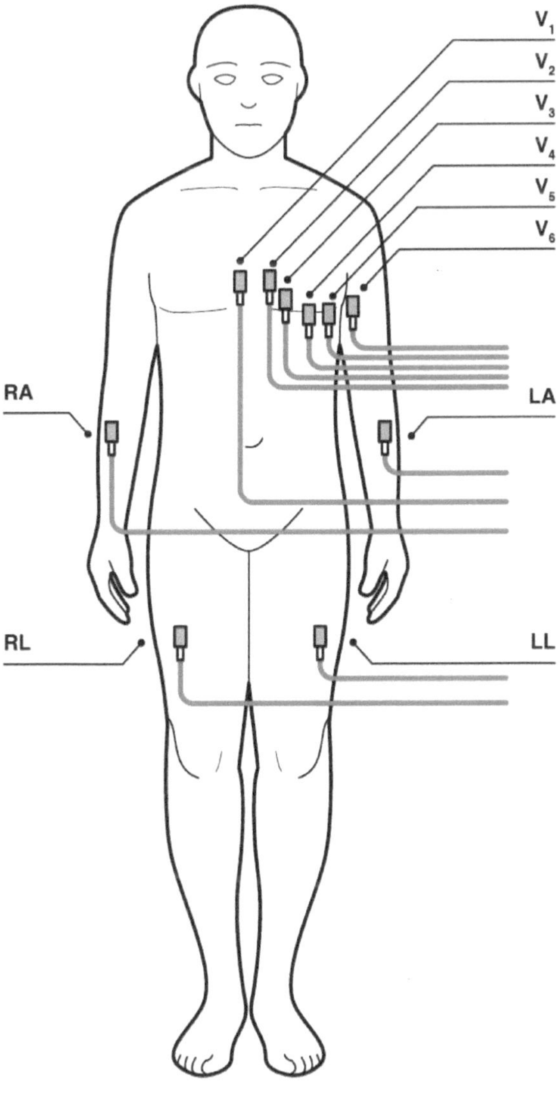

If electing to use a 15-lead placement system, the V4, V5, and V6 electrodes are instead placed posteriorly on the patient's left scapula and referred to as V7, V8, and V9. For quick recall when placing a 5-lead system, the nurse can remember the mnemonic "smoke over fire," which represents black above red, and "snow over grass," which represents white above green. The nurse ensures to note any clinical manifestations present during the ECG reading to provide a thorough clinical picture of activity.

In addition to cardiac monitoring, the nurse should review the homeostatic state of the patient to include primary diagnosis, comorbidities, and lifestyle. Cardiovascular hemodynamics include blood pressure, heart rate, respiratory rate, cardiac output, mean arterial perfusion, systemic vascular resistance, systolic time intervals, and lung congestion. When electing to use noninvasive monitoring systems, the nurse should detect cardiovascular homeostasis via external applications of automated or manual detection devices; such devices include manual blood pressure cuff, stethoscope, automated blood pressure cuff with pulse detection, and pulse oximetry. The nurse should also assess capillary refill for color and timing, skin temperature through a thermometer and via physical assessment, and quality of pulse.

Invasive hemodynamic monitoring may be necessary if the care team deems that a highly accurate and reliable reading is necessary for the severity of the patient's vulnerable condition. Invasive monitoring typically takes place in critical care environments and includes devices such as pulmonary artery catheter and arterial line. The need to monitor via invasive devices typically revolves around obtaining precisely accurate reviews of blood pressure and cardiac function when early intervention is crucial to avoid devastating outcomes. Some examples of conditions that may warrant invasive monitoring include myocardial injury, ischemic stroke, renal injury, and myocardial infarction, along with the postoperative period following cardiac surgeries such as aortocoronary bypass. Once homeostasis has been maintained and the patient is stable, the care team may opt to return to less invasive monitoring. The nurse implements care plans with evolving interventions that follow unique changes to hemodynamic status.

Acute Coronary Syndromes

Acute coronary syndrome (ACS) is the term used to describe the clinical symptoms caused by the sudden reduction in blood flow to the heart, but it is also known as **acute myocardial ischemia**. This syndrome commonly results in stable or unstable angina (UA), non-ST elevation myocardial infarction (NSTEMI), or ST elevation myocardial infarction (STEMI), which is shown in the figure below.

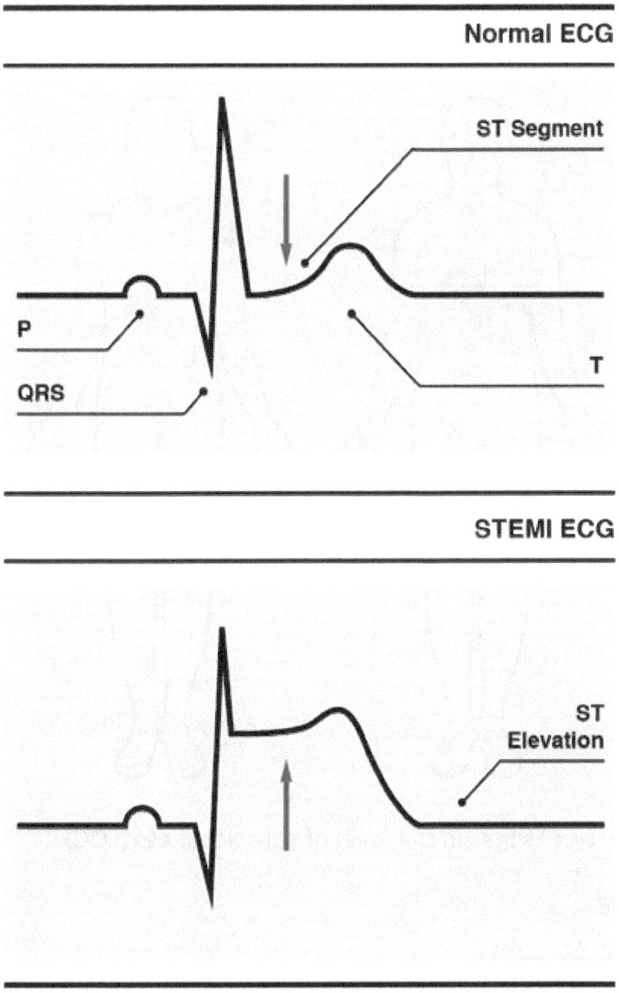

All three categories can occur with increased oxygen demand in the heart tissue, such as that caused by exercise and emotional distress.

In any of the three cases, major determining factors for tissue damage include how severe the blockage of the arteries is, how long the arteries are blocked, how much of the heart is affected, how high the demand for oxygen is in the heart, and how well the heart can compensate for the oxygen loss.

Common symptoms of a patient presenting with ACS include:

- Chest pain or discomfort in the upper body that radiates to the arms, back, neck, jaw, or stomach, as shown in the image below

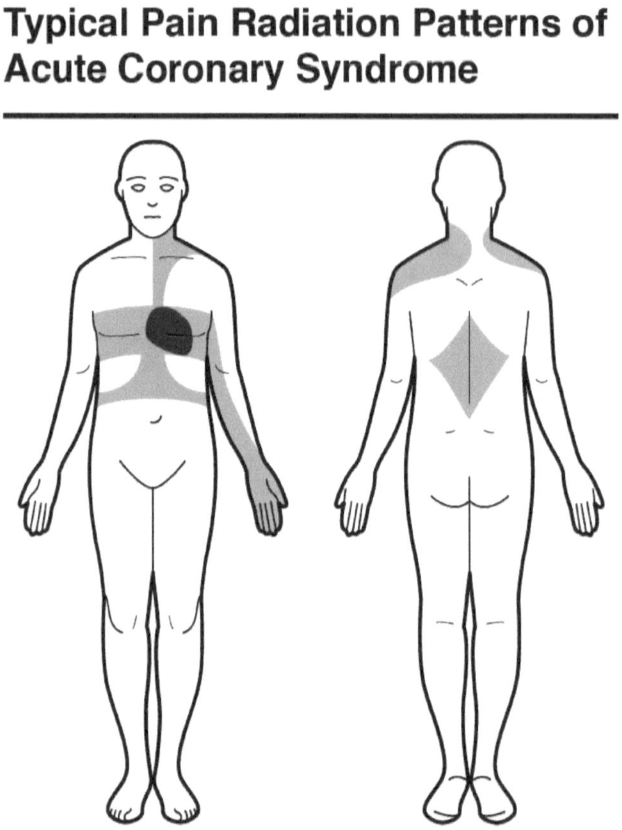

- Dizziness, syncope, or changes in the level of consciousness (LOC)
- Nausea or vomiting
- Palpitations or tachycardia
- Shortness of breath (SOB) or dyspnea
- Unusual fatigue

A patient may be experiencing a different condition than acute coronary syndrome, such as an anxiety attack or acid reflux, that may mimic the same signs and symptoms. The clinician must be aware of this when making a clinical judgment. An accurate assessment will be made based on patient history, clinical presentation, and events leading up to the current symptoms.

The most common symptom that signals acute coronary syndrome is chest pain. The chest pain of a heart attack has been described as "crushing pressure," "heavy weight," "tightness," and/or "fullness" in the chest area above the heart. Other accompanying symptoms include a shooting pain up and down one or either arm, along the jawline, or even in the back or abdomen. The patient may complain of "not being able to catch their breath," breathing rapidly, with shallow depth of breath. Dizziness, lightheadedness, nausea, and profuse drops of sweat may be part of the patient's presentation.

It is important to note that gender plays a role in how patients may present with a heart attack. Considering that heart disease is the leading cause of death for women in the United States, the nurse should be aware that women may not exhibit the classic signs of a heart attack. A woman is more likely to have non-chest-related symptoms, such as nausea, anxiety, and radiating pain in the upper or lower back and jaw region. These symptoms may occur weeks before the actual attack, making correct diagnosis even more difficult to pinpoint. That being said, knowing that there may be a different presentation will help the nurse make the correct clinical judgment regarding the situation, considering all involved factors.

Non-ST Segment Elevation Myocardial Infarction

A **Non-ST Segment Elevation Myocardial Infarction** (NSTEMI) does not produce changes in the ST segment of the ECG cycle. However, troponin levels are positive. Patients with a confirmed NSTEMI are hospitalized. Treatment includes aspirin, nitroglycerin (if not compromised hemodynamically), and morphine for high amounts of pain. Oxygen may be used if patient oxygen saturation is less than 90%. Additional pharmacological agents for treatment are beta-blockers, ACE inhibitors, statins, and antiplatelet medications. Coronary angiography and revascularization may be necessary.

The primary difference between UA and an NSTEMI is whether the ischemia is severe enough to damage the myocardium to the extent that cardiac markers indicative of injury are released and detectable through laboratory analysis. A patient is diagnosed with an NSTEMI when the ischemia is severe enough to cause myocardial damage and the release of a myocardial necrosis biomarker into the circulation (usually cardiac-specific troponins T or I). In contrast, a patient is diagnosed with UA if such a biomarker is undetectable in their bloodstream hours after the ischemic chest pain's initial onset.

ST Segment Elevation Myocardial Infarction

An **ST Segment Elevation Myocardial Infarction** (STEMI) is the most serious form of MI. It occurs when a coronary artery is completely blocked and unable to receive blood flow. Emergent revascularization is needed either through angioplasty or a thrombolytic medication.

UA and NSTEMIs generally indicate a partial-thickness injury to the myocardium, but a STEMI indicates injury across the full thickness of the myocardium, as shown in the image below. The etiology behind ischemia is partial or full occlusion of coronary arteries.

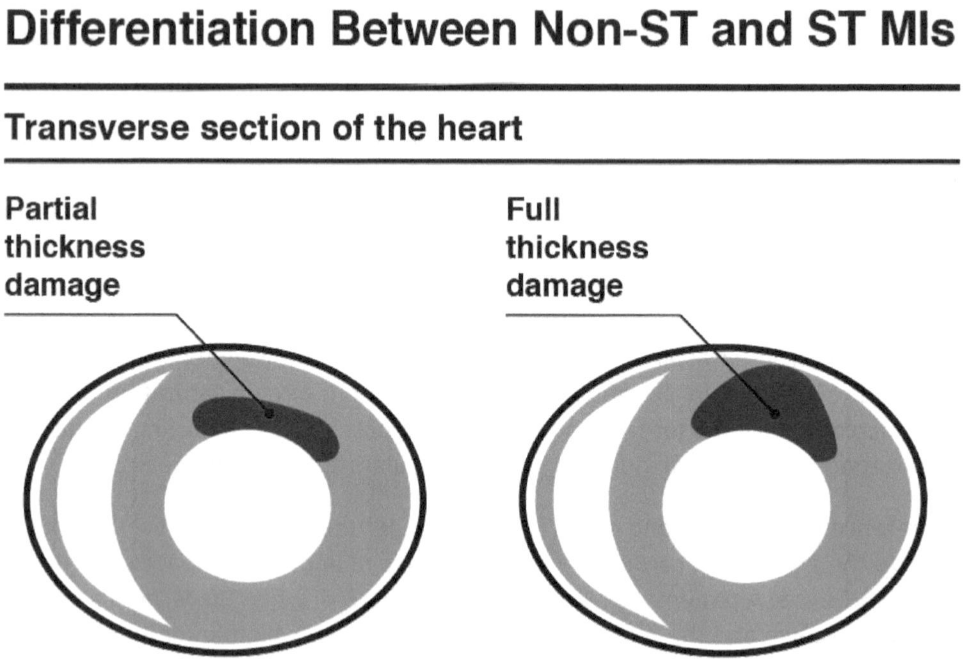

Angina

Angina is the term used to describe chest pain caused by decreased blood flow to the myocardium. The two primary categories of angina are stable or unstable, with stable angina being more common. It presents in a predictable pattern for patients, responds quickly to cessation of exertion or medication, and while it increases the likelihood of a future heart attack, it is not necessarily indicative of such an event occurring imminently. Unstable angina is often more frequent and severe. It may occur without physical exertion and be unresponsive to medication or activity cessation. It should be treated as an emergency and can signal an imminent heart attack.

Treatment for angina depends on the severity of the symptoms and can range from lifestyle modifications to surgical intervention. Pharmacological treatments for angina include beta-blockers, calcium channel blockers (CCBs), angiotensin-converting enzyme (ACE) inhibitors, statins, and antiplatelet and anticoagulant medications. These medications treat the symptoms related to angina by lowering blood pressure (BP), slowing heart rate (HR), relaxing blood vessels, reducing strain on the heart, lowering cholesterol levels, and preventing blood clot formation. Generally, the risk factors for the development of angina include:

- Diabetes
- Dietary deficiency (fruits and vegetables)
- Excessive alcohol consumption
- Family history of early coronary heart disease

- Hypertension (HTN)
- High LDL (low-density lipoprotein)
- Low HDL (high-density lipoprotein)
- Males
- Obesity
- Old age
- Sedentary lifestyle

Stable Angina

Atherosclerotic buildup generally occurs slowly over time. Because the buildup is gradual, the heart can usually continue to meet the body's oxygen demands despite the narrowing lumen of the vessel. However, in situations with increased oxygen demand, such as exercise or stress, the myocardium may not be able to meet the increased demands, thereby causing angina. The angina subsides with rest. Stable angina is predictable; it occurs in association with stress or certain activities. It does not increase in intensity or worsen over time. Nitroglycerine is effective in the treatment of stable angina because it dilates the blood vessels, reducing the resistance to blood flow, which decreases the demand on the myocardium. Lifestyle modifications such as smoking cessation and a regular exercise program are needed to slow atherosclerotic buildup.

Unstable Angina

Unstable angina (UA) is a more severe form of heart disease than stable angina. The angina associated with UA is generally related to small pieces of atherosclerotic plaque that break off and cause occlusions. The occlusions suddenly decrease blood flow to the myocardium, resulting in angina, without causing an actual MI. The pain symptomatic of UA occurs suddenly without a direct cause, worsens over a short period of time, and may last 15 to 20 minutes. Dyspnea (shortness of breath) and decreased blood pressure are also common. Because the angina is related to an acute decrease in blood flow, rest does not alleviate symptoms. Generally, UA does not respond to the vasodilatory effect of nitroglycerine. Laboratory values are typically negative for cardiac enzymes related to cardiac damage, but they can be slightly elevated. Therefore, a comprehensive history and physical exam that properly identify pertinent risk factors are critical for early diagnosis and treatment.

Depending on the severity of symptom presentation, pharmacological treatment for UA will include one or more antiplatelet medications and a cholesterol medication. In addition, medications to treat hypertension, arrhythmias, and anxiety may be necessary. The recommended intervention is angioplasty with coronary artery stenting. A **coronary artery bypass grafting** (CABG) surgery may be necessary in the case of extensive occlusion of one or more of the coronary arteries.

Treatment and Risk Scoring

Treatment for UA and NSTEMI is planned according to a risk score using the **Thrombolysis in Myocardial Infarction** (TIMI) tool. In the presence of UA or an NSTEMI, seven categories are scored: age, risk factors, a prior coronary artery stenosis, ST deviation on ECG, prior aspirin intake, presence and number of angina episodes, and elevated creatinine kinase (CK-MB) or troponins. In the presence of a STEMI, the TIMI tool scores eleven categories: age, angina history, hypertension, diabetes, systolic BP, heart rate, Killip class, weight, anterior MI in an ECG, left bundle branch block (LBBB) in an ECG, and a treatment delay after an attack. The **Global Registry of Acute Coronary Events** (GRACE), or ACS risk calculator, is a common tool used to predict death during admission and six months, as well as three years after a diagnosis of Acute Coronary Syndrome (ACS).

ACS can be life threatening. Treatment and survival are time-dependent. Quick recognition by the nurse followed by a thorough focused assessment that includes evaluation of pain type, location, characteristic, and onset is essential. The American Heart Association algorithm for Acute Coronary Syndrome should be followed immediately. The nurse should obtain a family, social, and lifestyle assessment to identify high-risk patients. An evaluation of recent medical history is imperative, since most ACS patients experience prodromal symptoms a month or more prior to the acute event. Establishing IV access is paramount for rapid administration of medications. Obtaining and reviewing an ECG and drawing and reviewing labs including troponins, CK-MB, complete blood count (CBC), C-reactive protein (CRP), electrolytes, and renal function will provide critical diagnostic data. A chest x-ray and echocardiogram will also add to the differential diagnosis. Immediate and long-term complications of ACS are cardiac dysrhythmia, heart failure (HF), and cardiogenic shock. Education should be provided to each patient about the diagnosis, risk factors, lifestyle modifications, and medications once the acute event has stabilized.

Acute Inflammatory Disease

Endocarditis

By definition, **endocarditis** is the inflammation of the endocardium, or innermost lining of the heart chambers and valves. It is also called **infective endocarditis**, or **bacterial endocarditis**.

To review, there are three layers of tissue that comprise the heart. A double-layer serous membrane, known as the **pericardium**, is the outermost layer. The pericardium forms the pericardial sac that surrounds the heart. The middle and largest layer is the **myocardium**. Since an MI occurs when the heart muscle is deprived of oxygen, the myocardial layer of the heart is where the damage due to lack of oxygen occurs. The innermost layer that lines the heart chambers and also the heart valves is called the **endocardium**. Endocarditis occurs when the endocardial layer and heart valves become infected and inflamed.

The most common cause of endocarditis is a bloodstream invasion of bacteria. ***Staphylococci*** and ***Streptococci*** account for the majority of infective endocarditis occurrences. During medical or dental procedures—such as a colonoscopy, cystoscopy, or professional teeth cleaning—bacteria may enter the bloodstream and travel to the heart. Inflammatory bowel disease and sexually transmitted diseases also foster bacterial transmission to the bloodstream and, ultimately, the heart.

Risk factors for the development of endocarditis include valve and septal defects of the heart, an artificial heart valve, a history of endocarditis, an indwelling long-term dialysis catheter, parenteral nutrition or central lines in the right atrium, IV drug use, and body piercings. Patients taking steroids or immunosuppressive medications are susceptible to fungal endocarditis. Regardless of the source, the bacteria infect the inside of the heart chambers and valves. Clumps of infective bacteria, or vegetation, develop within the heart at the site of infection. The heart valves are a common infection site, which often results in incomplete closure of the valves.

The classic symptoms of endocarditis are fever, cardiac murmur, and petechial lesions of the skin, conjunctiva, and oral mucosa. However, symptoms can range in severity. Flu-like symptoms, weight loss, and back pain may be present. Dyspnea and swelling of the feet and ankles may be evident. Endocarditis caused by ***Staphylococcus*** has a rapid onset, whereas ***Streptococcus*** occurs more slowly with a prolonged course.

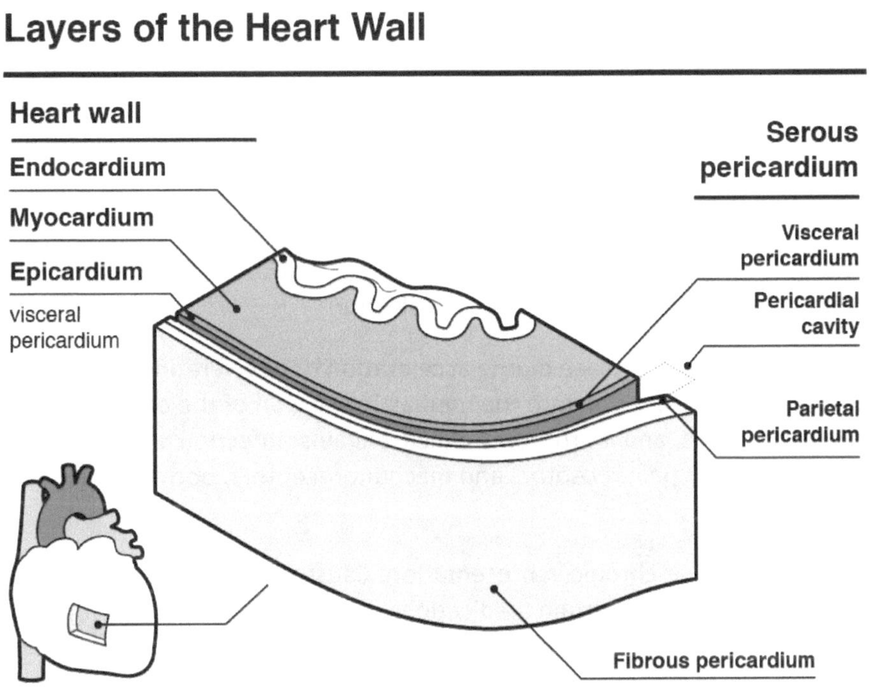

Antimicrobial treatment for four to six weeks is the standard of care. In some cases, two antimicrobials are used to treat the infection and prevent drug resistance. The objective of treatment is to eradicate the infection and treat complications. Surgery may be required for persistent recurring infections, one or more embolic occurrences, or if heart failure develops.

Left untreated, endocarditis can result in stroke or organ damage, as the vegetation breaks off and travels through the bloodstream and blocks circulation. The spread of infection and subsequent formation of abscesses throughout the body may also occur. Heart failure may develop when the infection hampers the heart's ability to pump effectively or with perforation of a valve.

A complete history and physical that includes inquiry about medications, recent surgeries, screening, and diagnostic testing may provide the crucial piece of information that identifies endocarditis in the face of otherwise vague symptom presentation. The nurse should anticipate the order for blood cultures, an erythrocyte sedimentation rate (ESR), a CBC, an ECG, a chest x-ray, and a transthoracic or transesophageal echocardiogram to identify the location of the infected area.

An in-depth patient interview and assessment by the nurse are essential. Diagnostic and laboratory results coupled with data from the patient interview will aid in early recognition and treatment of endocarditis. Because an incident of endocarditis places one at a higher risk for future infections, patient teaching should include informing all providers and dentists prior to treatment. Antibiotic prophylaxis may be indicated.

Pericarditis

Pericarditis is inflammation of the pericardium, which forms the pericardial sac that surrounds the heart. The pericardial sac consists of two layers. The **pericardium**, or outer layer of the heart wall, is a two-layer membrane that forms the pericardial sac, which envelops the heart.

The **visceral** (inner) layer of the pericardium is a double-layered membrane. One layer is affixed to the heart. The second layer lines the inside of the parietal layer (outer layer). The small space between the parietal and visceral layers is the pericardial space. The space normally contains between 15 and 50 milliliters of pericardial fluid. The pericardial fluid lubricates the membranes and allows the two layers to slide over one another as the heart beats.

The **parietal** (outer) layer of the pericardium is made of tough, thickened fibrous tissue. This layer is attached to the mid-diaphragm and to the back of the sternum.

These attachments keep the heart in place during acceleration or deceleration. The fibrous nature of the parietal layer prevents cardiac distention into the mediastinal region of the chest. It separates the heart from the surrounding structures, and it protects the heart against infection and inflammation from the lungs. The pericardium contains pain receptors and mechanoreceptors, both of which prompt reflex changes in the BP and HR.

Pericarditis can be either acute or chronic in presentation. Causes are varied and include an acute MI; bacterial, fungal, and viral infections; certain medications; chest trauma; connective tissue disorders such as lupus or rheumatic fever; metastatic lesions from lung or breast tumors; and a history of radiation therapy of the chest and upper torso. Frequent or prolonged episodes of pericarditis can lead to thickening and scarring of the pericardium and loss of elasticity. These conditions limit the heart's ability to fill with blood, and therefore limit the amount of blood being pumped out to the body. The result is a decrease in CO. Pericarditis can also cause fluid to accumulate in the pericardial cavity, known as **pericardial effusion**.

A characteristic symptom of pericarditis is chest pain. The pain is persistent, sharp, pleuritic, felt in the mid-chest, and aggravated by deep inhalation. Pericarditis may also cause ST elevation, thereby mimicking an acute MI, or it may be asymptomatic.

A pericardial friction rub is diagnostic of pericarditis. It is a creaky or scratchy sound heard at the end of exhalation. The rub is best heard when the patient is sitting and leaning forward. Stethoscope placement should be at the left lower sternal border in the fourth intercostal space. The rub is audible on auscultation and synchronous to the heartbeat. A pericardial friction rub is differentiated from a pleural friction rub by having patients hold their breath. The pericardial friction rub will remain constant with the heartbeat. Other presenting symptoms include a mild fever, cough, and dyspnea. Common laboratory findings are elevated white blood cell (WBC), ESR, or CRP levels.

The diagnosis of pericarditis is based on history, signs, and symptoms. Treatment goals are to determine the cause, administer therapy for treatment and symptom relief, and detect signs of complications. A thorough medical and surgical history will identify patients at risk for developing pericarditis. The physical assessment should evaluate the reported pain level during position changes, inspiration, expiration, coughing, swallowing, and breath holding. In addition, flexion, extension, and rotation of the neck and spine should be assessed for their influence on reported pain.

Aneurysm

An **aneurysm** is an abnormal bulge or ballooning that can form on an artery wall, as seen in the image below. Depending on the location, the rupture of an aneurysm can result in hemorrhage, stroke, or death. The most common places for the formation of an aneurysm are the left ventricle (LV) of the heart, the aorta, the brain, and the spleen.

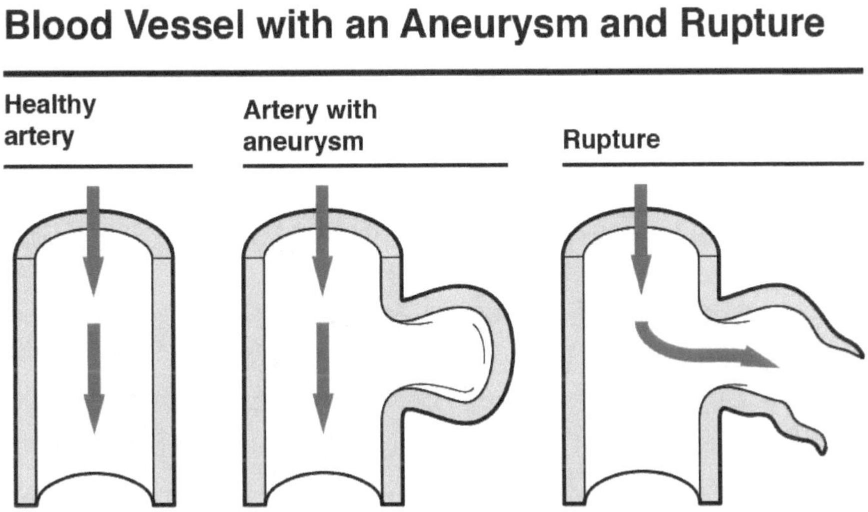

Generally, arteries carry oxygenated blood away from the heart to the organs and tissues of the body. The largest artery is the aorta, which receives blood directly from the LV of the heart. Oxygen-carrying blood continues to travel down the arterial system through successively smaller arteries that supply organs, ending with the arterioles that empty into the capillary bed.

Pulmonary and Systemic Circulation

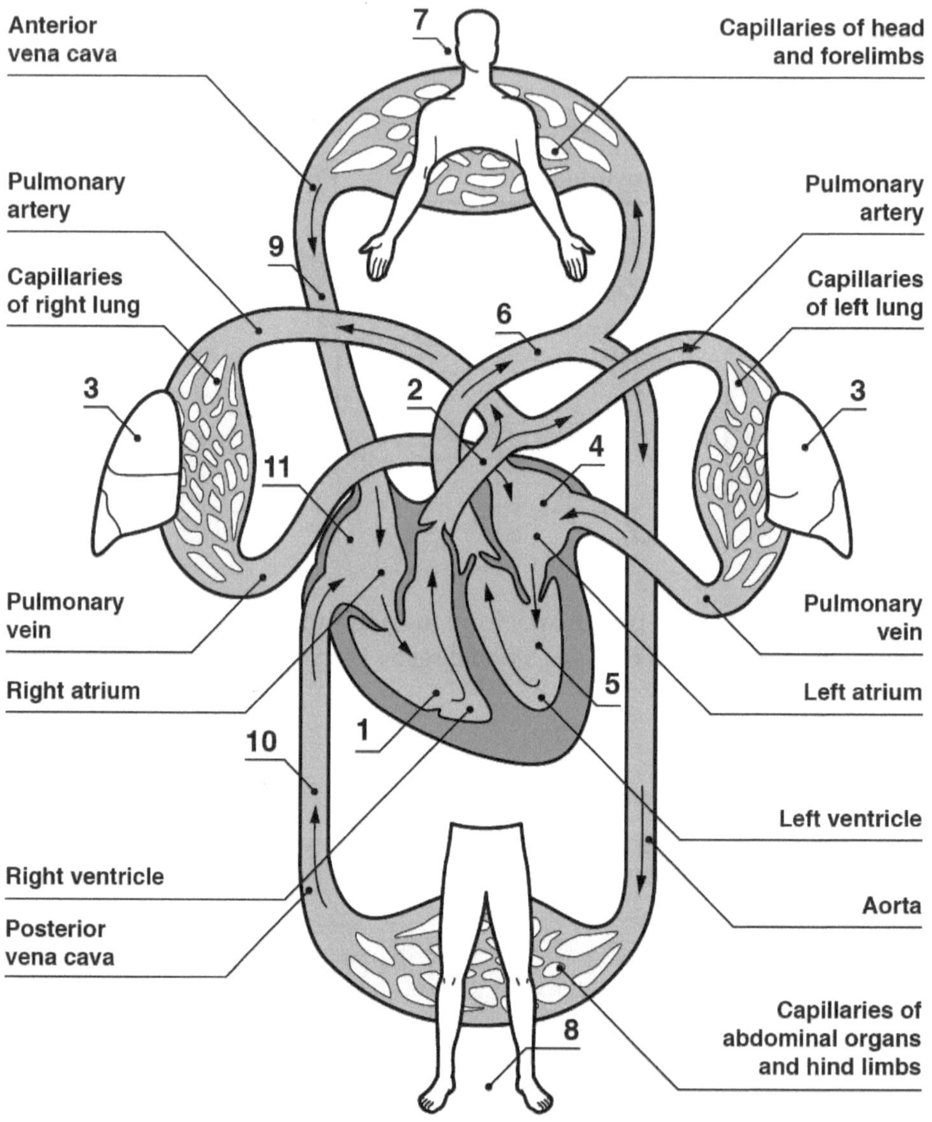

The capillary beds are drained on their opposite side by the venules, which return the now-deoxygenated blood back to the right atrium through progressively larger veins, ending in the great veins of the heart, known as the superior and inferior vena cava. The deoxygenated blood from the great veins moves into the right atrium, then the right ventricle, which pumps the blood to the lungs via the pulmonary artery to become oxygenated once again. The oxygenated blood flows from the pulmonary vein into the left atrium, then the LV, and into the aorta to repeat the cycle.

There are three tissue layers in the structure of arteries and veins. The **endothelium**, or **tunica intima**, forms the inner layer. The middle layer, the **tunica media**, contains elastin and smooth muscle fibers, and connective tissue forms the outside coating, called the **tunica externa**.

Arteries have a thicker elastin middle layer that enables them to withstand the fluctuations in pressure, which result from the high-pressure contractions of the LV. **Arterioles** regulate blood flow into the capillary bed through constriction and dilation, so they are the primary control structures for blood pressure regulation. Meanwhile, the venous side of circulation operates under very low pressures, so **veins** have no elastin in their structure; instead, they use valves to prevent backflow in those vessels working against gravity, as shown in the image below.

Structure of an Artery and Vein

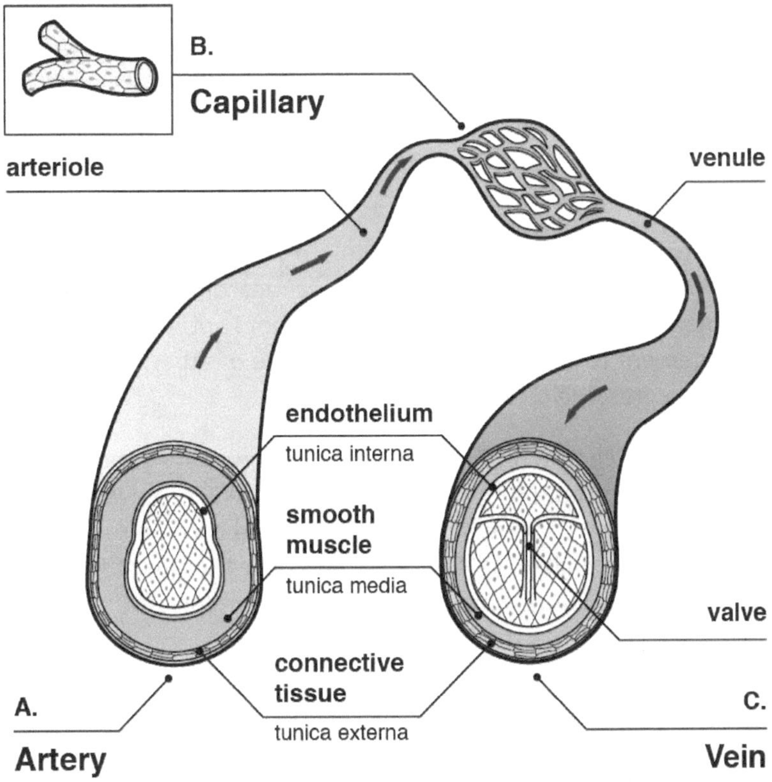

The aorta stretches from the LV through the diaphragm into the abdomen and pelvis. In the groin, the aorta separates into two main arteries that supply blood to the lower trunk and the legs. An aneurysm can occur anywhere along the aorta; an **abdominal aortic aneurysm** (AAA) is the most common. Atherosclerosis, hypertension, diabetes, infection, inflammation, and injury such as from a fall or auto accident are frequent causes. The most common presenting symptoms with an AAA are chest pain and back pain. The clinician may be able to palpate a pulsating bulge in the abdomen. Nausea and vomiting may be present. Other symptoms include lightheadedness, confusion, dyspnea, rapid heartbeat, sweating, numbness, and tingling. When an AAA develops slowly over a period of years, it is less likely to rupture, in which case the patient should be regularly monitored with ultrasound imaging. Aneurysms greater than 2 inches (5.5 centimeters) will generally require surgical repair.

A **thoracic aortic aneurysm** occurs in the stretch of the aorta that lies within the chest cavity. The critical size for surgical intervention of a thoracic aortic aneurysm is 2.3 inches (6 centimeters). As with all surgeries in such close proximity to the heart, the risk-to-benefit ratio must be carefully weighed.

A **left ventricular aneurysm** (LVA) is a bulge or ballooning of a weakened area of the LV, generally caused by an MI. There are no symptoms of an LVA, which should be diagnosed with an echocardiogram and angiogram. Small LVAs usually do not require treatment. Clot formation is a common occurrence with LVAs. In the body's attempt to repair the aneurysm, the inflammatory process and the clotting cascade are initiated, both of which increase the propensity for clot formation. Patients are most likely prescribed anticoagulants. Rapid treatment for an MI reduces the incidence of LVA formation.

A patient experiencing a sudden onset of tearing chest pain may be experiencing a rupture or dissection of an aortic aneurysm. Aortic aneurysms may occur at the top of the aorta, right after exiting the heart, termed **thoracic aortic aneurysms**. Aortic aneurysms may also occur farther down the aorta, then called either **thoracoabdominal aortic aneurysms** or **abdominal aortic aneurysms**. An aneurysm is any ballooning or enlargement of a blood vessel, often caused by atherosclerosis. When an aneurysm suddenly tears apart, massive amounts of the patient's blood start surging out with each and every heartbeat, making it an immediate medical emergency. A patient experiencing an aortic aneurysm dissection needs immediate surgical repair followed by intense cardiac and hemodynamic monitoring until stabilized.

Patients with unruptured aortic aneurysms may be completely asymptomatic. Detection of an aortic aneurysm occurs through ultrasonography, abdominal CT, echocardiography, and/or transesophageal echocardiography. Treatment for aortic aneurysms that have not ruptured includes elective surgical repair along with encouragement to quit smoking, a major cause of atherosclerosis, and drug therapy including antilipids and blood pressure control.

A family history of aneurysm and certain other aneurysm risk factors are genetic. Other predisposing factors are an arteriovenous malformation (AVM) at the circle of Willis, polycystic kidney disease (PKD), and Marfan syndrome. Poor lifestyle choices, such as smoking and cocaine use, greatly increase the risk for aneurysm formation. There is a higher risk for individuals over the age of forty, women, patients who have experienced a traumatic head injury, and patients with hypertension.

Dissecting

Dissection is a condition in which the layers of the arterial wall become separated and blood leaks in between the layers of the vessel, as shown in the image below. A dissection represents damage through at least the first layer of an artery. It is a more serious form of aneurysm because all the layers are compromised.

A dissection is different from a rupture. With a dissection, blood leaks in and through the layers of an artery, but the artery remains structurally intact, albeit weakened. Blood is still contained within the vessel. When a rupture occurs, it is similar to the popping of a balloon. The integrity of the artery is disrupted, and blood leaks out of the artery. Dissections increase the risk of rupture. Medical management with beta-blockers is the treatment of choice for stable aortic dissections.

Repair

If the AAA is small and slow-growing, a watch-and-wait approach is often taken. An abdominal ultrasound, computed tomography (CT), and MRI will aid in the determination of the most appropriate treatment. Surgical repair involves removing the damaged portion of the aorta and replacing it with a graft. Another minimally-invasive technique involves reinforcing the weakened area with metal mesh.

Summary

Symptoms of an aneurysm/dissection may be absent, vague, or difficult to identify. The consequences of a rupture are life-threatening. The expert clinician will ascertain a thorough patient and family history, including social factors and lifestyle choices. Autoimmune disorders, age, gender, a sedentary lifestyle, smoking, and drug or alcohol abuse are contributing factors to the development of an aneurysm. Rapid assessment, diagnosis, and treatment are essential. Vital signs, neurological status, and loss of consciousness should be closely monitored.

Cardiac Surgery

The postoperative course for a patient following the insertion of a coronary bypass graft is influenced by the patient's preoperative baseline health status and level of cardiac function; the vessel chosen for the graft, which is commonly the internal mammary artery or the great saphenous vein; whether or not the extracorporeal pump was used, and if used, the length of time that was required to complete the procedure; and the extent of the inflammatory response that can occur as a result of the circulating blood volume being perfused through the non-endothelialized surface of the bypass pump. Commonly, forty-eight hours postoperatively, patients are sufficiently stable to be transferred to a "step-down" medical unit. The nursing care of these patients is then focused on continued surveillance for changes that signal the onset of possible complications that include, but are not limited to, infection, occlusion of the graft, bleeding, acute inflammation or thrombophlebitis of the peripheral veins, acute kidney injury, alterations in respiratory function, dysrhythmias, and myocardial infarction or other cardiac events. In addition, the patient requires expert pain management, identification and management of elevated cardiac biomarkers such as troponin and creatine kinase MB fraction (CK-MB), and patient and family discharge teaching.

Cardiac/Vascular Catheterization

Cardiac catheterization is a procedure during which a catheter is inserted in the artery or vein to either diagnose or treat a disease. Unstable angina is a common indication for cardiac catheterization, among others. A sheath functions as a protective covering while placing or advancing a cardiac catheter. Depending on the procedure, a sheath can be used to protect an artery, a vein, or at times both. The femoral artery is a common place to use a sheath during cardiac catheterization due to its large size. Nursing care post cardiac catheterization with sheath placement includes the administration of anticoagulant and antithrombotic medication. As this medication comes with the risk of bleeding, the nurse also monitors for signs and symptoms of hematoma formation or hemorrhage. Care considerations also include monitoring the sheath site for inflammation, obtaining vital signs and pedal pulses, and assessing chest pain and shortness of breath. Laboratory testing for coagulation, along with a complete blood count, assists in determining when the patient is ready for sheath removal, which is then performed by a specially trained nurse or a physician. After the sheath is removed, the nurse will very closely monitor vital signs along with femoral and pedal pulses, especially during the first twenty-four hours.

Cardiac Tamponade

Cardiac tamponade, or **pericardial tamponade**, is a syndrome caused by the excessive accumulation of blood or fluid in the pericardial sac, resulting in the compression of the myocardium and reduced ventricular filling. It is a medical emergency with complications of pulmonary edema, shock, and death, if left untreated.

The **pericardium**, or outer layer of the heart wall, is a two-layer membrane that forms the pericardial sac, which envelops the heart. The parietal (outer) layer of the pericardium is made of tough, thickened fibrous tissue. This layer is attached to the mid-diaphragm and to the back of the sternum. These attachments keep the heart in place during acceleration or deceleration. The fibrous nature of the parietal layer prevents cardiac distention into the mediastinal region of the chest.

The **visceral** (inner) layer of the pericardium is a double-layered membrane. One layer is affixed to the heart. The second layer lines the inside of the **parietal** (outer) layer. The small space between the parietal and visceral layers is the **pericardial space**. The space normally contains between 15 and 50 milliliters of **pericardial fluid**. The pericardial fluid lubricates the membranes and allows the two layers to slide over one another as the heart beats.

A **pericardial effusion** develops when excess blood or fluid accumulates in the pericardial sac. If the effusion progresses, a pericardial tamponade will ensue. Because the fibrous parietal layer prevents cardiac distention, the pressure from the excessive blood or fluid is exerted inward, compressing the myocardium and reducing space for blood to fill the chambers. The normally low-pressure right ventricle and atrium are the first structures to be impacted by tamponade. Therefore, signs of right-sided heart failure such as jugular vein distention, edema, and hepatomegaly may be present.

Symptoms of a pericardial tamponade are dyspnea, chest tightness, dizziness, tachycardia, muffled heart sounds, jugular vein distention, and restlessness. **Pulsus paradoxus** is an important clinical finding in tamponade; it represents an abnormal BP variation during the respiration cycle and is evidenced by a decrease of 10 mmHg or more in systolic BP during inspiration. Pulsus paradoxus represents decreased diastolic ventricular filling and reduced volume in all four chambers of the heart. The clinical signs associated with tamponade are distended neck veins, muffled heart sounds, and hypotension. These clustered symptoms are known as **Beck's triad**.

Removal of the pericardial fluid via pericardiocentesis is the definitive therapy. A **pericardiocentesis** is immediately necessary, in which a needle is inserted and the leaked blood aspirated, to relieve pressure surrounding the heart and normalize BP. Fluid removed during the procedure is analyzed to determine the cause of the effusion. Malignancies, metastatic disease, and trauma are major causes of the development of pericardial effusions.

Identification and treatment of a tamponade requires emergent medical intervention. A rapid focused assessment of heart sounds and BP, including assessing for pulsus paradoxus, is a critical first step. An in-depth medical and surgical history can aid in identifying the etiology.

Cardiogenic Shock

The clinical definition of **cardiogenic shock** is decreased CO and evidence of tissue hypoxia in the presence of adequate intravascular volume. It is a medical emergency and the most severe expression of LV failure. It is the leading cause of death following an MI with mortality rates between 70 and 90 percent without aggressive treatment. When a large area of the myocardium becomes ischemic, the heart cannot pump effectively. Therefore, SV, CO, and BP drastically decline. The result is end-point hypoperfusion and organ failure. Characteristics of cardiogenic shock include ashen, cyanotic, or mottled extremities; distant heart sounds; and rapid and faint peripheral pulses. Additional signs of hypoperfusion such as altered mental status and decreased urine output may be present.

Cardiogenic shock often occurs following an acute MI. The ischemia that results from this condition causes the heart to fail in its ability to adequately circulate blood in the body. Mortality rates for cardiogenic shock are high if swift, aggressive intervention does not occur as soon as possible.

Cardiogenic shock is an emergency, and the patient must be treated immediately to prevent death. Admission to an ICU is likely, where the patient may have a central line put in to ensure rapid volume replacement and allow for multiple infusions of medicines to help maintain BP and cardiac output. The patient may have an arterial line placed to monitor BP continuously while BP is treated. Pharmacologic therapy will likely include drugs to improve cardiac contractility, such as dopamine, and diuretics to maintain volume and prevent volume overload during fluid resuscitation. If dopamine does not do an adequate job of maintaining BP, a stronger option would be norepinephrine, a potent vasoconstrictor. Any electrolyte abnormalities such as acidosis, hypokalemia, or hypomagnesemia will be corrected.

Some patients will have an intra-aortic balloon pump inserted in the aorta to assist the heart's function. When the heart pumps, during systole, the balloon is deflated. When the heart rests, during diastole, the balloon inflates. This inflation helps push blood into the coronary arteries, reperfusing them. The deflation allows for more space in the aorta and thus more blood to flow out to the body and the tissues needing oxygen.

Patients in cardiogenic shock are likely candidates for a percutaneous intervention (PCI) or coronary artery bypass graft (CABG) surgery to immediately correct the issue. Research has shown that a PCI is most effective within 90 minutes of patient presentation to prevent mortality and long-term damage.

Obstructive Shock

Obstructive shock occurs when the heart or the great vessels are mechanically obstructed. A cardiac tamponade or massive PE is a frequent cause of obstructive shock. Systemic circulatory collapse occurs because blood flow in or out of the heart is blocked. Generalized treatment goals for shock are to identify and correct the underlying cause. In the case of obstructive shock, the goal is to remove the obstruction.

Treatment begins simultaneously with evaluation. Stabilization of the airway, breathing, and circulation are primary, followed by fluid resuscitation to increase BP. Vital signs, urine flow, and mental status using the GCS should be monitored. Shock patients should be kept warm. Serial measurements of renal and hepatic function, electrolyte levels, and ABGs should be monitored.

Summary

Shock is characterized by organ blood flow that is inadequate to meet the oxygen demands of the tissue. The management goal for shock is to restore oxygen delivery to the tissues and reverse the perfusion deficit. This is accomplished through fluid resuscitation, increasing CO with inotropes, and raising the SVR with vasopressors.

Cardiomyopathies

A **cardiomyopathy** is any condition in which the heart muscle is diseased. There are four categories of cardiomyopathy that will be discussed here: dilated, hypertrophic, idiopathic, and restrictive cardiomyopathy.

Dilated

Dilated cardiomyopathy is a primary myocardial disorder, meaning it occurs on its own without any coronary artery disease or anything else. Usually both ventricles will be affected, dilating, thinning, becoming hypertrophic, and causing systolic dysfunction. Mitral and tricuspid regurgitation often develop because of the dilation. When the left ventricle is affected, the patient will have exertional dyspnea and fatigue because the left ventricle diastolic pressure rises and cardiac output is lowered. When the right ventricle is affected, the patient may present with edema of the legs and arms along with jugular vein distention. The symptoms of dilated cardiomyopathy typically develop slowly over time, except for acute cases such as takotsubo.

Takotsubo cardiomyopathy, also known as **acute apical ballooning cardiomyopathy** or **broken heart syndrome**, is triggered by a sudden and extreme amount of emotional distress. The patient may have experienced the loss of a loved one or some other catastrophic life event, which set in motion a hyperadrenergic state in the body. ***Takotsubo*** is a Japanese word for a fishing pot used for capturing octopuses, which is what the left ventricle has been said to look like during this type of cardiomyopathy. Patients typically present in ways like those experiencing an ischemic event, with dyspnea, chest pain, nausea, and vomiting, among other symptoms. This type of heart failure is typically reversible, requiring acute hemodynamic support and similar treatment to patients with acute coronary syndrome.

Typical dilated cardiomyopathy has several different potential causes, including chronic tachycardia, connective tissue disorders such as rheumatoid arthritis, drugs and toxins such as alcohol and cocaine, inherited genetic factors, infections, and metabolic disorders such as diabetes mellitus. Viral infections are a well-known cause of dilated cardiomyopathy, with over twenty different viruses identified, such as human immunodeficiency virus (HIV) infection.

A patient with dilated cardiomyopathy will be diagnosed using a chest x-ray, which will show the enlargement of the heart, called **cardiomegaly**. The chest film may also show pleural effusions, a result of ventricular failure. Serological markers such as troponin may be elevated in dilated cardiomyopathy. Tissue samples from the heart muscle may be obtained for biopsy in some cases. ECG and imaging studies such as echocardiography and cardiac magnetic resonance imaging (MRI) will also be used to make a diagnosis of dilated cardiomyopathy.

Patients with dilated cardiomyopathy will be treated with angiotensin-converting enzyme (ACE) inhibitors, beta blockers, angiotensin-receptor blockers (ARBs), diuretics, and digoxin, among other pharmacologic therapies. These drugs are often used in heart failure with a lowered ejection fraction. **Ejection fraction** is a term of measurement used to quantify the percentage of blood leaving the heart with each beat. A patient with heart failure, as is the case with dilated cardiomyopathy, will have a much lower ejection fraction than normal. A normal ejection fraction is around 55 to 70 percent.

Hypertrophic

Hypertrophic cardiomyopathy is an inherited condition due to a genetic mutation. In very rare cases, this type of cardiomyopathy may be acquired, as is the case in patients with acromegaly. **Hypertrophy**

refers to a thickening of the cardiac muscle, often becoming stiff and noncompliant. Ejection fraction in patients with hypertrophic cardiomyopathy may be elevated as the smaller heart chamber empties completely with each beat to maintain cardiac output.

This type of cardiomyopathy often occurs in athletes, frequently causing sudden death and the official diagnosis made upon autopsy. Symptoms are like acute coronary artery occlusion, such as chest pain, dyspnea, and syncope. Patients will be diagnosed using echocardiography or cardiac MRI, where the heart structures are visualized and the severity of the hypertrophy is analyzed.

Family history of sudden death or patient history of unexplained syncope are clues that the patient may have this type of cardiomyopathy.

The treatment plan for a patient diagnosed with hypertrophic cardiomyopathy usually includes beta-blockers such as metoprolol and calcium channel blockers such as verapamil. Beta-blockers and calcium channel blockers help with this type of cardiomyopathy because they slow the heart rate, decrease contractility, and prolong the time the heart chambers can fill between beats. Nitrates, diuretics, and ACE inhibitors should be avoided because they reduce preload, which worsens the condition. Implantable cardioverter defibrillator (ICD) is recommended to prevent death in patients with a history of cardiac arrest and syncope.

Idiopathic

When the cause of the cardiomyopathy is unknown, it is called an **idiopathic cardiomyopathy**. This type of cardiomyopathy occurs in up to half of the occurrences of heart failure. Patients with this type of cardiomyopathy are typically between twenty and sixty years of age. Their clinical presentation will be like other patients experiencing cardiomyopathy, with fatigue and dyspnea on exertion being a primary symptom if the left ventricle is affected. If the right ventricle is affected, jugular vein distention and edema may be present.

Like the other types of cardiomyopathies, idiopathic cardiomyopathy is believed to be the result of a viral infection, immune dysfunction, genetic factors, toxins, metabolism, and/or tachycardia-induced conditions. Alcohol and chemotherapeutic drugs are believed to be toxins that may cause cardiomyopathy.

The role of viruses must be investigated when determining the cause of idiopathic cardiomyopathy, as this root cause starts the chain reaction of inflammation and autoimmune dysfunction leading to cardiomyopathy. Viruses that have been associated with this type of cardiomyopathy include herpes, adenovirus, and enterovirus.

Treatment for the patient with idiopathic cardiomyopathy may include lifestyle modification of risk factors such as alcohol abuse; drug therapy with ACE inhibitors, beta-blockers, diuretics, and digitalis; and possible resynchronization therapy in patients experiencing dysrhythmias. Patients experiencing cardiomyopathy in the absence of a viral cause may be good candidates for immunosuppressive therapies such as prednisone, per the discretion of the physician.

Restrictive

A cardiomyopathy characterized by noncompliant heart walls that are resistant to filling during the diastolic period is termed **restrictive cardiomyopathy**. There are two categories of restrictive cardiomyopathy: obliterative and nonobliterative. **Obliterative** means that there is fibrosis within the endocardium and subendocardium, while **nonobliterative** entails that the myocardium has been infiltrated by an abnormal substance. One or both ventricles of the heart may be affected. Restrictive cardiomyopathy is much less common than dilated, idiopathic, and hypertrophic cardiomyopathies.

A patient with restrictive cardiomyopathy may present with fatigue and exertional dyspnea, like the other cardiomyopathic presentations. This is due to decreased cardiac output and oxygen delivery to the tissues and organs of the body.

Restrictive cardiomyopathy may arise because of genetic factors. The resistance to diastolic filling results in an increased filling pressure, followed by pulmonary venous hypertension.

A patient will be diagnosed with restrictive cardiomyopathy using echocardiography to visualize the ventricles and other structures of the heart. Cardiac MRI, heart catheterization, and biopsy may also be used to confirm the diagnosis.

A patient diagnosed with restrictive cardiomyopathy has a poor prognosis, unfortunately, as diagnosis is often made in the later stages of the disease. The cause will be treated if possible along with supportive treatment for symptoms. Diuretics will be used to relieve pulmonary vascular congestion if appropriate.

Illustration comparing a normal heart muscle with dilated, hypertrophic, and restrictive cardiomyopathies

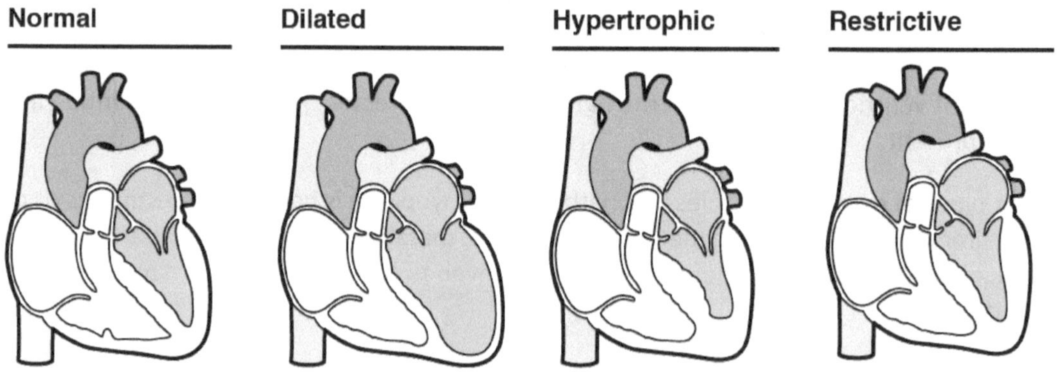

Dysrhythmias

Dysrhythmia, also known as **arrhythmia**, is abnormal electrical activity of the heart. The abnormal heartbeat may be irregular, too fast, or too slow.

Normally, the electrical conduction system of the heart begins with an impulse known as the **action potential** at the pacemaker sinoatrial (SA) node. The impulse travels across the right and left atria before activating the atrioventricular (AV) node.

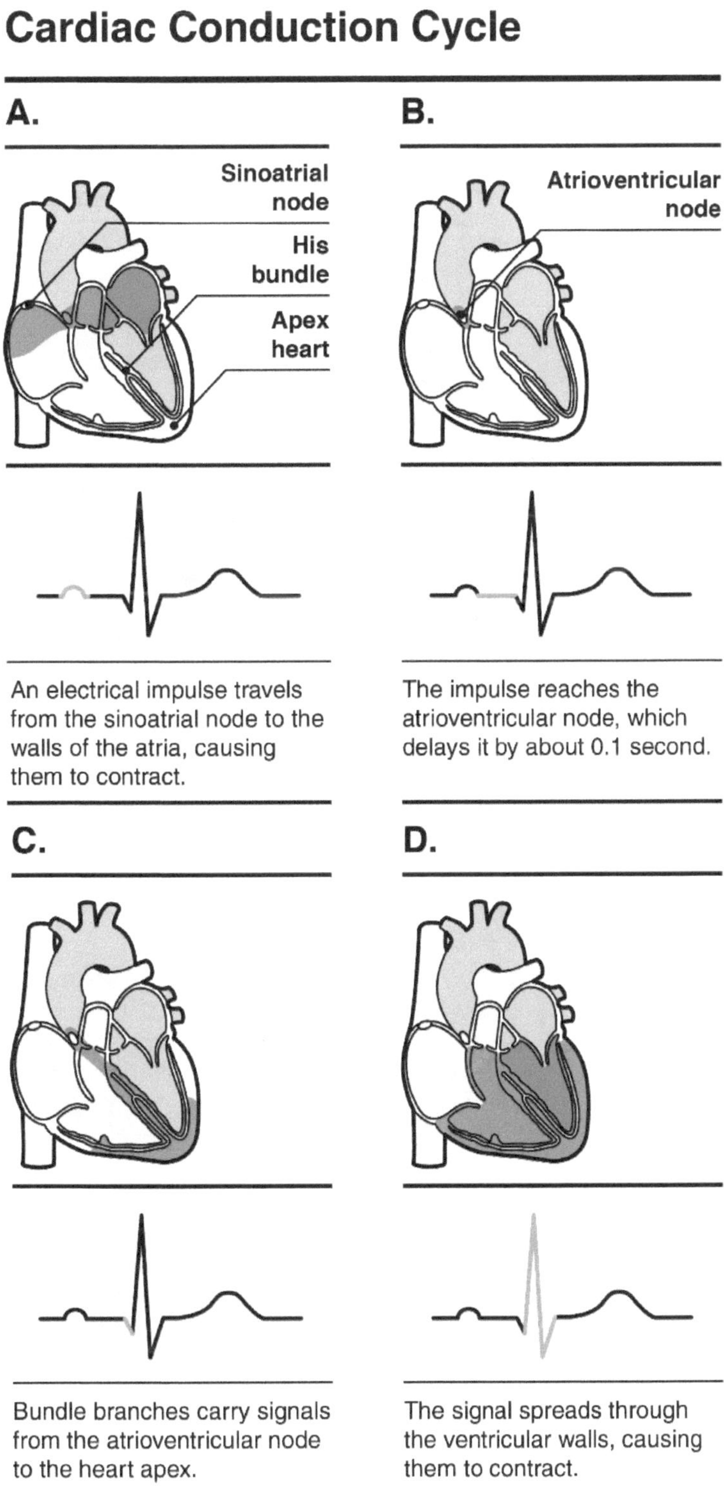
Cardiac Conduction Cycle
A.
Sinoatrial node
His bundle
Apex heart
An electrical impulse travels from the sinoatrial node to the walls of the atria, causing them to contract.
B.
Atrioventricular node
The impulse reaches the atrioventricular node, which delays it by about 0.1 second.
C.
Bundle branches carry signals from the atrioventricular node to the heart apex.
D.
The signal spreads through the ventricular walls, causing them to contract.

The pathway from the SA to the AV node is visualized on the ECG as the P wave. From the AV node, the impulse continues down the septum along cardiac fibers. These fibers are known as the **bundle of His**. The impulse then spreads out and across the ventricles via the Purkinje fibers. This is represented on the ECG as the QRS complex. The T wave represents the repolarization or recovery of the ventricles.

Electrical Events of the Cardiac Cycle

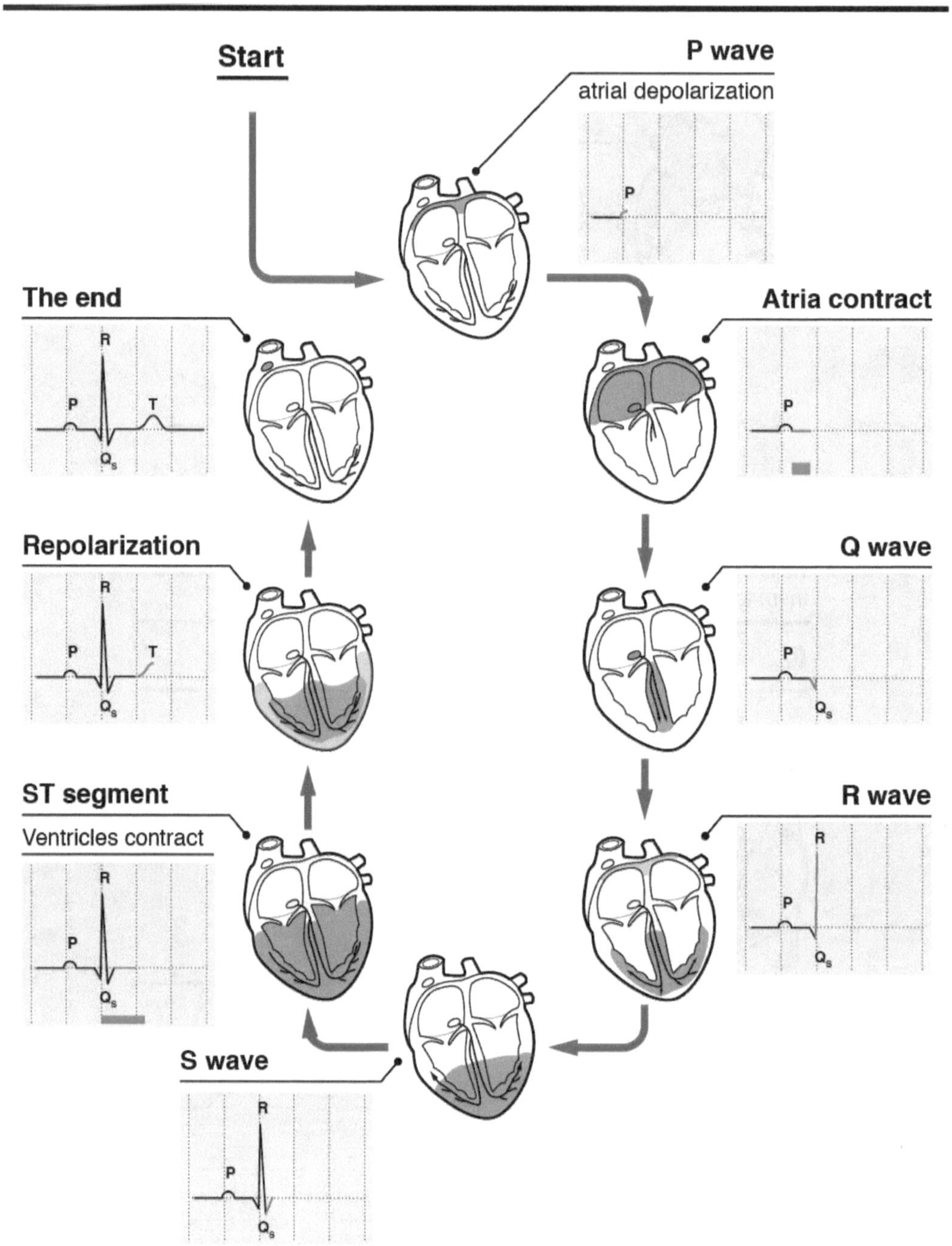

Cardiac cells have four important properties: excitability, conductivity, contractility, and automaticity. **Excitability** allows the heart to respond to stimuli and maintain homeostasis. **Conductivity** is the ability to transfer the electrical impulse initiated at the SA node across cardiac cells. **Contractility** is the cardiac cells' ability to transform an action potential into the mechanical action of contraction and relaxation. **Automaticity** is the ability of cardiac cells to contract without direct nerve stimulation. In other words, the heart initiates its own impulse. If the SA node fails to initiate the impulse, the AV node will fire the impulse at a slower rate. If neither the SA nor the AV node fires the impulse, the cells within the bundle of His and the Purkinje fibers will fire to start the impulse at an even slower rate.

The action potential is a representation of the changes in voltage of a single cardiac cell. Action potentials are formed as a result of ion fluxes through cellular membrane channels, most importantly, the sodium (Na+), potassium (K+), and calcium (Ca+) channels. Electrical activity requires an action potential. Contraction of the cardiac muscle fibers immediately follows electrical activity.

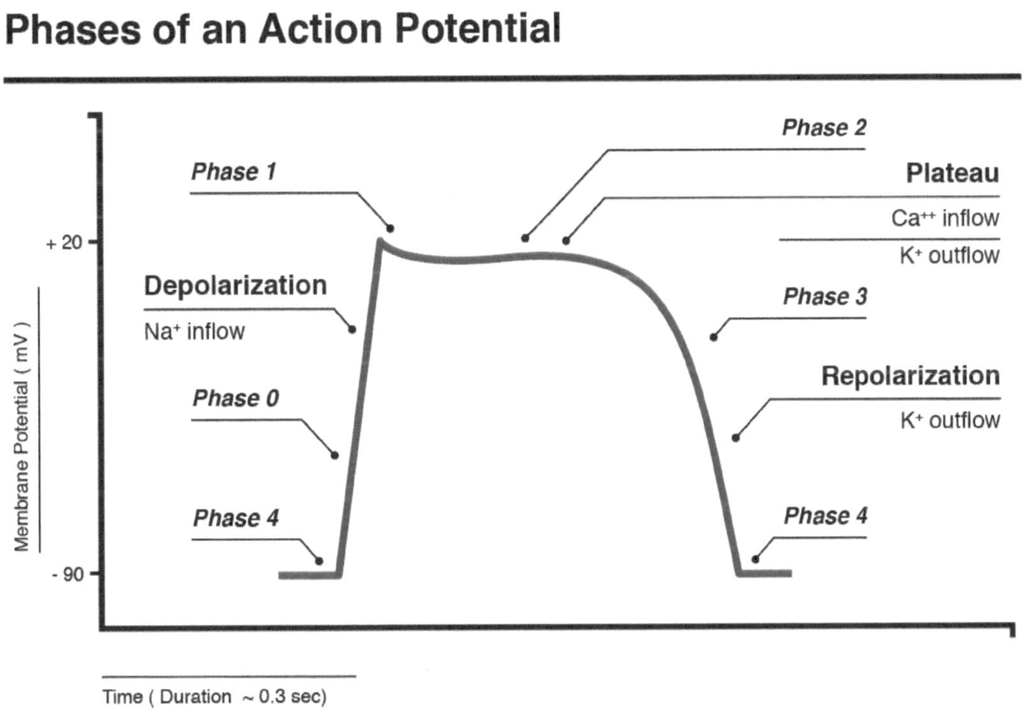

Phase 0: Depolarization

- Rapid Na^+ channels are stimulated to open.
- The cardiac cell is flooded with Na^+ ions, which change the transmembrane potential.
- The shift in potential is reflected by the initial spike of the action potential.
- Depolarization of one cell triggers the Na^+ channels in surrounding cells to open, which causes the depolarization wave to propagate cell by cell throughout the heart.

Phases 1 – 3: Repolarization phases

- During these phases, represented as the plateau, Ca^{2+} and some K^+ channels open.
- Ca^{2+} flows into the cells, and K^+ flows out.
- The cell remains polarized, and the increased Ca^{2+} within the cell trigger contraction of the cardiac muscle.

Phase 4: Completion of repolarization

- Ca^{2+} channels close.
- K^+ outflow continues.
- The cardiac cell returns to its normal state.

The cardiac cycle of **depolarization-polarization-depolarization** is represented on the ECG by the P wave, QRS complex, and T wave. A dysrhythmia can occur anywhere along the conduction system. It can be caused when an impulse from between the nodes or fibers is delayed or blocked. Arrhythmias also occur when an ectopic focus initiates an impulse, thereby disrupting the normal conduction cycle. Additional sources of damage to the conduction system include MIs, hypertension, coronary artery disease (CAD), and congenital heart defects.

Overview of Dysrhythmias

Abnormalities in the electrical conduction system of the heart may occur at the SA node, the AV node, or the His-Purkinje system of the ventricles. Careful evaluation of the ECG will aid in determining the location and subsequent cause of the dysrhythmia.

Dysrhythmias that occur above the ventricles in either the atria or the SA/AV nodes are known as **supraventricular dysrhythmias**. Common arrhythmias in this category are sinus bradycardia, sinus tachycardia, atrial fibrillation, atrial flutter, junctional rhythm, and sustained supraventricular tachycardia (SVT). **Atrioventricular (AV) blocks**, known as **heart blocks,** occur when the impulse is delayed or blocked at the AV node. The three types of **heart block** are first degree, second degree, and third degree, with first degree being the least severe and third degree being the most severe.

Ventricular dysrhythmias can be life-threatening because they severely impact the heart's ability to pump and maintain adequate cardiac output (CO). A bundle branch block (BBB), premature ventricular complexes (PVCs), sustained ventricular tachycardia (V-tach), ventricular fibrillation (V-fib), Torsades de pointes, and digoxin-induced ventricular dysrhythmias are the most common ventricular arrhythmias.

Atrial Fibrillation

Atrial fibrillation is the most common sustained dysrhythmia. It is caused when multiple foci in the atria fire randomly, thereby stimulating various parts of the atria simultaneously. The result is a highly irregular atrial rhythm. Ventricular rate may be rapid or normal. Fatigue, lightheadedness, chest pain, dyspnea, and hypotension may be present. Treatment goals are to improve ventricular pumping and prevent stroke. Beta-blockers and CCBs impede conduction through the AV node, thereby controlling ventricular rates, so they are the medications of choice. Cardioversion and ablation are also treatment options.

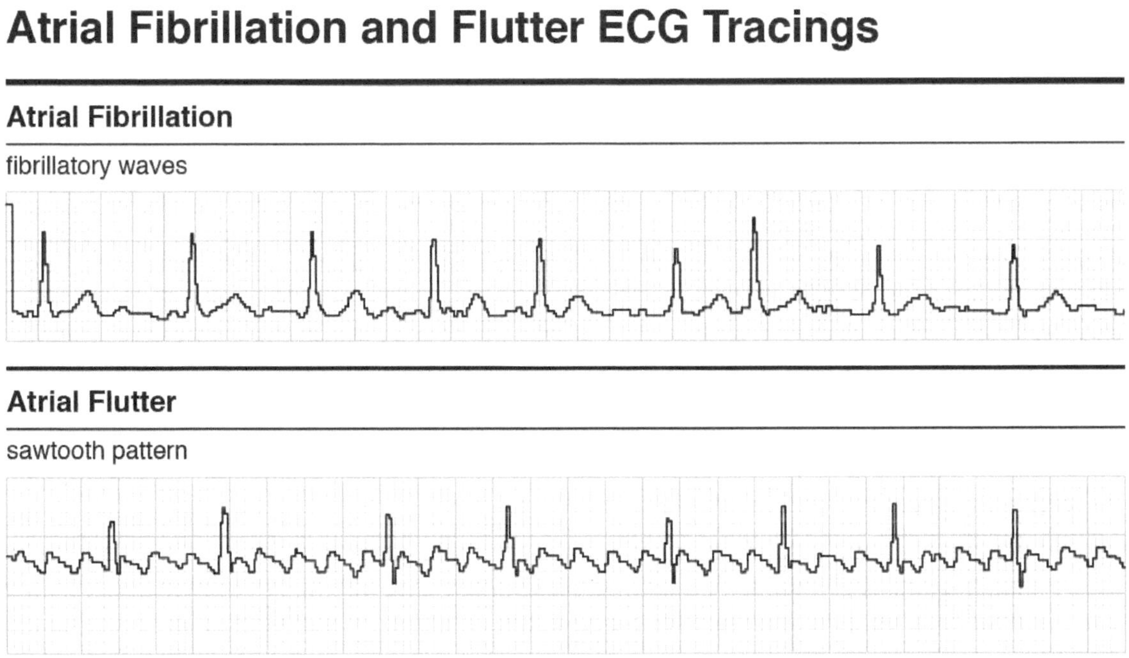

Atrial Flutter

Atrial flutter is caused by an ectopic atrial focus that fires between 250 and 350 times a minute. The AV node is unable to transmit impulses at that speed, so typically only one out of every two impulses reach the ventricles. Cardioversion is the treatment of choice to convert atrial flutter back to a sinus rhythm. Calcium channel blockers (CCBs) and beta-blockers are used to manage ventricular rates.

Junctional Dysrhythmias

If either the SA node slows or its impulse is not properly conducted, the AV node will become the pacemaker. The heart rate for an impulse initiated at the AV junction will be between 40 and 60 bpm. The P wave will be absent on an EKG. Suggested treatment is similar to that of sinus bradycardia: transcutaneous pacing, atropine, and epinephrine.

Bradydysrhythmias

Sinus bradycardia occurs when the SA node creates an impulse at a slower-than-normal rate—less than 60 beats per minute (bpm). Causes include metabolic conditions, calcium channel blockers (CCB) and beta-blocker medications, MIs, and increased intracranial pressure. If symptomatic, treatment involves transcutaneous pacing and atropine.

Conduction Defects and Blocks

Heart Block

In **first-degree heart block**, the impulse from the SA node is slowed as it moves across the atria. On an ECG, the P and R waves will be longer and flatter. First-degree block is often asymptomatic.

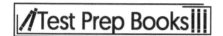

Second-degree heart block is divided into two categories known as Mobitz type I and Mobitz type II. In **Mobitz type I**, the impulse from the SA node is increasingly delayed with each heartbeat until eventually a beat is skipped entirely. On an ECG, this is visible as a delay in the PR interval. The normal PR interval is 0.12–0.20. The PR interval will get longer until the QRS wave doesn't follow the P wave. Patients may experience mild symptoms with this dysrhythmia.

When some of the impulses from the SA node fail to reach the ventricles, the arrhythmia is a **Mobitz type II** heart block. Some impulses move across the atria and reach the ventricles normally, and others do not. On an ECG, the QRS follows the P wave at normal speed, but some QRS complexes are missing because the signal is blocked. Patients experiencing this dysrhythmia usually need a pacemaker.

A **third-degree heart block** is also known as **complete heart block**, or **complete AV block**. The SA node may continue to initiate the impulses between 80 and 100 bpm, but none of the impulses reach the ventricles. The automaticity of cardiac cells in the Purkinje fibers will prompt the ventricles to initiate an impulse; however, beats initiated in this area are between 20 and 40 bpm. The slower impulses initiated from the ventricles are not coordinated with the impulses from the SA node. Therefore, third-degree heart block is a medical emergency that requires a temporary to permanent pacemaker.

Bundle Branch Block

A **bundle branch block** (BBB) occurs when there is a delay or defect in the conduction system within the ventricles; a BBB may be designated as "left" or "right" to specify the ventricle at fault or as "complete" or "partial." The QRS complex will be widened or prolonged. Treating the underlying cause is the goal.

Premature Ventricular Complex

A **premature ventricular complex** (PVC) occurs when a ventricular impulse is conducted through the ventricle before the next sinus impulse. This may be caused by cardiac ischemia, heart failure, hypoxia, or hypokalemia. Treatment is to correct the cause, and long-term treatment is not indicated unless the patient is symptomatic.

Device Related Dysrhythmias

The use of an **implantable cardiac device** (ICD) is associated with three forms of arrhythmias: inappropriate shocks, appropriate shocks, and "phantom shocks." There are two concerns related to the frequency of the ICD shocks; any time the ICD fires there is a risk of stimulating a life-threatening rhythm, and reports of depression, anxiety, and pain related to these shocks are noted in more than seventy-five percent of patients with an ICD. An **inappropriate shock** occurs when the ICD delivers the shock for any rhythm other than ventricular tachycardias. The most common cause is the presence of a supraventricular tachycardia because the rate of the dysrhythmia is within the programmed range of the ICD. The rate of appropriate shocks, and thereby the patient's concerns are kept to a minimum by antiarrhythmic therapy; however the medications can affect the defibrillation threshold of the ICD and are used with caution. **Phantom shocks** are sensed by the patient when no shock was delivered. This abnormal sensation most often decreases over time.

DDD Pacemakers

The **DDD pacemaker** (dual chamber activity sensing and response pacemaker) is associated with three specific dysrhythmic events. *Crosstalk* occurs when the pacemaker senses a signal as an R wave thereby interrupting the signal to the ventricle, inhibiting output and resetting the timing of the next signal. If the pacemaker fails to fire for any reason, the failure can result in a "native tachycardia," which inhibits the pacemaker action until the tachycardia subsides. Pacemaker-mediated tachycardias are associated with native atrial tachycardias or retrograde transmission or endless loop tachycardias. These conditions are commonly asymptomatic in patients with normal AV conduction but may be lethal with any degree of AV block.

Digoxin-Induced Ventricular Dysrhythmias

Digoxin is a cardiac glycoside medication that increases the strength and regularity of the cardiac rhythm. It has a very narrow therapeutic range. Toxicity occurs when therapeutic levels are exceeded. Digoxin toxicity can mimic all types of dysrhythmias. Digoxin acts by increasing automaticity in the atria, ventricles, and the His-Purkinje system. It also decreases conduction through the AV node. Therefore, an AV block is the most common form of presenting dysrhythmia in the general population. Among the elderly, chronic toxicity is common as well, as it can be easily caused by drug-to-drug interactions and declining renal function.

Lethal Ventricular Dysrhythmias

There are four lethal dysrhythmias that originate in the ventricles: ventricular tachycardia, ventricular fibrillation, torsades de pointes, and asystole.

Ventricular Tachycardia

Ventricular tachycardia (V-tach) occurs from a single, rapidly firing ectopic ventricular focus that is typically at the border of an old infarct (MI). This dysrhythmia is usually associated with CAD. Ventricular rates can be 150 to 250 bpm. However, the heart cannot pump effectively at those increased rates. Immediate cardioversion is the treatment of choice. Antidysrhythmic medications such as amiodarone, lidocaine, or procainamide may be given. An implantable cardioverter defibrillator (ICD) may be necessary.

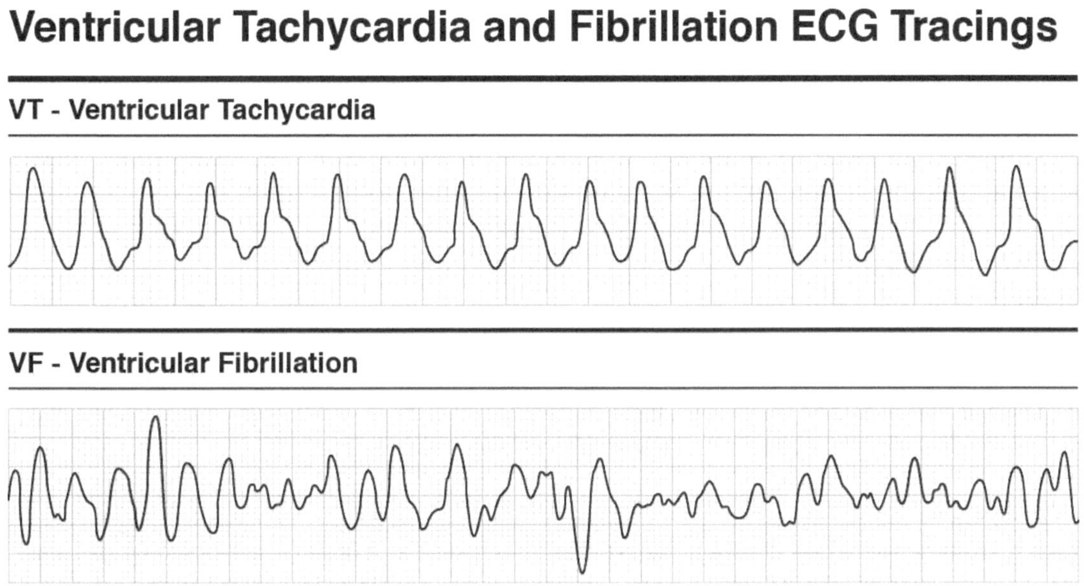

Ventricular Fibrillation

Ventricular fibrillation (V-fib) is a life-threatening emergency that requires immediate treatment. It is caused by multiple ventricular ectopic foci firing simultaneously, which forces the ventricles to contract asynchronously. Coordinated ventricular contraction is impossible in this scenario. The result is reduced cardiac output, and defibrillation is required. Lidocaine, amiodarone, and procainamide may be used.

Torsade de Pointes

Torsade de pointes is an atypical rapid undulating ventricular tachydysrhythmia. This rhythm has a prolonged QT interval. A variety of drugs cause QT-interval prolongation. The treatment is intravenous magnesium and cardioversion for sustained V-tach.

Torsade de Pointes ECG Tracing

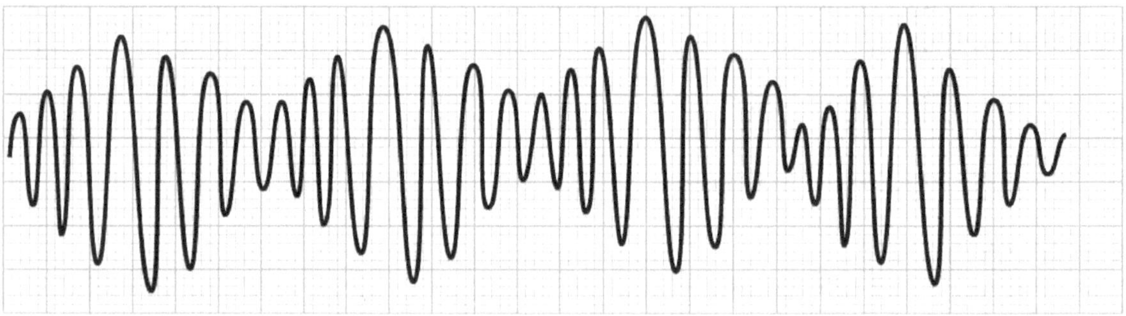

Asystole

Asystole is defined as sudden cardiac arrest (SCA) or death (SCD) that is manifested by a lack of electrical activity of the cardiac muscle resulting in an isoelectric ECG pattern. In monitored patients, asystole is most commonly preceded by ventricular dysrhythmias; however, bradyarrhythmias also may result in asystole. These lethal dysrhythmias often occur after a period of increasing premature ventricular activity. The most common cause of asystole is coronary artery disease; however, SCD is also associated with heart failure, structural heart diseases such as myocarditis and cardiomyopathy, and primary electrical diseases such as Brugada syndrome and Wolff-Parkinson-White syndrome. In addition, non-cardiac events such as traumatic injuries, hemorrhage, recreational drug intoxication, head injuries, and sudden airway obstruction due to disease or drowning may result in asystole.

Tachydysrhythmias

Supraventricular Tachycardia

Sustained **supraventricular tachycardia** (SVT) is usually caused by an AV nodal reentry circuit. Heart rate can increase to 150 to 250 bpm. Interventions that increase vagal tone such as the Valsalva maneuver or carotid massage may slow the heart rate. Beta-blockers and CCBs may be given intravenously for immediate treatment or may be taken orally to prevent reoccurrence.

Sinus Tachycardia

Sinus tachycardia occurs when the SA node creates an impulse at a faster-than-normal rate, also characterized as a rate greater than 100 bpm. Causes include physiological stress such as shock, volume loss, and heart failure, as well as medications and illicit drugs. Sinus tachycardia is typically treated by treating the underlying cause.

Summary

Dysrhythmias range from asymptomatic to life-threatening. They can be divided into three major groups: supraventricular dysrhythmias, heart block, and ventricular dysrhythmias. Treatment is necessary when ventricular pumping and cardiac output are impacted. There are two phases of treatment. The first is to terminate the dysrhythmia using medications, defibrillation, or both. The second is long-term suppression with medications.

A complete medical history with an emphasis on current medications, comorbidities, and family history is paramount. Immediate nursing priorities include establishing IV access, monitoring vital signs, and administering oxygen as needed. Evaluation of the ECG, chest x-ray, and both laboratory and diagnostic values is required. Defibrillation, cardioversion, and transcutaneous pacing are other possibilities.

Genetic Cardiac Disease

Long QT Syndrome

Long QT syndrome occurs when the QT segment of the ECG wave form is prolonged, representing the electrical activity in the ventricles. This hereditary and rare disorder usually occurs in healthy adults and children and is characterized by fainting episodes, feelings of "fluttering" in the chest, and abnormal heart rate or rhythm. Diagnosis occurs with ECG and stress testing. Long QT syndrome may be fatal, as it could potentially cause sudden cardiac arrest. A treatment plan for long QT syndrome may include beta-blockers, avoiding drugs that aggravate the syndrome, and possibly implantation of an ICD or pacemaker.

Brugada Syndrome

Brugada syndrome is the result of an inherited defect in the cardiac sodium channels gene. It is characterized by an ECG pattern of right bundle branch block with ST-segment elevation in leads V1, V2, and V3. This syndrome is associated with a significant risk of sudden cardiac arrest (SCA), with or without syncopal episodes, which is most often preceded by polymorphic ventricular ectopy. Two additional conditions, agonal nocturnal respiration and sudden unexpected nocturnal death syndrome (SUNDS), are also associated with the risk of SCA, characterized by similar ECG patterns, and related to a genetic defect in a cardiac sodium channel. SUNDS was first studied in a population of young men in Thailand where researchers proposed that the incidence of SCA was also related to the presence of hypokalemia. The treatment for Brugada includes antiarrhythmic therapy, ICD placement, and the avoidance of calcium channel blocker medications.

Structural Defects

The most common types of heart defects occur in developing fetuses and are diagnosed shortly after the child is born. Some common types of congenital defects are **atrial septal defects** (ASDs), **patent foramen ovale** (PFO), patent ductus arteriosus, coarctation of the aorta, and tetralogy of Fallot.

ASD and PFO are similar in that there is a hole between the two atria of the heart, and oxygen-rich blood leaks from the left chamber to the right. In ASD, the tissue never forms, and in PFO, the hole that is normally there does not close after birth as it should. An ASD hole is generally larger than a PFO.

Patent ductus arteriosus occurs when the **ductus arteriosus**, the vessel that connects the pulmonary artery and the aorta, does not close as it should after birth. The ductus arteriosus is vital for fetal development, but if it remains open after birth, the oxygen-rich blood of the aorta that is meant for body circulation gets mixed with the oxygen-poor blood of the pulmonary artery, resulting in increased pulmonary pressures and stress on the heart.

A narrowing of the aorta in a baby is called **coarctation of the aorta** and results in hypertension and heart damage.

Tetralogy of Fallot is a complex congenital heart defect involving four defects: a hole between the two ventricles called a **ventricular septal defect** (VSD), pulmonary valve stenosis, an aorta that is located between the two ventricles and above the VSD, and hypertrophy, or a thickening of the right ventricle due to working harder because of the pulmonary valve stenosis. Patients with tetralogy of Fallot must have open heart surgery to repair the defects.

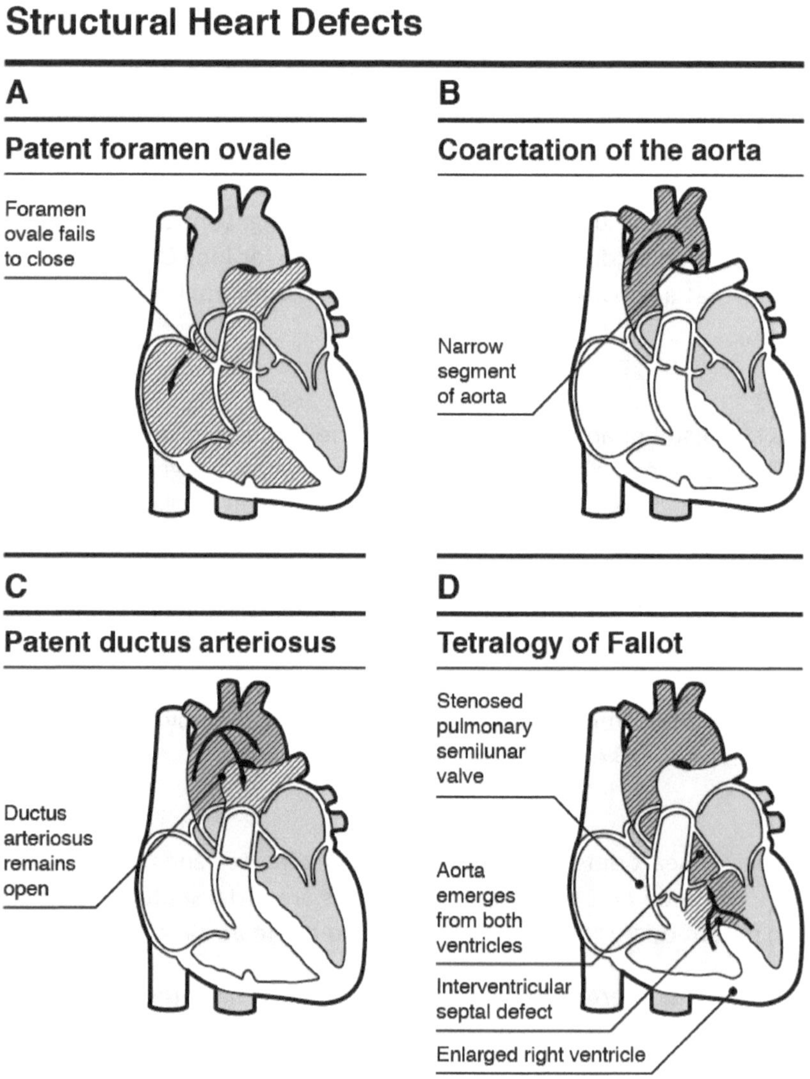

Structural heart defects occurring in adulthood include valvular disease. There are four valves in the heart: mitral, tricuspid, aortic, and pulmonary. These valves control the flow of blood between the chambers of the heart as well as the lungs for oxygenation and the body for circulation. Valvular defects occur because of normal aging and degeneration, infections, high BP, atherosclerosis, ischemic conditions such as heart attack, tumors, radiation, and even some medications. Valve dysfunctions can include stiffening, in which blood is forced backward rather than forward, or weakening, in which blood leaks inappropriately between chambers. The severity of the valve dysfunction determines the number of symptoms and the amount and type of treatment needed. Patients with valvular disease may experience palpitations, fatigue, dizziness, and/or chest pain. Diagnosis is made with an ECG, stress tests, chest x-rays, echocardiograms, and/or cardiac catheterization. Smoking cessation will be encouraged, antithrombotics or anticoagulants may be used to prevent dangerous clotting, and surgery to repair the valves may be a possibility for the patient with valvular disease.

Heart Failure

Mechanism

Defined as the failure of the heart to meet the metabolic demands of the body, **heart failure** (HF) is a general term that refers to the failure of the heart as a pump. Heart failure is a syndrome with diverse clinical features and various etiologies. The syndrome is progressive and often fatal. It may involve either or both sides of the heart. Based on an ejection fraction (EF), it can be further categorized as **diastolic** or **systolic** HF.

Left-sided HF is also referred to as congestive heart failure (CHF) because the congestion occurs in the **pulmonary** capillary beds. As mentioned previously, oxygenated blood flows from the pulmonary artery into the left atrium, then the LV, and into the aorta for distribution through the systemic circulation.

Once the oxygenated blood has been delivered to end-point tissues and organs, it arrives at the capillary bed. The now-deoxygenated blood begins the return journey back to the heart by passing from the capillary beds into small veins that feed into progressively larger veins and, ultimately, into the superior and inferior vena cava. The vena cava empties into the right atrium. From the right atrium, blood flows into the right ventricle and then into the pulmonary system for oxygenation.

When the right ventricle is impaired, it cannot effectively pump blood forward into the pulmonary system. The ineffective forward movement of blood causes an increase of venous pressure. When venous pressures rises, the blood backs up and leaks into the tissues and the liver. The end result is edema in the extremities and congestion within the liver.

When the LV is impaired, it cannot effectively pump blood forward into the aorta for systemic circulation. The ineffective forward movement of blood causes an increase in the pulmonary venous blood volume, which forces fluids from the capillaries to back up and leak into the pulmonary tissues. This results in pulmonary edema and impaired oxygenation.

Ejection fraction (EF) is the percentage of blood volume pumped out by the ventricles with each contraction. The normal EF is 50 to 70 percent. An EF of 60 percent means that 60 percent of the available blood volume was pumped out of the LV during contraction. It is an important measurement for diagnosing and tracking the progression of HF. The EF also differentiates between diastolic and systolic HF.

Diastolic HF is currently referred to as HF with normal ejection fraction (HFNEF). The heart muscle contracts normally, but the ventricles do not adequately relax during ventricular filling. In systolic HF, or heart failure with reduced ejection fraction (HFrEF), the heart muscle does not contract effectively, so less blood is pumped out to the body.

There are several variables that both impact and are impacted by HF. A review of these variables will provide the backdrop for a closer look at the classification, sequelae, symptoms, and treatment of HF.

Cardiac output (CO, or Q) is the volume of blood being pumped by the heart in one minute. It is the product of heart rate multiplied by stroke volume. **Stroke volume** (SV) is the amount of blood pumped out of the ventricles per beat; $CO = HR \times SV$. Normal CO is between four and eight liters per minute. Both CO and SV are reduced in HF.

Systemic vascular resistance (SVR) is related to the diameter and elasticity of blood vessels and the viscosity of blood. For example, narrow and stiff vessels and/or thicker blood will cause an increase in SVR. An increase in SVR causes the LV to work harder to overcome the pressure at the aortic valve. Conversely, larger and more elastic vessels and/or thin blood will decrease SVR and reduce cardiac workload.

Pulmonary vascular resistance (PVR) is the vascular resistance of the pulmonary circulation. It is the difference between the mean pulmonary arterial pressure and the left atrial filling pressure. Resistance and blood viscosity impact both SVR and PVR. However, pulmonary blood flow, lung volume, and hypoxic vasoconstriction are unique to the pulmonary vasculature.

Preload is defined as the amount of ventricular stretch at the end of diastole, or when the chambers are filling. In other words, preload is the amount of pressure from the blood that is being exerted against the inside of the LV. It is also known as left ventricular end-diastolic pressure (LVEDP) and reflects the amount of stretch of cardiac muscle sarcomeres. **Afterload** is the amount of resistance the heart must overcome to open the aortic valve and push the blood volume into the systemic circulation.

Sequelae

Heart failure may have an acute or chronic onset, but it is progressive. When CO is diminished, tissues are not adequately perfused, and organs ultimately fail. When the LV works harder because of increased preload or afterload, its muscular walls become thick and enlarged, resulting in ventricular hypertrophy. Ventricular hypertrophy causes ventricular remodeling (cardiac remodeling), which is a change to the heart's size, shape, structure, and physiological function.

The sympathetic nervous system responds to a diminished CO by increasing the heart rate, constricting arteries, and activating the renin-angiotensin-aldosterone system (RAAS). Elevated angiotensin levels raise BP and afterload, thereby prompting the heart to work harder. The reduced CO caused by HF can diminish blood flow to the kidneys. The kidneys respond to the decreased perfusion by secreting renin and activating the RAAS. As a result, the increase in aldosterone signals the body to retain Na^+ and water. Retained Na^+ and water leads to volume overload, pulmonary congestion, and hypertension. The body's response to reduced CO caused by HF can perpetuate a downward spiral. However, there are naturally-occurring natriuretic peptides that are secreted in response to elevated pressures within the heart. These peptides counteract fluid retention and vasoconstriction.

Atrial natriuretic peptide (ANP) is secreted by the atria. **B-type natriuretic peptide** (BNP) is secreted by the ventricles. Both ANP and BNP cause diuresis, vasodilation, and decreased aldosterone secretion, thereby balancing the effects of sympathetic nervous system response and RAAS activation. Elevated levels of BNP are a diagnostic indication of HF.

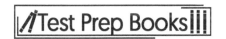

Acute Exacerbations

Either an MI or a dysrhythmia can precipitate HF. The clinical presentation reflects congestion in the pulmonary and/or systemic vasculature. Treatment depends on the clinical stage of the disease. Common symptoms include:

- Dyspnea on exertion
- Fatigue
- Pulmonary congestion, which causes a cough and difficulty breathing when lying down
- Feelings of suffocation and anxiety that are worse at night
- Peripheral edema

Heart failure symptoms may vary based on the side of the heart affected. Symptoms of left-sided heart failure are tachycardia, shortness of breath, and the expectoration of frothy pink sputum. Pitting edema is symptomatic of right-sided heart failure and increased venous pressure that backs up into the tissues, causing edema. Ascites is a result of diffuse congestion in the liver caused by the increased venous pressure that characterizes right-sided heart failure.

The most common cause of HF exacerbation is fluid overload due to nonadherence to sodium and water restrictions. Patient education is extremely critical to avoiding and managing exacerbations. Congestive heart failure is a core measure, tied to patient satisfaction, patient education, subsequent readmissions in a defined period of time, and ultimately, to reimbursements.

Chronic

HF is closely associated with chronic hypertension, CAD, and diabetes mellitus. The New York Heart Association (NYHA) classification tool is most frequently used to categorize the stages and symptom progression of HF as it relates to heart disease.

- Stage I: Cardiac disease; no symptoms during physical activity
- Stage II: Cardiac disease; slight limitations on physical activity
- Stage III: Cardiac disease; marked limitations during physical activity
- Stage IV: Cardiac disease; unable to perform physical activity; symptoms at rest

Therapy for HF focuses on three primary goals: reduction of preload, reduction of afterload (SVR), and inhibition of the RAAS and vasoconstrictive mechanisms of the sympathetic nervous system. Pharmacotherapy includes ACE inhibitors, angiotensin II receptor blockers (ARBs), diuretics, beta-blockers, vasodilators, and cardiac glycosides.

The ACE inhibitors and ARBs interfere with the RAAS by preventing the body's normal mechanism to retain fluids and constrict blood vessels. Diuretics decrease fluid volume and relieve both pulmonary and systemic congestion. Beta-blockers and cardiac glycosides slow the HR and strengthen the myocardium to improve contractility. Vasodilators decrease SVR. In addition to a thorough physical exam and complete medical history, a clinical work-up will include a chest x-ray, a BNP and other laboratory values, an ECG, and perhaps an echocardiogram or MUGA scan to measure EF.

HF is a common debilitating syndrome characterized by high mortality, frequent hospitalizations, multiple comorbidities, and poor quality of life. A partnership between providers, nurses, and patients is paramount to managing and slowing disease progression. Patient education should include a discussion of the disease process, prescribed medications, diet restrictions, and weight management. Patients should know which symptoms require immediate medical care. Self-care can be the most important aspect of HF management. The nurse as educator performs an essential role in this and all disease management.

Hypertension

Hypertension (HTN) is an abnormally high BP (140/90 mmHg or higher). The diagnosis is based on two or more accurate readings that are elevated. HTN is known as *the* **silent killer** because it is asymptomatic. Several variables impact BP, and understanding them is essential.

Variables

BP is the product of CO multiplied by SVR; $BP = CO \times SVR$. CO is the volume of blood being pumped by the heart in one minute. It is the product of HR multiplied by SV; $HR \times SV = CO$. SV is the amount of blood pumped out of the ventricles per beat.

SVR is related to the diameter of blood vessels and the viscosity of blood. The narrower the vessels or the thicker the blood, the higher the SVR. Conversely, larger-diameter vessels and thinner blood decrease SVR.

Mechanism

For HTN to develop, there must be a change in one or more factors affecting SVR or CO and a problem with the control system responsible for regulating BP. The body normally maintains and adjusts BP by either increasing the HR or the strength of myocardial contraction or by dilating or constricting the veins and arterioles.

When veins are dilated, less blood returns to the heart, and subsequently, less blood is pumped out of the heart. The result is a decrease in CO. Conversely, when veins are constricted, more blood is returned to the heart, and CO is increased. The arterioles also dilate or constrict. An expanded arteriole reduces resistance, and a constricted arteriole increases resistance. The veins and arterioles impact both CO and SVR. The kidneys contribute to the maintenance and adjustment of BP by controlling Na^+, chloride, and water excretion and through the RAAS. Management of HTN will focus on one or more of the factors that regulate BP. Those regulatory factors are SVR, fluid volume, and the strength and rate of myocardial contraction.

Classification

HTN is classified as **primary** or **secondary** depending on the etiology. In primary HTN, the cause is unknown, but the primary factors include problems related to the natriuretic hormones or RAAS or electrolyte disturbances. Primary HTN is also known as **essential** or **idiopathic** HTN.

In secondary HTN, there is an identifiable cause. Associated disease states include kidney disease, adrenal gland tumors, thyroid disease, congenital blood vessel disorders, alcohol abuse, and obstructive sleep apnea. Products associated with secondary HTN are nonsteroidal anti-inflammatory drugs (NSAIDs), birth control pills, decongestants, cocaine, amphetamines, and corticosteroids.

HTN normally increases with age, and it is more prominent among African Americans. BP is classified according to treatment guidelines as normal, pre-HTN, Stage 1 HTN, and Stage 2 HTN. **Pre-HTN** is defined as systolic pressures ranging from 120 to 139 mmHg and diastolic pressures ranging from 80 to 89 mmHg. **Stage 1 HTN** ranges from 140 to 159 mmHg systolic and 90 to 99 mmHg diastolic pressures. In the more severe Stage 2 HTN, systolic pressures are 160 mmHg or higher, and diastolic pressures are 100 mmHg or higher.

Sequelae

Systolic pressure is the amount of pressure exerted on arterial walls immediately after ventricular contraction and emptying. This represents the highest level of pressure during the cardiac cycle. Diastolic pressure is the amount of pressure exerted on arterial walls when the heart is filling. This represents the lowest pressure during the cardiac cycle. In general, hypertension increases the risk of cardiovascular disease; diastolic HTN poses a greater risk.

Prolonged HTN damages the delicate endothelial layer of vessels. The damaged endothelium initiates the inflammatory response and clotting cascade. As mentioned, the diameter of veins, arterioles, and arteries changes SVR. When SVR is increased, the heart must work harder to pump against the increased pressure. In other words, the pressure in the LV must be higher than the pressure being exerted on the opposite side of the aortic valve by systemic vascular pressure. The ventricular pressure must overcome the aortic pressure for contraction and ventricular emptying to occur. When the myocardium works against an elevated systemic pressure for a prolonged period of time, the LV will enlarge, and HF may ensue.

Risk Factors

There are both modifiable and nonmodifiable risk factors associated with the development of HTN. Modifiable risk factors include obesity, a sedentary lifestyle, tobacco use, a diet high in sodium, dyslipidemia, excessive alcohol consumption, stress, sleep apnea, and diabetes. Age, race, and family history are nonmodifiable risk factors.

Treatment

First-line treatments include lifestyle changes and pharmacologic therapy.

Initial therapy includes diuretics, CCBs, ACE inhibitors, and ARBs. Diuretics decrease fluid volume. CCBs decrease myocardial contractility. Both ACE inhibitors and ARBs interfere with the RAAS by preventing the normal mechanism that retains fluids and narrows blood vessels. The result is decreased volume and SVR.

Summary

The astute nurse will conduct an in-depth patient interview to identify prescribed and illicit drug use, alcohol and tobacco use, family history, sleep patterns, and dietary habits. Patient education should include information about the Dietary Approach to Stop Hypertension (DASH) diet and alcohol in moderation with a limit of one to two drinks per day. Aerobic exercise and resistance training three to four times weekly for an average of 40 minutes is recommended. Information about prescribed hypertensive medications should also be reviewed with the patient.

Hypertensive Crisis

A **hypertensive crisis** is defined as a BP higher than 180/120 mmHg. BP must be lowered quickly to prevent end organ damage. Pregnancy, an acute MI, a dissecting aortic aneurysm, and an intracranial hemorrhage are associated with a hypertensive crisis. The therapeutic goal is to reduce the BP by 25 percent within the first hour of treatment with a continual reduction over the following 2 to 6 hours and an ongoing reduction to the target goal over a period of days. Short-acting antihypertensive medications administered intravenously is the primary treatment.

Minimally-Invasive Cardiac Surgery

Endarterectomy

The patient with atherosclerosis of the carotid artery may be a candidate for a surgical procedure called an **endarterectomy**. In this surgery, the carotid artery is accessed by a surgeon, incised, and the problematic plaque carefully removed. The artery is then sutured closed, and the patient will likely be sent to an intensive care unit (ICU) to recover.

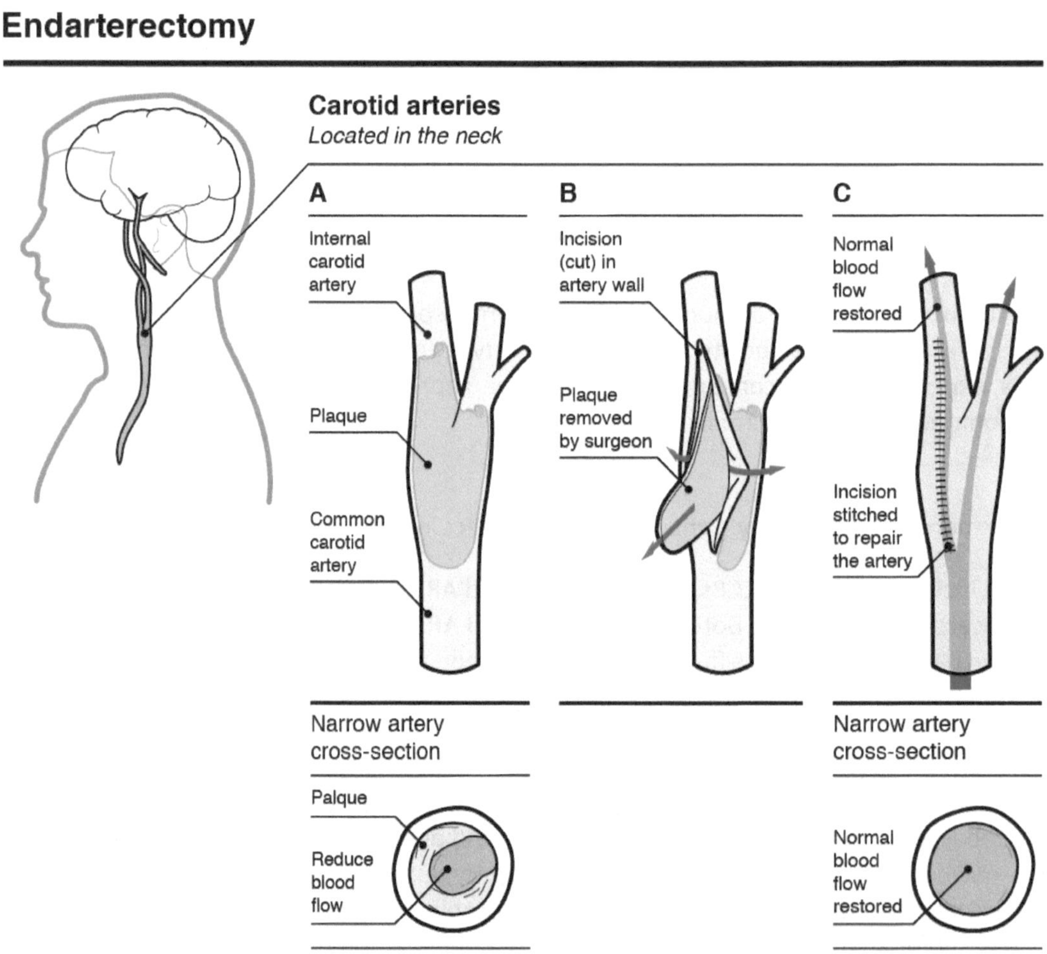

The progressive care nurse will be carefully monitoring the patient in the hours and days following the surgery. Since a major artery was accessed, bleeding is the first and most obvious complication to be monitored for. The incision site will be monitored not only for signs of becoming infected, but for hematoma or signs of bleeding. There may be wound drains for which patency needs to be maintained. The patient must be taught to support their head with their hands when moving to minimize strain of the neck muscles. Clots are still a threat to this patient's well-being, so the nurse will monitor for any signs that the carotid artery has become occluded again or that the patient is experiencing a CVA. Signs of a CVA include sudden onset of neurologic deficits such as confusion, dizziness, slurred speech, or paralysis of the arms and/or legs.

Hemodynamic monitoring is critical to determine if a patient is developing complications. Though previously only available for patients in ICUs with invasive monitoring devices, now many facilities are now able to provide hemodynamic monitoring via non-invasive devices, so progressive care nurses should be familiar with normal parameters. Commonly assessed normal parameters for hemodynamic values are listed below, but of course, normal values may vary from patient to patient depending on diagnosis, fluid volume status and age.

- Cardiac Output (CO): 4.0-8.0 l/min
- Cardiac Index (CI): 2.5-4.0 $l/min/m_2$
- Systemic Vascular Resistance: 800-1200 dynes · sec/cm_5
- Right Atrial Pressure: 1-8 mmHg

If there are large changes in hemodynamics the progressive care nurse should be ready to contact the provider to report changes and be anticipating orders based on hemodynamics. Progressive care nurses should also be familiar with signs of hemodynamic instability in patients without devices. For example, hypotension could indicate volume loss or possibly lead to myocardial ischemia. Hypertension puts the patient at risk of developing a CVA, as well as putting added pressure on the recently incised and healing artery.

The progressive care nurse will monitor for signs of respiratory distress, such as a change in rate, rhythm, depth, and effort of breath. The nurse will also be mindful of tracheal deviation from the midline and patient restlessness, as well as difficulty swallowing. These could be signs of excessive swelling and could lead to further respiratory distress. It is recommended that a patient who has had an endarterectomy have a tracheostomy kit at their bedside, in case of an emergency.

The patient will likely be put on antiplatelet therapy in the postop period, including aspirin at 100 mg daily and clopidogrel at 75 mg daily for at least the first thirty days, starting day one post op. A major complication in the postoperative period is clotting and/or restenosis of the artery, and this therapy aims to prevent that.

Cardiac/Vascular Catheterization

A progressive care nurse is well acquainted with the **cardiac catheterization** procedure, as it is a powerful and frequently used tool to determine if a patient has cardiac disease. The test involves the threading of a small, thin catheter through peripheral arteries or veins up to the heart, obtaining information about the chambers, valves, and structures therein, the pulmonary artery, the coronary arteries, and the veins.

There are two different approaches to cardiac catheterization: left heart and right heart. **Left heart catheterization** is commonly used to determine anatomy of the heart, blood pressure in the aorta, or to assess aortic or mitral valve function. If the cardiologist wishes to use this approach, they will access the femoral artery and enter the heart through the aorta on the left side. For left heart catheterization, the subclavian, radial, or brachial arteries may also be accessed, but less commonly.

For **right heart catheterization**, the venous system is accessed. The heart is approached from the right side, entering through the right atrium where venous blood is returning. Right heart cardiac catheterization is used to determine the pressures in the right atria, right ventricle, and pulmonary arteries, as well as the pulmonary artery occlusion pressure (PAOP). Common venous access sites used for right heart catheterization are the femoral, subclavian, internal jugular, or antecubital veins.

The method of visualization used in cardiac catheterization is through the injection of radiopaque contrast into the heart chambers and surrounding structures while x-ray images are taken to produce images. This is called **angiography**. Another visualization technique uses tiny ultrasound transducers placed at the end of the catheter to produce images. Angiography and ultrasonography can be used at the same time.

Patients with kidney disease may not be good candidates for undergoing a cardiac catheterization due to the contrast that is used. When this dye is shot into the heart, it must be metabolized by the kidneys, which in a damaged kidney could lead to further damage. Patients with active infections, fever, heart failure, heart arrhythmias, and coagulopathies may also be poor candidates for cardiac catheterizations, at the discretion of the physician.

To prepare for a cardiac catheterization, the patient will be kept nil per os (NPO) for 4 to 6 hours pre-catheterization. During the procedure, the patient will be given medication to help them relax, but will not be put under general anesthesia. Patients traditionally go to a cath lab recovery unit until anesthetics wear off and the plastic sheath that was inserted in the femoral or radial artery is usually removed there. When patients return to the nursing unit after having cardiac catheterization, the site of insertion should be closely monitored for minimally four hours, checking for hematoma or bleeding at the site as well as signs of good circulation below the site- color, pulses, paresthesias/paralysis, and cap refill. If patients have coughing or vomiting, check the site immediately. If bleeding is noted, pressure should be held to the puncture site until hemostasis can be achieved. Patients' vital signs and cardiac rhythm should also be closely observed, notifying provider of abnormalities.

There are two uses for cardiac catheterization: diagnostic and interventional. The diagnostic approach means the cardiologist is looking to assess the anatomy of the heart and determine its functioning ability. Disease states will be evaluated. Common diagnostic uses of cardiac catheterization include angiography, intravascular ultrasonography, measuring of cardiac output, biopsy of tissues within the heart, shunt detection, and measurement of the heart's metabolic function.

The second approach to cardiac catheterization is interventional, often occurring during a diagnostic procedure. A problem is seen, and action is taken to correct it. Common interventions during cardiac catheterization are percutaneous transluminal coronary angioplasty and stent insertion.

The tip of the cardiac catheter is a tiny balloon that can be inflated to open occluded arteries, a procedure termed **angioplasty**. After balloon inflation, the cardiologist may choose to insert a stent into the reopened artery to maintain patency of the vessel, as shown in the image below. Stent placement is used often in the case of acute MI. This intervention helps restore blood flow to areas of ischemia in the heart following a coronary artery occlusion.

Illustration of catheter insertion, balloon inflation, and stent placement during cardiac catheterization

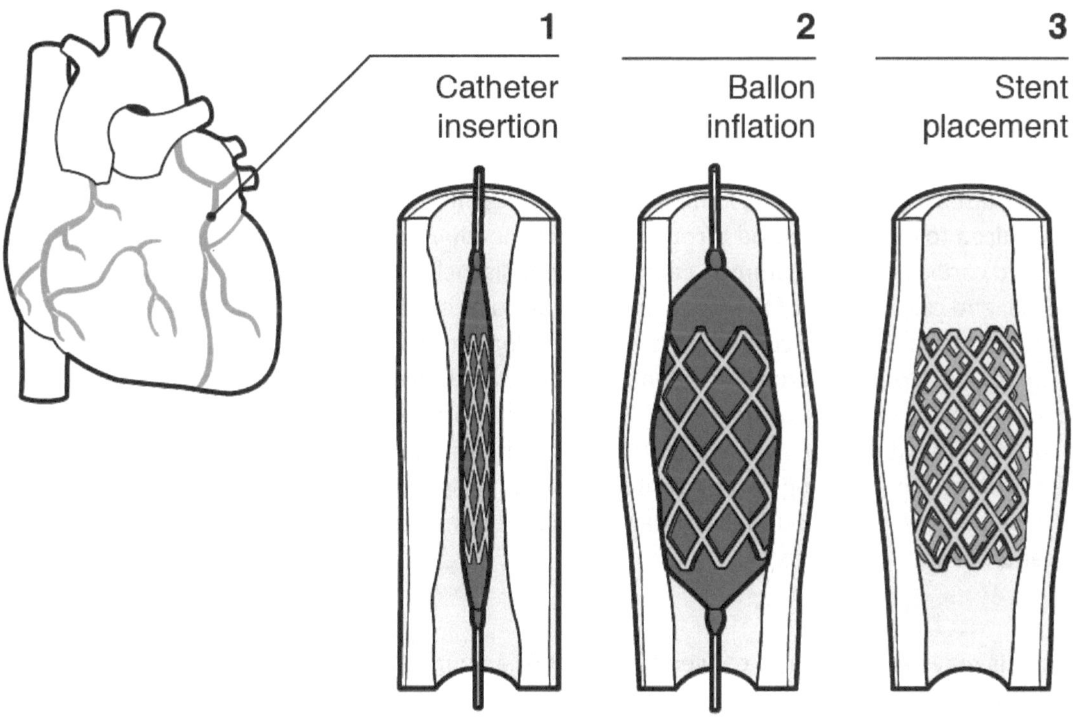

Septal Defects

Congenital Septal Defects

The **adult atrial septal defect** (ASD) results from an error in the early embryonic development of the primum and secundum septa between the right and left atria. At birth, the changes in pressure due to respiration compress the septum primum against the septum secundum to seal the foramen ovale. In 20% of the population, the foramen ovale either does not seal completely or is left open. The degree of left to right shunting of blood that occurs with either of these conditions may be well tolerated into middle or late adulthood. The defects increase in size over time, resulting in the onset of pulmonary hypertension, atrial dysrhythmias, dyspnea, exercise intolerance, and possible progression to heart failure. The defect may be repaired with open or percutaneous procedures depending on the extent of the defect.

Congenital ventricular septal defects are less common than atrial defects. These defects often present with the onset of heart failure in infants or children depending on the size of the defect. Smaller defects may remain asymptomatic until adulthood, but the development of aortic regurgitation or endocarditis is possible. Although smaller defects may close spontaneously, surgery is recommended for all symptomatic patients.

Acquired Septal Defects

Trauma and endocarditis from all sources are the most common causes of acquired septal defects in adults. The manifestations are related to whether the onset is acute or progressive and the patient's compensatory response to the event. Trauma to the valves represents a surgical emergency, while inflammation of the endocardium and its effects may be managed medically in some patients. In either case, the treatment is centered on the underlying pathology and resulting cardiac events.

Valvular Heart Disease

Stenosis and insufficiency due to regurgitation are the two most common processes associated with valvular heart disease. **Stenosis** is described as a stiffening of the valvular leaflets which increases the pressure required to move the blood through the valve, leading to enlargement of the cardiac chambers and decreased cardiac output. Common causes of stenosis include congenital abnormalities, rheumatic heart disease, and calcification of the valve leaflets due to altered mineral metabolism and atherosclerosis. **Insufficiency** occurs when the valvular leaflets do not close completely, allowing regurgitation of the blood back to the original chamber, which eventually decreases cardiac output. Insufficiency is most often due to congenital defects, rheumatic fever, endocarditis, and coronary artery disease. The patient with mild valvular dysfunction may be asymptomatic; however, valvular disease is most often progressive, resulting in the eventual onset of fatigue, dyspnea, syncope, and chest tightness. Open and percutaneous valve repair or replacement procedures are considered based on the individual and the specific defect.

Aortic

Aortic stenosis may be caused by a congenital defect or acquired. The most common congenital defect of the aortic valve is an alteration in the number of valvular leaflets. The resulting anatomical shape of the valve increases the bending motion of the valve during systole which restricts the opening of the valve and increases friction on the valve as it closes. The resulting damage to the endothelium and the formation of fibrotic areas results in symptomatic disease in younger patients. The most common acquired defect is the calcification of the valve leaflets that appears to be associated with the development of atherosclerosis and calcification in other areas of the cardiac vasculature.

Aortic regurgitation or insufficiency may be caused by endocarditis with vegetative growth on the valve leaflets, rheumatic fever, collagen vascular diseases, chest trauma, or damage related to the use of a left ventricular assist device (LVAD).

Mitral

Mitral valve stenosis can be caused by rheumatic fever, or more rarely by a congenital defect. The condition evolves slowly with the gradual deposition of vegetative growths that eventually thicken and calcify the leaflets resulting in the narrowing of the pathway from the left atria to the left ventricle.

Mitral valve insufficiency occurs as a result of mitral valve prolapse, endocarditis, rheumatic disease, and ischemic heart disease. The regurgitation of the blood from the left ventricle to the left atrium results from any alteration in the valve structure. This condition often develops gradually; however, rapid onset of the insufficiency is common when occurring concurrently with left-sided heart failure.

Mitral valve prolapse results from enlargement of the bicuspid leaflets and redundancy of the chordae tendineae that attach to the ventricular endocardium. This process may be the result of an inherited disorder, Marfan syndrome, hyperthyroidism, or alterations in the autonomic nervous system. The condition is more prevalent in women.

Vascular Disease

Peripheral vascular disease (PVD) refers to diseases of the blood vessels that are outside the heart and brain. The term PVD is used interchangeably with **peripheral arterial disease** (PAD). It is the narrowing of peripheral vessels caused by atherosclerosis. The narrowing can be compounded by emboli or thrombi. Limb ischemia due to reduced blood flow can result in loss of limb or life. The primary factor for the development of PVD is atherosclerosis.

PVD encompasses several conditions: atherosclerosis, Buerger's disease, chronic venous insufficiency, deep vein thrombosis (DVT), Raynaud's phenomenon, thrombophlebitis, and varicose veins.

CAD, atrial fibrillation, cerebrovascular disease (stroke), and renal disease are common comorbidities. Risk factors include smoking, phlebitis, injury, surgery, and hyperviscosity of the blood. Autoimmune disorders and hyperlipidemia are also common factors. The two major complications of PVD are limb complications or loss and the risk for stroke or heart attack.

Intermittent claudication (cramping pain in the leg during exercise) may be the sole manifestation of early symptomatic PVD. It occurs with exercise and stops with rest. Physical findings during examination may include the classic **five P's**: pulselessness, paralysis, paresthesia, pain, and pallor of the extremity.

The most critical symptom of PVD is **critical limb ischemia** (CLI), which is pain that occurs in the affected limb during rest. Manifestations of PVD may include the following symptoms:

- Feet that are cool or cold to the touch
- Aching or burning in the legs that is relieved by sitting
- Pale color when legs are elevated
- Redness when legs are in a hanging-down (dependent) position
- Brittle, thin, or shiny skin on the legs and feet
- Loss of hair on feet
- Nonhealing wounds or ulcers over pressure points
- Loss of muscle or fatty tissue
- Numbness, weakness, or heaviness in muscles
- Reddish-blue discoloration of the extremities
- Restricted mobility
- Thickened, opaque toenails

The **ankle-brachial index** (ABI) should be measured. The ABI is the systolic pressure at the ankle, divided by the systolic pressure at the arm. It is a specific and sensitive indicator of peripheral artery disease (PAD). The **Allen test** looks for an occlusion of either the radial or ulnar arteries. A Doppler ultrasonography flow study can determine the patency of peripheral arteries.

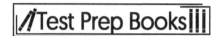

The patient should be assessed for heart murmurs, and all peripheral pulses should be evaluated for quality and bruit. An ECG may reveal an arrhythmia. Because the presence of atherosclerosis initiates an inflammatory response, inflammatory markers such as the D-dimer, CRP, interleukin 6, and homocysteine may be present. Blood urea nitrogen (BUN) and creatinine levels may provide indications of decreased organ perfusion. A lipid profile may reveal the risk for atherosclerosis. A stress test or angiogram may be necessary.

The two main goals for treatment of PVD are to control the symptoms and halt the progression to lower the risk of heart attack and stroke. Specific treatment modalities depend on the extent and severity of the disease, the patient's age, overall medical history, clinical signs, and their preferences. Lifestyle modifications include smoking cessation, improved nutrition, and regular exercise. Aggressive treatment of comorbidities can also aid in stopping the progression. Pharmacotherapy may include anticoagulants and vasodilators.

Carotid Artery Stenosis

Carotid artery stenosis is a subcategory of peripheral vascular insufficiency involving the arteries of the neck that supply the brain with nutrient-filled blood. This condition may exist long before symptoms occur, as the narrowing may not be severe enough to significantly reduce blood flow to the brain. Stenosis, the narrowing of a blood vessel, in this case is most often caused by atherosclerosis. This entails a building up of a fatty substance called *plaque* inside the artery walls, which leads to reduced blood flow.

An acute condition involving carotid artery stenosis is when a clot occurs at the site of the stenosis, interrupting blood flow completely. This leads to a **transient ischemic attack** (TIA), or worse, a **cerebrovascular accident** (CVA), commonly referred to as a **stroke**. A TIA is an episode that mimics stroke symptoms, such as slurring of speech, drooping of face, and other neurologic deficits, and lasts for less than an hour but greater than 5 minutes. There is no long-term damage, as the episode is transient enough that no brain tissue is injured. A TIA may be the first clue the patient has that they have carotid artery stenosis, as there are few to no symptoms beforehand.

Risk factors for developing carotid artery stenosis include alcohol abuse, high BP, smoking, high cholesterol, diabetes, obesity, stress, heart disease, drug abuse (especially cocaine and amphetamines), vascular inflammation, history of stroke, and old age. Smoking cessation information should be given to the patient to encourage them to quit.

Carotid artery stenosis is diagnosed most commonly with carotid ultrasound, using sonography to visualize the arterial structures in the neck. Other tests that may be ordered include carotid angiography, magnetic resonance angiography, and computerized tomography angiography (CAT).

The arteries may be stented or partially removed to correct the stenosis. Antiplatelet therapy will ensue as well as anticoagulants to prevent future blood clots.

Minimally Invasive Interventions

Endografts

Peripheral vascular disease is broadly defined as atherosclerotic alterations in the vasculature outside of the heart; however, the common understanding of the term refers to occlusive disease of the arms or legs that most commonly affects the aortic-iliac segment, the femoropopliteal segment, and the tibial arteries. The manifestations are related to the progressive decrease in the arterial circulation to the legs and may include intermittent claudication, pain at rest, development of arterial ulcers, pallor, and diminished peripheral pulses. The most common risk factors associated with the development of the disease are hypertension, smoking, male gender, history of the disease in a first-degree relative, obesity, atherosclerosis with abnormal cholesterol levels, diabetes, and chronic renal failure.

The disease can compromise circulation to the extremities by gradually decreasing the lumen of the vessels by plaque formation or by sudden total occlusion due to thrombus formation. The manifestations are associated with the etiology and the extent of the available collateral circulation to the limb. Treatment is aimed at eliminating or treating the risk factors, and restoring the arterial blood supply. Angioplasty with the placement of a peripheral endograft in the occluded artery is a common choice. The vessel is expanded to allow normal blood flow, the endograft is placed to maintain the patency of the vessel. Continued surveillance of the integrity of the endograft is necessary to identify and treat possible leakage from that area.

Peripheral stents

Peripheral stents are another option to attempt to open occluded arteries in a patient with peripheral arterial disease (PAD). Stent placement occurs at the same time as angioplasty, in which a small thin catheter is threaded into the affected blood vessel, and a tiny balloon is inflated to "pop" open the lumen of the blood vessel. Then, stent placement can occur.

The stent is, in most cases, a tiny metal, mesh-like tube that provides a scaffolding or support structure to keep a blood vessel open. The stent remains in the patient's blood vessel permanently, although it is possible to remove a stent if absolutely necessary.

Antiplatelet and antithrombotic therapies are used in the postoperative period.

Peripheral Arterial Occlusions

When an artery or vein is blocked by a clot, the occlusion is termed a **thrombosis**. Clot formation is a normal hemostatic adjustment that occurs in a healthy individual to prevent excessive bleeding and promote wound healing. Inappropriate clotting, however, can interrupt critical blood flow and thus oxygen delivery to the tissues of the body. Interruption in oxygen delivery, if not corrected, will lead to tissue damage and death.

Occlusion of an artery may sometimes occur because of atherosclerosis, in which fatty deposits, called **plaques**, build up over time, sticking to the walls of the vessels. These fatty deposits are composed of lipids, inflamed smooth muscle cells, and a connective tissue matrix composed of thrombi in various stages, as well as calcium deposits.

A person may not know that they have atherosclerosis until a plaque bursts or occludes blood flow, causing ischemic conditions such as stroke or heart attack.

Persons who smoke should be encouraged to cease, as smoking is one of the greatest risk factors for developing atherosclerosis. Nicotine and other chemicals found in cigarette or cigar smoke are toxic to the inner lining of blood vessels. These toxins inflame and scar the vascular endothelium, not only increasing the risk of plaque accumulation, but also causing vasoconstriction. Vasoconstriction in already narrowed blood vessels increases BP and puts the smoker in danger of other life-threatening events such as clots and IAs.

Other risk factors for atherosclerosis include high cholesterol, diabetes, family history, sedentary lifestyle, obesity, and high BP.

To confirm a diagnosis of atherosclerosis, the affected blood vessels need to be visualized by imaging techniques such as angiography or ultrasonography.

Modifications in lifestyle such as diet, exercise, and smoking cessation will be encouraged for the patient with atherosclerosis. Drug therapy will include antiplatelets such as aspirin at 100 mg daily and statins for targeting lipids such as atorvastatin at 40–80 mg per day.

Peripheral Surgical Interventions

Femoropopliteal bypass

A **femoropopliteal (fem-pop) bypass graft** is a surgical procedure that reroutes blood in the leg past an occluded section of artery, caused by atherosclerosis. The patient's own vein may be used, or an artificial vein will be used, though this presents a risk for narrowing over time. The vein bypasses the occlusion starting at the femoral artery and ending at the popliteal artery in the knee.

Femoropopliteal Bypass

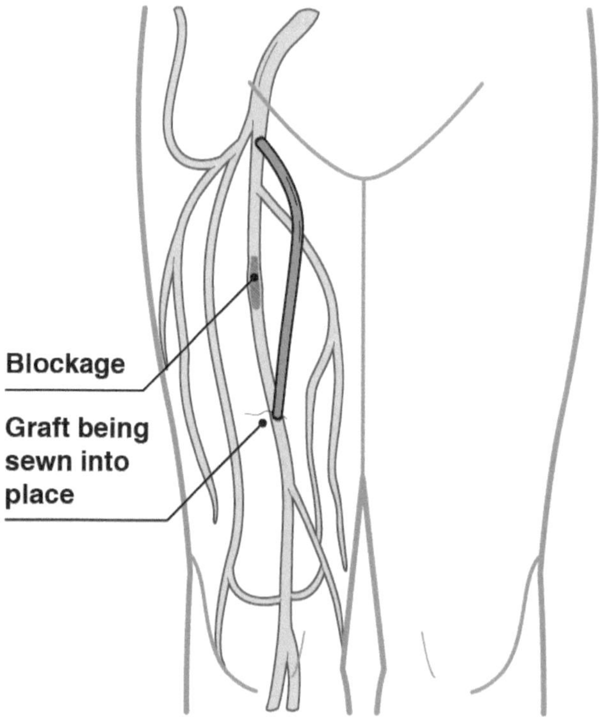

This procedure is used for patients with severe claudication. **Claudication** is a word of Latin origin, originally meaning "limp," but in this case, it means severe pain in the legs caused by restricted blood supply. Claudication may occur in the feet or, most commonly, in the calves. The patient may also be experiencing sores that will not heal or gangrene due to restricted blood flow. The bypass will reinstate healthy blood flow to previously ischemic areas, hopefully alleviating symptoms.

Patients should be encouraged to quit smoking before the procedure to prevent complications and promote overall health. Smoking cessation information and resources should be shared early and often.

Patients will be anesthetized for the procedure. Blood transfusion is a distinct possibility to maintain volume and replace blood loss. The incision made by the surgeon is generally 4 to 8 inches in length, in the groin area where the femoral artery is located. Internal stitches will be made to secure the graft in place. The patient may be in surgery anywhere from 1 to 6 hours depending on the complexity of the surgery.

The nurse in the unit receiving the patient post op will want to monitor the incision site for infection, bleeding, and/or hematoma. Hemodynamic monitoring will be in place to watch for hypotension, which could indicate bleeding, or hypertension, which could put added pressure on the healing graft. Like postoperative therapy for a carotid endarterectomy, the patient will be put on antiplatelet and antithrombotic therapy to prevent clotting and restenosis of the vessels.

Peripheral Venous Thrombosis

A common venous occlusion is a **deep vein thrombosis** (DVT). Although DVTs may be asymptomatic, the common presentation is redness, pain, and swelling over the site of the clot. Common sites for DVT are the lower extremities, specifically the superficial femoral, popliteal, posterior tibial, or peroneal veins in the calves. DVTs come about because of impaired venous return, an injury to the endothelium such as leg fractures, or in states of hypercoagulability in which the body is more apt to make clots. Impaired venous return is common in immobile patients. Therefore, early ambulation is encouraged as well as mobility exercises while the patient is still in bed, to prevent clots.

DVTs in the lower extremities have a high correlation with patients also developing pulmonary embolisms (PEs), or blood clots that travel to the lungs. This is a life-threatening situation. Other complications of DVTs include a chronic insufficiency of the veins and postphlebitic syndrome, in which a patient feels aching, cramping, pain, and other symptoms in the legs that worsen with walking or standing and are relieved by resting.

A **D-dimer** is the test used to help diagnose a DVT. A negative result rules out a DVT, while a positive is not 100 percent conclusive. A positive d-dimer requires further testing, usually ultrasonography, to confirm the diagnosis. History and physical examination are also helpful in determining the probability of a DVT.

If left untreated, there is a high likelihood that the patient with a DVT will develop a PE and die; therefore, detection and treatment are vital. Treatment is usually with anticoagulants such as subcutaneous heparin for a short period followed by a longer period of oral warfarin. Pain control with nonsteroidal anti-inflammatory drugs (NSAIDs) may be included in the treatment plan, along with leg elevation with pillows while the patient is at rest, being careful to avoid venous compression, which could lead to clot dislodgement.

Practice Quiz

1. What emergency surgery is necessary to relieve cardiac tamponade?
    a. Thoracocentesis
    b. Pericardiocentesis
    c. Left heart cardiac catheterization
    d. Open heart surgery

2. A progressive care nurse is caring for a patient who is being treated with a DDD pacemaker. Which of the following ECG findings is the nurse's main concern?
    a. The interval between the pacing spike and the R wave is consistent.
    b. The R wave of the captured beats is a negative complex.
    c. The patient's native rhythm is a second degree AV degree block.
    d. Every complex has a 0.20 second PR interval.

3. The nurse is aware that the congenital and acquired alterations in the mitral and aortic valves have a significant impact on the function of the valve. Which of the following statements correctly identifies the resulting pathology?
    a. A tricuspid aortic valve causes stenosis, but does not result in regurgitation.
    b. A quadri-cuspid mitral valve has 5 leaflets, which causes heart failure in the elderly.
    c. Acquired alterations are symptomatic earlier than congenital alterations.
    d. Endocarditis results in the deposition of vegetative complexes that prevent valve closure.

4. What is the pathway of oxygenated blood from the lungs?
    a. Lungs to the left atrium, through the mitral valve into the left ventricle, pumped into the aorta upon contraction, then dispersed to tissues via a network of arteries and capillaries
    b. Lungs to the right atrium, through the mitral valve into the right ventricle, pumped into the aorta upon contraction, then dispersed to tissues via a network of arteries and veins
    c. Lungs to the left atrium, directly to the right aorta, then dispersed to tissues via a network of arteries and capillaries
    d. Lungs to the left atrium, through the septum valve, stored in the left ventricles, then dispersed to tissues via a network of arteries and capillaries

5. What procedure uses a small inflated balloon to treat arterial blockages?
    a. Coronary bypass surgery
    b. Defibrillation
    c. Coronary angioplasty
    d. Laparoscopy

See answers on the next page.

Answer Explanations

1. B: Pericardiocentesis is indicated in the emergent situation of cardiac tamponade. A needle is inserted, and the hemorrhaging blood is aspirated from the pericardial sac. Thoracocentesis, or pleural tap, can be used for hemothorax or pneumothorax. Left cardiac catheterization is used in acute myocardial infarctions to open obstructed coronary vessels. Open heart surgery can be performed in emergency situations involving thoracic trauma, but not specifically for cardiac tamponade.

2. B: The function of the DDD pacemaker can result in asystole if the patient has an underlying AV block because any R wave that is incorrectly identified by the pacemaker inhibits ventricular output, and resets the refractory period. In this instance, the atrial pacemaker is functioning properly, but the signals from the atria are blocked in the diseased AV pathways. Choices *A* and *C* are normal patterns for paced rhythms. Choice *D* represents a normal sinus rhythm, rather than a paced rhythm.

3. D: Endocarditis results in areas of inflammation along the surface of the valve that support vegetative growth, which eventually occupies space thereby preventing the adequate closure of the valve leaflets. Alterations in the number of cusps in the mitral or aortic valves are associated with both stenosis and regurgitation because the anatomical shape of the valve is distorted. The repeated bending of the misshapen valve and the resulting stress on the chordae tendineae can affect either the diameter of the open valve leading to stenotic changes, or incomplete closure of the valve leading to regurgitation. A unicuspid mitral valve has one cusp, which results in heart failure in the neonate. Congenital valve defects most commonly are diagnosed before adulthood depending on the characteristics of the alteration. Acquired defects are associated with progressive vascular events such as atherosclerosis and the effects of diabetes.

4. A: This path correctly describes where blood flows after leaving the lungs in order to reach the tissues of the body. The other paths listed are incorrect, out of order, and list fictitious structures.

5. C: This procedure inflates a small balloon inside the blocked artery to break down the blockages and widen the pathway through which blood can flow. A coronary bypass surgery reroutes blood from unhealthy vessels to healthier ones. Defibrillation tries to reset the electrical rhythm of the heart. Laparoscopy refers to surgical procedures that take place in the torso.

Pulmonary

Working in tandem with the cardiac system is the pulmonary system, composed of the two lungs and the airway. Airway and breathing are part of the airway, breathing, circulation (ABC) mnemonic representing the patient's most vital functions. The progressive care nurse knows that taking good care of the patient's pulmonary system using critical thinking and sound clinical judgments is crucial to the patient's overall well-being.

The nursing assessment of the respiratory system is multifaceted and includes an in-depth review of the patient's overall pulmonary status. First, the nurse should assess the depth of respirations and note if breaths are shallow or deep, and then assess the rhythm and note whether it is even or uneven. Next, the nurse should assess the level of effort needed to breathe. Continuing on, the nurse should note chest expansion (including symmetry), along with any presence of a cough (productive or nonproductive). Finally, the nurse should auscultate the lungs to assess air exchange throughout and determine the presence of adventitious, absent, lowered, diminished, or distant sounds.

Various patterns of respiration exist; therefore the nurse must closely examine to ensure accuracy in the assessment. Normal respirations are regular, comfortable, and at a rate of 12-20 breaths per minute. If the rate is lower than 12 breaths per minute, the patient is displaying **bradypnea**; if the rate is higher than 20 breaths per minute, the patient is displaying **tachypnea**. **Hyperventilation**, also known as **hyperpnea**, is when the rate is higher than 20 breaths per minute, accompanied by deep breathing. **Cheyne-Stokes** involves varying periods of increased depth, alternating with periods of **apnea**, which is breathlessness. **Kussmal respirations** involve rapid, deep, and labored breaths. **Biot respirations** are irregular and disorganized periods of apnea, while **ataxic breathing** is similar but with the addition of varying depths of respiration.

In order to measure the oxygen level of the blood, the nurse should place a pulse oximeter on the patient's finger; this device provides an indirect reading that displays how well oxygen is reaching peripheral areas of the body, noted as SpO_2. The pulse oximetry must be interpreted, and then appropriate action must take place, including determining the patient's need for continuous or intermittent monitoring. When additional information is warranted, such as during periods of alterations from normal (whether that is outside of typical range or outside of the patient's usual baseline), an invasive measurement can be obtained via laboratory blood work. This method is used to gather direct arterial oxygen saturation levels (SaO_2). While both laboratory analysis and pulse oximetry display the arterial oxygen saturation level, noting the finding through the use of SpO_2 terminology simply denotes that the level was obtained via pulse oximetry rather than via arterial blood gas sampling. **End-tidal carbon dioxide** ($EtCO_2$) monitoring is a noninvasive technique used to measure the amount of CO_2 at the end of exhalation, which is displayed as a plateau waveform in terms of mmHg. The normal range values are 5%-6% CO_2, indicating 35-45 mmHg. Nasal prongs with two sensors are placed to measure capnography, the concentration or partial pressure of CO_2, for the patient who is breathing. These values are important for understanding cardiac output and pulmonary blood flow.

A two-step system should be used when assessing arterial blood gases (ABGs). First, the care team should check the pH level to determine if an imbalance exists; however, it is important to note that even if the pH is normal, the patient may still be suffering from a disturbance as the system attempts to compensate to maintain homeostasis. Review of various levels, including pH, pCO_2, pO_2, HCO_3, BXS, and O_2 saturation, helps the care team to understand a complete clinical picture of acid-base manifestations.

If acidosis is present, the pH will be below 7.35, while a pH above 7.45 is indicative of alkalosis, as normal blood pH is 7.4. If an imbalance is detected, the care team must determine the primary cause of the disturbance. If the CO_2 is above 40 mmHg in a case of acidosis, the patient is suffering from respiratory acidosis. If the HCO3 is below 24 mmHg in a case of acidosis, the patient is suffering from metabolic acidosis. When alkalosis is present, the cause is respiratory if the CO_2 is less than 40 mmHg or metabolic if the HCO_3 is greater than 24 mmHg. ABG monitoring includes pH, pCO_2, pO_2, HCO_3, BXS, and O_2 saturation levels.

Arterial blood gases are drawn through the use of a heparinized syringe. The blood must not come in contact with room air and should be kept on ice and transported to the lab immediately. Simple hypoxia may be seen in acute respiratory distress and pneumonia. Acidosis is seen in chronic obstructive pulmonary disease (COPD), lung edema, shock, and diabetes mellitus. Alkalosis is seen in anxiety disorders, vomiting, and diuretic use. The nurse must understand that hypoventilation may lead to respiratory acidosis, while hyperventilation may lead to respiratory alkalosis. Alterations in acid-base status are closely monitored and fluctuations in ABGs are reported to the care team and the patient. Patient education involves changes to functioning and how symptoms of clinical conditions impact ABGs, so that as a collaborative team homeostasis can be achieved.

Normal ABG values:

- pH: 7.35-7.45
- pCO2: 35-45 mmHg
- p02: 80-100 mm Hg
- HCO3: 21-28 mEq/L
- BXS: 0%-2%
- 02 sat: 95%-100%

Acute Respiratory Distress Syndrome

Acute respiratory distress syndrome (ARDS) is the widespread inflammation of the lungs and capillaries of the alveoli and results in the rapid development of pulmonary system failure. It can occur in both adults and children and is considered the most severe form of acute lung injury. Presence of the syndrome is determined by:

- Timing: Onset of symptoms within one week of inciting incident
- Chest x-ray: Bilateral lung infiltrates not explained by consolidation, atelectasis, or effusions
- Origin of Edema: Not explained by heart failure or fluid overload
- Severity of Hypoxemia

It should be noted that the severity of hypoxemia is based on PaO_2/FiO_2 ratio while on 5 cm of continuous positive airway pressure (CPAP). PaO_2 is the partial pressure of oxygen, while FiO_2 is the fraction of inspired oxygen. Categories are:

- Mild (PaO_2/FiO_2 = 200–300)
- Moderate (PaO_2/FiO_2 = 100–200)
- Severe ($PaO_2/FiO_2 \leq 100$)

ARDS has a high mortality rate (30–40%), which increases with advancing age. It also leads to significant morbidity because of its association with extended hospital stays, frequent nosocomial (hospital-acquired) infections, muscle weakness, significant weight loss, and functional impairment. The most common cause of ARDS is sepsis, a life-threatening bacterial infection of the blood. Other common causes include:

- Severe pneumonia
- Inhalation of toxic fumes
- Trauma (such as falls, bone fractures, motor vehicle accidents, near drowning, and burns)
- Massive blood transfusion

It should also be noted that, for one in five patients with ARDS, there will be no identifiable risk factors. Therefore, the cause of ARDS may not be evident.

The onset of ARDS symptoms is fairly rapid, occurring 12 to 48 hours after the inciting incident. Many of the signs and symptoms of ARDS are nonspecific. Signs and symptoms of ARDS can include:

- Dyspnea (initially with exertion, but rapidly progressing to occurring even at rest)
- Hypoxia
- Tachypnea
- Tachycardia
- Fever
- Bilateral rales
- Cyanosis
- Hypotension
- Fatigue

The diagnosis of ARDS is clinical since there's no specific test for the condition. Diagnosing ARDS is done by exclusion, ruling out other diseases that mimic its signs and symptoms. Tests used to diagnose ARDS can include:

- Chest x-ray, which, by definition, should reveal bilateral lung infiltrates
- ABG analysis (usually reveals extreme hypoxemia and respiratory alkalosis or metabolic acidosis)
- CBC with differential (can reveal leukocytosis, leukopenia, and/or thrombocytopenia)
- Plasma B-type natriuretic peptide (BNP), a level < 100 pg/mL favors ARDS rather than CHF
- CT scan
- Echocardiography, which is helpful in excluding CHF (cardiogenic pulmonary edema)
- Bronchoscopy with bronchoalveolar lavage (BAL), which is helpful in excluding lung infections

Numerous medications, such as corticosteroids, synthetic surfactant, antibody to endotoxin, ketoconazole, simvastatin, ibuprofen, and inhaled nitric oxide, have been used for the treatment of ARDS, but none have proven effective. Therefore, treating the underlying symptoms of ARDS and providing supportive care are the most crucial components of therapy. The only therapy found to improve survival in ARDS is intubation and mechanical ventilation using low tidal volumes (6 mL/kg of ideal body weight). Because sepsis, an infection, is the most common etiology of ARDS, early administration of a broad-spectrum antibiotic is crucial.

Treatment also includes fluid management and nutritional support. For individuals with shock secondary to sepsis, initial aggressive fluid resuscitation is administered, followed by a conservative fluid management strategy. It is best to institute nutritional support within 48 to 72 hours of initiation of mechanical ventilation.

Important preventative measures include DVT prophylaxis with enoxaparin, stress ulcer prophylaxis with sucralfate or omeprazole, turning and skin care to prevent decubitus ulcers, and elevating the head of the bed and using a subglottic suction device to help prevent ventilator-associated pneumonia.

Severe Asthma

Status asthmaticus is an acute episode of worsening asthma that's unresponsive to treatment with bronchodilators. Even after increasing their bronchodilator use to every few minutes, individuals still experience no relief. Status asthmaticus represents a respiratory emergency that can lead to respiratory failure. Airway inflammation, bronchospasm, and mucus plugging highlight the condition. Common triggers include exposure to an allergen or irritant, viral respiratory illness, and exercise in cold weather. Status asthmaticus is more common among individuals of low socioeconomic status, regardless of race.

The main symptoms of status asthmaticus are wheezing, cough, and dyspnea; however, severe airway obstruction can result in a "silent chest" without audible wheezes. This can be a sign of impending respiratory failure. Other signs and symptoms of status asthmaticus include:

- Chest tightness or pain
- Tachypnea
- Tachycardia
- Cyanosis
- Use of accessory respiratory muscles
- Inability to speak more than one or two words at a time
- Altered mental status
- Pulsus paradoxus >20mm Hg
- Syncope
- Hypoxemia
- Hypercapnia
- Retractions and the use of abdominal muscles to breathe
- Hypertension
- Seizures (late sign)
- Bradycardia (late sign)
- Hypotension (late sign)
- Agitation (late sign)

Useful tests for the diagnosis of status asthmaticus include:

- Chest x-ray (for the exclusion of pneumonia, pneumothorax, and CHF)
- ABG analysis can be diagnostic as well as therapeutic (tracking response to treatment measures). Assess cost/benefit for children due to pain associated with ABG sampling.

- CBC with differential can reveal an elevated WBC count with left shift (possible indication of a microbial infection)

- Peak flow measurement can be diagnostic as well as therapeutic (tracking response to treatment measures)

- Pulse oximetry provides continuous measurement of O_2 saturation. Reading is affected by decreased peripheral perfusion, anemia, and movement.

- Blood glucose levels, stress, and therapeutic medications can lead to hyperglycemia. Younger children may exhibit hypoglycemia.

- Blood electrolyte levels (therapeutic medications can lead to hypokalemia)

Intubation and mechanical ventilation should be used with extreme caution in individuals with status asthmaticus. It's usually considered a therapy of last resort due to its inherent dangers: air trapping leading to an increased risk for barotrauma (especially pneumothorax); decreased cardiac output; and increasing bronchospasm. Mechanical ventilation of individuals with status asthmaticus often requires controlled hypoventilation with low tidal volumes, prolonged exhalation times, low respiratory rates, and tolerance of permissive hypercapnia. The majority of individuals needing mechanical ventilation can be extubated within 72 hours.

Supportive Treatment

- O_2 therapy to maintain O_2 saturation > 92%; non-rebreathing mask can deliver 98% O_2
- Hydration
- Correction of electrolyte abnormalities
- Antibiotics only with evidence of concurrent infective process

Pharmacological Agents Used for Acute Asthma

Various classes of pharmacological agents are used for the treatment and control of status asthmaticus. The following discussion concentrates on pharmacological agents to treat and control acute asthma rather than chronic asthma. Urgent care of asthma can include the following:

Beta-2 Adrenergic Agonists (Beta-2 Agonists)

Short-acting preparations of Beta-2 agonists are the first line of therapy for the treatment of status asthmaticus. These medications relax the muscles in the airways, resulting in **bronchodilation** (expanding of the bronchial air passages) and increased airflow to the lungs. It is important to remember that one of the underlying factors in asthma is bronchoconstriction. Albuterol is the most commonly used short-acting Beta-2 agonist. Dosing for acute asthma is 2.5 mg to 5 mg once, then 2.5 mg every twenty minutes for 3 doses via nebulizer, and finally 2.5 mg to 10 mg every one to four hours as needed. Adverse effects of albuterol include tachycardia, tremors, and anxiety. Another short-acting Beta-2 agonist used to treat acute asthma is levalbuterol (Xopenex™). This medication is related to albuterol and has the same result, but without the adverse effects. Dosage for acute asthma is 1.25 mg to 2.5 mg every twenty minutes for 3 doses, then 1.25 mg to 5 mg every one to four hours as needed. However, it must be noted that the frequent use of adrenergic agents prior to receiving emergency care can decrease a patient's response to these medications in a hospital setting.

Anticholinergics

Anticholinergics block the action of the neurotransmitter acetylcholine which, in turn, causes bronchodilation. Anticholinergics can also increase the bronchodilating effects of short-acting Beta-2 agonists. The most commonly used anticholinergic is ipratropium (Atrovent™), which is used in combination with short-acting Beta-2 agonists for the treatment of status asthmaticus. Dosing for acute asthma is 2.5 mL (500 mcg) every twenty minutes for 3 doses via nebulizer, then as needed. Adverse effects can include dry mouth, blurred vision, and constipation.

Corticosteroids

Corticosteroids are potent anti-inflammatory medications that fight the inflammation accompanying asthma. Corticosteroids commonly used in the treatment of status asthmaticus include prednisone, prednisolone, and methylprednisolone. Methylprednisolone (Solu-Medrol™) is administered once in doses of 60 mg to 125 mg intravenously (IV) in cases of status asthmaticus and then followed by a taper of oral prednisone over seven to ten days. The intravenous administration of corticosteroids is equal in effectiveness to oral corticosteroid administration. Corticosteroids have numerous adverse effects, and they should not be used for more than two weeks. Adverse effects of long-term corticosteroid use can include weight gain, osteoporosis, thinning of skin, cataracts, easy bruising, and diabetes. Therefore, it is necessary to monitor blood glucose routinely and use regular insulin on a sliding scale. Electrolytes (particularly potassium) must also be monitored.

Methylxanthines

Methylxanthines are used as bronchodilators and as adjuncts to Beta-2 agonists and corticosteroids in treating status asthmaticus. The primary methylxanthines are theophylline and aminophylline. At therapeutic doses, methylxanthines are much weaker bronchodilators than Beta-2 agonists. The adverse effects of methylxanthines can include nausea, vomiting, tachycardia, headaches, and seizures. As a result, therapeutic monitoring is mandatory. Therapeutic levels of theophylline range from 10 mcg/mL to 20 mcg/mL. Dosing of theophylline is a loading dose of 6 mg/kg, followed by a maintenance dose of 1 mg/kg/h IV. Methylxanthines aren't frequently used to treat status asthmaticus because of their possible adverse effects and the need for close monitoring of drug blood levels.

Magnesium Sulfate

Magnesium sulfate is a calcium antagonist that relaxes smooth muscle in the lung passages leading to bronchodilation. Clinical studies indicate it can be used as an adjunct to Beta-2 agonist therapy during status asthmaticus. A dose of 30 mg/kg to 70 mg/kg is administered by IV over 20 to 30 minutes. It is given slowly to prevent adverse effects such as bradycardia and hypotension. The use of magnesium sulfate is controversial.

Leukotriene Inhibitors

Leukotriene inhibitors target inflammation related to asthma. Typically used for the long-term control of asthma, this class of medication can be helpful for a minority of individuals with status asthmaticus. The primary leukotriene inhibitors used in the treatment of asthma are zafirlukast (Accolate™) and zileuton (Zyflo™). Zafirlukast can be administered orally in doses of 10 mg to 20 mg twice daily. Zileuton can be administered in a dose of 600 mg four times daily. Adverse effects of leukotriene inhibitors include headache, rash, fatigue, dizziness, and abdominal pain.

Heliox

Heliox, administered via face mask, is a mixture of helium and oxygen that can help relieve airway obstruction associated with status asthmaticus. Benefits of heliox include decreased work of breathing, decreased carbon dioxide production, and decreased muscle fatigue. It can only be used in individuals who are able to take a deep breath or while on mechanical ventilation. The 80/20 mixture of helium to oxygen has been the most effective in clinical trials. One limitation to using heliox is the amount of supplemental oxygen required by an individual suffering from status asthmaticus. Heliox loses its clinical efficacy when the fraction of inspired oxygen (FiO_2) is greater than 40%. No significant adverse effects have been reported with heliox.

Medication Monitoring

Beta-2 agonists used for pulmonary system support, such as albuterol and terbutaline, can cause side effects that include tremor, dizziness, and palpitations. Nursing interventions include ensuring the correct dosing and contacting the prescriber if the patient becomes non-responsive to the prescriber dose. Corticosteroids can induce Cushing's syndrome, which includes signs and symptoms such as fat loss from arms and legs, muscle weakness, anxiety, moon face, diaphoresis, fatty deposits around upper back, and abdominal weight gain. Corticosteroids should be weaned following a gradual titration, as abrupt discontinuation may trigger an adrenal insufficiency crisis. Theophylline, a methylxanthine, can cause arrhythmias and seizures. The nurse must carefully monitor vital signs and provide patient education on maintenance, which should include taking the medication at regular intervals during the day.

COPD Exacerbation

Chronic Obstructive Pulmonary Disease (COPD) is characterized by an airflow obstruction that's not fully reversible. It's usually progressive and is associated with an abnormal inflammatory response in the lungs. The primary cause of COPD is exposure to tobacco smoke, and is one of the leading causes of death in the United States. COPD includes chronic bronchitis, emphysema, or a combination of both. Though asthma is part of the classic triad of obstructive lung diseases, it is not part of COPD. However, someone with COPD can have an asthma component to their disease. **Chronic bronchitis** is described as a chronic productive cough for three or more months during each of two consecutive years. **Emphysema** is the abnormal enlargement of **alveoli** (air sacs) with accompanying destruction of their walls. Signs and symptoms of COPD can include:

- Dyspnea
- Wheezing
- Cough (usually worse in the morning and that produces sputum/phlegm)
- Cyanosis
- Chest tightness
- Fever
- Tachypnea
- Orthopnea
- Use of accessory respiratory muscles
- Elevated jugular venous pressure (JVP)
- Barrel chest
- Pursed lip breathing
- Altered mental status

As smoking is the most common cause of COPD, smoking cessation should be encouraged to decrease exacerbations and slow the progression of the disease. Over the course of several years, the disease will worsen, starting with a productive cough and leading to trouble with breathing. Patients with COPD will often complain of a recurring headache in the morning. Their chest may become barrel-like in appearance due to hyperinflation of the lungs. Weight loss and muscle wasting are common signs of advanced disease. The patient may breathe with their lips pursed, a sign of "**auto-PEEPing**." This means they are creating their own PEEP by making the hole their air passes through smaller, like breathing through a straw. As the disease progresses, their exacerbations will increase. An exacerbation is when, for whatever reason—often unknown—their symptoms worsen, and hospitalization often occurs.

A diagnosis of COPD can be made through **pulmonary function tests** (PFTs), a chest x-ray, blood chemistries, ABG analysis, or a CT scan. A formal diagnosis of COPD can be made through a PFT known as spirometry, which measures lung function. PFTs measure the ratio of forced expiratory volume in one second over **forced vital capacity** (FEV_1/FVC) and should normally be between 60% and 90%. Values below 60% usually indicate a problem. The other diagnostic tests mentioned are useful in determining the acuity and severity of exacerbations of the disease. In acute exacerbations of COPD, ABG analysis can reveal respiratory acidosis, hypoxemia, and hypercapnia. Generally, a pH less than 7.3 indicates acute respiratory compromise. Compensatory metabolic alkalosis may develop in response to chronic respiratory acidosis. A chest x-ray can show flattening of the diaphragm and increased retrosternal air space (both indicative of hyperinflation), cardiomegaly, and increased bronchovascular markings. Blood chemistries can suggest sodium retention or hypokalemia. A CT scan is more sensitive and specific than a standard chest x-ray for diagnosing emphysema.

Treatment for acute exacerbations of COPD can include oxygen supplementation, short-acting Beta-2 agonists, anticholinergics, corticosteroids, and antibiotics. Oxygen should be titrated to achieve an oxygen saturation of at least 90%. Low-flow oxygen is used, while the nurse understands that patients with chronically high CO2 levels may be triggered to cease respirations when given pure oxygen. Short-acting Beta-2 agonists (albuterol or levalbuterol) administered via nebulizer can improve dyspnea associated with COPD. The anticholinergic medication ipratropium, administered via nebulizer, can be added as an adjunct to Beta-2 agonists. Short courses of corticosteroids can be given orally or intravenously. In clinical trials, the administration of oral corticosteroids in the early stage of a COPD exacerbation decreased the need for hospitalization. Also in clinical trials, the use of antibiotics was found to decrease the risk of treatment failure and death in individuals with a moderate to severe exacerbation of COPD. If the patient has a PaO_2 that is less than 55 mmHg, the patient may be discharged on home oxygen therapy. Discharge education should include how to use home oxygen, benefits of smoking cessation, and importance of avoiding airway infections, along with education pertaining to diaphragmatic and pursed-lip breathing techniques.

Obstructive Sleep Apnea

Apnea refers to temporary pauses in breath in which the lung volume stagnates. The musculature involved in respiration temporarily ceases function. Apnea can be caused by distress, laughing, trauma, or neurological disease. It is also a common sleep condition, in which a patient can stop breathing up to 30 times per hour.

Obstructive sleep apnea is the most common type of sleep apnea, although there are others. It occurs when the muscles in the throat and soft palate relax during sleep, blocking the passage of air. While loud snoring is a classic symptom, headaches upon waking, excessive daytime sleepiness, and waking up abruptly with a gasp or choke are also common.

Risk factors include excessive weight, smoking, asthma or breathing disorders, male sex, and hypertension. Without detection or treatment, sleep apnea can greatly tax the cardiovascular system and lead to cardiac events, due to the long periods of time without oxygen circulation. Sleep apnea is often an undetected condition. The condition can be treated with a mouthpiece to thrust the jaw forward or a CPAP machine, which helps keep a patent airway.

A nurse caring for an acutely ill patient, should be especially vigilant to monitor patients showing signs or symptoms of sleep apnea, especially after that patient has been given anesthesia or pain medication. This may include staying close and monitoring a patient the first time they have been given a new medication that could cause respiratory distress and having continuous SpO_2 monitoring on the patient.

Pleural Space Abnormalities and Complications

Pneumothorax

Pneumothorax is the abnormal presence of air in the **pleural cavity**, which is the space between the parietal and visceral pleurae. Pneumothorax can be categorized as:

Pneumothorax can be categorized as:

- Spontaneous Pneumothorax: This can be classified as either primary or secondary. Primary spontaneous pneumothorax (PSP) occurs in individuals with no history of lung disease or inciting event. Those at risk for PSP are typically eighteen to forty years old, tall, thin, and smokers. There's also a familial tendency for primary spontaneous pneumothorax. Secondary spontaneous pneumothorax occurs in individuals with an underlying lung disease such as COPD, cystic fibrosis, asthma, tuberculosis (TB), or lung cancer.

- Traumatic Pneumothorax: This occurs as a result of blunt or penetrating trauma to the chest wall. The trauma disrupts the parietal and/or visceral pleura(e). Examples of inciting events include: gunshot or stab wounds; air bag deployment in a motor vehicle accident; acute respiratory distress syndrome (ARDS); and medical procedures such as mechanical ventilation, lung biopsy, thoracentesis, needle biopsy, and chest surgery.

- Tension Pneumothorax: This is the trapping of air in the pleural space under positive pressure. It causes a mediastinal shift toward the unaffected lung and a depression of the hemidiaphragm on the side of the affected lung. Shortly after, the event is followed by severe cardiopulmonary compromise. Tension pneumothorax can result from any of the conditions or procedures listed for Spontaneous and Traumatic Pneumothorax.

Signs and symptoms of pneumothorax depend on the degree of lung collapse (partial or total) and can include:

- Chest pain
- Dyspnea
- Cyanosis
- Tachypnea
- Tachycardia

- Hypotension
- Hypoxia
- Anxiety
- Adventitious breath sounds
- Unilateral distant or absent breath sounds
- Jugular venous distention (JVD)
- Tracheal deviation away from the affected side (with tension pneumothorax)

Diagnosis of pneumothorax is primarily clinical (based on signs and symptoms), but can involve an upright posteroanterior chest x-ray, chest CT scan (the most reliable imaging for diagnosis), ABG analysis, and ultrasonography of the chest. Treatment of a pneumothorax depends on the severity of the condition and can include:

- Supplemental oxygen
- The standard of treatment for all large, symptomatic pneumothoraces is a tube thoracostomy (chest tube).
- Observation (a reasonable option for small asymptomatic pneumothorax; multiple series of chest x-rays are needed until resolution)
- Simple needle aspiration (an option for small, primary spontaneous pneumothorax)
- Because they can quickly cause life-threatening cardiopulmonary compromise, the standard of treatment for all tension pneumothoraces is an emergent needle thoracostomy.

Hemothorax

Hemothorax, the presence of blood in the pleural space, is most commonly the result of blunt or penetrating chest trauma. The pleural space lies between the parietal pleura of the chest wall and the visceral pleura of the lungs. A large accumulation of blood in the pleural space can restrict normal lung movement and lead to hemodynamic compromise. Common signs and symptoms of hemothorax include chest pain, dyspnea, and tachypnea. When there is substantial systemic blood loss, tachycardia and hypotension can also be present.

Diagnosis of hemothorax primarily involves a chest x-ray, which reveals blunting at the costophrenic angle on the affected side of the lung. A helical CT scan has a complementary role in the management of hemothorax, and it can localize and quantify the retention of blood or clots within the pleural space.

Small hemothoraces usually require no treatment, but need close observation to ensure resolution. Tube thoracostomy drainage is the mainstay of treatment for significant hemothoraces. Needle aspiration has no place in the management of hemothorax. Blood transfusions can be necessary for those with significant blood loss or hemodynamic compromise. Complications from hemothorax can include **empyema** (secondary bacterial infection of a retained clot) or **fibrothorax** (fibrosis of the pleural space, which can trap lung tissue and lead to decreased pulmonary function).

Pleural Effusion

A **pleural effusion** is an abnormal accumulation of fluid in the pleural space. The **pleural space** is located between the parietal and visceral pleurae of each lung. The **parietal pleura** covers the inner surface of the chest cavity, while the **visceral pleura** surrounds the lungs. Approximately 10 milliliters of pleural fluid is maintained by oncotic and hydrostatic pressures and lymphatic drainage and is necessary for normal respiratory function. Pleural effusions can be categorized as transudates or exudates. **Transudates** result from an imbalance between oncotic and hydrostatic pressures, so they are characterized by low protein content. The transudates are often the result of congestive heart failure (CHF), cirrhosis, low albumin blood levels, nephrotic syndrome, and peritoneal dialysis. **Exudates** result from decreased lymphatic drainage or inflammation of the pleura, so they are characterized by high protein content. The exudates are often the result of malignancy, pancreatitis, pulmonary embolism, uremia, infection, and certain medications.

The main symptoms of a pleural effusion include dyspnea, cough, and chest pain. Diagnosis of a pleural effusion can include chest x-ray, chest CT scan, ultrasonography, and thoracentesis. Thoracentesis can provide pleural fluid for analysis such as LDH, glucose, pH, cell count and differential, culture, and cytology. Pleural fluid should be distinguished as either transudate or exudate. Exudative pleural effusions are characterized by:

- Ratio of pleural fluid to serum protein > 0.5
- Ratio of pleural fluid to serum LDH > 0.6
- Pleural fluid LDH > 2/3 of the upper limit of normal blood value

Treatment of a pleural effusion is usually dictated by the underlying etiology; however, the treatment of a very large pleural effusion can include:

- Thoracentesis
- Chest tube (also known as tube thoracostomy)
- **Pleurodesis** (instillation of an irritant to cause inflammation and subsequent fibrosis to obliterate the pleural space)
- Indwelling tunneled pleural catheters

Chylothorax

Chylothorax involves an accumulation of lymph formed in the digestive system (chyle) in the pleural cavity. This complication typically arises from trauma, aortitis, filariasis, or tuberculosis lymphadenitis, or is found as a congenital condition potentially co-occurring with other malformations of the lymphatic system. As chylothorax is a lymphatic flow disorder impacting the space between the lung and chest wall, shortness of breath, chest pain, and cough typically develop. When this disorder progresses, the care team provides treatment to reduce the likelihood of the patient succumbing to this condition. Nursing care targets symptom resolution via the delivery of parenteral nutrition and arranging dietary consult with the dietician to implement a therapeutic dietary plan. If these interventions fail, the patient and care team may consider surgical interventions. In the case of surgery to perform ligation of the thoracic duct, insert a shunt, or otherwise directly target the trauma or malformation, the nurse navigates preoperative supportive care that may include medication management, patient comfort, and respiratory support.

Empyema

In patients with pneumonia, thoracic surgery or chest trauma, the development of empyema may be a complication. Empyema occurs when pathogens enter the pleural area and form pus. The exudate made is usually protein rich and can hinder lung expansion. *Streptococcus pneumoniae* and *staphylococcus aureus* are the two most commonly found pathogens that result in an empyema. Patients already in the hospital on appropriate antibiotics who show worsening chest x-rays should be evaluated for empyema, unless another diagnosis fits the patient's clinical picture. On a physical exam, percussion of the area with the empyema will sound dull, with breath sounds decreased. Patients may also present with elevated temperature, dyspnea, and productive cough. Once an empyema has been visualized on a chest x-ray, patients may either undergo CT or ultrasonography to assess the empyema further and decide on an approach to treatment. Most patients with moderate to large empyemas will undergo diagnostic thoracentesis, which can be done concurrently with therapeutic thoracentesis if drainage is considered necessary for relieving symptoms. Prior to sending a patient for thoracentesis, the nurse should assess that the consent has been completed and that the patient understands the procedure in their own words.

The nurse should discuss with the provider if the patient is taking a blood thinner, as some providers will want these held but some will have them given. Fluid gathered from thoracentesis should be sent for cell count with differential, cytology and microbiology. Some patients will require that the tube for drainage be left in place. If so, follow-up chest CT is usually done immediately to assess the placement of the tube. The thoracostomy drainage tube and drainage must be frequently assessed and documented, including color and amount of drainage volume and any redness, bleeding or leaking around the site. Provider should be notified immediately of any change in respiratory status, especially dyspnea or chest pain. If patients develop a new fever, this should also be reported. If the patient fails to improve with drainage and antibiotics, other treatments may be considered, including video assisted thoracoscopy (VATS).

Pulmonary Embolism

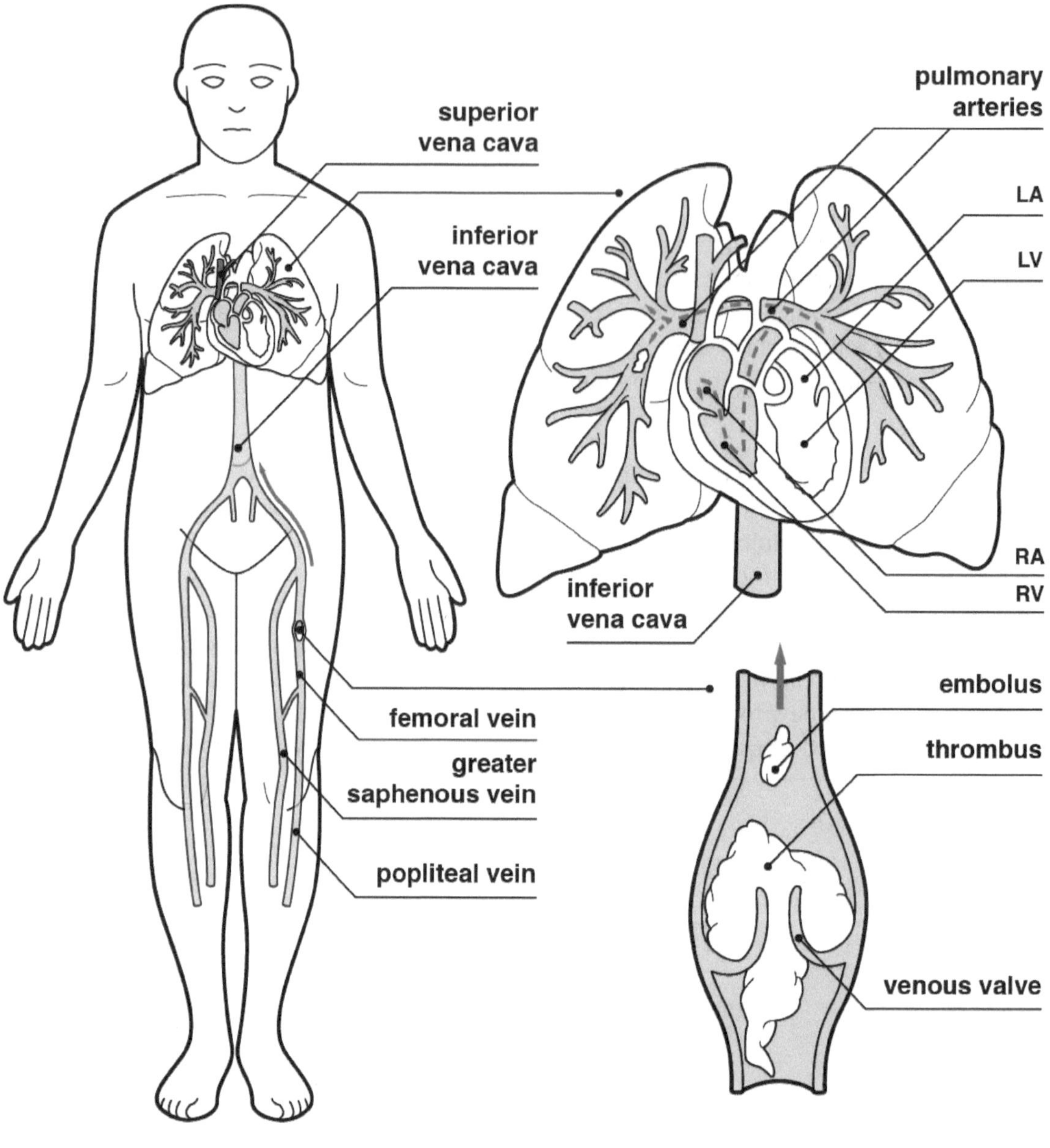

A **pulmonary embolism** (PE) is the abnormal presence of a blood clot, or thrombus, causing a blockage in one of the lungs' pulmonary arteries. It is not a specific disease, but rather a complication due to thrombus formation in the venous system of one of the lower extremities, which is termed **deep venous thrombosis** (DVT). Other rarer causes of PEs are thrombi arising in the veins of the kidneys, pelvis, upper extremities, or the right atrium of the heart. Occasionally, other matter besides blood clots can cause pulmonary emboli, such as fat, air, and septic (infected with bacteria) emboli. PE is a common and potentially fatal condition.

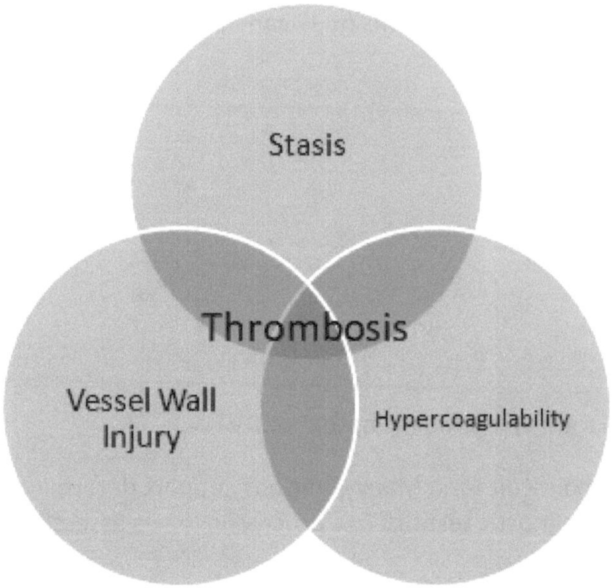

The primary influences on the development of DVT and PE are shown in **Virchow's triad**: blood hypercoagulability, endothelial injury/dysfunction, and stasis of blood. Risk factors for DVT and PE include:

- Cancer
- Heart disease, especially congestive heart failure (CHF)
- Prolonged immobility (such as prolonged bedrest or lengthy trips in planes or cars)
- Surgery (one of the leading risk factors, accounting for up to 15% of all postoperative deaths)
- Overweight/obesity
- Smoking
- Pregnancy
- Supplemental estrogen from birth control pills or estrogen replacement therapy (ERT)

There are three categories of PEs based on severity: small, submassive, and massive. **Small PEs** may exist without any symptoms. **Submassive PEs** may slightly impair right ventricular function, but hypotension is absent. A **massive PE** impairs the function of the right ventricle, causes a hypotensive crisis, and presents a serious risk of death for the patient.

A **saddle PE** is a particularly dangerous type of clot in which the pulmonary embolus has lodged itself in the bifurcation between the main pulmonary artery and the left and right pulmonary arteries. Saddle PEs usually impair right ventricular function with or without hypotension.

The signs and symptoms of PE are nonspecific, which often presents a diagnostic dilemma and a delay in diagnosis. Nearly half of all individuals with PE are asymptomatic. The signs and symptoms of PE can vary greatly depending on the size of the blood clots, how much lung tissue is involved, and an individual's overall health. Signs and symptoms of PE can include:

- Pleuritic chest pain
- Dyspnea
- Cough
- Tachypnea
- Hypoxia
- Fever
- Diaphoresis
- Rales
- Cyanosis
- Unilateral lower extremity edema (symptom of DVT)

The diagnosis of PE can be a difficult task. Many clinicians support determining the clinical probability of PE before proceeding with diagnostic testing. This process involves assessing the presence or absence of the following manifestations:

- Pulmonary Signs: Tachypnea, rales, and cyanosis

- Cardiac Signs: Tachycardia, S3 - S4 gallop, attenuated second heart sound, and cardiac murmur

- Constitutional Signs: Fever, diaphoresis, signs and symptoms of thrombophlebitis, and lower extremity edema

Once the clinical probability of PE has been determined, diagnostic testing ensues. Duplex ultrasonography is the standard for diagnosing a DVT. A spiral computed tomography (CT) scan with or without contrast has replaced pulmonary angiography as the standard for diagnosing a PE. If spiral CT scanning is unavailable or if individuals have a contraindication to the administration of intravenous contrast material, ventilation-perfusion (V/Q) scanning is often selected. Magnetic resonance imaging (MRI) is usually reserved for pregnant women and individuals with a contraindication to the administration of intravenous contrast material. A D-dimer blood test is most useful for individuals with a low or moderate pretest probability of PE, since levels are typically elevated with PE. Arterial blood gas (ABG) analysis usually reveals hypoxemia, hypocapnia, and respiratory alkalosis.

A chest x-ray, though not diagnostic for PE since its findings are typically nonspecific, can exclude diseases that mimic PE, as can an echocardiography. Electrocardiography is also useful because it can assess right ventricular heart function and be prognostic, since there's a 10% death rate from PE with right ventricular dysfunction. Lastly, transesophageal echocardiography (TEE) can reveal central PE.

The first step in treating a PE is determining the patient's stability. Patients with hypotension are categorized as unstable, while patients without hypotension are generally considered stable. For hemodynamically unstable patients presenting with a PE, treatment should focus on stabilizing the patient, including vasopressors or intubation if needed. Treatment of PE should begin to prevent complications or death. PE treatment is focused on preventing an increase in size of the current blood clots and the formation of new blood clots. Supportive care treatment of PE can include:

- Supplemental oxygen to ease hypoxia/hypoxemia
- Dopamine (Inotropin®) or dobutamine (Dobutrex®) administered via IV for related hypotension
- Cardiac monitoring in the case of associated arrhythmias or right ventricular dysfunction
- Intubation and mechanical ventilation

Medications involved in treatment can include: thrombolytics or clot dissolvers (such as tissue plasminogen activator (tPA), alteplase, urokinase, streptokinase, or reteplase). These medications are reserved for individuals with a diagnosis of acute PE and associated hypotension (systolic BP < 90 mm Hg). They are not given concurrently with anticoagulants. Anticoagulants or blood thinners may also be used. The historical standard for the initial treatment of PE was unfractionated heparin (UFH) administered via IV or subcutaneous (SC) injection, which requires frequent blood monitoring. Current treatment guidelines recommend low-molecular weight heparin (LMWH) administered via SC injection over UFH IV or SC as it has greater bioavailability than UFH and blood monitoring is not necessary. Fondaparinux (Arixtra®) administered via SC injection is also recommended over UFH IV or SC; blood monitoring is not necessary.

Warfarin (Coumadin®), an oral anticoagulant was the historical standard for the outpatient prevention and treatment of PE. It is initiated the same day as treatment with UFH, LMWH, or fondaparinux. It is recommended INR of 2-3 with frequent blood monitoring, at which time IV or SC anticoagulant is discontinued. Alternatives to Warfarin include oral factor Xa inhibitor anticoagulants such as apixaban (Eliquis®), rivaroxaban (Xarelto®), and edoxaban (Savaysa®), or dabigatran (Pradaxa®), an oral direct thrombin inhibitor anticoagulant. Blood monitoring is not necessary with these medications. The most significant adverse effect of both thrombolytics and anticoagulants is bleeding.

An embolectomy (removal of emboli via catheter or surgery) is reserved for individuals with a massive PE and contraindications to thrombolytics or anticoagulants. Vena cava filters (also called inferior vena cava (IVC) filters or Greenfield filters) are only indicated in individuals with an absolute contraindication to anticoagulants, a massive PE who have survived and for whom recurrent PE will be fatal, or documented recurrent PE.

Pulmonary Hypertension

When the pressure in the pulmonary circulation rises, it is termed **pulmonary hypertension**. The blood vessels within the pulmonary beds of circulation become constricted and sometimes even obstructed. This raised BP may cause failure of the right ventricle of the heart.

Causes of pulmonary hypertension may be idiopathic, but left heart failure, diastolic dysfunction, parenchymal lung disease, and a PE have been known to raise the pulmonary pressures.

A patient with pulmonary hypertension may complain of exertional dyspnea and chronic fatigue, experience loss of consciousness, and feel chest discomfort. Diagnosis is made via echocardiography, which estimates the pressures, and confirmed by right heart catheterization.

Pulmonary hypertension can be treated through use of vasodilators and diuretics. Sildenafil is an example of a phosphodiesterase inhibitor used to treat pulmonary hypertension and is helpful in increasing blood flow in the lungs. Amlodipine is an example of a calcium channel blocker, a class of drugs that may be helpful for pulmonary hypertension. Epoprostenol is a drug specifically formulated for use in patients with pulmonary hypertension. Lung transplantation may be an option in advanced disease states.

Respiratory Depression

Respiratory depression, defined as **hypoventilation**, occurs when the amount of inhaled air or tidal volume is insufficient for normal gas exchange at the alveolar membrane. If hypoventilation is severe or prolonged, the saturation of oxygen in the circulating blood volume falls, while the carbon dioxide level rises. This results in tissue hypoxia and additional depression of the respiratory drive, due to the onset of respiratory acidosis. The most common causes of hypoventilation include narcotic, barbiturate, and benzodiazepine medication overdoses; however, if the specific agent is not known, the naloxone protocol is used to determine the if a narcotic medication is the source of the hypoventilation.

Depressed respiratory function can also result from any traumatic injury, hemorrhagic or occlusive event that damages the brainstem, increased intracranial pressure or status epilepticus, or rarely from adult congenital central hypoventilation syndrome. Direct injury to the brainstem results in damage to the chemoreceptors that control respiration, and the brain stem is also adversely affected by the decreased blood pressure and ischemia associated with increased intracranial pressure. Anxiety and restlessness, which can occur before any overt signs of respiratory depression, are associated with the onset of hypoventilation, which may be rapid or slowly progressive. Depending on the patient's baseline health status and the cause of the hypoventilation, the treatment includes the elimination of the cause and ventilatory support.

SaO_2 Monitoring

If the SaO_2 obtained via blood analysis is greater than 94%, the partial pressure of arterial blood oxygen (PaO_2) is greater than 70 mmHg, requiring no immediate action aside from continuing to intermittently monitor. When the SaO_2 is between 90% and 94%, the PaO_2 falls within 60-70 mmHg, leading the progressive care nurse to reposition the probe to ensure accuracy then continue via intermittent or continuous monitoring depending on the patient's overall pulmonary status and pattern of results. If the SaO_2 is between 85% and 90%, the PaO_2 is within 50-60 mmHg, requiring the patient be placed in high-Fowler's position and instructed to take slow, deep breaths. If this does not raise the SaO_2, the nurse should notify the provider and prepare to administer oxygen. When the SaO_2 drops below 85%, the PaO_2 is below 55 mmHg, necessitating the administration of oxygen, provider notification, and the progressive care nurse at the bedside to closely monitor.

Respiratory Failure

Any case in which oxygen exchange in the alveoli of the lungs is impaired, whether due to impaired respiration, weakness of respiratory effort, or obstruction of the airway, is called **respiratory failure**. Though respiratory arrest and cardiac arrest are two different events, one always leads to another if one is left untreated. Lack of oxygen will cause permanent damage to vital organs if respiratory arrest goes on for much longer than five minutes. Many patients the progressive nurse cares for will have acute (short term) respiratory failure, which can develop very quickly from non-respiratory causes and may need emergency care. However a great number of patients cared for in progressive care units suffer from chronic (long term) respiratory failure, which comes on slowly and is usually the result of a lung issue. Patients with diseases such as COPD, asthma, and cystic fibrosis are at a much higher risk of developing chronic respiratory failure.

The nursing responsibility in respiratory management involves understanding when and how to use oxygen delivery devices, along with monitoring for effectiveness. Five commonly used devices include the nasal cannula, simple mask, venturi mask, partial rebreathing mask, and nonrebreathing mask. When using a venturi mask, an appropriate entrainment port is also included. A key consideration to remember for using the partial rebreathing mask and the nonrebreathing mask is that the reservoir bag should never fully collapse. In order to select an appropriate device, a few key considerations must be reviewed. First, the care team must determine the targeted percentage of oxygen to be delivered. Next, safe flow rates are set based on device.

Let's review the flow rates and percentages of oxygen delivered based on device. The nasal cannula can be set at the following rates with correlating percentage of oxygen delivered: 1 L/min (24%), 2 L/min (28%), 3 L/min (32%), 4 L/min (36%), 5 L/min (40%), and 6 L/min (40%). The simple mask can be set at the following rates with correlating percentage of oxygen delivered: 5-6 L/min (40%), 7-8 L/min (50%), and 10 L/min (60%). The venturi mask can be set at the following rates with correlating percentage of oxygen delivered: 4 L/min (24%), 4 L/min (28%), 6 L/min (31%), 8 L/min (35%), 8L/min (40%), and 10 L/min (50%). The partial rebreathing mask can be set to a rate of 6-10 L/min to deliver up to 80% oxygen, while the nonrebreathing mask can be set to a rate of 10 L/min to deliver 80-100% oxygen.

If the patient is a candidate for non-invasive mechanical ventilation, other devices may be used to deliver pressurized air into the patient's airways to improve oxygenation. Continuous positive airway pressure (CPAP) machines provide respiratory therapy via the use of one pressure, while bilevel positive airway pressure (BiPAP) machines provide two pressures. When CPAP does not adequately treat the patient's needs, BiPAP machines are considered. BiPAP is typically used for patients diagnosed with sleep apnea, lung disease, or congestive heart failure. Nursing analysis includes impaired gas exchange and ineffective airway clearance due to secretions.

Pulmonary care involves assessing for hypoxia, which includes symptoms such as anxiety, irritability, and confusion, along with signs such as tachypnea, tachycardia, and mottled extremities. The nurse should also monitor for signs of respiratory distress such as nasal flaring and intercostal retractions. Respiratory failure can occur because of an upper or lower airway obstruction. Upper airway obstructions include blood, mucus, foreign object, tumor, inflammation, or edema. Lower airway obstructions include aspiration, bronchospasm, pneumonia, pulmonary edema or hemorrhage, or drowning.

Patients with central nervous system deficits may have a decreased respiratory effort, leading to respiratory failure. Examples of this include brain stem injuries as is the case with strokes and tumors. An adverse medication effect may cause decreased respiratory effort. Alcohol, opioids, and sedatives are all examples of drugs that can depress respiratory effort to the point of failure.

Hypoglycemia and hypotension are examples of metabolic disorders that may weaken respiratory effort.

The progressive care nurse will recognize a patient going into respiratory distress by observing lowered respiratory effort, difficulty breathing, unconsciousness, cyanosis, and lowered pulse oxygenation percentages. Patients that may be on the cusp of a respiratory arrest may exhibit signs of decreasing neurologic function such as agitation, confusion, and oxygen hunger. They may be sweating profusely with a rapid heart rate. It is imperative that the progressive care nurse maintain the patient's airway to keep the patient from going from respiratory distress to arrest. Interventions to maintain an airway include optimally positioning the patient, doing a head-tilt chin-lift to help with occlusions, removing and minimizing sputum and other airway secretion, and assessing, intervening and reporting respiratory distress early to the provider for orders such as oxygen and medications. Most hospitals also have a rapid response team (also called a medical emergency or high acuity response team) which should be called as soon as symptoms of respiratory distress appear.

Diagnosis of respiratory failure will be based on clinical observation, and treatment will depend on finding and reversing the cause. If there is an obstruction present, it will need to be removed. If failure was caused by an adverse drug effect, an antidote may be given if appropriate. Titration of oxygen and non-invasive ventilation may be tried, but if those are unsuccessful, or if the patient is in extreme distress, they may have to be intubated and ventilated using mechanical ventilation if necessary to prevent impending cardiac arrest. Oxygenation and ventilation are the high priority at this point.

Failure to Wean

While using mechanical respiratory assistive devices for breathing, the progressive care nurse ensures the patient maintains a patent airway that is clear and free from obstruction and provides routine oral care and suction. The nurse assesses vital signs, oxygen saturation, bilateral breath sounds, and breathing rate. While barriers may exist, the nurse navigates assessing the patient's pain, anxiety, and sedation level, and administering supportive medication to relieve distress when indicated. The endotracheal tube must be well secured to prevent unplanned extubation. Sedation and neuromuscular blocking agents are reduced while weaning, which is the process of decreasing ventilator support, however if the patient is unable to remain hemodynamically stable and maintain their respiratory function independently, the medications are increased.

A spontaneous breathing trial is used to assess the patient's ability to breathe on their own once the underlying condition causing the respiratory failure is thought to have been resolved. If the weaning attempt fails, the nurse continues to provide supportive care including assessing sleep quality, handgrip strength, and diaphragmatic function. As the ultimate goal is to successfully wean off of mechanical ventilation, the nurse monitors for patient readiness to engage in another spontaneous breathing trial. Typical criteria include adequate cough, reduction of trachea-bronchial secretion, stable cardiovascular status, adequate hemoglobin level, afebrile, and a tidal volume greater than 5 mL/kg.

Tracheostomy Care

A patient may require the establishment of a tracheostomy if long-term care via invasive mechanical ventilation is warranted. In addition to the nursing care consideration present with mechanical ventilation, the nurse also assumes practices focused on tracheostomy care. The progressive care nurse ensures that the site remains clean, intact, and free from infection, assesses lung fields, and suctions secretions. For patients vulnerable to decreased oxygen levels, such as those receiving mechanical ventilation, the nurse provides suction for shorter, more frequent durations to avoid hypoxia. Nursing documentation involves detailed assessment of color, amount, and consistency of secretions, site and dressing condition, and respiratory status. The nurse should understand the length of time since the tracheostomy was placed, along with the type and size of the tracheostomy tube. While the patient is under sedation and unable to verbally respond, the nurse should also be cognizant of the patient's potential to be present for the interventions and verbally explain the process to the patient to reduce anxiety, maintain dignity, and provide patient-centered care.

Respiratory Infections

Bronchiolitis

Bronchiolitis is inflammation of the **bronchioles** (the small airways in the lungs) and is most commonly caused by **respiratory syncytial virus** (RSV). It typically affects children under the age of two, with a peak onset of three to six months of age. The disease is spread through direct contact with respiratory droplets. Bronchiolitis results in hospitalization of approximately 2% of children, the majority of which are under six months of age. Criteria for hospitalization can include prematurity, under three months of age, diagnosis of a congenital heart defect, respiratory rate >70-80 bpm, inability to maintain oral hydration, and cyanosis.

Signs and symptoms of bronchiolitis include:

- Difficulty feeding
- Fever
- Congestion
- Cough
- Dyspnea
- Tachypnea
- Nasal flaring
- Tachycardia
- Wheezing
- Fine rales
- Hypoxia
- Retractions
- Apnea

A diagnosis of bronchiolitis is usually established through a clinical examination. The most common diagnostic tests for the disease are: a rapid, viral antigen test of nasopharyngeal secretions for RSV; white blood cell (WBC) count with differential; ABG analysis; a chest x-ray; and a test of C-reactive protein (a marker of inflammation).

Although highly contagious, the disease is self-limiting and typically resolves without complication in one to two weeks. Treatment of bronchiolitis is supportive and can include oxygen supplementation, maintenance of hydration, fever reducers, nasal and oral suctioning, and intubation and mechanical ventilation.

Acute Laryngotracheobronchitis

Acute laryngotracheobronchitis, or classic **croup**, is a common viral illness in children. It results in inflammation of the larynx, trachea, and occasionally the bronchi. As a result, croup can be life-threatening in some children. Croup is primarily a disease of infants and toddlers, peaking between the ages of six months and three years. It rarely occurs after age six. The most common cause of croup is the parainfluenza viruses (types 1, 2, and 3), accounting for approximately 80% of the diagnosed cases. Other viral causes include adenovirus, rhinovirus, RSV, enterovirus, coronavirus, echovirus, and influenza A and B.

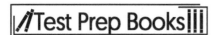

Croup is the most common pediatric ailment that causes stridor, an abnormal, high-pitched breath sound indicating partial or complete airway obstruction. Other signs and symptoms of the disease can include:

- Barking cough
- Pharyngitis
- Rhinorrhea
- Wheezing
- Tachypnea
- Tachycardia
- Fever
- Cyanosis
- Agitation
- Hypoxemia
- Respiratory failure

Croup is primarily a clinical diagnosis that relies on clues from the patient history and physical examination. In children, a chest x-ray occasionally reveals the "**steeple sign**," which indicates airway narrowing at the level of the glottis.

Treatment of croup can include:

- Corticosteroids, especially dexamethasone administered intravenously (IV), intramuscularly (IM), or orally (PO)

- Nebulized racemic epinephrine (typically reserved for hospital use; effects last only one and a half to two hours and require observation for at least three hours after dose)

- Cool mist (once the mainstay of treatment, but little evidence supports its clinical utility)

- Intubation and mechanical ventilation (for severe cases)

Acute Epiglottitis

Acute epiglottitis (also known as **supraglottitis**) is inflammation of the epiglottis. The **epiglottis** is the small piece of cartilage that's pulled forward to cover the windpipe when a person swallows. The cause of the condition is usually bacterial, with *Haemophilus influenzae* type B being the most common. Other bacterial causes include *Streptococcus pneumoniae*, *Streptococcus* groups A, B, and C, and non-typeable *Haemophilus influenzae*. The disease is most commonly diagnosed in children, but can be seen in adolescents and adults. A decline in the number of cases of acute epiglottitis has been noted since the introduction of the *Haemophilus influenzae* type B (Hib) vaccine in the 1980s.

Acute epiglottitis is usually accompanied by the classic triad of symptoms: dysphagia, drooling, and respiratory distress. Other signs and symptoms can include:

- Fever
- Sore throat
- Inability to lay flat
- Voice changes (can be muffled or hoarse)

- Tripod breathing position (a position said to optimize the mechanics of breathing where an individual sits up on their hands, head leaning forward, and tongue protruding)
- Tachypnea
- Hypoxia
- Agitation
- Cyanosis

Direct visualization of the epiglottis via a nasopharyngoscopy/laryngoscopy is the gold standard for diagnosing acute epiglottitis since an infected epiglottis has a cherry red appearance.

Acute epiglottitis is a potentially life-threatening medical emergency and should be treated promptly. It can quickly progress to total obstruction of the airway and death. Treatment of the condition can include:

- IV antibiotics (after blood and epiglottic cultures have been obtained)
- Analgesic-antipyretic agents such as aspirin, acetaminophen, and nonsteroidal anti-inflammatory drugs (NSAIDs), such as ibuprofen
- Intubation with mechanical ventilation, tracheostomy, or needle-jet insufflation (options for immediate airway management, if needed)
- Racemic epinephrine, corticosteroids, and Beta-2 agonists are also sometimes used; however, they have yet to been proven as useful treatments

Acute Tracheitis

A rare condition, **acute tracheitis**, is the inflammation and infection of the trachea (windpipe). The majority of cases occur in children under the age of sixteen. The etiology of acute tracheitis is predominantly bacterial, with *Staphylococcus aureus* being the leading cause. Community-associated, methicillin-resistant *Staphylococcus aureus* (CA-MRSA) has recently emerged as an important causative agent. Other bacterial causes of acute tracheitis include *Streptococcus pneumoniae, Haemophilus influenzae,* and *Moraxella catarrhalis*.

Acute tracheitis is often preceded by an upper respiratory infection (URI). Signs and symptoms of acute tracheitis can include:

- Bark-like cough
- Dyspnea
- Fever
- Tachypnea
- Respiratory distress
- Stridor
- Wheezing
- Hoarseness
- Nasal flaring
- Cyanosis

The only definitive means of diagnosis is the use of a laryngotracheobronchoscopy to directly visualize mucopurulent membranes lining the mucosa of the trachea. Additional tests can include pulse oximetry, blood cultures, nasopharyngeal and tracheal cultures, and neck x-rays.

Treatment of acute tracheitis should be prompt because of the increased likelihood of complete airway obstruction leading to respiratory arrest and death. Treatment can include:

- IV antibiotics (if living in an area with high or increasing rates of CA-MRSA, the addition of vancomycin should be considered)
- Intubation and mechanical ventilation or tracheostomy (rarely needed) are options if immediate airway management is needed
- Fever reducers

Viral Pneumonia

Viral pneumonia is more common at the extremes of age (young children and the elderly). It accounts for the majority of cases of childhood pneumonia. Cases of viral pneumonia have been increasing over the past decade, mostly as a result of immunosuppression (weakened immune system). Common causes of viral pneumonia in children, the elderly, and the immunocompromised are the influenza viruses (most common), RSV, parainfluenza virus, and adenovirus.

Signs and symptoms of viral pneumonia largely overlap those of bacterial pneumonia and can include:

- Cough (nonproductive)
- Fever/chills
- Myalgias
- Fatigue
- Headache
- Dyspnea
- Tachypnea
- Tachycardia
- Wheezing
- Cyanosis
- Hypoxia
- Decreased breath sounds
- Respiratory distress

Viral pneumonia is diagnosed via a chest x-ray and viral cultures. The chest x-ray usually reveals bilateral lung infiltrates, instead of the lobar involvement commonly seen in bacterial causes. Viral cultures can take up to two weeks to confirm the diagnosis. Rapid antigen testing and gene amplification via polymerase chain reaction (PCR) have been recently incorporated into the diagnostic mix to shorten the diagnosis lag.

Treatment of viral pneumonia is usually supportive and can include:

- Supplemental oxygen
- Rest

- Antipyretics
- Analgesics
- Intravenous fluids
- Parenteral nutrition
- Intubation and mechanical ventilation

Specific causes of viral pneumonia can benefit from treatment with antiviral medications. Influenza pneumonia can be treated with oseltamivir (Tamiflu®) or zanamivir (Relenza®). Ribavirin® is the only effective antiviral agent for the treatment of RSV pneumonia.

Acute Respiratory Tract Infections

Acute Bronchitis

Acute bronchitis is inflammation of the bronchial tubes (bronchi), which extend from the trachea to the lungs. It is one of the top five reasons for visits to healthcare providers and can take from ten days to three weeks to resolve. Common causes of acute bronchitis include respiratory viruses (such as influenza A and B), RSV, parainfluenza, adenovirus, rhinovirus, and coronavirus. Bacterial causes include *Mycoplasma species, Streptococcus pneumoniae, Chlamydia pneumoniae, Haemophilus influenzae,* and *Moraxella catarrhalis*. Other causes of acute bronchitis are irritants such as chemicals, pollution, and tobacco smoke.

Signs and symptoms of acute bronchitis can include:

- Cough (most common symptom) with or without sputum
- Fever
- Sore throat
- Headache
- Nasal congestion
- Rhinorrhea
- Dyspnea
- Fatigue
- Myalgia
- Chest pain
- Wheezing

Acute bronchitis is typically diagnosed by exclusion, which means tests are used to exclude more serious conditions such as pneumonia, epiglottitis, or COPD. Useful diagnostic tests include a CBC with differential, a chest x-ray, respiratory and blood cultures, PFTs, bronchoscopy, laryngoscopy, and a procalcitonin (PCT) test to determine if the infection is bacterial.

Treatment of acute bronchitis is primarily supportive and can include:

- Bedrest
- Cough suppressants, such as codeine or dextromethorphan
- Beta-2 agonists, such as albuterol for wheezing
- Nonsteroidal anti-inflammatory drugs (NSAIDs) for pain
- Expectorants, such as guaifenesin

Although acute bronchitis should not be routinely treated with antibiotics, there are exceptions to this rule. It's reasonable to use an antibiotic when an existing medical condition poses a risk of serious complications. Antibiotic use is also reasonable for treating acute bronchitis in elderly patients who have been hospitalized in the past year, have been diagnosed with congestive heart failure (CHF) or diabetes, or are currently being treated with a steroid.

Pneumonia

Pneumonia is an infection that affects the functional tissue of the lung. Microscopically, it is characterized by consolidating lung tissue with exudate, fibrin, and inflammatory cells filling the alveoli (air sacs). Pneumonia can represent a primary disease or a secondary disease (e.g., post-obstructive pneumonia due to lung cancer), and the most common causes of pneumonia are bacteria and viruses. Other causes of pneumonia include fungi and parasites.

Pneumonia can be categorized according to its anatomic distribution on a chest x-ray or the setting in which it is acquired. Pneumonia categorized according to its anatomic distribution on chest x-ray can be:

- Lobar: Limited to one lobe of the lungs. It can affect more than one lobe on the same side (multilobar pneumonia) or bilateral lobes ("double" pneumonia).
- Bronchopneumonia: Scattered diffusely throughout the lungs
- Interstitial: Involving areas between the alveoli

Pneumonia categorized according to the setting in which it is acquired can be:

- **Community-Acquired Pneumonia** (CAP): Pneumonia in an individual who hasn't been recently hospitalized, or its occurrence in less than 48 hours after admission to a hospital.
- **Hospital-Acquired** (Nosocomial) Pneumonia: Pneumonia acquired during or after hospitalization for another ailment with onset at least 48 hours or more after admission.
- **Aspiration Pneumonia**: Pneumonia resulting from the inhalation of gastric or oropharyngeal secretions.

Community-Acquired Pneumonia (CAP)

Common causes of community-acquired pneumonia (CAP) include:

- Streptococcus pneumoniae
- Haemophilus influenzae
- Moraxella catarrhalis
- Atypical organisms (such as Legionella species, Mycoplasma pneumoniae, and Chlamydia pneumoniae)
- Staphylococcus aureus
- Respiratory viruses

Streptococcus Pneumoniae

Streptococcus pneumonia (also known as **S. pneumonia** or **pneumococcus**) is a gram-positive bacterium and the most common cause of CAP. Due to the introduction of a pneumococcal vaccine in 2000, cases of pneumococcal pneumonia have decreased. However, medical providers should be aware there is now evidence of emerging, antibiotic-resistant strains of the organism. Signs and symptoms of pneumococcal pneumonia can include:

- Cough productive of rust-colored sputum (mucus)
- Fever with or without chills
- Dyspnea
- Wheezing
- Chest pain
- Tachypnea
- Altered mental status
- Tachycardia
- Rales over involved lung
- Increase in tactile fremitus
- E to A change
- Hypotension
- Lung consolidation

Diagnosis of pneumococcal pneumonia can include:

- CBC with differential
- Chest x-ray
- CT scan (if underlying lung cancer is suspected)
- Sputum gram stain and/or culture
- Blood cultures
- Procalcitonin and C-reactive protein blood level tests
- Sputum, serum, and/or urinary antigen tests
- Immunoglobulin studies
- Bronchoscopy with bronchoalveolar lavage (BAL)

Treatment of pneumococcal pneumonia can include:

- Antibiotics, such as ceftriaxone plus doxycycline, or azithromycin

- Respiratory quinolones, such as levofloxacin (Levaquin®), moxifloxacin (Avelox®), or gemifloxacin (Factive®)

- Supplemental oxygen

- Beta-2 agonists, such as albuterol via nebulizer or metered-dose inhaler (MDI), as needed for wheezing

- Analgesics and antipyretics

- Chest physiotherapy

- Active suctioning of respiratory secretions

- Intubation and mechanical ventilation

Mycoplasma Pneumoniae

Mycoplasma pneumonia, also known as **M. pneumoniae**, is a bacterium that causes atypical CAP. It is one of the most common causes of CAP in healthy individuals under the age of forty. The most common symptom of mycoplasmal pneumonia is a dry, nonproductive cough. Other signs and symptoms can include diarrhea, earache, fever (usually ≤ 102 °F), sore throat, myalgias, nasal congestion, skin rash, and general malaise. Chest x-rays of individuals with mycoplasmal pneumonia reveal a pattern of bronchopneumonia. Cold agglutinin titers in the blood can be significantly elevated (> 1:64). Polymerase chain reaction (PCR) is becoming the standard confirmatory test for mycoplasmal pneumonia, though currently it is not used in most clinical settings. Other diagnostic tests for M. pneumoniae are usually nonspecific and therefore do not aid in its diagnosis.

Treatments for mycoplasmal pneumonia are no different than for CAP, except for antibiotic choices, which include:

- Macrolide antibiotics, such as erythromycin, azithromycin (Zithromax®), clarithromycin (Biaxin®, Biaxin XL®)
- Doxycycline (a tetracycline antibiotic derivative)

Methicillin-Resistant Staphylococcus Aureus

Community-Acquired Methicillin-Resistant Staphylococcus Aureus (CA-MRSA) has emerged as a significant cause of CAP over the past twenty years. It also remains a significant cause of hospital-acquired pneumonia. The majority (up to 75%) of those diagnosed with CA-MRSA pneumonia are young, previously healthy individuals with influenza as a preceding illness. Symptoms are usually identical to those seen with other causes of CAP. Chest x-ray typically reveals multilobar involvement with or without cavitation/necrosis. Gram staining of sputum and/or blood can reveal gram-positive bacteria in clusters. Other diagnostic tests are nonspecific and do not aid in the diagnosis of CA-MRSA pneumonia.

Treatment of CA-MRSA should be prompt as it has a high mortality rate. Supportive measures are needed as in other cases of CAP. CA-MRSA is notoriously resistant to most antibiotics with the exception of the following:

- Vancomycin: The mainstay and only treatment for CA-MRSA pneumonia for many years (unfortunately with a disappointing cure rate). A loading dose of 25 mg/kg (max 2,000 mg) is needed with a maintenance dose based on creatinine clearance and body weight (in kg). Vancomycin trough should be drawn prior to the fourth dose with a target goal of 15-20 mcg/mL (mg/L).
- Linezolid: An alternative to vancomycin and quickly becoming the agent of choice for the treatment of CA-MRSA pneumonia. It is administered 600 mg PO/IV every twelve hours.

Thoracic Surgery

In certain conditions of the lung, thoracic surgery may be considered. A **thoracic surgeon** is one who specializes in operations on the thoracic region of the body, involving the organs of the chest. The heart and lungs are the primary targets of these surgical procedures.

Surgeries may be performed to remove cancerous tumors of the lung. Possible procedures a patient would undergo for this purpose would be a pneumonectomy, lobectomy, wedge resection, or sleeve resection. Pneumonectomy removes the entire lung. Lobectomy removes the entire lobe containing the cancerous tumor. Wedge resection removes part of the affected lobe. Sleeve resection refers to "trimming" the affected part of the airway and sewing it back together, like cutting a stain off a sleeve and reattaching the upper and lower portions.

If a thoracic surgeon wishes to visualize the interior of the chest wall and surrounding tissues, they may opt to perform a thoracoscopy. During this procedure, small incisions are made into the chest wall, and a thin tube with a camera at the end, called a *scope,* is inserted. The surgeon then explores the interior cavity and visualizes the area they wish to view. This procedure may be used to biopsy tissue for histological analysis. A more invasive procedure used to visualize the interior chest cavity is called a **thoracotomy**, where the chest is opened directly.

Thoracic surgery involves either percutaneous or open incisions into the thorax for the purpose of removing cancerous or benign lesions, diseased tissue that may result from tuberculosis or other infections, or non-functioning tissue that increases the respiratory effort in patients with chronic obstructive pulmonary disease (COPD). The choice of the exact procedure is dependent on the type, size, and location of the lesion, and common approaches include lobectomy and pneumonectomy as noted below.

Lobectomy

A **lobectomy** refers to the removal of an entire lobe of one lung with ligation of its vasculature and lobular bronchi. Lobectomy is most commonly performed for the treatment of primary and metastatic lung cancer, bronchiectasis, and traumatic injury.

There are two basic approaches to the removal of the tissue including an anatomical approach and a non-anatomical approach. Anatomical approaches include the pneumonectomy, lobectomy, segmentectomy, and the sleeve resection, which require ligation and attachment of the "feeding vessels" and the airways to a portion of unresected lung tissue.

The specific surgical approach is based on a rigorous preoperative evaluation and risk assessment and may be either an open procedure, or a minimally invasive procedure such as video-assisted thoracoscopic surgery (VATS), or robotic-assisted thoracoscopic surgery (RATS). **Video-assisted thoracoscopic surgery** (VATS) results in fewer hospital days and a quicker recovery as compared to the open approach. In addition, the VATS approach has gained wider acceptance than the RATS approach due to the expense of the system and the provider learning curve. Video-assisted thoracoscopic surgery (VATS) uses a small video camera called a thoracoscope to diagnose and treat chest conditions. The camera is inserted into the chest via one or more small incisions. The surgeon is guided through the procedure via chest images projected onto the video screen. This technique may be performed to assist with multiple surgical procedures, such a lung biopsy, hiatal hernia repair, or thymus gland removal, among many other chest-related issues.

Possible complications include hemorrhage, nerve damage, and pneumonia. Compared with more invasive options such as thoracotomy, VATS may improve outcomes by reducing complications and shortening recovery time. Nursing care involves frequent respiratory and cardiac monitoring, pain assessment and management, and patient education regarding condition-specific care. Wound assessment and management is conducted to reduce post-operative risk for infection and bleeding. As VATS is used to support the investigation and treatment of a large variety of chest conditions, additional care considerations should be tailored to the underlying reason for the VATS, along with condition-specific discharge planning.

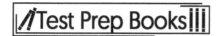

Post-operative care following any type of lobectomy is focused on providing pain management, treating the underlying cause and maintenance of optimal respiratory function.

Pneumonectomy

A **left pneumonectomy** is the removal of both the upper and lower lobes, while a **right pneumonectomy** refers to the removal of the upper, middle and lower lobes. Indications for pneumonectomy include stage I and II primary tumors, selected metastatic lesions, pulmonary TB, fungal infections, and traumatic trachea-bronchial injuries. Pneumonectomy is an anatomic approach to thoracic surgery that requires securing the fragile pulmonary vasculature and the pulmonary airway structures to maintain the integrity of the surviving lung. The preoperative evaluation for pneumonectomy includes a comprehensive risk assessment that compares all elements of the patient's pulmonary and constitutional status to the projected outcome of the surgical procedure. In addition, all imaging studies will be completed, and if necessary repeated, in order to provide surgeons with information related to the patient's current status.

Currently, pneumonectomy commonly requires an open surgical approach that corresponds to the anatomical position of the disease; however, in patients with small growths that are favorably positioned, the use of VATS, a minimally-invasive approach, may be an option. The less invasive surgical approach is associated with improved patient outcomes and decreased length of stay, which offsets the initial expenses of the VATS technology.

After thoracic surgery, an incentive spirometer is usually used during a patient's postop recovery. Incentive spirometry encourages maximal inspirations and promotes lung expansion to prevent atelectasis. The progressive care nurse uses an incentive spirometer to assess patient signs of atelectasis, such as decreased breath sounds and shallow respirations, while reviewing respiratory rate and depth along with vital signs. This process provides identification of respiratory conditions impeding breathing and also supports healthy respiratory function. The nurse must take great care to consider discontinuation of use if the patient is uncooperative or if hypoxia develops secondary to the interruption of other prescribed therapies. After educating the patient on the procedure, the nurse assists them to an upright position and uses pillows for splinting support when necessary. The nurse instructs the patient to exhale, and then inhale slowly to full lung capacity while maintaining sealed lips around the spirometry mouthpiece. At this point, the nurse instructs the patient to hold their breath for three to five seconds and notes the highest level the volume indicator reaches to gather the inspiratory capacity.

Nursing care for pneumonectomy or lobectomy involves assisting with ambulation and cardiopulmonary therapies as indicated. Air leaks are significant post-operative complications requiring expiratory chest tube management, while prolonged air leaks lasting a week may require subsequent surgical intervention to correct. The nurse should focus on respiratory assessment to discover early warning signs of complication and proactively support healing that reduces the risk for the development of atelectasis, mucous plugging, and pneumonia. Patient education should involve the importance of smoking cessation and strategies for goal attainment, which ideally had been initiated pre-operatively and continued. Chest physiotherapy, antibiotic treatment, and pain management techniques should be included as needed. Additional complications vary by procedure specifics, which may include pulmonary edema, cardiac herniation, hemothorax, bronchopleural fistula, wound infection, chylothorax, hemorrhage, and nerve injury.

The progressive care nurse should closely monitor for early complications, and then report abnormal findings to the care team for continued monitoring and diagnosis, which may involve imaging, laboratory assessment, and invasive procedures. Length-of-stay and discharge instructions rely on the particular procedure performed and the patient's individualized responsiveness to it. The nurse prioritizes sustained patient ventilation, which is evidenced by smooth, non-labored respiration and a rate within the patient's typical baseline or normal baseline for specifics of condition, along with breath sounds present in all lobes prior to discharge.

Practice Quiz

1. Apnea and loss of normal oxygenation during a spontaneous breathing trial are signs that what should occur?
    a. Sedation should be increased.
    b. The breathing trial should continue for a few more minutes.
    c. An antidote for respiratory distress should be administered.
    d. Mechanical ventilation should continue.

2. Which of the following procedures confirms a diagnosis of pulmonary hypertension?
    a. Transesophageal echocardiography
    b. Right cardiac catheterization
    c. Left cardiac catheterization
    d. Lung transplantation

3. Pulmonary hypertension will likely be treated with all but which of the following drug therapies?
    a. Sildenafil
    b. Amlodipine
    c. Epoprostenol
    d. Diazepam

4. Which of the following terms refers to severe bronchoconstriction with wheezing that does not respond to the usual bronchodilation treatment?
    a. Delirium tremens
    b. Status asthmaticus
    c. Pulsus paradoxus
    d. Febre rubra

5. Which of the following is a more invasive procedure performed by a thoracic surgeon involving opening the chest wall to visualize the interior structures?
    a. Thoracotomy
    b. Thoracocentesis
    c. Thoracobronchotomy
    d. Thoracoscopy

See answers on the next page.

Answer Explanations

1. D: If a patient becomes apneic and oxygenation drops off during a spontaneous breathing trial, it is a sign that the patient should be placed back on mechanical ventilation, as they are not ready to breathe on their own. Increasing the sedation will worsen the patient's breathing function. Continuing the breathing trial will lead to organ damage due to lack of oxygenation and perfusion. An antidote is not appropriate in this scenario.

2. B: Right cardiac catheterization is a procedure that will confirm a diagnosis of pulmonary hypertension. Transesophageal echocardiography is useful in visualizing the back side of the heart but does not fit with this specific scenario. Left cardiac catheterization enters the opposite side of the heart and is not helpful in confirming diagnosis. Lung transplantation is a surgical procedure used to treat severe cases of pulmonary hypertension.

3. D: Diazepam is an anxiolytic that is not specifically used for the treatment of pulmonary hypertension. Diuretics, calcium channel blockers, and vasodilators may all be used to treat pulmonary hypertension. Sildenafil is an example of a phosphodiesterase inhibitor and is helpful in increasing blood flow in the lungs. Amlodipine is an example of a calcium channel blocker, a class of drugs that may be helpful for pulmonary hypertension. Epoprostenol is a drug specifically formulated for use in patients with pulmonary hypertension.

4. B: *Status asthmaticus* is the Latin term for a severe asthma attack, characterized by wheezing and bronchoconstriction, that is unresponsive to the usual therapy of bronchodilators. *Delirium tremens* is the set of symptoms experienced by an alcoholic in withdrawal. *Pulsus paradoxus* is defined as a drop in the systolic blood pressure by ten points and a decrease in the amplitude of pulse waves while the patient breathes in. It can be observed during cardiac tamponade. *Febre rubra* is the Latin term for scarlet fever.

5. A: A thoracotomy is the opening of the chest by a thoracic surgeon to visualize the interior structures and tissue of the chest. Thoracocentesis is an invasive procedure where small incisions are made in the chest wall with the purpose of removing air or fluid and inserting a chest tube to drain. Thoracocentesis is also called a *pleural tap*. Thoracobronchotomy is a procedure where an incision is made into the bronchus and thorax, usually to remove a tumor or foreign object. Thoracoscopy is a less invasive procedure involving small incisions and the insertion of a thin tube with a camera affixed to the end, called a scope, to visualize the interior structure and tissues of the chest.

Endocrine/Hematology/Neurology/Gastrointestinal/ Renal

The progressive care nurse will encounter several conditions affecting the hormonal regulation of the human body, the blood and its unique chemistry, the digestive tract, the kidneys and their filtration processes, and the largest organ of the body, the skin, which protects the interior of the body from the exterior environment. This section comprises a discussion of those body systems, including the endocrine, hematological, gastrointestinal, renal, and integumentary systems.

Endocrine

The hormones of the body play a key role in metabolism and the regulation of body processes. Each hormone, produced in various glands throughout the body, has a specific target tissue that it acts upon, producing a specific result. Dysfunction of hormonal regulation can lead to disease states.

Major Human Endocrine Glands and Some of Their Hormones

Gland		Hormone	Chemical Class	Representative Actions	Regulated By
 **Hypothalamus**		Hormones released from the posterior pituitary and hormones that regulate the anterior pituitary *see below*			
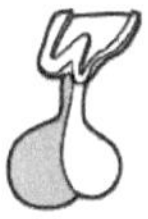 **Posterior pituitary gland** *Releases neurohormones made in hypothalamus*		Oxytocin	Peptide	Stimulates contraction of uterus and mammary gland cells	Nervous system
		Antidiuretic hormone **ADH**	Peptide	Promotes retention of water by kidneys	Water/salt balance
 **Anterior pituitary gland**		Growth hormone **GH**	Protein	Stimulates growth (especially bones) and metabolic functions	Hypothalamic hormones
		Prolactin **PRL**	Protein	Stimulates milk production and secretion	Hypothalamic hormones
		Follicle-stimulating hormone **FSH**	Glycoprotein	Stimulates production of ova and sperm	Hypothalamic hormones
		Luteinizing hormone **LH**	Glycoprotein	Stimulates ovaries and testes	Hypothalamic hormones
		Thyroid-stimulating hormone **TSH**	Glycoprotein	Stimulates thyroid gland	Hypothalamic hormones
		Adrenocorticotropic hormone **ACTH**	Peptide	Stimulates adrenal cortex to secrete glucocorticoids	Hypothalamic hormones
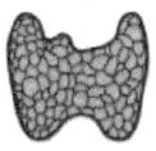 **Thyroid gland**		Triiodothyrocine $\mathbf{T_3}$ Thyrocine $\mathbf{T_2}$	Amine	Stimulate and maintain metabolic processes	TSH
		Calcitonine	Peptide	Lowers blood calcium level	Calcium in blood
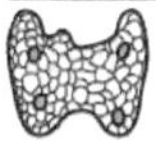 **Parathyroid glands**		Parathyroid hormone **PTH**	Peptide	Raises blood calcium level	Calcium in blood
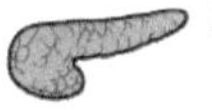 **Pancreas**		Insulin	Protein	Lowers blood glucose level	Glucose in blood
		Glucagon	Protein	Raises blood insulin level	Glucose in blood
 **Adrenal glands**	*Adrenal medulla*	Epinephrine Norepinephrine	Amines	Raises blood glucose level; Increases metabolic activities; Constrict certain blood vessels	Nervous system
	*Adrenal cortex*	Glucocorticoids	Steroid	Raises blood glucose level	ACTH
		Mineralocorticoids	Steroid	Promote reabsorbtion of Na^+ and excretion of K^+ in kidneys	K^+ in blood; angiotensin II
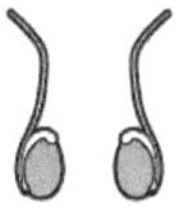 **Gonads**	*Testes*	Androgens	Steroid	Support sperm formation; Promote development and maintenance of male secondary sex characteristics	FSH LH
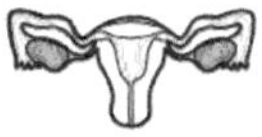	*Ovaries*	Estrogens	Steroid	Stimulate uterine lining growth; Promote development and maintenance of female secondary sex characteristics	FSH LH
		Progestins	Steroid	Promote uterine lining growth;	FSH and LH
 **Pineal gland**		Melatonin	Amine	Involved in biological rhythms	Light/dark cycles

The endocrine system is maintained through homeostatic balance of a variety of hormones. To ensure proper maintenance and detection of disease, laboratory values are monitored via individualized, patient-centered treatment plans regarding frequency and response to results. If medication management is initiated in response to laboratory and clinical findings, repeat laboratory values should be assessed on an individualized basis to provide follow-up response to treatment.

Diabetes Mellitus

Diabetes Mellitus is a condition that affects how the body responds to the presence of glucose. Glucose is needed for cell functioning, and all consumable calories eventually are converted to glucose in the body. A hormone produced by the pancreas, called **insulin**, is needed to break down food and drink into glucose molecules. In patients with type 1 diabetes, the pancreas fails to produce insulin, leading to high levels of glucose in the bloodstream. This can lead to organ damage, organ failure, or nerve damage. Patients with **type 1 diabetes** receive daily insulin injections or have a pump that continuously monitors their blood insulin levels and releases insulin as needed. In patients with **type 2 diabetes**, the pancreas produces insulin, but the body is unable to use it effectively. Patients with type 2 diabetes typically need to manage their condition through lifestyle changes, such as losing weight and eating fewer carbohydrate-rich and sugary foods. There are also some medications that help the body use the insulin that is present in the bloodstream.

Gestational diabetes is a form of diabetes that some women develop during the second to third trimester of pregnancy, when their systems temporarily become resistant to insulin. High blood sugar in a pregnant woman can affect fetal growth and influence the baby's risk of becoming obese. Pregnant women with gestational diabetes are encouraged to exercise daily, avoid excessive weight gain, and carefully monitor their diet. Gestational diabetes is similar to type 2 diabetes in the way symptoms present and in treatment options.

Diabetes mellitus type I is an autoimmune condition that requires insulin therapy for disease management, as these patients do not produce insulin. Diabetes mellitus type II often requires oral agents for disease management; however, as the disease progresses, patients may require insulin therapy, as they do not respond to insulin effectively and later struggle to produce insulin. **Diabetic ketoacidosis** is a medical emergency that involves the body's overproduction of blood acids called ketones in response to too little insulin. Warning signs and symptoms of this serious condition include abdominal pain, extreme thirst, frequent urination, fruity breath odor, confusion, and high blood sugar levels. Upon further examination, the care team finds high levels of ketones in the blood and urine, referred to as ketosis. During diabetic ketoacidosis management, the progressive care nurse provides care to reduce unpleasant symptoms while closely monitoring blood glucose levels, intake and output, diabetic diet, vital signs, and level of orientation. Emergency treatment involves insulin therapy and intravenous fluids to prevent dehydration and maintain electrolyte balance.

Nursing considerations for insulin administration include ensuring the correct route, either subcutaneous or intravenous (regular insulin). For subcutaneous administration, the injection angle should be at forty-five to ninety degrees and sites should be rotated. When not in use, insulin vials are stored in the refrigerator once open. If the patient's blood sugar level is well maintained using mixed insulin, the care team typically continues this treatment plan, which requires the nurse to first draw up the short-acting insulin and then the long-acting insulin into the syringe. The insulin should not be diluted unless the prescriber gave direction to do so. Fast-acting insulin should be injected approximately fifteen minutes before meals. Nursing care considerations include thorough knowledge of common hypoglycemic agents, including types, peak, and duration. Before administering hypoglycemic agents, the progressive care nurse should review the indications and directions approved for each medication, as wide variation exists. In general, oral agents typically peak within an hour to several hours, with the onset of action one hour for fast-acting, two to four hours for intermediate-acting, and four to six hours for long-acting insulin therapies.

Diabetic Ketoacidosis

A patient diagnosed with diabetes mellitus may be prone to a complication of this condition called **diabetic ketoacidosis** (DKA). The process of developing DKA is a complex metabolic pathway in which the body seeks alternative energy sources to glucose and an acidotic state results.

At the beginning of DKA, the body is in a state of insulin deficiency. This at times happens as a result of diabetes mellitus, and the body must compensate to continue operations as usual. The body begins to metabolize triglycerides and amino acids to create energy. In a normal state, the body breaks down glucose as an energy source. However, when insulin is deficient and blood glucose supply is in flux all the time, as is the case with diabetes mellitus, the body searches for alternatives.

The breakdown of triglycerides and amino acids then causes an increase in serum levels of glycerol and free fatty acids as a byproduct of **lipolysis**, or fat breakdown. Alanine also rises in the serum as a byproduct of muscle breakdown, as another energy source when the body cannot find enough glucose. This rise in alanine and glycerol stimulate the liver to produce its own glucose as an energy source. Glucagon, which is produced in the pancreas and used as an emergency source of energy when outside glucose sources drop, rises to excessive levels and stimulates free fatty acids to be converted to ketones. This process is called **ketogenesis** and is normally blocked by sufficient levels of insulin. Ketogenesis results in ketoacids, such as acetone, which create the acidic environment of DKA. Acetone is released from the body by way of respiration, which is why a patient with DKA has a "fruity" smell to their breath.

When the blood sugar rises during DKA, it causes substantial amounts of fluids to be excreted through the urine, called **osmotic diuresis**. This leads to fluid and electrolyte imbalances. Potassium levels must be carefully monitored during DKA. They may not initially fall in serum tests because, despite great loss of potassium through the urine, there is also a great release of potassium from the cells into the bloodstream. Potassium will be ushered back into the cells when insulin levels return to normal.

Presenting symptoms of DKA include polyuria, polydipsia, nausea, and abdominal pain. Diagnosis will be made based on symptoms and measurements of arterial blood gases. Presence of ketones in the bloodstream, an anion gap of >12, and a pH of < 7.30 are considered positive diagnostic signs of DKA.

Treatment of DKA will include insulin administration, correction of fluid and electrolyte imbalances (especially potassium), and possibly bicarbonate to correct severe cases of acidosis. Most facilities have policies in place for DKA, with the key components including isotonic saline, potassium to replace deficit, and IV insulin at low doses once potassium is within normal range. Frequent blood sugars and ABGs will be drawn per institution protocol.

Titrating IV insulin drips is a very critical and serious matter for the nurse. The progressive care nurse should feel adequately trained in hospital policy and always have a second nurse verify the insulin drip protocol order and pump settings. Often, once potassium levels are safe, an initial bolus of 0.1 units/kg of regular insulin is given and then a continuous drip of 0.1 units/kg/hr is usually started. From there, titrations occur per protocol based on blood glucose levels, which should be checked hourly while titrations occur and with any symptoms of hypoglycemia.

Hyperglycemic Hyperosmolar Syndrome (HHS)

A patient with diabetes type II still produces insulin, though the insulin response is limited as the cells have developed a resistance to insulin. When blood sugar rises to unhealthy levels, it stimulates the kidneys to drop large amounts of urine, a condition called **polyuria**. The blood volume is thus depleted, causing a state of dehydration and abnormal concentration of the blood. Concentration of the blood creates a hyperosmolar state in the bloodstream. When the blood is concentrated yet not acidotic as a result of fat cells breaking down, it is called **hyperglycemic hyperosmolar nonketotic syndrome**.

HHS can result from a patient not taking their prescribed diabetic medications appropriately, causing a hyperglycemic state. At other times, an infection or illness unrelated to diabetes mellitus may cause a hyperglycemic state. Corticosteroids are known to cause a rise in blood sugar, thus their use must be administered with caution. If the patient also suffers from high blood sugar and has been prescribed diuretics, a hyperosmolar state may result.

The concentrated blood of HHS will primarily cause neurological deficits such as confusion, disorientation, drowsiness, and even coma. Certain patients will experience seizures or stroke-like syndromes. Death may occur if HHS is left untreated.

HHS will be diagnosed based on symptoms of confusion and blood tests to look for hyperosmolarity of the blood, as well as decreased blood volume signaling dehydration. Treatment will occur via intravenous (IV) therapy to correct fluid and electrolyte imbalances. Treatment of HHS is very similar to treatment of DKA.

Hypoglycemia

In the body, a normal amount of blood glucose is necessary as an energy source for metabolic processes. The brain relies on glucose as an energy source to perform its functions. The term "**blood sugar**" refers to the amount of glucose circulating in one's blood at any given time. A normal blood sugar before a person eats falls into the 70 mg/dl to 99 mg/dl range. After one eats, blood sugar rises, but should be no more than 140 mg/dl a few hours after a meal. When the blood glucose level falls below 50 mg/dl, the person is considered to be **hypoglycemic**, meaning they are in a state of low blood sugar.

Hypoglycemia may occur with or without symptoms. The body has a number of regulatory activities that are performed to correct low blood sugar. As a compensatory mechanism, the levels of glucagon and epinephrine may rise, and growth hormone and cortisol levels may increase. These regulatory mechanisms may occur and correct the hypoglycemia before any noticeable symptoms arise.

Symptoms of hypoglycemia are reflective of the autonomic activity occurring within the body. The patient may be sweating, feel warm, or experience nausea, anxiety, and palpitations. The patient may be trembling, complain of headache, experience blurry or double vision, become confused, slur their speech, or even begin to have a seizure or enter a comatose state. Many of these symptoms are caused by the lack of blood glucose to the brain causing neurological symptomology.

The cause of an acute hypoglycemic state is almost always drug-induced, especially if the patient is receiving insulin therapy. Overtreatment with insulin without proper balance with the patient's mealtime schedule will result in hypoglycemia. Patients in the hospital setting often fall victim to hypoglycemia due to an ever-changing schedule of tests, procedures, and periods of time where they are required to fast.

Treatment of hypoglycemia usually includes administration of dextrose or some other form of sugar. Oral glucagon is an option in the alert patient who can swallow. Symptoms should be corrected upon normalization of blood sugar.

Metabolic Syndrome

Metabolic syndrome, or **Syndrome X**, refers to the presence of comorbid cardiovascular and insulin-related conditions. Patients diagnosed with metabolic syndrome must have three or more of the following conditions: hypertension, elevated fasting blood glucose levels, low HDL cholesterol, high triglycerides, and excess belly fat. This syndrome is believed to result from insulin resistance, causing high blood glucose, insulin, and lipid levels. Patients with metabolic syndrome tend to be overweight or obese and at an increased risk of organ failure, heart attacks, and strokes. They often suffer from another underlying condition, such as diabetes or polycystic ovary syndrome, that leads to metabolic syndrome. Metabolic syndrome is often treated with prescription medications that lower cholesterol and blood pressure, but diet and exercise changes are strongly recommended. Weight loss is a key component in managing metabolic syndrome.

Other Endocrine Disorders

Conn's syndrome represents primary hyperaldosteronism often in response to adrenal adenoma, congestive heart failure, liver cirrhosis, or nephrotic syndrome. Sodium retention leads to hypertension, while potassium loss leads to muscle weakness. Laboratory assessment of fluid and electrolyte balance is necessary for analysis. The progressive care nurse monitors intake and outpost, ECG, and dietary maintenance to reduce risk for sodium and potassium imbalances. Spironolactone should be administered with milk or antacids. Patient education should include the requirement for lifelong use of gluco- and mineralocorticosteroids for patients with bilateral adrenalectomy.

Addison's disease involves adrenal hypofunction usually in response to autoimmune disease. Laboratory testing is used to determine whether the patient is suffering from a lack of glucocorticosteroids and mineralocorticosteroids, along with hypoglycemia and electrolyte imbalances. The progressive care nurse should assess the patient for signs and symptoms of weight loss, apathy, stress incontinence, and hyperpigmentation of skin folds. More hormone replacement is often needed during times of stress. Lifelong replacement of gluco- and mineralocorticosteroids is typically necessary. An addisonian crisis due to a lack of glucocorticoids may be fatal. The nursing assessment includes the review of acute hypotension, shock, and renal failure. Intravenous administration of sodium chloride (NaCl) and hydrocortisone, along with strict intake and output monitoring and assessment of vital signs every fifteen minutes is often warranted, mitigating risk and improving patient outcomes.

Hypothyroidism, often seen in the autoimmune condition of Hashimoto's thyroiditis, leads to symptoms of fatigue, weight gain, loss of appetite, bradycardia, cold intolerance, puffy face, and dry skin. In the severe case of myxedema coma, the nurse should assess for hypotension, hypothermia, hypoglycemia, enlarged tongue, and slow, slurred speech. Laboratory testing may reveal elevated thyroid-stimulating hormone (TSH), along with either reduced or normal levels of triiodothyronine (T3) and thyroxine (T4). Thyroxine hormone replacement is typically delivered via natural or synthetic preparations. Close monitoring for signs and symptoms of hyperthyroidism during treatment should be maintained.

Hyperthyroidism, often seen in the autoimmune condition of Grave's disease, leads to symptoms of nervousness, weight loss, increased appetite, tachycardia, heat intolerance, hand tremor, protruding eyes, and warm, moist skin. In the severe case of thyroid storm or thyrotoxic crisis, the nurse should pay close attention to the presence of palpitations, fever, and delirium. Nursing care involves ensuring balanced nutrition with a high-caloric diet during this hyperbolic state and monitoring vital signs and cardiac output. Laboratory testing may reveal decreased thyroid-stimulating hormone (TSH) and elevated or normal levels of triiodothyronine (T3) and thyroxine (T4). Medication management involves propranolol, propylthiouracil, and iodine. If exophthalmos is present, the nurse should ensure that conjunctivas remain moist and administer eye drops if necessary.

Hematology/Immunology/Oncology

Anemia

There are certain components in blood that have the capacity to carry oxygen to the tissues of the body. These components are called the red blood cells (RBCs), hematocrit, and hemoglobin. When any of these three components drops in number, oxygen-carrying capacity also drops. A hemoglobin of less than 14 g/dL, a hematocrit of less than 42%, or a red blood cell count of less than 3.4 million/mL are all general ranges of what is considered anemic.

Often anemia is not a disease in and of itself but rather a symptom of an underlying disorder. The practitioner will investigate for underlying causes of anemia to make sure nothing is missed.

There are three broad categories of anemias, not including blood loss: microcytic anemias, normocytic anemias, and macrocytic anemias. In **microcytic anemias**, including iron-transport deficiency, lead poisoning, and thalassemia, the heme and globin synthesis is defective or deficient. Testing for microcytic anemias will include an analysis of the patient's iron stores. In **normocytic anemias**, the RBC is normal in size but deficient in number. Examples of normocytic anemias include anemia of chronic disease and aplastic anemia acquired from primary bone marrow disorders. **Macrocytic anemias**, caused by abnormal DNA synthesis, lead to large RBCs that do not have sufficient oxygen-carrying ability.

The symptoms commonly experienced by patients with anemia include fatigue, weakness, difficulty breathing during exercise, and a pale skin tone. **Pallor**, or paleness, can be assessed in a dark-skinned patient by looking at the bottoms of their feet, palms, lips, buccal mucosa, and conjunctiva of the eye. Dark-skinned patients will usually have a warm tone, but when anemic or cyanotic, they will have a more gray or ashen hue.

As mentioned, there are a variety of different types of anemias. **Thalassemia**, common in those of Mediterranean descent, is one type in which the amount of oxygen-carrying hemoglobin is decreased causing pallor, weakness, fatigue, and poor growth. **Folate deficiency anemia**, associated with alcoholism, is a result of poor absorption of nutrients and decreases the amount of folate available to RBCs, thus decreasing oxygen delivery to tissues. Infections, cancers, and many other illnesses may destroy RBCs, hemoglobin, and/or hematocrit, causing anemia.

The treatment of anemia will depend on the underlying cause and the patient's symptomology. If the patient is anemic because of massive blood loss, blood transfusions will be required. If the anemia is caused by deficient erythropoiesis, the process by which blood is formed, drugs like erythropoietin will be used to stimulate blood production.

In a patient requiring blood transfusion, prior to initiating a blood transfusion, the progressive care nurse assesses the patient's baseline status by examining vital signs and laboratory data. Blood product is obtained from the blood bank with a licensed member of the care team, and then both licensed clinicians verify the product (patient name, blood type, Rh factor, blood product order, unit number matches arm band and blood bank form, expiration date/time noted on bag). Once ready to infuse, the nurse spikes a bag of normal saline with a Y blood tubing set and primes the blood tubing line and filter, clamps tubing, then inserts spike into the blood bag. The blood product should be administered slowly, at least for the first fifteen minutes, and the nurse should closely monitor for any signs and symptoms of a transfusion reaction while staying at the bedside. Anaphylactic allergic reactions and acute hemolytic reactions typically occur within the first fifteen minutes, while febrile, non-hemolytic reactions usually occur within thirty minutes and mild to moderate allergic reactions within the first hour. If signs of a serious reaction are noted, the nurse should stop the transfusion, keep intravenous access while running the normal saline, and call the provider. Epinephrine should be available for administration if the patient shows signs of anaphylaxis. Types of blood products include: whole blood, packed red blood cells, fresh frozen plasma, platelets, and albumin.

Coagulopathies

Hemophilia is a hereditary blood disorder in which an individual's blood lacks proteins (specifically, clotting factors VIII or IX) that aid in clotting, resulting in wounds bleeding for a longer period of time. Hemophiliacs are not usually in danger if they have a small or superficial cut, but the risk of excessive bleeding with deeper cuts or internal wounds is especially critical. This can result in hemorrhage or damage to the internal organs. In addition to excessive bleeding in response to relatively normal situations such as minor surgery, symptoms of hemophilia include abnormal and frequent bruising, abnormal and frequent nosebleeds, joint pain, and blood in the urine or stool. Hemophiliac episodes that constitute a medical emergency include extreme swelling of large joints, prolonged headaches, chronic vomiting, neck pain, vision problems, major injuries, and lethargy. Hemophilia and associated emergencies are usually treated by manually replacing the insufficient clotting protein via drip or injection directly into the hemophiliac's vein.

Medication-Induced Thrombocytopenia

Thrombocytopenia is a disease that causes individuals to have platelet counts significantly below normal healthy levels, usually without symptoms. But some individuals may experience increased nosebleeds, bleeding wounds, or bruising, and women may experience longer menstruation periods. Another obvious indicator of thrombocytopenia is the presence of visible blood-filled sacs in the mouth. This disease can be genetic but can also result from dehydration, malnutrition, the use of certain medications, liver failure, sepsis, Lyme disease, or snake bites. Treatment will vary by individual case and cause and may include steroid therapy.

Some diseases require the formation of clots to be slowed or decreased. For example, patients who have congenital heart disease or a lifestyle disease that requires any kind of heart surgery or who are at high risk of heart attack or stroke are often required to take anticoagulants. **Anticoagulants** thin the blood to decrease or prevent the formation of clots, which can obstruct other blood vessels and lead to a heart attack or travel to the brain and cause a stroke. The most common anticoagulants include the medications warfarin and heparin. These medications work by blocking the body's ability to adhere platelets together or by limiting the ability to produce clotting factors. The medications can be delivered orally (a slower release) or intravenously (more rapid results); the attending physician will usually decide what is best on an individual basis.

Heparin-induced thrombocytopenia (HIT) occurs when the anticoagulation caused by the administration of heparin leads to thrombosis and thus, thrombocytopenia. This condition results when the patient's body has an abnormal antibody response to the heparin that activates platelets. Heparin must be promptly stopped and alternative medicines must be administered.

Two forms of heparin-induced thrombocytopenia have been identified: HIT type I and HIT type II. **HIT type I**, which occurs at the beginning of therapy, is most often a benign condition that does not result in thrombotic events, is not the end-product of an immune response and quickly resolves spontaneously with continued exposure to the medication. HIT I results in a transient decrease in the platelet count, which recovers rapidly when heparin is discontinued.

HIT type II is defined as an immune-mediated reaction that occurs as a result of the activation of platelets by HIT substances in the presence of heparin or other similar trigger medication. This antibody activation also initiates platelet aggregation which can result in the risk of a thrombotic event or life-threatening gangrene. Warfarin (Coumadin®) is associated with a delayed HIT reaction, which means that any associated thrombotic events or the onset of thrombocytopenia will occur up to five days after the warfarin is discontinued. Research indicates that even when the warfarin is opposed by a direct thrombin inhibitor (lepirudin), life-threatening thrombotic events are still possible if a subtherapeutic level of the anticoagulant dose is present. Warfarin is recommended as a secondary source of anticoagulation due to this association with HIT II.

Immunosuppressive Disorders

An **immunocompromised** person refers to any individual who has a less than optimally functioning immune system. This could be the result of a genetic disorder, a viral or cancerous disease, medication, injury, surgery, age, or nutrition. An immunocompromised person is more susceptible to infection and illness than someone whose immune system is functioning optimally.

HIV/AIDS

The **human immunodeficiency virus** (HIV) is a sphere-shaped virus that is a fraction of the size of a red blood cell. There are primarily two types of HIV: HIV-1 and HIV-2. **HIV-2** is not highly transmissible and is poorly understood. It has mainly affected people in West Africa. **HIV-1** is more severe and more highly transmissible. It is the dominant strain among global HIV cases, and when literature and media refer to HIV, this is usually the type that is being referred to.

HIV is highly contagious. It is found in human bodily fluids and can be transmitted through infected breast milk, blood, mucus, and sexual fluids. The most common forms of transmission are through anal or vaginal sex, but transmission can also occur through contaminated syringe use, blood transfusions, or any other method where membranes are compromised. Once in the body, HIV attacks and destroys CD4/T cells. These cells are responsible for attacking foreign bodies (e.g., bacteria, infections, other viruses). As the body's CD4/T-cell count diminishes, the patient is left immunocompromised.

The HIV-1 type can be broken further into four groups: M, N, O, and P. M is the most commonly seen group globally. Within group M, there are nine different subtypes of HIV. These are noted as A, B, C, D, E, F, G, H, J, and K. Subtype B is prevalent in the Western world, and most research has been conducted on this subtype. This research has led to the manufacturing of antiretroviral (ARV) drugs. Antiretroviral therapy (ART) has been a major breakthrough in the management of HIV and in the quality of life for patients with HIV. In conjunction with medical care, many patients with HIV are able to have completely normal, healthy, active lives. It is important to treat HIV as early as possible. The better a patient's HIV is managed, the lower their viral load. Viral load refers to how much HIV is present in a patient's blood; when a viral load is low, transmission of the disease is far less likely to occur. With ART, many patients with HIV are viral-suppressed, and some even have an undetectable viral load. Viral load in other transmitting fluids, such as semen, cannot be detected but the virus is still present. Therefore, transmission is still possible, and all precautions should be taken.

Globally, most HIV patients have subtype C, but subtypes are mixing as travel and migration become more widespread. Most subtypes can be treated with ART, though these drugs were researched and manufactured to treat subtype B. However, ART is not always physically available or financially accessible in countries that need it most.

Without early intervention or adequate managed care of HIV, the virus can deteriorate the host body's immune system to a point where it cannot be rehabilitated. This stage is marked by extremely low levels of CD4/T cells (less than two hundred cells per cubic millimeter of blood) and is referred to as **acquired immunodeficiency syndrome** (AIDS). When a patient's HIV diagnosis progresses to AIDS, he or she often succumbs to serious chronic diseases, such as cancer. Mild illnesses, such as a cold or flu, can also be fatal to someone with AIDS. Not everyone who is diagnosed with HIV will also be diagnosed with AIDS. Once diagnosed with AIDS, the patient has approximately one to three years to live unless he or she receives adequate treatment.

Patients Receiving Chemotherapy

Chemotherapy is a broad term referring to the use of drugs in cancer treatment. This type of therapy is intended to target and treat the entire body, especially in advanced stages of cancer where malignant cells may be widespread. However, it may also be used in earlier stages of cancer to eliminate many of the cancerous cells. This is done with the intention that the patient will go into remission and potentially not experience cancer again in the future. If this does not seem like a viable prognosis, chemotherapy can be used to control early stages of cancer from advancing. In advanced stages of cancer, chemotherapy can be used to manage pain and suffering from cancerous tumors, even if the patient's prognosis is poor.

The aggressiveness of chemotherapy (such as which drugs are used, dosing amount, and frequency) is contingent on many factors, such as the type and stage of cancer. Chemotherapy treatment plans also consider the patient's personal and medical history. Since this form of treatment is so aggressive, it is often effective in reducing or eliminating cancer cells. However, chemotherapy can also kill healthy cells in the process. The intensity of this side effect varies by person, but almost all patients experience some degree of immunocompromise. This is because chemotherapy almost always inadvertently targets bone marrow, where white blood cells are made. White blood cells, especially neutrophils, play an important role in fighting infection. When there are not enough white blood cells present in the patient's blood, he or she can become seriously ill from sickness or infection that would be mild in a healthy person. Medical personnel usually monitor neutrophil counts during and between chemotherapy cycles to make sure these levels do not fall too low. Chemotherapy cycles can last up to six months, and patients are considered to have a compromised immune system for the entire time they are undergoing chemotherapy. Once a full cycle of chemotherapy ends, it takes approximately one month for the immune system to return to its normal state.

Patients undergoing chemotherapy should be especially mindful of personal hygiene habits such as handwashing and showering, as well as avoiding cuts, scrapes, insect bites, or other instances where the skin may break. They may also need help taking care of a pet and handling pet waste or other trash. Additionally, it is important to practice extra caution when handling foods, such as cooking meats well, avoiding unpasteurized foods, washing produce with produce cleaner, cooking many foods that typically could be eaten raw, and avoiding certain moldy cheeses. They also need to be more careful of their surroundings in public places; since these areas tend to be dirtier and more populated, there is an increased risk of contracting infections. Medical personnel and those visiting the patient should be aware of these practices as well.

Cancer

Cancer is a large group of diseases that are commonly expressed as carcinomas, sarcomas, melanomas, lymphomas, and leukemia. The normal cells experience mutation due to one or multiple carcinogens such as diesel exhaust, radiation, or viruses, which results in changes in the cell membrane that inhibit the tumor-suppressing action of the normal cell and alter the cell surface antigens. This, in turn, diminishes the immune response. The abnormal cell matures through the process already described and eventually manifests the following characteristics: abnormal cell structure; haphazard, uncontrolled cellular replication; and destructive invasiveness. Malignant cells cause harm not only by occupying space, but by invading adjacent and distant tissues, and although benign tumors can also cause harm by occupying space, the tumors remain encapsulated and do not invade surrounding tissues. In addition, oncology nurses understand that if a carcinoma originates in the breast and subsequently metastasizes to the brain, the tumor in the brain will resemble breast cancer, the original tumor type that has invaded distant tissues.

Once the normal tissue has been invaded, the malignant cells are able to create an extracellular environment that supports the growth of the tumor and facilitates ongoing metastasis by making alterations in three processes that control normal cellular proliferation: density-dependent inhibition, cell-surface adhesion, and contact inhibition. The proliferation of normal cells depends on the level of growth hormones and the action of the cellular growth factors. When the cell density is sufficient for normal function, the levels of the hormones and growth factors decrease, which slows proliferation. Malignant cells continue to replicate because the cells are independently capable of producing sufficient growth factors even when hormone levels do not support growth. Normal cells create an orderly matrix that is supported by cell surface adhesion molecules, however, malignant cells are able to suppress these molecules, which allows the malignant cells to more easily invade normal tissue. During normal cellular growth, when cells come in contact with one another replication is stopped according to the concept of cell contact inhibition, however, malignant cells do not respond to those signals. When a new tumor grows to a density of approximately one million cells, malignant cells are capable of initiating **angiogenesis**, which is the development of new blood vessels that support tumor growth and provide new pathways for metastasis.

Neurology

Encephalopathy

Any form of brain damage, disease, or dysfunction can fall under the umbrella term of **encephalopathy**. There are numerous different causes and forms of encephalopathy, including hypoxic, metabolic, hepatic and infectious. A patient whose mental state is altered may be suffering from a form of encephalopathy and the cause should be investigated.

Infections, trauma, adverse drug effects, metabolic abnormalities, and states of oxygen deprivation to the brain tissue can all cause encephalopathic states. Encephalopathy is then a symptom itself of an underlying disease. Encephalopathy can be prevented as well and some forms of encephalopathy can be reversed.

Encephalopathy may be diagnosed using blood and urine tests to determine the cause as well as imaging studies such as CT scans and MRIs. Once the cause is found, reversal of the cause can occur. If the cause is anoxia, oxygen therapy will be applied. If the cause is alcohol toxicity, fluid resuscitation and possibly oral lactulose will be administered. If the cause originates from the kidney and is severe enough, the patient may receive dialysis treatments. If the encephalopathy was caused by a hyper- or hypoglycemic state as a result of uncontrolled diabetes, measures will be taken to correct the blood glucose level to normal with insulin and other diabetic drugs.

One type of encephalopathy that is slow in onset and results from repeated injuries to the head is called **chronic traumatic encephalopathy** or CTE. This is a disease that has been around for a long time, but only recently named as the function of the brain. CTE is common to contact sport athletes such as boxers and football players who have received several blows to the head during their career. Symptoms include chronic headaches, dizziness, disorientation, and memory loss. This type of encephalopathy is usually irreversible. In those cases, symptom management and improving quality of life for the patient and the caregivers take priority.

Seizure Disorders

A **seizure** is defined as a chaotic period of uncoordinated electrical activity in the brain, which results in one of several characteristic behaviors. Although the exact cause is unknown, several possible triggers have been proposed as noted below. The recently revised classification system categorizes seizure activity according to the area of the brain where the seizure initiates, the patient's level of awareness during the seizure, and other descriptive features such as the presence of an aura. The unclassified category includes seizure patterns that do not conform to the primary categories. Seizures that originate in a single area of the brain are designated as **focal seizures**, while seizures that originate in two or more different networks are designated as **generalized seizures**. The remaining seizures in the onset category include seizures without an identified point of onset and seizures that progress from focal seizures to generalized seizures.

Risk factors associated with seizures include genetic predisposition, illnesses with severe temperature elevation, head trauma, cerebral edema, inappropriate use or discontinuance of antiepileptic drugs (AEDs), intracerebral infection, excess or deficiency of sodium and glucose, toxin exposure, hypoxia, and acute drug or alcohol withdrawal. Patients are encouraged to identify any conditions that may be triggers for their seizure activity. Although the triggers vary greatly from one patient to another, commonly identified events include increased physical activity, excessive stress, hyperventilation, fatigue, acute ETOH (ethyl alcohol) ingestion, exposure to flashing lights, and inhaled chemicals, including cocaine.

The **tonic phase** presents as stiffening of the limbs for a brief period, while the **clonic phase** is evidenced by jerking motions of the limbs. These manifestations may be accompanied by a decreased level of consciousness, respiratory alterations and cyanosis, incontinence, and biting of the tongue. **Absence seizures** are manifested by a decreased level of awareness without abnormal muscular activity. The manifestations of the postictal phase include alterations in consciousness and awareness and increased oral secretions. Seizure disorders are diagnosed by serum lab studies to assess AED levels and to identify excess alcohol and recreational drugs, metabolic alterations, and kidney and liver function. Electroencephalography (EEG) and the enhanced magnetoencephalography are used to identify the origin of the altered electrical activity in the brain, and MRI, skull films, and CSF analysis are used to rule out possible sources of the seizure disorder such as tumor formation.

Seizure disorders are treated with AEDs that stabilize the neuron cell membrane by facilitating the inhibitory mechanisms or opposing the excitatory mechanisms. Patients with a chronic seizure disorder, or epilepsy, usually require a combination of medications to minimize seizure activity. Elderly patients respond differently to the AEDs and may require frequent assessment and revision of the care plan. The emergency care of the patient with seizures is focused on patient safety during and after the seizure and the cessation and prevention of the seizure activity. Prolonged seizure activity is defined as **status epilepticus**, which is the occurrence of multiple seizures, each lasting more than 5 minutes over a 30-minute period. This life-threatening condition is commonly the result of incorrect usage of AEDs or the use of recreational drugs. Care of this condition includes the immediate administration of phenytoin and benzodiazepines, in addition to possible general anesthesia if the medication therapy is not effective.

Stroke

A **stroke** is defined as the death of brain tissue due to ischemic or hemorrhagic injury. **Ischemic strokes** are more common than **hemorrhagic strokes**; however, the differential diagnosis of these conditions requires careful attention to the patient's history and physical examination. In general, an acute onset of neurological symptoms and seizures is more common with hemorrhagic stroke, while ischemic stroke is more frequently associated with a history of some form of trauma. The National Institutes of Health (NIH) **Stroke Scale** represents an international effort to standardize the assessment and treatment protocols for stroke. The scale includes detailed criteria and the protocol for assessment of the neurological system. The stroke scale items are to be administered in the official order listed and there are directions that denote how to score each item. The NIH scale has the examiner test for level of consciousness, gaze, visual fields, palsy of the face, motor deficits, sensory loss, language deficits, and neglect by asking the patient to answer a series of questions and perform actions. Each answer/action is graded on a scale and tracked frequently throughout the patient's stay to assess the efficacy of different treatment options and for an objective measure of patients "getting better" or "getting worse" symptomatically.

Ischemic Stroke

Ischemic strokes result from occlusion of the cerebral vasculature as a result of a thrombotic or embolic event. At the cellular level, the ischemia leads to hypoxia that rapidly depletes the ATP stores. As a result, the cellular membrane pressure gradient is lost, and there is an influx of sodium, calcium, and water into the cell, which leads to cytotoxic edema. This process creates scattered regions of ischemia in the affected area, containing cells that are dead within minutes of the precipitating event. This core of ischemic tissue is surrounded by an area with minimally-adequate perfusion that may remain viable for several hours after the event. These necrotic areas are eventually liquefied and acted upon by macrophages, resulting in the loss of brain parenchyma. These affected sites, if sufficiently large, may be prone to hemorrhage, due to the formation of collateral vascular supply with or without the use of medications such as recombinant tissue plasminogen activator (rtPA). The ischemic process also compromises the blood-brain barrier, which leads to the movement of water and protein into the extracellular space within 4 to 6 hours after the onset of the stroke, resulting in vasogenic edema.

Nonmodifiable risk factors for ischemic stroke include age, gender, ethnicity, history of migraine headaches with aura, and a family history of stroke or transient ischemic attacks (TIAs). Modifiable risk factors include hypertension, diabetes, hypercholesterolemia, cardiac disease including atrial fibrillation, valvular disease and heart failure, elevated homocysteine levels, obesity, illicit drug use, alcohol abuse, smoking, and sedentary lifestyle. The research related to the occurrence of stroke in women indicates the need to treat hypertension aggressively prior to and during pregnancy and prior to the use of contraceptives to prevent irreversible damage to the microvasculature. In addition, it is recommended that to reduce their risk of stroke, women with a history of migraine headaches preceded by an aura should ameliorate all modifiable risk factors, and all women over seventy-five years old should be routinely assessed for the onset of atrial fibrillation.

Heredity is associated with identified gene mutations and the process of atherosclerosis and cholesterol metabolism. Hypercholesterolemia and the progression of atherosclerosis in genetically-susceptible individuals are now regarded as active inflammatory processes that contribute to endothelial damage of the cerebral vasculature, thereby increasing the risk for strokes. There are also early indications that infection also contributes to the development and advancement of atherosclerosis.

The presenting manifestations of ischemic stroke must be differentiated from other common diseases, including brain tumor formation, hyponatremia, hypoglycemia, seizure disorders, and systemic infection. The sudden onset of hemisensory losses, visual alterations, hemiparesis, ataxia, nystagmus, and aphasia are commonly, although not exclusively, associated with ischemic strokes. The availability of reperfusion therapies dictates the emergent use of diagnostic imaging studies, including CT and MRI scans, carotid duplex scans, and digital subtraction angiography to confirm the data obtained from the patient's history and physical examination. Laboratory studies include CBC, coagulation studies, chemistry panels, cardiac biomarkers, toxicology assays, and pregnancy testing as appropriate.

Care of the patient with symptoms of an ischemic stroke is focused on the stabilization of the patient's ABCs, completion of the physical examination and appropriate diagnostic studies, and initiation of reperfusion therapy as appropriate. The time of initial onset of stroke symptoms should be documented exactly, as many reperfusion therapies must be started within 4.5 hours of onset of symptoms. Reperfusion therapies include the use of alteplase (the only fibrinolytic agent that is approved for the treatment of ischemic stroke), antiplatelet agents, and mechanical thrombectomy. Healthcare providers must also be alert for hyperthermia, hypoxia, hypertension or hypotension, and signs of cardiac ischemia or cardiac arrhythmias.

Hemorrhagic Stroke

Hemorrhagic strokes are less common than ischemic strokes; however, a hemorrhagic stroke is more likely to be fatal than an ischemic stroke. A hemorrhagic stroke is the result of bleeding into the parenchymal tissue of the brain due to leakage of blood from damaged intracerebral arteries. These hemorrhagic events occur more often in specific areas of the brain, including the thalamus, cerebellum, and brain stem. The tissue surrounding the hemorrhagic area is also subject to injury due to the mass effect of the accumulated blood volume. In the event of subarachnoid hemorrhage, intracranial pressure (ICP) becomes elevated with resulting dysfunction of the autoregulation response, which leads to abnormal vasoconstriction, platelet aggregation, and decreased perfusion and blood flow, resulting in cerebral ischemia.

Risk factors for hemorrhagic stroke include older age; a history of hypertension, which is present in 60 percent of patients; personal history of stroke; alcohol abuse; and illicit drug use. Common conditions associated with hemorrhagic stroke include hypertension, cerebral amyloidosis, coagulopathies, vascular alterations including arteriovenous malformation, vasculitis, intracranial neoplasm, and a history of anticoagulant or antithrombotic therapy.

Although the presenting manifestations for hemorrhagic stroke differ in some respect from those associated with ischemic stroke, none of these manifestations is an absolute predictor of one or the other. In general, patients with hemorrhagic stroke present with a headache that may be severe, significant alterations in the level of consciousness and neurological function, hypertension, seizures, and nausea and vomiting. The specific neurological defects depend on the anatomical site of the hemorrhage and may include hemisensory loss, hemiparesis, aphasia, and visual alterations.

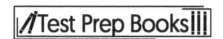

Diagnostic studies include CBC, chemistry panel, coagulation studies, and blood glucose. Non-contrast CT scan or MRI are the preferred imaging studies. CT or magnetic resonance angiography may also be used to obtain images of the cerebral vasculature. Close observation of the patient's vital signs, neurological vital signs, and ICP is necessary.

The management of the patient with hemorrhagic stroke is focused on the ABC protocol, in addition to the control of bleeding, seizure activity, and increased ICP. There is no single medication used to treat hemorrhagic stroke; however, recent data suggests that aggressive emergency management of hypertension initiated early and aimed at reducing the systolic BP to less than 140 millimeters of mercury may be effective in reducing the growth of the hematoma at the site, which decreases the mass effect. Beta-blockers and ACE inhibitors are recommended to facilitate this reduction. Endotracheal intubation for ventilatory support may be necessary; however, hyperventilation is not recommended due to the resulting suppression of cerebral blood flow. While seizure activity will be treated with AEDs, there is controversy related to the prophylactic use of these medicines. Increased ICP requires osmotic diuretic therapy, elevation of the head of the bed to 30 degrees, sedation and analgesics as appropriate, and antacids. Steroid therapy is not effective and is not recommended.

Patients who present with manifestations of hemorrhagic stroke with a history of anticoagulation therapy present a special therapeutic challenge due to the extension of the hematoma formation. More than 50 percent of patients taking warfarin who suffer a hemorrhagic stroke will die within thirty days. This statistic is consistent in patients with international normalized ratio (INR) levels within the therapeutic range, with increased mortality noted in patients with INRs that exceed the therapeutic level. Emergency treatment includes fresh frozen plasma, IV vitamin K, prothrombin complex concentrates, and recombinant factor VIIa (rFVIIa). There are administration concerns with each of these therapies that must be addressed to prevent any delays in the reversal of the effects of the warfarin.

Dysphagia

A patient with either type of stroke is at increased risk of dysphagia. Bedside swallow screens are usually part of hospital protocol for any patient that presents with a stroke prior to receiving anything orally. These screens should be done per protocol and documented. Some other conditions that may place a patient at higher risk for dysphagia or aspiration include Parkinson's disease, muscular dystrophies, and Sjogren's syndrome. While a speech therapist is often acutely involved in the bedside swallow screen for dysphagia, the nurse may assist or be responsible for some aspects of the assessment depending on policy and protocol. Bedside swallow screens involve the assessment of level of consciousness, ability to close lips and clench teeth, formation of speech, tongue and uvula positioning, face symmetry, presence of gag and swallow reflexes, cough, and the buildup of secretions. With the patient in an upright position, the screening process moves on to the oral delivery of water to assess ability to swallow, which is first administered in a small dose (i.e. a teaspoon) and then gradually increased as tolerated. Abnormal screening results are documented and elevated to the speech therapist when noted.

Transient Ischemic Attack

A **transient ischemic attack** (TIA) is defined as a short-term episode of altered neurological function that lasts for less than one hour; it may be imperceptible to the patient. The deficit may be related to speech, movement, behavior, or memory and may be caused by an ischemic event in the brain, spinal cord, or retina. The patient's history and neurological assessment according to the NIH Stroke Scale establish the diagnosis. Additional diagnostic studies include CBC, glucose, sedimentation rate, electrolytes, lipid profile, toxicology screen, 12-lead ECG, and CSF analysis. Imaging studies include non-contrast MRI or CT, carotid Doppler exam, and angiography.

Initial care of the patient with a TIA is focused on the assessment of any neurological deficits and the identification of comorbid conditions that may be related to the attack. Hospital admission is required in the event of an attack that lasts more than one hour, if the patient has experienced more than a single attack in a one-week period, or if the attack is related to a cardiac source such as atrial fibrillation or a myocardial infarction. The **ABCD2 stroke risk score** calculates the patient's risk for experiencing a true stroke within two days after the TIA based on five factors (see the table below). Interventions aimed at stroke prevention in relation to the risk stratification as calculated by the $ABCD^2$ score are specific to underlying comorbidities; however, treatment with ASA and clopidogrel is commonly prescribed.

$ABCD^2$ Stroke Risk Score		
	1 Point	2 Points
Age	$\geq$ 60 years	
Blood Pressure	SBP $\geq$ 140 mmHg DBP $\geq$ 90 mmHg	
Clinical Features	Speech impairment but no focal weakness	Focal weakness
Duration of Symptoms	$\leq$ 59 minutes	$\geq$ 60 minutes
Diabetes	Diagnosed	
Total Score (denotes risk for stroke (CVA) within 2 days after TIA)	0-3 points = 1% risk 4-5 points = 4.1% risk 6-7 points = 8.1% risk	

Cerebrovascular Malformation

Aneurysm

Bulging or ballooning in a blood vessel within the brain is the second most common site for an aneurysm (after the abdominal aorta). Another common site for aneurysms is where the internal carotid artery (ICA) enters the cranium; it branches into a system of arteries that provide blood flow to the brain, known as **the circle of Willis**. Most small brain aneurysms do not rupture and are found during various tests. An aneurysm may press on brain tissue and present with ocular pain or symptoms. However, a rupture is a medical emergency that can lead to stroke or hemorrhage. The most common symptom described by patients is "the *worst* headache of my life." A sudden, severe headache, stiff neck, blurred or double vision, photophobia, seizure, loss of consciousness, and confusion may also be reported.

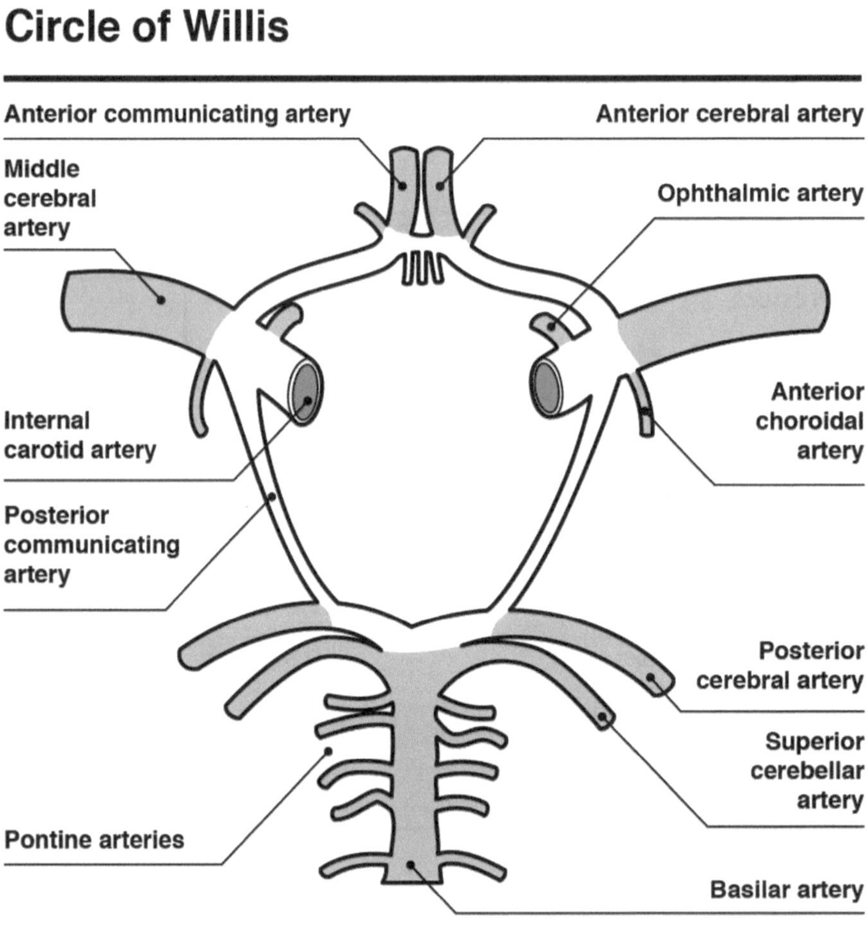

A family history of aneurysm and certain other aneurysm risk factors are genetic. Other predisposing factors are an arteriovenous malformation (AVM) at the circle of Willis, polycystic kidney disease (PKD), and Marfan syndrome. Poor lifestyle choices, such as smoking and cocaine use, greatly increase the risk for aneurysm formation. There is a higher risk for individuals over the age of forty, women, patients who have experienced a traumatic head injury, and patients with hypertension.

Depending on a brain aneurysm's cause, size, and symptoms, and the patient's general health, there are several treatment options. The most common surgical treatment is clipping. The bulge is clipped at the base to prevent blood from entering. The clip remains in place for life. Eventually, the bulge will shrink.

If the artery has been damaged by the aneurysm, an occlusion and bypass surgical procedure may be performed. The affected artery is closed off, and a new route that allows circulation to bypass the damage is created. The artificial development of an embolism, known as **endovascular embolization**, is another treatment option. A variety of substances such as plastic particles, glue, metal, foam, or balloons are coiled and inserted into the aneurysm to block blood flow.

A liquid embolic surgical glue is a new option to the standard coiling procedure: Onyx HD 500 is a vinyl alcohol copolymer that solidifies on contact with the blood in the aneurysm, sealing it. In the case of smaller aneurysms, a watch-and-wait approach may be taken. Bleeding, vasospasm, seizures, and hydrocephalus are the main complications related to a brain aneurysm.

AV Malformation

An **AV malformation** is the congenital mutation of the vasculature in the brain that results in a tangled web of arteries that communicate directly with the veins without any intervening capillary structure. The resulting mass is unstable and has the potential to cause an intracranial hemorrhage and seizure activity. It is estimated that AV malformation is the cause of two percent of all cerebral vascular accidents (CVAs). Children are more likely to present with intracranial hemorrhage; however, adults may present with intracranial hemorrhage, the new onset of seizure activity that may progress to epilepsy, or rarely, a focal neurologic deficit. The risk of subsequent hemorrhage following presentation is increased when hemorrhage is the original presenting symptom, if an **aneurysm** (a weakness in the wall of the artery) is present, or if the lesion is positioned in a deep brain location.

Angiography is the "gold standard" for diagnosing AV malformation and also for obtaining specific information that may be required for surgical treatment of the lesion. Treatment choices include surgical excision, radiosurgery, and endovascular embolization. The decision is most often based on the results of a surgical risk analysis with the Spetzler-Martin grading scale or some similar instrument. The treatment approach depends on the location of the lesion, the presenting manifestations, and the patient's gender and baseline health status.

Intracranial Hemorrhage

Hemorrhage, a term referring to a bleed within the body cavity, can occur anywhere there is a vascular path, including the brain. The following discussion compares different types of brain bleeds, including intracranial, intraventricular, and subarachnoid.

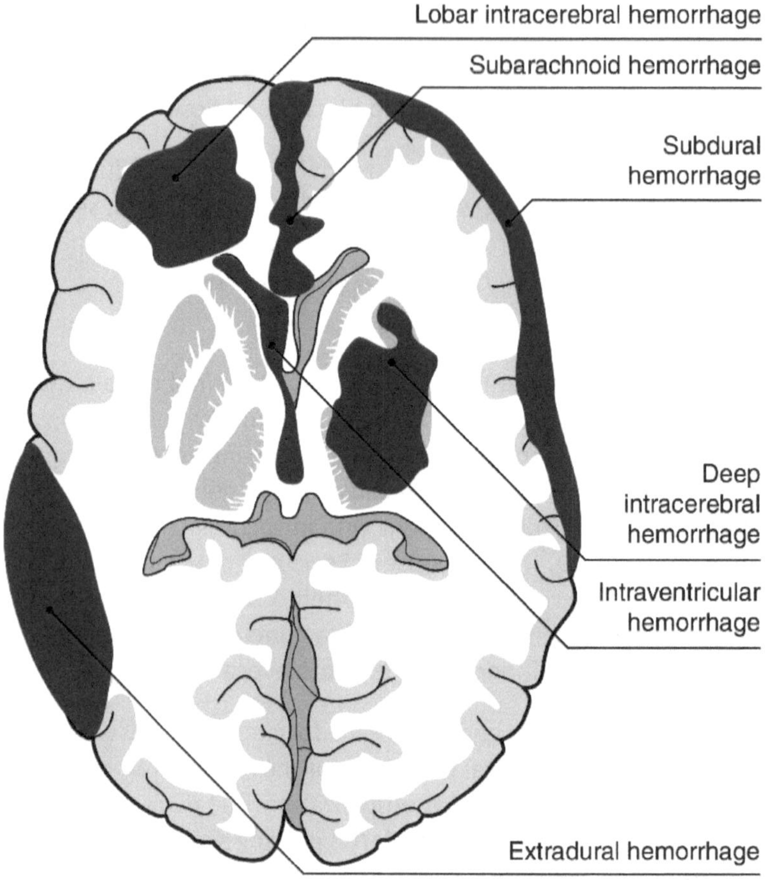

Intracranial (ICH)

Intracranial bleed is a broad term referring to hemorrhaging inside the cranial vault. This type of bleed may affect the functional tissue of the brain, called *parenchyma*, or the meninges that surround the parenchyma. This type of bleed is likely to cause mortality or serious debilitation in patients, more so than an ischemic stroke or subarachnoid hemorrhage.

Intracranial hemorrhaging is most often caused by high blood pressure, but may also be caused by eclampsia and drug abuse that damage the walls of blood vessels. A ruptured arteriovenous malformation (AVM) or aneurysm may also cause an intracranial bleed.

As the blood accumulates in the cranial vault, it compresses the brain tissue, causing an increase in intracranial pressure (ICP) and the neurological symptoms associated with this type of hemorrhage. Within minutes to hours of the start of internal bleeding, the patient will have altered mentation, headache, nausea and vomiting, and possibly even seizures.

If an intracranial bleed is suspected, the patient will be worked up with laboratory tests and imaging procedures. A CT scan will show hemorrhaging and is helpful for diagnosis. A complete blood count (CBC) as well as a prothrombin time/partial thromboplastin time (PT/PTT) will help identify platelet counts, hemoglobin and hematocrit counts, and if there is coagulopathy present.

Depending on the severity of the bleed, surgery may be an option. A craniotomy would be performed, opening up a small section of the skull, followed by a clot evacuation at the site of the bleed. Stereotactic aspiration of the bleed using thrombolytic agents is an option as well. As far as medical care of the patient goes, maintaining a normal to low blood pressure is key to controlling the damage done by the hemorrhaging. The less pressure pushing on the compromised area of the brain, the better, and the lesser the neurological side effects and damage.

Intraventricular (IVH)

An **intraventricular hemorrhage** is a type of intracranial bleed in which the ventricles are involved. The **ventricles** of the brain function to produce cerebrospinal fluid or CSF, a special fluid of the nervous system that cushions, protects, and nourishes the neurological tissues therein.

Ventricles of the Brain

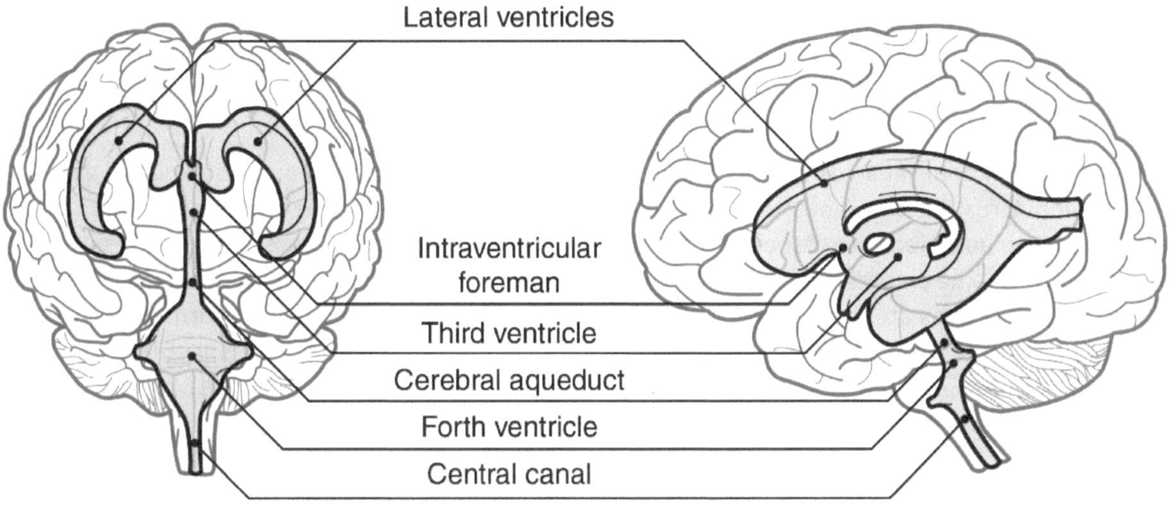

In adults, an intraventricular hemorrhage usually occurs along with a cerebral hemorrhage. An intraventricular hemorrhage that occurs on its own without cerebral hemorrhage usually develops in premature babies. These neonates have immature or poorly developed brain tissue, leading to the bleed. Early respiratory distress syndrome and cerebral palsy are associated with this type of bleed in neonates.

Symptoms of intraventricular hemorrhage in adults are like those of intracranial bleeds, with headache, neurological deficits, and nausea and vomiting being most prevalent. Diagnosis and treatment will also follow the same pattern, with CT scanning, hemodynamic monitoring and stabilization, as well as potential surgical intervention to drain hemorrhaging blood that is compressing brain tissue.

Subarachnoid (Traumatic or Aneurysmal)

When a hemorrhage occurs in the subarachnoid space between the pia and arachnoid membranes of the brain, it is called a **subarachnoid hemorrhage**. This type of brain bleed is usually traumatic or aneurysmal in nature, meaning a traumatic blow or the rupture of an aneurysm is the cause.

A patient experiencing a subarachnoid brain bleed will present with headache, pain around the eyes or orbital pain, dizziness, double vision or diplopia, and/or loss of vision. Some patients may experience prodromal symptoms or symptoms that occur before the actual event, such as sensory or motor disturbances, seizures, ptosis or droopy eyelids, bruits, and/or dysphasia. Upon assessment, the nurse may find the patient tachycardic, feverish, hypertensive, with swelling around the eyes and hemorrhage of the retinas.

If subarachnoid hemorrhage is suspected, a CT will likely be performed to image the brain tissue. If diagnosed with a subarachnoid hemorrhage, the patient's blood pressure will need to be stabilized with IV beta blockers, followed by a visit to the surgical suite to clip the ruptured aneurysm if that is the cause.

The patient who has had a subarachnoid bleed must be monitored for the development of complications such as re-bleed, vasospasm, seizures, hyponatremia, and hydrocephalus.

Gastrointestinal

Functional GI Disorders

Obstruction

There are three anatomical areas of the GI system that are prone to obstruction, including the gastric outlet at the pylorus, the small intestine, and the bowel. The small intestine is the most commonly affected site, and adhesions are responsible for more than 60 percent of all obstructions. These conditions may also be categorized as mechanical or nonmechanical depending on the cause, where mechanical obstructions are due to some extrinsic source such as adhesions, tumor formation, intussusception, or hernias, and nonmechanical obstructions are due to decreased peristalsis, neurogenic disorders, vascular insufficiency, or electrolyte imbalance. The mechanical obstruction of the biliary tract is due to effects of cirrhosis and hepatitis.

The manifestations are specific to the anatomical site of obstruction. The gastric outlet obstruction occurs most commonly in the pylorus and is associated with upper abdominal distention, nausea, vomiting, weight loss, and anorexia. Diagnostic tests include endoscopy and assessment of nutritional deficits, in addition to testing to eliminate *H. pylori* or diabetic gastric paresis as the cause. Obstruction of the small bowel is associated with severe fluid and electrolyte losses, metabolic acidosis, nausea and vomiting, fever, and tachycardia, and may lead to strangulation of the affected bowel segment. Bowel obstruction, most frequently due to tumor formation or stricture resulting from diverticular disease, is manifested by lower abdominal distention, possible metabolic acidosis, cramping abdominal pain, and minimal fluid and electrolyte losses. Common diagnostic studies include endoscopy, common lab studies, flat plate of the abdomen to assess for free air, and CT imaging.

Treatments are specific to the cause and may include tumor excision, antibiotic therapy for *H. pylori*, colectomy to remove the affected bowel segment, and/or colostomy placement. Although some obstructions may be treated with gastric or enteric decompression, bowel rest, and fluids, emergency intervention is usually necessary to prevent complications such as peritonitis and hemorrhage.

Ileus

An **ileus** refers to a segment of the large intestine that has lost forward propulsive movement, allowing the accumulation of gas and fluid. This pathology is most likely due to the interplay between the autonomic nervous system and the central nervous system, which is necessary to maintain bowel motility under normal circumstances. An ileus is most commonly seen following abdominal surgery and the development of an ileus is related to the type of surgery and the anesthetic. Spinal anesthesia and sympathectomy target the long reflex arcs that can contribute to the ileus, thereby reducing the incidence of the condition. The stress response related to the surgical intervention also contributes to the development of the altered motility by secreting inflammatory mediators that are capable of altering the function of the bowel wall.

A partial list of the most common causes includes sepsis, head injuries, heart failure, adrenal disease, spinal trauma, hypokalemia, and post-operative opioid pain management. An ileus is most often a temporary event; however, if the condition is not resolved after successful treatment of the underlying cause and symptom management, imaging studies are done to identify a possible mechanical bowel obstruction. Symptomatic interventions include nasogastric suctioning, fluid volume maintenance, and electrolyte homeostasis.

Diabetic Gastroparesis

Diabetic gastroparesis is defined as delayed gastric emptying that can be objectively measured and is not associated with mechanical intestinal obstruction. The most common manifestations include nausea, vomiting, early satiety, and upper abdominal pain. The condition is associated with several possible alterations in the function of the autonomic nervous system, which result in general nervous impairment of gastric function.

In type I diabetics with any degree of autonomic neuropathy, there is a bi-directional relationship between gastric emptying and blood glucose levels. Acute hyperglycemia delays gastric emptying under fasting or postprandial conditions. The opposite reaction occurs in the state of hypoglycemia, and the rate of gastric emptying is increased. The degree of gastroparesis also affects carbohydrate absorption and the absorption of some medications including oral hypoglycemic medications. Common manifestations include nausea, vomiting, satiety, abdominal pain, fullness, and bloating after meals, and possible weight loss. Diagnostic studies that include scintigraphy, endoscopy, CT, and MRI, are aimed at confirming the presence of gastroparesis and eliminating any additional causes that may be responsible for the patient's symptoms. Treatment is aimed at glycemic control, diet changes, and prokinetic and antiemetic medications.

Gastroesophageal Reflux

The lower esophagus is sealed off from the acidic environment of the stomach by way of a muscular sphincter. When this sphincter weakens and contents of the stomach leak up into the esophagus, it is called **gastroesophageal reflux disease** (GERD). The burning sensation caused by stomach acid coming in contact with the lining of the lower esophagus is the tell-tale sign of GERD.

Risk factors for the development of GERD include weight gain, cigarette smoking, and drug side effects. Antihistamines, tricyclic antidepressants, nitrates, and calcium channel blockers are all examples of drugs that may contribute to the development of GERD.

A patient will be diagnosed with GERD based on symptomology, with the occasional endoscopy used to confirm the diagnosis. The patient will be encouraged to make dietary changes, be prescribed proton pump inhibitors and, in very severe cases, surgical repair may be recommended.

Dietary changes should include avoiding consuming substances that aggravate the condition such as coffee, alcohol, and fatty foods. Smoking cessation will be encouraged as this also can be an aggravating factor.

Omeprazole is a commonly prescribed proton pump inhibitor used in the treatment of GERD, along with lansoprazole, pantoprazole, and esomeprazole.

Long-standing GERD may lead to further complications, such as esophagitis, peptic esophageal ulcer, esophageal stricture, Barrett esophagus, and even cancerous tumors of the esophagus.

Irritable Bowel Syndrome

Irritable bowel syndrome (IBS) is characterized as a constitutional illness that is associated with somatic complaints that are not related to a specific disease entity. The syndrome is very common in the adult population; however, many patients do not seek medical attention. The course and syndrome manifestations are patient-specific but will include some pattern of remitting and relapsing of abdominal pain and/or cramping that may or may not be relieved with defecation, and most often alternating periods of diarrhea and constipation. Conditions such as fibromyalgia, chronic fatigue syndrome, GERD, non-cardiac chest pain, and depression and anxiety often are concurrent with the manifestations of IBS.

The physical examination is the priority assessment method used to establish the diagnosis if there is no evidence of any additional pathology. The exception is if the patient has any "alarm" manifestations, which include melena, nighttime diarrhea, increasing abdominal pain, abnormal laboratory studies, unexplained weight loss, and a family history of IBS or colon cancer. Treatment is focused on identifying and managing the underlying pathology, and the patient-specific manifestations.

Inflammatory Bowel Syndrome

Inflammatory bowel disease (IBD) is an idiopathic disease that results from a harmful immune response to normal intestinal flora. Two types of IBD include Crohn's disease and ulcerative colitis (UC). Crohn's disease is characterized by inflammatory changes in all layers of the bowel. Although the entire length of the GI tract may be involved, the ileum and colon are affected most often. The inflamed areas are commonly interrupted by segments of normal bowel. Endoscopic views reveal the cobblestone appearance of these affected segments. UC is characterized by inflammatory changes of the mucosa and submucosa of the bowel that affect only the colon. There is a genetic predisposition for Crohn's disease, and there is also an increased incidence of cancer in patients with either form of IBD. Additional risk factors include a family history of IBD or colorectal cancer, NSAID and antibiotic use, smoking, and psychiatric disorders. IBD is diagnosed by a patient's history, including details of any recent foreign travel or hospitalization to rule out tuberculosis or *C. difficile* as the precipitating cause, in addition to endoscopy, CT and magnetic resonance imaging (MRI), serum and stool studies, and histologic studies.

Manifestations are nonspecific and are most often associated with the affected bowel segment. Common manifestations of IBD include diarrhea with blood and mucus and possible incontinence; constipation primarily with UC that is associated with progression to obstipation and bowel obstruction; rectal pain with associated urgency and tenesmus; and abdominal pain and cramping in the right lower quadrant with Crohn's disease, and in the umbilical area or left lower quadrant with UC. In addition, anemia, fatigue, and arthritis may be present.

The treatment of IBD focuses on attaining periods of remission and preventing recurrent attacks by modifying the inflammatory response. The stepwise treatment protocol begins with aminosalicylates and progresses to antibiotics, corticosteroids, and immunomodulators. Emergency care of the patient with IBD is focused on assessment and treatment of possible hemorrhage, megacolon, or bowel obstruction.

GI Bleed

Gastrointestinal (GI) bleeding is defined according to the area of the defect. Upper GI bleeding occurs superiorly to the junction of the duodenum and jejunum. Lower GI bleeding occurs in the large and small intestine. Conditions associated with upper GI bleeding include esophageal varices, gastric and duodenal ulcers, cancer, and Mallory-Weiss tears. Risk factors include age, history of gastroesophageal reflux disorder (GERD), use of nonsteroidal anti-inflammatory drugs (NSAIDs) and steroids, and alcoholism. Acute presenting manifestations include hematemesis, melena, hematochezia, and lightheadedness or fainting. The diagnosis is made by the patient's history and physical examination, routine lab studies including complete blood count (CBC) and coagulation tests, endoscopy, and chest films. Treatment is specific to the cause; for example, peptic ulcer disease will be treated with the appropriate antibiotic and a proton-pump inhibitor (PPI).

Causative factors for GI bleeding of the lower intestine include anatomical defects such as diverticulosis, ischemic events of the vasculature related to radiation therapy or other embolic events, cancer, and infectious or noninfectious inflammatory conditions. Manifestations that are specific to the cause and location of the hemorrhage include melena, maroon stools or bright red blood, fever, dehydration, possible abdominal pain or distention, and hematochezia. Common diagnostic studies include routine lab studies, endoscopy, radionucleotide studies, and angiography. Treatment is focused on the identification and resolution of the source of the bleeding and correction of any hematologic deficits that resulted from the hemorrhage. Orthostatic hypotension is defined as a decrease in diastolic blood pressure (BP) of 10 millimeters of mercury or more is associated with a blood loss of approximately 1000 milliliters. Therefore, care of massive GI bleeding requires aggressive fluid volume replacement with isotonic crystalloids while the exact source of the bleeding is being confirmed.

In order to target the source of the bleed, a tool called an endoscope will often be used. Depending on the suspected region of the GI tract, whether upper or lower, an upper endoscopy or lower endoscopy may be used. Colonoscopy is the term used to refer to a scope of the colon, part of the lower GI tract. Esophagogastroduodenoscopy or EGD is a long and medically accurate way to say an endoscopy that looks at the esophagus, stomach, and duodenum. In endoscopy, a thin tube with a camera affixed to the end of it is threaded into the body and images are produced. During endoscopy, areas that are bleeding may be cauterized to stop bleeding. **Cauterization** is the application of heat to the lesion to bring about hemostasis. Once a patient has had an endoscopy of either type ordered and scheduled, they will usually be NPO for 4-8 hours or longer.

While many providers will allow patients to take their oral medications with a sip of water on the day of the procedure, some medications may need to be specifically clarified, such as diabetic medications (as the patient will be NPO for an extended time) and anticoagulants (for which risk and benefit for each patient will need to be considered by the provider). For patients undergoing a colonoscopy, thorough education and assistance must be provided regarding the colon preparation. Patients should understand that prepping the bowels appropriately will lead to watery amber to yellow diarrhea, if the prep has been effective. Patients should have informed consent before having this procedure done and before receiving any medications for anesthesia. When patients return to their room following either an EGD or colonoscopy, they should be immediately assessed for level of consciousness and vital signs. Frequent monitoring of the patient post-procedural sedation is vital as well as monitoring for any unexpected bleeding. Patients should be educated that feeling bloated, belching, and even cramping after these procedures is generally considered normal because of air used during the procedure.

Ulcers

Ulcers of the GI tract are categorized as to the anatomical site of injury. **Gastric ulcers** are located in the body of the stomach, and **peptic ulcers** are located in the duodenum. The presenting symptom is abdominal pain 2 to 4 hours after eating for duodenal ulcers, in addition to hematemesis and melena. The defect is due to erosion of the mucosal lining by infectious agents, most commonly *H. pylori;* extreme systemic stress such as burns or head trauma; ETOH abuse; chronic kidney and respiratory disease; and psychological stress. Untreated, the mucosal erosion can progress to perforation, hemorrhage, and peritonitis.

Laboratory studies include examination of endoscopic tissue samples for the presence of the *H. pylori* organism, urea breath test, CBC, stool samples, and metabolic panel. Endoscopy, which is used to obtain tissue samples and achieve hemostasis, and double barium imaging studies made be obtained. The treatment depends on the extent of the erosion and will be focused on healing the ulcerated tissue and preventing additional damage. The treatment protocol for *H. pylori* infection includes the use of a PPI, amoxicillin, and clarithromycin for a minimum of seven to fourteen days. Subsequent testing will be necessary to ensure that the organism has been eradicated. Patients infected with *H. pylori* also must discontinue the use of NSAIDs or continue the long-term use of PPIs. Surgery may be indicated for significant areas of hemorrhage that were not successfully treated by ultrasound, and the procedure will be specific to the anatomical area of ulceration.

GI Infections

Most commonly, the identification of the causative agent for self-limiting foodborne illness of the gastrointestinal tract requires additional information beyond the presenting symptoms; however, there are some characteristic manifestations that indicate the exact nature of the agent. Diarrhea that is "watery" is known to be specific to organisms of the small bowel, while infection by pathogens native to the large intestine produce inflammatory manifestations such as mucoid or bloody diarrhea with fever. Additional clues to the causative agent are provided by the exposure history, especially when the infection is the result of an outbreak that is associated with a known source. Other exposure sources include animal contact, travel to high-risk areas, occupational exposure, water-borne outbreaks, and recent antibiotic use.

Additional manifestations include vomiting (which may or may not be present), abdominal cramping and bloating, systemic manifestations, neurological manifestations due to the ingestion of toxins, and hepatitis. Diagnostic studies include stool cultures, fecal occult analysis, CBC, and other organism-specific studies. In general, the onset of symptoms is twenty-four to forty-eight hours after the initial exposure to the pathogen, and recovery occurs within an additional forty-eight to seventy-two hours. The plan of care focuses on treatment of the underlying cause, fluid volume maintenance, and symptom management.

Difficile

Clostridium difficile (*C. diff*) is a bacterium known for causing infectious diarrhea and a more serious condition called *C. diff* colitis. The symptoms of infection can range from minor (frequent watery diarrhea, abdominal pain and tenderness) to lethal (as many as fifteen watery stools/day, severe abdominal pain, anorexia, fever, weight loss, and blood or pus in stool).

If an individual suspects that he or she may be infected, that person may want to consult a physician before self-administering an antidiarrheal medication, as stopping the diarrhea will almost certainly make the *C. diff* infection worse, thus leading to other complications.

In the health care setting, *C. diff* is spread mainly by hand-to-hand contact. Healthy people can occasionally fall prey to *C. diff* infection; however, individuals at greatest risk for contracting *C. diff* are mainly those who are hospitalized or in long-term care (LTC) facilities. Patients who are under a multiple-antibiotic regimen also have an increased chance to be infected, as the wide range of broad-spectrum antibiotics administered will eradicate the "good" intestinal bacteria that can prevent overgrowth of *C. diff*. Other risk factors include (but are not limited to) GI tract surgery, certain diseases of the colon such as inflammatory bowel disease and colorectal cancer, use of chemotherapy drugs, previous infection with *C. diff*, age sixty-five years or older, and kidney disease.

Nursing considerations when caring for a patient presenting for *C. diff* will focus on immediate hydration and pain management. Stabilization of vital signs is required if the patient presents with fever and hematochezia (bright red blood in stool). A CBC as well as a basic metabolic panel (BASEMET) or comprehensive metabolic panel (COMPMET) will be collected to determine any metabolic disturbances as a result of frequent diarrhea, and a stool sample may be necessary. A physician will typically prescribe a ten- to fourteen-day course of antibiotic therapy consisting of one of the following: metronidazole (Flagyl®), fidaxomicin (Dificid®), or vancomycin (Vancocin®). An improvement of symptoms will usually occur about 72 hours after starting antibiotics, but diarrhea may still reappear briefly. In addition to prescribed medications, probiotics may also be considered as an alternative treatment. Upon discharge from the health care facility, the patient will need to remember to continue drinking a lot of water to prevent dehydration from recurrent diarrhea (if and when it persists).

Prevention of the illness focuses on excellent hygiene; frequent handwashing after coming into contact with an infected individual, using chlorine bleach-based cleaning agents for home use, and washing soiled clothing with detergent and bleach are a few of the ways to reduce or eliminate the possibility of a *C. diff* infection.

GI Surgeries

There are many conditions of the various organs of the abdomen that may need surgical intervention to fix.

A cholecystectomy is a procedure in which the entire gallbladder is removed. The gallbladder is a pear-shaped organ that is positioned below the liver and adjacent to the stomach. The decision to take out the gallbladder is based on patient condition and, specifically, if gallstone formation is causing pain.

Cholecystectomy begins with the physician inflating the abdomen for a clear view with which to work. After this, the physician makes small incisions and insets a thin tube with a camera at the end into the abdomen. The physician visualizes the gallbladder and then removes it.

This type of surgical procedure, in which there is minimal invasion, a camera or scope is used, and smaller incisions are made, is called a laparoscopic procedure.

Illustration showing cholecystectomy using the minimally-invasive laparoscopic procedure

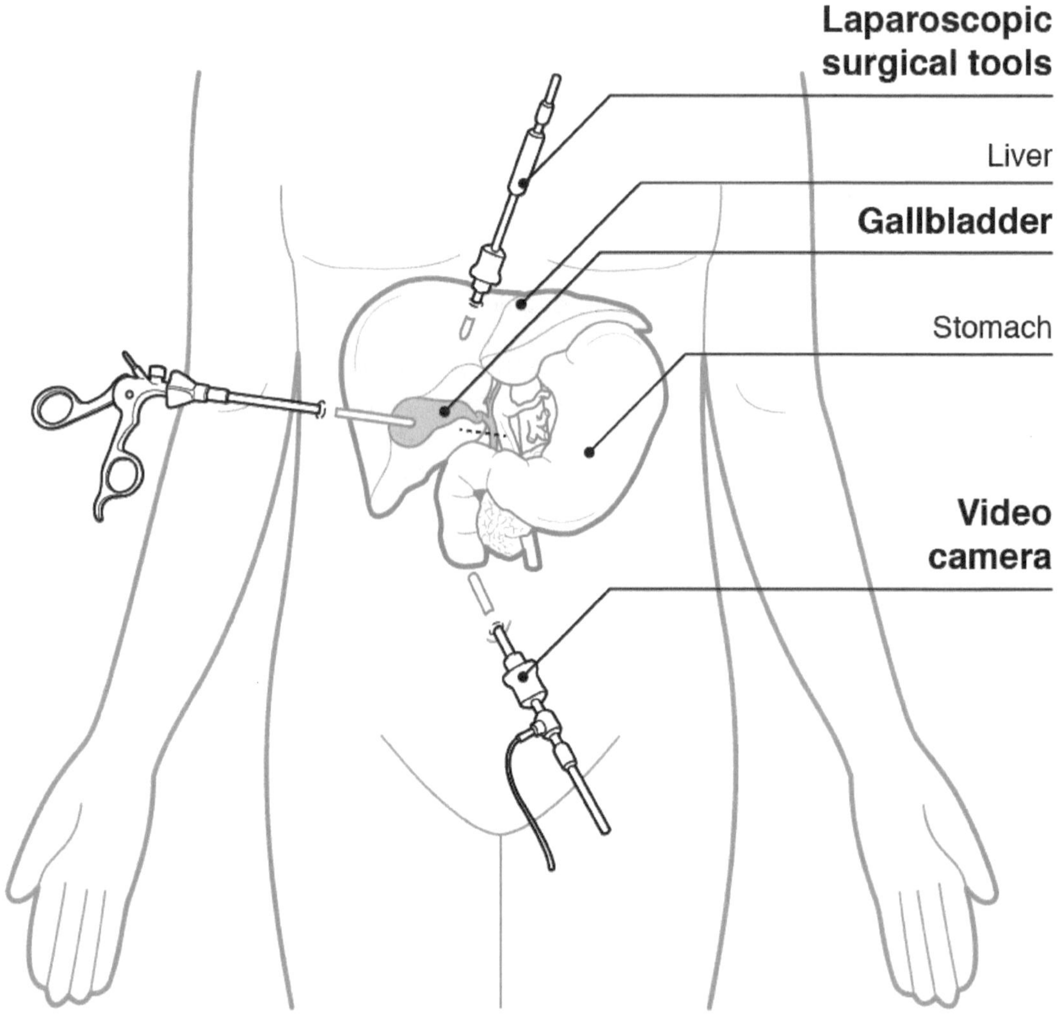

Other surgical interventions of the upper organs of the GI tract include hiatal hernia repair, removal of cancerous tumors, removal of hepatic cysts, and repair of ulcerative conditions.

Surgeries involving the lower GI tract include hemorrhoidectomy (removal of hemorrhoids), repair of anal fistulas, resection of the bowels, ileostomy, and colostomy.

Ileostomy and colostomy are surgical procedures in which a portion of the bowel is rerouted up through a hole in the abdomen. Ileostomy involves the small intestine or ileum, while colostomy involves the large intestine or colon. These two procedures are performed in the cases of severe bowel disease, such as bowel cancer, diverticulitis, and inflammatory bowel disease.

The patient with a stoma as a result of an ileostomy or colostomy will need to be educated on how to care for it. A bag is attached to the stoma for the purpose of collecting fecal matter. This bag can be taken off and replaced as needed. The stoma needs to be assessed regularly to make sure it has not become infected. The stoma should be pink, and the area surrounding it should be kept clean and dry.

Healthy stoma site postcolostomy

Stoma is pink; area surrounding is clean and dry

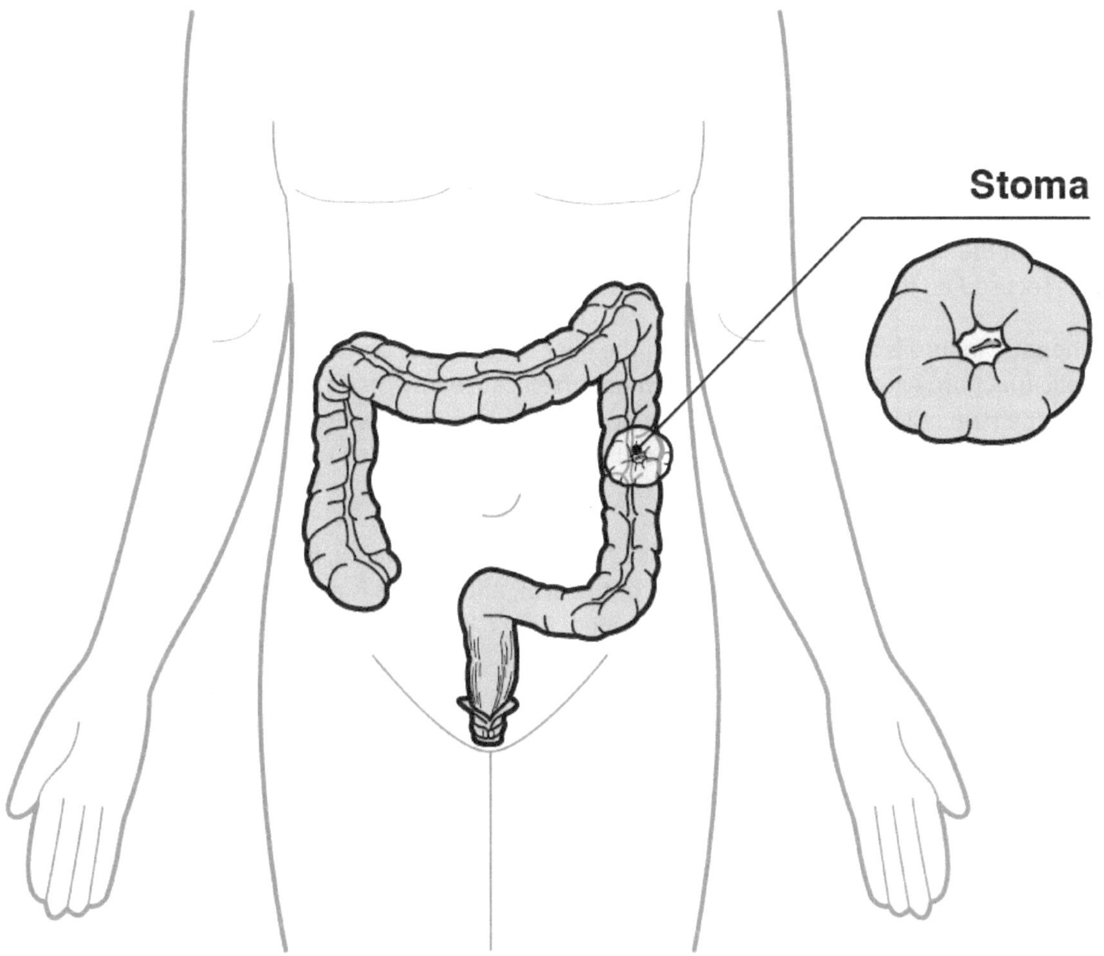

Hepatic Failure

Hepatitis is an inflammatory condition of the liver, which is further categorized as infectious or noninfectious. Causative infectious agents for hepatitis may be viral, fungal, or bacterial, while noninfectious causes include autoimmune disease, prescription and recreational drugs, alcohol abuse, and metabolic disorders. More than 50 percent of the cases of acute hepatitis in the United States are caused by a virus. Transmission routes include fecal-oral, parenteral, sexual contact, and perinatal transmission. There are four phases of the course of viral hepatitis. During phase 1, which is asymptomatic, the host is infected, and the virus replicates; the onset of mild symptoms occurs in phase 2; progressive symptoms of liver dysfunction appear in phase 3; and recovery from the infection occurs in phase 4. These phases are specific to the causative agent and the individual.

The most common viral agents are hepatitis A (HAV), hepatitis B (HBV), and hepatitis C (HCV). Less commonly, hepatitis D (HDV), hepatitis E (HEV), CMV, Epstein-Barr virus, and adenovirus may cause hepatitis. HAV and HBV often present with nausea, jaundice, anorexia, right upper quadrant pain, fatigue, and malaise. HCV may be asymptomatic or, alternatively, may present with similar symptoms. Approximately 20 percent of acute infections with HBV and HCV result in chronic hepatitis, which is a risk factor for the development of cirrhosis and liver failure. The care of the patient with acute hepatitis due to HAV and HCV is focused on symptom relief, while the antiviral treatment for HBV is effective in decreasing the incidence of adenocarcinoma.

Chronic hepatitis is a complication of acute hepatitis and frequently progresses to hepatic failure, which is associated with deteriorating coagulation status and the onset of hepatic encephalopathy due to alterations in the blood-brain barrier that result in brain cell edema. Care of the patient with hepatic failure is focused on fluid volume and coagulation homeostasis and reduction of encephalopathy.

Acute hepatic failure is a condition in which the liver is no longer performing at its normal level of metabolic function. Acute hepatic failure is most often caused by drug toxicity or viral infection. For instance, the pain reliever and fever reducer acetaminophen is known to cause liver damage and failure in toxic overdoses. The common viral culprit of liver failure is hepatitis B, with hepatitis C being less common.

A patient experiencing liver failure will exhibit signs of encephalopathy, including confusion, as well as jaundice and ascites. Jaundice is a yellowing of the skin, and ascites is a severe bloat of the abdomen as a result of massive collection of free fluid. In severe cases, this fluid will be drained off the abdomen to relieve pressure.

Portal hypertension is a condition most often caused by cirrhosis or scarring of the liver in which the pressure of the portal vein is elevated. The portal vein drains blood from the organs of the upper GI tract, such as the spleen, intestines, and pancreas into the liver. When the liver cannot receive the normal amount of blood due to scarring or disease, the resistance to the incoming blood rises, resulting in the higher pressure. Complications of portal hypertension include ascites, splenomegaly, and acute variceal bleeding. Variceal bleeding has a high mortality rate as it is difficult to control.

Treatment of portal hypertension includes monitoring, banding via endoscopy, and pharmacologic therapy, such as beta-blockers.

Cirrhosis is a scarring of the liver tissue over time and is an associated condition of acute liver failure. Chronic alcoholism is a leading cause of cirrhosis. The scarring of the liver can be slowed with treatment and alcohol abuse cessation, but ultimately is irreversible.

Esophageal varices are dilated veins located in the esophagus and are a result of portal hypertension. These varices are highly vulnerable to massive bleeding, but are otherwise asymptomatic. Esophageal varices may be treated with banding procedures as well as intravenous administration of octreotide.

Fulminant hepatitis is a type of acute liver failure that occurs without the presence of pre-existing, chronic disease states. This type of liver failure is usually preceded by hepatic viruses, exposure to toxins, or drug injury. Fulminant hepatitis causes a large amount of necrosis or tissue death in the liver. As a result, liver transplantation may be needed in order for the patient to fully recover.

Biliary atresia is a condition of the bile duct in which it is blocked or possibly even absent. This condition occurs in newborns because of abnormal fetal development. Newborns with biliary atresia are jaundiced because of the bile-duct atresia. A procedure called the **Kasai procedure** is often used to repair biliary atresia. In this procedure, the small intestine is attached to the liver to create a new pathway for bile to drain. The intestine is then reattached to a lower portion of the small intestine to reconnect it with the GI tract. Many infants with biliary atresia will develop liver failure later in life and will likely need liver transplants.

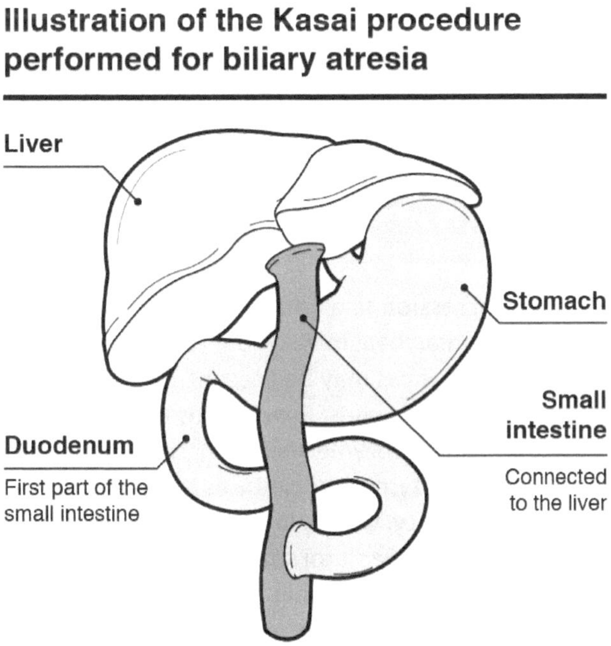

Ischemic Bowel

Ischemic bowel disease is a potentially serious condition in which an artery that should be perfusing the intestines is narrowed or blocked, causing inadequate blood flow. A blockage in the arteries can be due to a blood clot or tumor, while narrowing is usually due to atherosclerosis. Inadequate blood flow to the intestines can also be due to an obstruction in the colon, hypotension, or certain medications, such as non-steroidal anti-inflammatories, diuretics, and some chemotherapy agents.

Symptoms of ischemic bowel disease include abdominal pain and cramping, diarrhea and a frequent urge to defecate, bloody stools, abdominal distension, and nausea and vomiting.

Malnutrition

Malnutrition is a disorder that includes overnutrition and undernutrition. **Overnutrition** is a form of malnutrition that is associated with obesity and metabolic syndrome, in which a person is consuming far more calories from food than needed for healthy body function. **Undernutrition** is a result of deficient consumption of necessary nutrients for the body's function. Nutrients can be lost as a result of diarrhea or vomiting, leading to an undernourished state. Anorexia, a psychological condition in which a person refrains from eating in order to lose weight to achieve an unrealistic body image, is another form of undernutrition.

Progression of malnutrition may be slow or rapid, depending on the case. Anorexia is a slow decline in nourishment, while the body wasting or cachexia associated with cancers may result in rapid undernourishment.

Undernutrition often manifests as weakness, muscle wasting, weight loss, and irritability. The patient may become pale and fatigued.

Treatment of undernutrition includes diet control, correction of fluid and electrolyte irregularities, and correction of complications that may have developed.

Malabsorption is a disorder of the small intestine in which nutrients are not properly absorbed into the bloodstream, resulting in a malnourished state of the body. Chronic diarrhea is the most common manifestation of malabsorption. **Steatorrhea**, or fatty stools, is a common sign of malabsorption, reflecting the fat loss of the body. Treatment of malabsorption will be aimed at correcting the cause. Common causes of malabsorption include bacterial overgrowth syndrome, celiac disease, Whipple disease, and short-bowel syndrome.

Pancreatitis

Pancreatitis has a rapid onset and progression to a critical illness, which is manifested by characteristic abdominal pain, nausea, vomiting, and diarrhea. In addition, fever, tachycardia, hypotension, and abdominal distention and rebound tenderness may be present. The exocrine function of the pancreas is the production and secretion of digestive enzymes. Pancreatitis exists when one of the causative agents inhibits the homeostatic suppression of the enzyme secretion, resulting in excessive amounts of the enzymes in the pancreas. This excess of enzymes precipitates the inflammatory response, which results in increased pancreatic vascular permeability, which, in turn, leads to edema, hemorrhage, and eventual necrosis of the pancreas. The inflammatory mediators can result in systemic complications that may include sepsis, respiratory distress syndrome, renal failure, and GI hemorrhage. Chronic alcoholism and biliary tract obstruction are the most common causes of pancreatitis; however, as many as 35 percent of the cases of pancreatitis are idiopathic. Pancreatitis can also occur after endoscopic retrograde cholangiopancreatography (ERCP) due to defects in the sphincter of Oddi. Aggressive pre-procedure hydration and rectal indomethacin post procedure are employed to prevent this complication. Less common causes include some antibiotics and chemotherapy agents.

Diagnosis is based on the patient's presenting history and routine lab studies that include amylase P, lipase, metabolic panel, liver panel, C-reactive protein, CBC, and arterial blood gases (ABGs). Imaging studies may be used if the diagnosis is unclear to rule out gallbladder disease. Nonsurgical treatment includes bowel rest with nasogastric decompression, analgesics, and IV fluid administration. Surgical procedures may be open or minimally invasive and are aimed at removing diseased tissue to limit the progression to systemic complications, to repair the pancreatic duct, or to repair defects in the biliary tree. The initial care of pancreatitis focuses on prompt diagnosis, aggressive fluid management, and treatment of the cause because the disease is associated with the rapid onset of systemic complications.

Renal

Acute Kidney Injury (AKI)

Acute kidney injury is a sudden decrease in performance by the kidneys, which leads to build up of wastes in the body. The kidneys are a pair of organs located in the posterior portion of the abdomen. They filter the blood for waste that later leaves the body in urine. The kidneys are also influenced by **antidiuretic hormone**, which signals when the kidneys should retain water. Consequently, the kidneys play an important role in electrolyte balance and hydration.

Kidney (or renal) failure is usually a gradual process; often, it is the last stage of chronic, progressive renal disease. However, renal failure can also be sudden. This is referred to as acute kidney injury and usually results from sudden trauma to the kidneys. Acute kidney injury is often caused by drug overdose, lengthy surgeries, heart attack, or crush syndrome.

Renal failure that results from chronic kidney disease is not treatable, but managed based on the progression of disease. Stage 1 kidney disease shows few symptoms. Stage 5 kidney disease requires dialysis and may result in the need for a kidney transplant. During the progression of these five stages, lifestyle changes are usually incorporated alongside medical interventions to manage symptoms and hinder disease progression. These changes usually include dietary modifications, such as decreasing red meat and sugar intake, along with smoking cessation and increasing exercise frequency and duration. These changes decrease the strain on the body's cardiovascular system, and therefore ease the process of blood filtration for the kidneys.

Renal failure results in the body's inability to filter waste and balance fluids and electrolytes. Symptoms include nausea, swelling of the extremities and abdomen, cramping, decreased urine output, blood or excess protein in the urine, excess waste products in the blood, acidic blood pH levels, and elevated or low electrolyte levels. Testing includes checking blood creatinine and urea levels and may also include comprehensive metabolic panels.

Chronic Kidney Disease (CKD)

While acute injury and failure of the kidney can often be corrected, **chronic kidney disease** is a slow, progressive, and irreversible decline in function of the kidney. The most common causes of CKD are diabetes, hypertension, and diseases of the glomerulus. Metabolic syndrome, in which the patient has both diabetes and hypertension, is a major factor in CKD development.

Over time, these causative factors slowly destroy vital cells in the renal tissue. Renal function first becomes insufficient and then fails altogether, which is called **end-stage renal disease** (ESRD).

As the kidney fails, waste products build up in the body. Creatinine and urea are markers for kidney decline, though they are not the only waste products that cause the symptoms of **uremia**, or "urine in the blood." Sodium, water, potassium, and other fluid and electrolyte imbalances will occur as a result of CKD.

The kidney is responsible for releasing **erythropoietin**, a hormone that stimulates the production of red blood cells. When kidneys fail, as is the case in CKD, erythropoietin release is decreased as well, resulting in decreased erythropoiesis, or RBC production. Thus, anemia results. Patients with CKD often must be treated for anemia along with many other conditions.

A patient with CKD will present with weight loss, anorexia, nausea, vomiting, and stomatitis. They may have a yellow-brown tint to their skin, as well as itchiness and crystallization of their sweat called uremic frost.

Treating a patient with CKD is a complicated matter, as so many other systems are involved as a result of the kidneys failing. Management of diabetes and hypertension is crucial, as these are often the underlying causes. Heart failure and anemia must be addressed. Patients should quit smoking, keep cholesterol levels, glucose levels and blood pressure within normal limits, and eat a reduced-salt diet to protect the kidneys. Patients with CKD should have a pharmacist carefully considering all medications to help look for drugs that are nephrotoxic such as many antibiotics (vancomycin) and analgesics (NSAIDS). Dialysis will likely be an option in the future of the CKD patient to replace the function of the kidney.

End-Stage Renal Disease (ESRD)

Chronic renal failure is defined by specific parameters for glomerular filtration rate, serum creatinine, and other clinical markers of kidney function; however, there is no generally accepted definition for the point at which chronic renal failure becomes **end-stage renal failure**. The initiation of dialysis, or a glomerular filtration rate (GFR) less than 15 mL per minute per $1.73m^2$, are cited as plausible definitions of ESRD; however, survival rates confirm that patients often survive months or years beyond the onset of these alterations.

The most common causes of the original damage to the kidneys include, hypertension, diabetes, nephrotoxic medications and radiocontrast dyes, severe dehydration and shock, altered calcium and phosphate metabolism, genetics, and smoking as shown in the figure below.

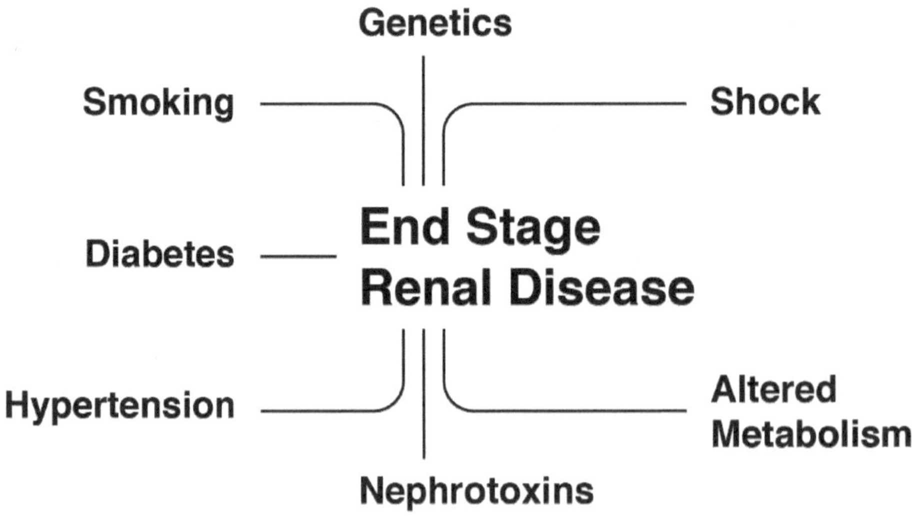

When nephrons are injured, the remaining nephrons are capable of increasing the filtration rate to maintain normal kidney function until fewer than 50 percent of functional nephrons remain. However, this adaptive response of hyperfiltration also damages the functioning nephrons due to the effects of capillary hypertension and hypertrophy of the nephrons resulting in glomerular sclerosis. Indications for renal replacement therapies such as peritoneal and hemodialysis and renal transplantation include hyperkalemia, metabolic acidosis, encephalopathy, peripheral neuropathy, and severe fluid overload. Asymptomatic patients with a GFR of 5 to 9 mL per minute per $1.73m^2$ will also require acute intervention. Prevention of the original injury is the focus of patient education.

Hemodialysis removes waste and fluid from the blood via a dialysis machine and filter for patients with renal failure. To gain venous access, the patient undergoes a minor surgical procedure. Potassium, calcium, and sodium are regulated through hemodialysis to promote homeostasis. Sedating medication is held prior to hemodialysis to avoid complications with reduced blood pressure. The nurse should maintain patency of the shunt, graft, or fistula and monitor for complications related to occlusion, infection, or cannula separation at the site. Documentation should include the status and location of the shunt, graft, or fistula, along with vital signs and pulses distal to shunt, graft, or fistula. Nursing care involves maintaining comfort and assessing color, temperature, and pain level of affected extremity (site). Dressing changes should be performed and documented as well. Cannula separation can lead to hemorrhage; therefore, the nurse ensures to clamp off the shunt until a new cannula is inserted. Patient education involves care of the access site and dressing management.

Electrolyte Imbalance

Electrolytes are minerals that, when dissolved, break down into ions. They can be acids, bases, or salts. In the body, different electrolytes are responsible for specific cellular functions. These functions make up larger, critical system-wide processes, such as hydration, homeostasis, pH balance, and muscle contraction. Electrolytes typically enter the body through food and drink consumption, but in severe cases of imbalance, they may be medically-administered. They are found in the fluids of the body, such as blood.

Key electrolytes found in the body include the following:

Sodium and Chloride

Sodium (Na^+) is mainly responsible for managing hydration, blood pressure, and blood volume in the body. It is found in blood, plasma, and lymph. It is important to note that sodium is primarily found outside of cells and is accessed by a number of different systems and organs to tightly regulate water and blood levels. For example, in cases of severe dehydration, the circulatory and endocrine systems will transmit signals to the kidneys to retain sodium and, consequently, water.

Sodium also affects muscle and nerve function. It is a positively-charged ion and contributes to membrane potential—an electrochemical balance between sodium and potassium (another electrolyte) that is responsible for up to 40 percent of resting energy expenditure in a healthy adult. This balance strongly influences the functioning of nerve impulses and the ability of muscles to contract. Healthy heart functioning and contraction is dependent on membrane potential.

Sodium is available in large quantities in the standard diets of developed countries, especially in processed foods, as it is found in table salt. Consequently, sodium deficiencies (**hyponatremia**) are possible, but rare, in the average person. Hyponatremia can result in endocrine or nervous system disorders where sodium regulation is affected. It can also result in excessive sweating, vomiting, or diarrhea, such as in endurance sporting events, improper use of diuretics, or gastrointestinal illness. Hyponatremia may be treated with an IV sodium solution. Too much sodium (**hypernatremia**) is usually a result of dehydration. Hypernatremia may be treated by introducing water quantities appropriate for suspending the sodium level that is tested in the patient's blood and urine.

Chloride (Cl^-) is a negatively-charged ion found outside of the cells that works closely with sodium. It shares many of the same physiologic responsibilities as sodium. Any imbalances (**hypochloremia** and **hyperchloremia**) are rare but may affect overall pH levels of the body. Chloride imbalances usually occur in response to an imbalance in other electrolytes, so treating a chloride imbalance directly is uncommon.

Potassium

Potassium (K^+) is mainly responsible for regulating muscular function and is especially important in cardiac and digestive functions. In women, it is believed to promote bone density. It works in tandem with sodium to create membrane potential. Potassium is a positively-charged ion and is usually found inside cells. It plays a role in maintaining homeostasis between the intracellular and extracellular environments.

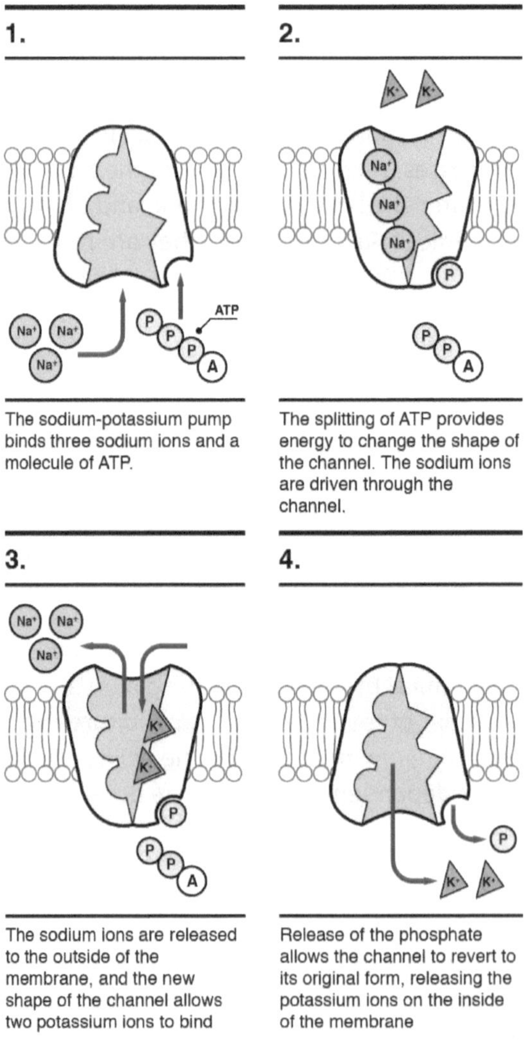

1. The sodium-potassium pump binds three sodium ions and a molecule of ATP.

2. The splitting of ATP provides energy to change the shape of the channel. The sodium ions are driven through the channel.

3. The sodium ions are released to the outside of the membrane, and the new shape of the channel allows two potassium ions to bind

4. Release of the phosphate allows the channel to revert to its original form, releasing the potassium ions on the inside of the membrane

Potassium is found in all animal protein and animal dairy products and in most fruits and vegetables. Low potassium levels (**hypokalemia**) may be caused by dehydration due to excessive vomiting, urination, or diarrhea. In severe or acute cases, hypokalemia may be a result of renal dysfunction and may cause lethargy, muscle cramps, or heart dysrhythmia. It may be treated by stopping the cause of potassium loss (e.g., diuretics), followed by oral or IV potassium replenishment.

High potassium levels (**hyperkalemia**) can quickly become fatal. Hyperkalemia is often the result of a serious condition, such as sudden kidney or adrenal failure, and may cause nausea, vomiting, chest pain, and muscle dysfunction. It is treated based on its severity, with treatment options ranging from diuretic use to IV insulin or glucose. IV calcium may be administered if potentially dangerous heart arrhythmias are present.

Calcium and Phosphorus

Calcium (Ca^{2+}) is plentiful in the body, with most calcium stored throughout the skeletal system. However, if there is not enough calcium in the blood (usually available through proper diet), the body will take calcium from the bones. This can become detrimental over time. If enough calcium becomes present in the blood, the body will return extra calcium stores to the bones. Besides contributing to the skeletal structure, this electrolyte is important in nerve signaling, muscle function, and blood coagulation. It is found in dairy products, leafy greens, and fatty fishes. Many other consumables, such as fruit juices and cereals, are often fortified with calcium.

Low calcium levels (**hypocalcemia**) can be caused by poor diet, thyroid or kidney disorders, and some medications. Symptoms can include lethargy, poor memory, inability to concentrate, muscle cramps, and general stiffness and achiness in the body. Supplementation can rapidly restore blood calcium levels. In cases where symptoms are present, IV calcium administration in conjunction with an oral or IV vitamin D supplement may be utilized.

High calcium levels (**hypercalcemia**) is usually caused by thyroid dysfunction but can also be the result of diet, limited mobility (such as in paralyzed individuals), some cancers, or the use of some diuretics. Symptoms can include thirst, excess urination, gastrointestinal issues, and unexplained pain in the abdominal area or bones. Severe or untreated hypercalcemia can result in kidney stones, kidney failure, confusion, depression, lethargy, irregular heartbeat, or bone problems.

There is an intricate balance between calcium levels and the levels of phosphorus, another electrolyte. Phosphorus, like calcium, is stored in the bones and found in many of the same foods as calcium. These electrolytes work together to maintain bone integrity. When too much calcium exists in the blood, the bones release more phosphorus to balance the two levels. When there is too much phosphorus in the blood, the bones release calcium. Therefore, the presence or absence of one directly impacts the presence or absence of the other. Indicators of hypocalcemia and hypercalcemia usually also indicate low levels of phosphorus (**hypophosphatemia**) and high levels of phosphorus (**hyperphosphatemia**), respectively.

Magnesium

Magnesium (Mg^{2+}) is another electrolyte that is usually plentiful in the body. It is responsible for an array of life-sustaining functions, including hundreds of biochemical reactions such as oxidative phosphorylation and glycolysis. It is also an important factor in DNA and RNA synthesis, bone development, nerve signaling, and muscle function. Magnesium is stored inside cells or within the structure of the bones. It can be consumed through leafy greens, nuts, seeds, beans, unrefined grains, and most foods that contain fiber. Some water sources may also contain high levels of magnesium.

Low levels of magnesium (**hypomagnesemia**) are primarily caused by chronic alcohol or drug abuse and some prescription medications and can also occur in patients with gastrointestinal diseases (such as celiac or Crohn's). Symptoms of hypomagnesemia include nausea, vomiting, depression, personality and mood disorders, and muscle dysfunction. Chronically depleted patients may have an increased risk of cardiovascular and metabolic disorders.

High levels of magnesium (**hypermagnesemia**) are rare and usually result in conjunction with kidney disorders when medications are used improperly. Symptoms include low blood pressure that may result in heart failure. Hypermagnesemia is usually treated by removing any magnesium sources (such as salts or laxatives) and may also require the IV administration of calcium gluconate.

Magnesium imbalance can lead to calcium or potassium imbalance over time, as these electrolytes work together to achieve homeostasis in the body.

Hydration is critical to fluid presence in the body, as water is a critical component of blood, plasma, and lymph. When fluid levels are too high or too low, electrolytes cannot move freely or carry out their intended functions. Therefore, treating an electrolyte imbalance almost always involves managing a fluid imbalance as well. Typically, as fluid levels rise, electrolyte levels decrease. As fluid levels decrease, electrolyte levels rise. Common tests to determine electrolyte fluid imbalances include basic and comprehensive metabolic panels, which test levels of sodium, potassium, chloride, and any other electrolyte in question.

Contrast-Induced Nephropathy

Contrast-induced nephropathy is defined as an episode of temporary damage to the kidney following the infusion of a radiocontrast dye as evidenced by either a 25 percent increase in serum creatinine or a 0.5 mg/dL increase in absolute creatinine within seventy-two hours of the infusion. There are two theories related to the development of acute tubular necrosis (ATN), which include renal medullary hypoxia due to vasoconstriction, and cytotoxic effects on the tubular cells exacerbated by the vasoconstriction. Unlike tubular necrosis associated with other causative agents, recovery from the contrast-induced ATN most often occurs within three to four days of onset, which may indicate less severe or different mechanisms of injury.

The creatinine levels most commonly decrease within three to seven days, and most patients do not experience oliguria; however, if oliguria does occur, the urinary output falls immediately after the procedure. Additional manifestations include hyperkalemia, metabolic acidosis, and hyperphosphatemia that resolve as the creatinine levels normalize. The possible residual effects include worsening of baseline kidney function in patients with a history of chronic kidney disease, an increased mortality rate, risk for cardiac events and heart failure, and lifetime use of dialysis in all patients with contrast-induced nephropathy.

Medication-Induced Renal Failure

There are a great number of medications that are associated with nephrotoxicity; however, there are only five mechanisms of injury: rhabdomyolysis, tubular cell toxicity, thrombotic microangiopathy, altered intraglomerular blood flow, and inflammation. Rhabdomyolysis occurs in the presence of a muscle injury that causes the release of myoglobin and creatine kinase into the plasma, resulting tubular toxicity and decreases in the glomerular filtration rate. Statins, recreational drugs, ketamine, methadone, and methamphetamines are associated with rhabdomyolysis. The proximal tubule cells are susceptible to toxic changes due to their function of concentrating and reabsorbing the glomerular filtrate, and these changes are commonly due to aminoglycosides, amphotericin B, antiretrovirals, and radiocontrast dyes.

Thrombotic microangiopathy, which results in platelet aggregation that causes endothelial toxicity in the vasculature of the kidney, is associated with the use of clopidogrel, cyclosporine, and quinine. The normal function of the renal vasculature is dependent on the balance between prostaglandin control of the vasodilation of the afferent arterioles and the angiotensin II constrictive control of the efferent arterioles. This means that prostaglandin inhibitors, such as nonsteroidal anti-inflammatory drugs (NSAIDs) and anti-angiotensin II medications such as angiotensin-converting enzyme inhibitors (ACE inhibitors) and angiotensin receptor blockers (ARBs), can result in altered renal hemodynamics in susceptible patients.

Inflammatory changes, both acute and chronic, can affect any area of kidney function and can result from a wide range of medications, including over the counter (OTC) medications such as long-term acetaminophen use, Chinese herbs, quinolone antibiotics, lithium, and phenytoin. Treatment is aimed at eliminating the use of the causative agent and restoring renal function.

Nephritic Syndrome

Nephritic syndrome is an inflammatory process that is often described interchangeably with glomerulonephritis and glomerular disease; however, a kidney biopsy may be required to differentiate nephritic syndrome from nephrotic syndrome. In fact, there is significant overlap in the presenting manifestations, and it is common for patients to exhibit evidence of both conditions. Nephritic syndrome is associated with mild to moderate albuminuria, leukocyturia, loss of leukocytes in the urine, and hematuria or the loss of red blood cells into the urine. Additional manifestations include a decline in the GFR, the onset or worsening of hypertension, and peripheral and periorbital edema. Nephritic syndrome is specifically associated with pulmonary hemorrhage, palpable purpura and generalized arthritis, and constitutional symptoms such as fever, chills, weight loss and night sweats.

Common diagnostic studies include glycated hemoglobin (HbA1C), anti-nuclear antibody, serum protein immunofixation, serum C3 and C4 complement levels, and testing for hepatitis B and C and human immunodeficiency virus (HIV). The patient's condition may be complicated by the concurrent effects of different glomerular conditions, which means patients often present with multiple extra-renal manifestations that affect the care and prognosis of the patient. Treatment is specific to the underlying cause and symptom management, which ultimately may progress to dialysis or renal transplantation.

Practice Quiz

1. Which of the following statements correctly identifies the relationship between hypokalemia and the development and duration of an ileus?
   a. K level of 6.0 mEq. causes metabolic alkalosis, which affects the bowel wall motility.
   b. K level of 2.6 mEq. causes muscle weakness that can progress to paralysis of the intestinal musculature.
   c. K level of 4.5 mEq. decreases the capillary permeability of the bowel wall, which decreases the amount of gastric fluid in the bowel.
   d. K level 3.7 increases the incidence of vomiting, which further decreases the bowel contents.

2. The nurse is caring for a patient with diabetic nephropathy. Which of the following statements correctly identifies the relationship between diabetes and kidney injury?
   a. Chronically elevated glucose levels damage the renal basement membrane.
   b. Oral hypoglycemic agents are nephrotoxic in the elderly population.
   c. Insulin administration decreases the glomerular capillary permeability, resulting in fluid overload.
   d. Only Type I diabetes is associated with renal injury.

3. What is the specific pathology responsible for brain damage in Alzheimer's disease?
   a. Invasion of the cortex by infectious prions
   b. Multiple hemorrhagic strokes
   c. Deposition of amyloid-β plaques
   d. Formation of Lewy bodies

4. Which of the following statements correctly identifies the difference between the forgetfulness that is common to the normal aging process and the memory alterations associated with Alzheimer's disease?
   a. The processes are the same; however, memory alterations associated with Alzheimer's disease include only short-term memory loss.
   b. Forgetfulness is progressive and eventually results in the individual's inability to perform ADLs independently.
   c. Memory lapses associated with Alzheimer's disease improve with frequent cueing.
   d. The end stage of memory impairment in Alzheimer's disease is the inability to recognize family members.

5. A progressive care nurse is providing discharge education for a sixty-six-year-old patient with type 2 diabetes who has had a TIA. Which of the following patient statements indicates that the teaching has been effective?
   a. "There is nothing I can do to change my risk for another episode."
   b. "The best thing I can do is to keep my A1C level below 6.5 like my doctor said."
   c. "I only have type 2 diabetes, so that doesn't affect my blood vessels."
   d. "I'm glad I don't have to take insulin to fix this."

See answers on the next page.

Answer Explanations

1. B: Serum potassium levels less than 3 mEq./L are associated with generalized muscle weakness, which includes the intestinal musculature. If hypokalemia is present in post-operative patients, the potential for the development of an ileus increases, and the duration of an existing ileus also increases. A potassium level of 6.0 mEq/L is associated with metabolic acidosis, rather than alkalosis, and there is no relationship between this potassium level and the motility of the bowel wall. The remaining potassium levels are normal and not associated with any alteration of the intestine.

2. A: Diabetic nephropathy is associated with alterations in the basement membrane that result in thickening and decreased filtration efficiency. Diabetes is also commonly associated with systemic hypertension which further damages the glomeruli. Pre-diabetes conditions such as obesity and metabolic syndrome are also associated with structural changes in the glomeruli that may be evidenced by microalbuminuria. Insulin protects the capillary permeability by controlling the serum glucose concentration. Oral hypoglycemic agents, which are principally sulfonylureas, are not nephrotoxic at therapeutic doses; however, the hypoglycemic effect of the medications is greatly increased in the presence of renal insufficiency. Either form of diabetes can affect kidney function because those effects are the result of an elevated serum glucose level, and both are commonly associated with systemic hypertension.

3. C: The destruction of brain tissue in Alzheimer's disease is the result of amyloid-β plaque formation in the cerebral cortex. Creutzfeldt-Jakob disease is a rare form of dementia that results from tissue damage caused by infectious prions; therefore, Choice *A* is incorrect. Multiple hemorrhagic strokes may be a trigger for the deposition of amyloid-β plaque formation; however, this form of damage can exist without causing Alzheimer's disease. It is not the specific causative process for the disease; therefore, Choice *B* is incorrect. The formation of Lewy bodies is responsible for the damage associated with Parkinson's disease, not Alzheimer's disease; therefore, Choice *D* is incorrect.

4. D: Early manifestations of memory impairment in Alzheimer's disease are associated with short-term memory loss and the inability to assimilate new knowledge, with progressive impairment that affects long-term memory, mood, and independent functioning. The end stage of this process is the inability to recognize family members. The processes are not the same. Memory lapses associated with forgetfulness improve with cueing and do not progress to the inability to recognize family members. Therefore, Choices *A*, *B*, and *C* are incorrect.

5. B: The elevated glucose levels associated with both type 1 and type 2 diabetes result in atherosclerosis, or wall thickening of the small arterioles and capillaries, which alters the circulation in the brain, retina, peripheral nerves, and kidneys. These changes are cumulative and irreversible; however, long-term control of the serum glucose level as measured by the A1C can limit the progression of this process. Current research indicates that the optimum A1C level is patient-specific. In this discussion, the patient knows his personal A1C target and understands the association between the elevated glucose levels and the occurrence of the TIA; therefore, Choice *B* is correct. Two of the $ABCD^2$ score categories are modifiable risk factors. Maintaining the systolic and diastolic blood pressure and blood glucose level as defined by the A1C within normal limits may lower the risk of a repeated attack. The patient should be encouraged to make the necessary lifestyle changes, including smoking cessation, dietary modifications, exercise participation, and compliance with the medication regimen that may include antihypertensive and glucose-lowering agents. Choice *A* is incorrect. There are differences in the pathophysiology between type 1 and type 2 diabetes; however, the complications are similar. In type 2 diabetes, hyperglycemia and insulin resistance contribute to increased low-density lipoproteins and triglycerides and decreased levels of high-density lipoproteins and alterations in microvasculature; therefore, Choice *C* is incorrect. To prevent further damage to the vascular system and reduce the risk of recurrent TIAs, the use of insulin may be necessary to control hyperglycemia as evidenced by the A1C level; therefore, Choice *D* is incorrect.

Musculoskeletal/Multisystem/Psychosocial

Musculoskeletal

Functional Issues

Walking is a complex motor function we take for granted. If you have an able body, you don't have to actively account for dexterity and fine motor control. Unfortunately, unassisted walking becomes much harder as a person grows older. Let's not forget individuals with physical and mental alignments that impair their ability to walk. Once you reach 70, your locomotion becomes more strenuous as muscles shrink and reactions slow.

As we get older, our bodies become more fragile. It's most noticeable in the way that we walk. Elderly adults are often stereotyped with shorter gaits, hobbling from one point to another. This is due to the fact an elderly adult's calf muscles have become weaker. They must place more force into their hips and extensor muscles. They also develop a more pronounced pelvic and spinal tilt. Some factors include weakened abdominal muscles, abdominal fat, and tighter flexor muscles. Many subtle changes in our bodies force gradual changes in our locomotion.

An individual may have trouble walking or consistently moving. They may struggle to shift their weight and can only stand in place. Many diseases and disorders can cause gait issues. A common disease that causes locomotion issues is Parkinson's disease. Individuals suffer from **festination**. They have to take small, rapid steps to stay upright. Otherwise, they may fall and injure themselves. They will often freeze in place out of caution or even fear. Parkinson's disease can even cause foot drop or dragging.

It's important to discuss any movement-related issues with elderly patients alongside their medical history. Primary care practitioners and physical therapists can conduct gait and mobility assessments if needed. MRI and CT scans help identify underlying neurological issues causing locomotion difficulties.

Prolonged bed rest and a sedentary lifestyle can result in physiological changes known as **deconditioning**. Deconditioning is a decline in an individual's physical and mental health. A loss in physical activity will cause muscle atrophy, which can inhibit essential motor functions. Individuals must get constant mental stimulation and communication because even mental health can reel backward. Limited socialization can cause depression, anxiety, loneliness, and more. Clinical studies have shown that the bedbound patient suffers a 20% decrease in muscle strength per week and a 50% decrease in muscle strength after a month in bed. There is also a 3% loss of muscle mass within the thigh muscles within seven days. Within seven days, the muscle fibers and connective tissues are maintained in a shortened position and contractures begin within three weeks.

Elderly patients, patients with cognitive dysfunction, and patients whose illnesses have left them debilitated and weak, are at a considerable risk of falling. Falls are a leading cause of injury and accidental deaths in the elderly. Gait and balance disorders, functional impairments, visual defects, cognitive impairments, and use of psychotropic medications are the most important risk factors for falls. Primary prevention of falls includes high levels of physical activity, even in patients with disease. Secondary prevention includes improving gait along with resistance and balance training. The effects of an active lifestyle on mood and confidence are probably as important as their effect on physiology.

All acutely ill patients should be considered fall risks. Environmental factors such as the lighting of the room, objects on the floor, and proximity to the call light must all be factored in to help prevent a fall. Most hospitals have a fall risk policy and a method to identify the high-risk patients. Indicators such as yellow fall arm bands, signs on doors, or yellow slippers can all alert the staff that the patient is a fall risk. The progressive care nurse should work closely with the family and caregivers so that patients at risk can have the monitoring they need to prevent a fall. Bed alarms and sitters may be indicated.

Multisystem

End-of-Life

Patients should be encouraged to discuss end-of-life wishes with their family members early on in the process when possible. The decision-making process can be complex, intense, and stressful for those left to make the decision for the patient. Having a plan in place that makes the patient's wishes clear can reduce the level of stress for both the family and the patient.

It is helpful for the patient to establish a plan that outlines specifically what their wishes are as relates to end-of-life care. A healthcare proxy can assist with ensuring such wishes are honored. Core topics and/or decisions a healthcare proxy can assist with include the location of healthcare (e.g., at home or in a facility) and resuscitation expectations.

Nurses may need to provide some guidance in pointing their patients in the right direction to complete an advanced directive and/or living will. Advanced directives and living wills are two additional resources that should be kept on file to assist with the documentation and communication of a patient's wishes.

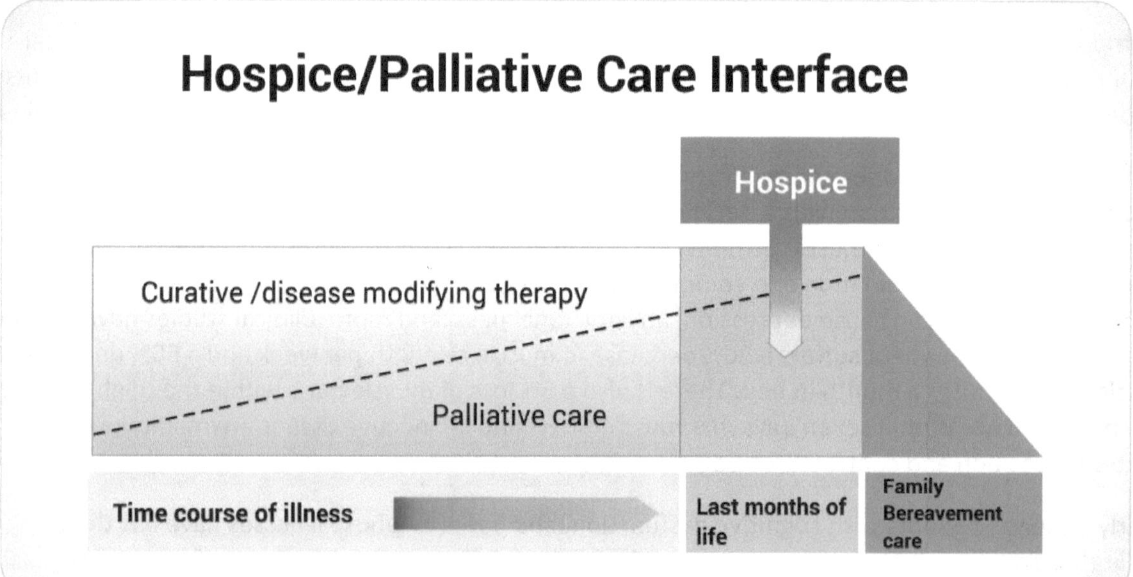

End-of-life issues can be complicated from both a logistical and an emotional perspective. For many patients, end-of-life issues may not have been discussed or resolved with family members; a nurse or other medical staff member may have to step in the role of facilitating this sensitive subject. Even when the situation has been planned for, it can come unexpectedly for both the patient and family members. Most end-of-life situations will require managing the physical and emotional pain of the patient and family members, helping the patient transition in a dignified manner, and dealing with legal paperwork. Many healthcare providers report not feeling emotionally equipped to handle these aspects, do not feel they have time on the job to adequately do so, or feel there is no financial compensation to provide these services. Being aware that job duties may require these uncomfortable tasks can be the first step in being able to provide some level of effective end-of-life support for the patient and family. Understanding common end-of-life issues can also help.

Organ and tissue donation refers to the process of removing healthy, functional organs and tissues from the patient's body after death and transplanting them to another patient in need. This may be a topic that the patient has already considered; for example, many people make this decision when applying for a driver's license and have it notated on their card. Common organs that can be donated include the heart, lungs, liver, and kidneys. Common tissues that can be donated include heart, skin, components of the eyeball, and bone.

Advanced directives are legal documents that note how a patient would like to receive or guide medical treatments in the case of terminal cases, cases where the patient is in a vegetative state, or in other end-of-life contexts. Having this document prepared in advance is extremely helpful for healthcare providers and the patient's family, as the patient's personal decisions are known and can be accounted for. However, many people do not take the time to develop these. Advance directives may only be utilized when a physician has declared the patient to be in an end-of-life state. Other rules may vary by state, so it is useful to be informed of the particular guidelines set forth by the state in which providers are practicing. In emergency cases, support staff do not usually have the legal rights to follow instructions written in an advanced directive until a physician confirms that the patient will not recover. Therefore, support staff must continue to provide comprehensive, life-sustaining care unless otherwise instructed.

More healthcare organizations are beginning to allow family members to be present during end-of-life procedures, including intense procedures that can be harrowing to watch. New research shows this can be beneficial for family members as they cope in the long-term. While remaining present with the patient is often the wish of family members, they may be unaware of the emotional upheaval they may feel when watching a loved one go through resuscitative procedures. Nursing staff should be equipped to be able to continue working even with the presence of distraught family members, and be able to provide compassionate and honest support if needed.

Withholding and withdrawing treatments are components of palliative care. They are most commonly seen in tragic, traumatic events or in hospice care. These procedures occur when a patient is believed to be terminal, and interventions that were previously being utilized to sustain the patient are gradually ceased in order to let the patient pass comfortably. Withholding and withdrawing treatments are often requested by patients who are aware of their situation and are ready to move on, but may also be done at the request of family members or medical proxy if the patient is in a vegetative state.

Healthcare-Acquired Infections

Hospital-acquired and health care–associated infections may occur in patients receiving healthcare. Common healthcare-acquired infections include surgical site infections, pneumonias, catheter-associated infections, and central-line associated infections. Surgical site infections are infections that occur in the region of the body a surgery has taken place in and can be either superficial infections or life threatening infections. Healthcare-acquired pneumonias occur in patients in medical settings, and is especially common in patients who require intubation. These patients are likely to have been infected with gram-negative bacilli such as *Pseudomonas aeruginosa* and antibiotic-resistant strains such as *methicillin-resistant Staphylococcus aureus.* Like the other pneumonias, diagnosis is based on clinical presentation and chest x-ray. Treatment is usually a regimen of broad-spectrum antibiotics. Prevention includes keeping the head of the bed greater than 30 degrees, assisting patients to keep good oral hygiene (suctioning subglottic secretions as needed), and general aspiration precautions.

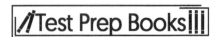

Catheter-Associated Urinary Tract Infections (CAUTIs)

Catheter-associated urinary tract infections (CAUTIs) are the most common hospital-acquired infection. The duration of use is directly associated with the incidence of infection especially in at-risk populations such as women, diabetics, and immobile patients. The most common causative agents are enteric pathogens; however, yeast infections are also common while the catheter is in place and after removal. The indwelling catheter is the source of the infection, and if left in place for two weeks, the biofilm formed on the surface of the catheter is totally "immune" to antibiotic therapy. There are currently efforts focused on reducing the incidence of CAUTI by limiting even the short-term or intermittent use of the catheter.

Central-Line Associated Bloodstream Infections

Central-line associated bloodstream infection (CLABSI) is the deadliest hospital-acquired infection with CDC reported mortality rates of 20 to 25 percent. The most common organisms are *Staphylococcus aureus*, gram negative bacilli, and candida, which gain entry to the bloodstream as a result of manipulation of the intravenous catheter. The rate of infection is associated with the duration of the therapy and the patient's baseline health status. As with the CAUTIs discussed previously, there are nation-wide efforts to decrease the incidence of the CLABSIs with meticulous care because the use of central lines is an essential therapy.

Infectious Diseases

Influenza

Influenza is a type of virus that causes an upper respiratory infection. True influenza comes in three varieties: A, B, and C. Some infections are mistakenly called the "flu," but are not actually caused by the influenza virus, resulting in a bit of confusion. A nasal swab can differentiate between influenza and other upper respiratory infection-causing organisms.

Symptoms of the flu include cough, coryza, fever, headache, and a generalized malaise. **Coryza** is the term for inflammation and mucus production in the airways.

There is a time of year in which flu commonly occurs, called flu season. Flu season differs around the world, occurring in the coldest months of the year when the flu virus thrives.

The number of influenza infections in a geographic region sometimes escalates rapidly, turning into an epidemic. The term **pandemic** refers to when the infection rate of the flu affects populations worldwide, not contained to one region.

Everyone over six months of age should be vaccinated against the flu annually, at the beginning of their respective flu season. Vaccination greatly decreases the prevalence of infections. Patients at high risk of developing a severe case of influenza infection may be given antivirals; others at lower risk may be treated for symptoms alone, allowing the virus to run its course naturally.

Influenza, when it occurs at the pandemic level, may be severe enough to cause even healthy, young patients to die. For this reason, vaccination of the population is vital. Progressive care nurses may do their part in educating and encouraging the public to get their vaccination so as to prevent large scale flu infections.

Multidrug Resistant Organisms

Multidrug-resistant organisms (MDROs) are defined as bacteria that have become impervious to certain antibiotics and can therefore no longer be used to kill the bacteria. MDROs commonly develop when antibiotics are self-administered longer than necessary or when they are not needed at all but still taken.

Staphylococcus aureus (*S. aureus*) is a bacterium that is generally located on the skin or in the nasal passages of healthy people. When present without symptoms, it is known as colonization, and when symptoms are present, it is an infection. ***Methicillin-resistant Staphylococcus aureus*** (MRSA) is a strain of *S. aureus* that is resistant to methicillin and most often occurs in individuals who have been hospitalized for an extended period of time or frequently visit a health care facility (hospital acquired) for treatment of an illness (e.g., dialysis).

Infection can also ensue as community-associated MRSA, which occurs in healthy individuals who have not recently been hospitalized or treated for an illness in a facility. People at risk for this type of MRSA consist of athletes, prisoners, daycare attendees, military recruits, IV drug abusers, and those who live in crowded settings, have poor hygiene practices, and are immunocompromised. Community-associated MRSA is communicated through human-to-human contact, contact with MRSA-contaminated items, or infection of a preexisting abrasion or wound that has not been dressed.

MRSA enters the bloodstream via this kind of abrasion and can cause sepsis, cellulitis, **endocarditis** (inflammation of the inner lining of the heart), osteomyelitis, septic arthritis, toxic shock syndrome, organ failure, and death. Prevention of infection focuses on strict handwashing, practicing good personal hygiene, avoiding sharing personal items (toothbrushes, mouth guards, clothing, bedclothes), and thoroughly cleansing an abrasion or wound.

The individual infected with MRSA will present with a fever and the appearance of an erythematous, edematous skin area, which is warm to the touch, painful, and draining pus. A more severe infection will manifest as the previously described rash, chest pain, cough, fatigue, chills, fever, malaise, headache, muscle aches, and shortness of breath.

Interventions to be implemented upon initiating care for the individual infected with MRSA consist of a detailed assessment of skin lesions; anticipation of drainage of an infected skin site and culturing of secretions; preparation of blood, sputum, and urine culture; administration of antibiotics; and in-depth education of the patient and caregivers with regard to causes and modes of transmission, signs and symptoms, and the importance of adherence to recommended treatment measures.

Vancomycin-resistant enterococci (VRE) are enterococci that have developed a resistance to many antibiotics, particularly vancomycin. Enterococci live in the intestines and on the skin and normally do not cause any issues until they become unaffected by certain antibiotic therapies. Common sites of infection include the intestines, the urinary tract, and wounds. VRE, similar to many other bacteria, can be spread by casual contact or contact with contaminated objects. Akin to MRSA, VRE are most commonly communicated from a health care worker to those who are hospitalized or in a nursing home.

Additionally, those who are immunocompromised, have long-term illnesses, have had a major surgery, or have been treated with multiple antibiotics have a greater chance of becoming infected. Understandably, VRE prevail most heavily in individuals who have used vancomycin often.

Signs and symptoms of a VRE infection depend largely on where the infection is located. If VRE are present in a wound, the affected area will be erythematous and painful to the touch. One who is suffering a urinary tract infection caused by VRE will exhibit flank pain and burning and pain upon urination. Some people have general symptoms such as fever, diarrhea, and generalized weakness.

Diagnosis of VRE starts with a blood, wound culture, urine, or stool sample to determine the cause of the illness. Severe VRE infections are treated with caution, and the hospitalized individual is placed in contact isolation to prevent the spread of infection to others. VRE infections, by nature, are difficult to manage due to the antibiotic resistance of the strain. Antibiotic treatment may consist of oral agents as well as IV, and blood, urine, and stool samples will be sent to the lab for testing after initiation of antibiotic therapy to determine if VRE bacteria are still present in the body.

Extended-spectrum beta-lactamases (ESBLs), found predominantly in gram negative bacteria, make these bacteria more resistant to many commonly used antibiotics. Patients are more at risk for ESBLs if they have catheters, have prolonged hospital stays, and have already received antibiotics during the hospital stay. ESBL infections are usually treated with a carbapenem, like meropenem.

Carbapenem-resistant enterobacteriaceae (CRE) are on the rise, especially in critical care areas. CREs are more common in patients with long hospitalizations, prior antibiotic use, and patients with comorbidities. Strict contact precautions must be used to prevent the spread of these drug resistant organisms to another patient.

Pain

Pain has been called the fifth vital sign. This is because along with heart rate, blood pressure, temperature, and rate of breathing, pain as reported by the patient is an important clue as to how well the patient is doing.

Pain is almost completely subjective data. Pain is as the patient reports it and is very difficult to measure otherwise. Whereas the heart rate can easily and accurately be counted in beats per minute, pain can only be described without much, if any, tangible evidence.

The common measure of pain is the **pain scale**, rated one to ten, with one being almost no pain at all and ten being the worst pain the patient has ever felt in their life.

The progressive care nurse will assess for pain by asking the patient what aggravates the pain and what alleviates the pain, in other words, what makes it worse and what makes it better. The nurse should ask the location of the pain, the quality, and its onset. The nurse should ask about when exacerbations occur and what signs and symptoms accompany an exacerbation. Finally, the nurse should assess how the pain affects the patient's overall functioning ability, how intense it becomes, and its temporal characteristics.

Grimacing, sweating, clutching, and guarding are all examples of non-verbal signs that pain is being experienced.

Pain can also be acute or chronic. **Acute pain** is pain that is generally related to an injury and slowly gets better over time as the injury heals. Acute pain usually lasts for less than three months. **Chronic pain** continues for at least three months and is often caused by underlying disease. Patients who come to the hospital setting may be experiencing acute on top of chronic pain, and their pain may be more difficult to manage, as they may have developed a tolerance to pain medications.

Pain Management and Procedural Sedation

Pain is one of the most commonly seen symptoms in progressive care settings, as many situations necessitating progressive care involve a high level of pain. However, since cases in healthcare settings often vary widely in scope and every patient will have a different personal threshold for pain tolerance, best practices are difficult to develop when it comes to pain management. It is often done on a case by case basis. However, when a patient's pain is not managed in a way that seems appropriate to that individual, it can cause patient and family dissatisfaction in the healthcare organization. As a result, medical staff must try to provide effective and safe pain management options that can make the patient comfortable at the present time, but that also do not cause harm over time. In some cases, like a sprained muscle, ice therapy and time can provide adequate pain management. More serious cases, defined as pain that does not subside after an objectively reasonable period of time for the injury, may require topical, intramuscular, or oral pain medication. These can include stronger doses of common over-the-counter pain medications, or prescription pain medications.

Prescription pain medications, especially opioids and muscle relaxers, are known for causing debilitating addiction, so when prescribing them to a patient, the lowest dose and dosing frequency necessary should be utilized. Additionally, patients should be closely monitored for their reactions to their pain medications. Finally, some individuals who are addicted to prescription painkillers and muscle relaxers may feign injuries in order to receive another prescription. Therefore, all patients' medical histories should be thoroughly evaluated to note their history of pain medication usage. Patients should also be assessed for showing any signs of drug abuse history and withdrawal symptoms (such as damaged teeth, shaking, and agitation).

Procedural sedation and analgesia (PSA) allows patients to remain somewhat alert during medical procedures that may be uncomfortable but not unbearably painful, such as resetting bones. Unlike general anesthesia, where patients are completely sedated and do not feel any sensations, PSA allows patients to be somewhat conscious and aware of bodily functions. It can be utilized with or without pain-relieving medications. Practitioner awareness is crucial when administering procedural sedation, especially when pain relief is also utilized. Progressive care nurses who will assist with PSA must be well trained, ACLS certified and know their related facility policies. Prior to a patient having procedural sedation, the nurse should confirm that the patient has informed consent on the chart and that pre-procedure vital signs and rhythm strips have been obtained. If procedural sedation is to be done at the bedside, the nurse should make sure that airway management devices are within reach of the bedside for the provider to use and the patient is being appropriately monitored with continuous oxygen saturation, heart rate and rhythm, respiratory rate, and end tidal carbon dioxide monitoring. During the procedure frequent blood pressure readings should be obtained. Any abnormalities should be immediately reported to the practitioner. The nurse should make sure meds for ACLS as well as reversal medications, such as naloxone and flumazenil, are available if needed and that the patient has patent IV access. Most hospital policies require 1:1 nursing care for the patient during procedural sedation and for 30 minutes after, provided the patient has returned to pre-procedure baseline.

Palliative Care

Palliative care is comprehensive care provided for symptoms and illness exacerbated by a chronic condition, including cancer, liver failure, dementia, and chronic obstructive pulmonary disease. Palliative care is delivered by a multidisciplinary team of physicians, nurses, nutritionists, pharmacists, social workers, case managers, and a number of specialists in a collaborative manner.

The characteristic that distinguishes palliative care from hospice care is the time at which palliative care may be offered. Progressive care nurses may advocate for palliative care to be administered at any stage of an illness or at any age. Ideally, palliative care should be initiated upon diagnosis for conditions like cancer and continue for the duration of therapy, follow-up care, and end-of-life care, as indicated.

Hospice care, though a form of palliative care, is typically administered as a component of end-of-life care to those who are suffering from terminal illness with less than six months to live.

Palliative care has the ability to improve one's quality of life, addressing physical, behavioral, spiritual, and practical needs. Palliative care delivers a variety of options to patients that go far beyond pain assessments.

Palliative care may be delivered in the patient's home as long as they are under the supervision of a physician, or it may be a component of hospice or provided in a facility. It is typically covered by health insurance and in some instances may be covered by Medicare and Medicaid. Those who do not qualify for palliative care by any of the identified entities may need further assistance from their progressive care nurse and/or social worker to identify potential resources that can provide the necessary support to receive services.

Pressure Ulcers

Most progressive care nurses that have had to deal with immobile, bedridden patients who are very ill are familiar with pressure ulcers. Because of immobility, pressure against vulnerable parts of the body results in tissue necrosis and ulceration. Bony prominences are especially susceptible to ulceration.

Risk factors for developing pressure ulcers include increased age, immobility, undernutrition, and urinary and/or fecal incontinence. Factors that contribute to pressure ulcers include shear, friction, pressure, and moisture. Increased exposure in compromised patients results in ulceration.

Ulcers can be staged into several categories, including stages I, II, III, and IV, unstageable, and suspected deep tissue injury (DTI). Each category looks at depth of wound and tissues affected. Wounds do not necessarily progress from one stage to the next; they can sometimes develop very quickly, skipping stages.

Prevention is obviously the best intervention when addressing pressure ulcers. The progressive care nurse can help prevent pressure ulcers by turning the patient every two hours, reducing pressure where possible with pillows and supports, encouraging early mobilization and proper nutrition, and meticulously caring for wounds that do develop to prevent infection and loss of tissue.

Rhabdomyolysis

Rhabdomyolysis occurs in the presence of a muscle injury that causes the release of myoglobin and creatine kinase into the plasma, resulting tubular toxicity and decreases in the glomerular filtration rate.

Statins, recreational drugs, ketamine, methadone, and methamphetamines are associated with rhabdomyolysis.

Sepsis Continuum

Sepsis is a serious condition in which the body has an out-of-control response to a wound, infection, or illness. It can progress through three stages of severity, with septic shock being the most life-threatening stage. It always accompanies the presence of an underlying condition, including pneumonia, kidney infections, and blood infections. The frequency of cases has been rising in the United States; this increase is attributed to aging populations, antibiotic resistance, increased chronic illness rates, and increased reporting of sepsis cases.

Systemic Inflammatory Response Syndrome

The inflammatory response of the body was defined in 25 CE by the Roman encyclopedist Celsius as rubor, calor, dolor, and tumor. These Latin terms mean redness, heat, pain, and swelling, the classic signs of inflammation the progressive care nurse is familiar with today.

In the case of **systemic inflammatory response syndrome**, or SIRS, two or more criteria must be met: a temperature of greater than 38 degrees Celsius or less than 36 degrees Celsius, a pulse of greater than 90 beats per minute, a respiratory rate of greater than 20 breaths per minute, or a white blood cell count of greater than 12,000. Two or more of these criteria being met in a critically ill patient would suggest that a systemic inflammatory response is afoot and potential complications may be up ahead for the patient.

SIRS is the first step in a continuum of worsening illness.

Sepsis

The next stage after SIRS is **sepsis**, in which criteria for SIRS has been met and there is a known source of infection. It is characterized by a high fever, extreme pain, sleepiness, an accelerated heart rate, and/or rapid breathing.

It is important to administer treatment as soon as possible to keep a sepsis diagnosis from progressing through the more severe stages. The first line of intervention usually includes antibiotics and IV fluid administration. In more severe cases, surgery to remove affected tissues may be necessary to prevent septic shock.

Severe Sepsis

If other serious physiological symptoms are also present with sepsis, such as low platelet count, low urine output, or mental confusion, the patient diagnosis shifts to **severe sepsis**—the third stage.

Sepsis Shock

Septic shock occurs when severe sepsis is present, hypotension is unresponsive to fluid resuscitation, and hypoperfusion abnormalities are present. Lactic acidosis, oliguria, and altered mental status are examples of hypoperfusion abnormalities.

Once a patient goes into septic shock, he or she may experience organ failure. Half of all septic shock cases are fatal. Prognosis after treatment for mild and severe sepsis varies. With early and adequate treatment, most people who experience mild sepsis return to their normal quality of life. However, immunocompromised patients or patients who have other health problems may quickly progress to severe sepsis status or go into septic shock. They may require surgical amputation if gangrene sets in or if all the tissues in an extremity die, experience irreparable organ damage, or suffer from other long-term complications. Even in the event of a full recovery, most of these patients remain with an increased risk of another sepsis episode in the future.

Multiple organ dysfunction syndrome or MODS is the final step in the continuum, with evidence of more than two organs failing.

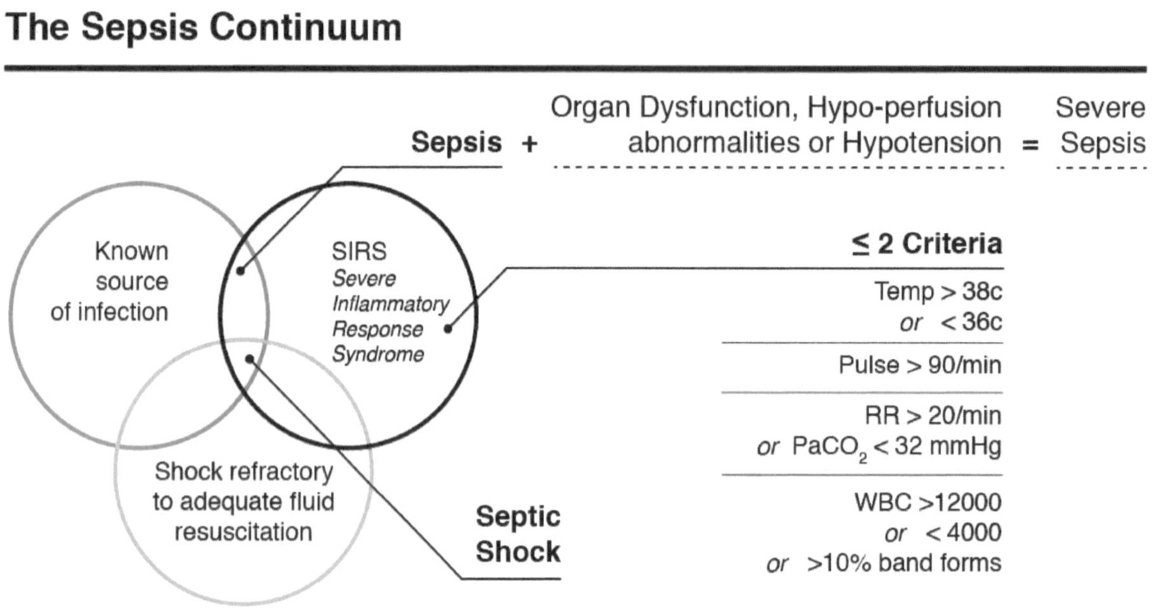

Treatment of the continuum of SIRS to MODS includes fluid resuscitation, cultures to identify the source of infection, empirical antibiotics to fight infection, vasopressors for hypotensive support, lactate level measurements, and central venous pressure measurement.

Shock States

Shock refers to any context where the body is unable to circulate an adequate amount of blood to carry out essential physiological functions. It commonly occurs in emergencies of the cardiovascular system.

Hypovolemic

Cardiogenic shock occurs as a result of direct cardiac muscle damage. It often presents due to heart attack or heart failure.

Hypovolemic

Hypovolemic shock occurs as a result of heavy bleeding and overall low blood volume, which prevents adequate circulation from occurring. Shock patients will always exhibit low blood pressure. They may also present with cold, clammy, bluish skin; dehydration; shallow breathing; chest pain; and abnormal pulses. Patients in a state of severe shock may be unconscious. Shock patients will likely need to be treated with chest compressions if they aren't breathing and don't have a pulse, suctioning and mechanical ventilation, and/or defibrillation before or during transport. Pediatric patients under three months of age and all immunocompromised patients who appear to be in shock should be treated as septic.

Anaphylactic

An allergic reaction occurs when an individual's body responds negatively to a substance it has come in contact with, either through touch, consumption, or inhalation. The substance that causes an allergic reaction in an individual is referred to as an **allergen**, and the reaction occurs as a result of the individual's immune system treating the allergen as a threat. Since immune systems between individuals vary widely, the presence and severity of an allergic reaction—even to the same allergen—varies also. A potential allergen (e.g., a plant pollen or a peanut) may cause no response in one individual, cause a mild uncomfortable response in a second individual, and be life-threatening to a third individual. Usually, allergic reactions happen relatively soon (immediately to within a few hours) after exposure to an allergen. Repeated exposure can eventually result in hypersensitivity to the allergen and produce more intense allergic reactions. Family history typically influences the presence and severity of allergies. Symptoms of a mild allergic reaction include rashes, itching, congestion, watery eyes, and other cold-like symptoms. Many mild allergic reactions can be treated by eliminating the presence of the allergen or taking anti-allergy medications.

More severe allergic reactions can include symptoms such as physical pain in the chest or stomach, diarrhea, skin swelling or redness, fainting, and trouble breathing deeply. The most severe allergic reactions occur almost instantly and can intensify to result in **anaphylaxis**, which is a medical emergency requiring immediate attention. Anaphylaxis comprises severe swelling of the tongue or throat (which can result in suffocation), vomiting, dizziness, or rashes. If anaphylaxis goes untreated, it can result in death. The most common treatment of anaphylaxis is an epinephrine injection, and many individuals who know they have a severe allergy carry an epinephrine injection pen (EpiPen®) with them.

Common allergens include nuts, shellfish, some fruits, eggs, dairy, gluten, a variety of pollen types, latex, animal dander and hair, and insect or reptilian venom. Some of these allergens, like food allergens, can be present from birth onward; others will develop later in life. Allergens such as bee venom or snake venom may remain unknown unless there is an attack.

Toxic Ingestions and Inhalations

Any chemical that can cause harm to the body when ingested or inhaled is considered **toxic**. Exhaust fumes from cars, lead in drinking water, asbestos in old buildings, and pesticides on plants can all cause harm to the body if ingested or inhaled. Ingestion occurs through eating or swallowing the substance, which then travels through the body's GI tract and is absorbed into the circulatory system from the small intestine. A short-term effect would be headache and vomiting, while long-term effects could include cancer and other disease states. Substances that are inhaled travel through the airways, into the lungs, and are absorbed into the circulation through the pulmonary capillary beds.

Treatment of toxic ingestions depends on the toxic substance ingested as well as the amount ingested. Patient monitoring usually includes level of consciousness, cardiac monitoring, pulse oximetry and vital signs as well as blood glucose measurements. Many patients can be managed with supportive care or activated charcoal may be necessary to rid the body of the toxin. Activated charcoal works by absorbing the toxin before the body gets a chance to, decreasing its toxic effects. If activated charcoal is not effective, for some patients the benefits may outweigh the risks for hemodialysis, hemoperfusion, or urinary alkalization. For certain poisonings, there are specific treatments that may decrease hepatotoxicity, for example giving N-acetylcysteine for patients with acetaminophen poisoning. When poisoning is confirmed, progressive care nurses should follow institution protocols for reporting to poison control centers, and when appropriate, obtain psychiatric consultation if the poisoning may be suicide-attempt related.

Wounds

Knowing how to care for each wound type is crucial to restoring the patient back to their normal functioning ability. There are three distinct types of wounds that a progressive care nurse may encounter in their practice: infectious, surgical, and traumatic.

Infectious

A wound that has become infected is called an **infectious wound**. This means that bacteria and other microorganisms have invaded and colonized. This infection can delay healing and spread to other tissues of the body or even to the body's internal system. Any wound a patient develops, whether a pressure ulcer, trauma wound, or surgical wound, may become infected; thus, the progressive care nurse must be aware of signs and symptoms.

An infectious wound may become reddened or painful, swell as a result of inflammation, discharge a pus-like fluid that is green or yellow, be malodorous, and not heal as a result of the infection.

Staphylococcus aureus is a common bacterial invader of wounds, as it is often found on normal skin. The wound is its entryway to becoming a full-blown infection.

Those at risk for developing infectious wounds are the elderly, diabetics, and those who are immunocompromised, such as patients with the HIV infection.

Surgical

A **surgical wound** is a natural byproduct of any surgery. Whether a small or large incision, the surgeon has to open the body cavity in some way, shape, or form to access the internal tissue or organ he/she needs to operate on. Surgical wounds will usually be dressed by the operating room (OR) team, but the progressive care nurse will be in charge of monitoring the wound and changing the dressing while the patient is in the unit. A surgical wound will often have sutures, or tiny stitches that are sewn onto the patient's skin, in place. Sometimes these sutures will dissolve and be absorbed by the patient, and sometimes they will need to be removed after a certain amount of time, depending on the procedure, the surgeon, and the facility policy on the subject.

The signs of a surgical wound that has become infected are the same as any infectious wound: redness, swelling, discharge of pus, odor, pain, and lack of healing.

Trauma

A **trauma wound** differs from a surgical wound in that its openings will usually be irregular and large. Bleeding is a major factor in traumatic wounds due to their depth and size. Bleeding must be stopped, and the wound must be closed before any dressing may be placed and healing can begin. This will be likely handled in the emergency department or the surgical suite, but the progressive care nurse receiving the patient to the unit will be responsible for further monitoring of the wound, dressing changes, and assessing for healing.

Most dressing changes are recommended daily, usually to be administered with an antibiotic cream. Dressing changes may be more or less frequent depending on the wound and the surgeon's orders. The progressive care nurse will follow suit.

Wound Drains

Multiple wound drains and evacuators exist including: Penrose, Hemovac, Jackson-Pratt, and T-tube. The progressive care nurse should carefully remove dressings to not dislodge the drain or evacuator and then dispose in a biohazard bag. Wound assessment should include the amount, color, and consistency of drainage along with general wound appearance and signs of infection. After cleaning the wound from the drain/evacuator outward in a circular motion, a clean dressing should be applied around the insertion site, and timed and dated. The nurse should then check that the tubing is not kinked or dislodged. When emptying the drain of an evacuator to prevent overfilling, the nurse should apply tension to the suture site and facilitate the flow of clots by gently squeezing the evacuator. Applying compression to the evacuator maintains suction pressure, which is needed to maintain evacuation. Drain tubes should be emptied to prevent overfill and tension on the suture site. Documentation should include the status and condition of the wound, incision site, drain, and dressing, along with the solution used to clean and medications applied to the wound. The nurse should note the patient's tolerance to the procedure and address knowledge deficits, while providing emotional support.

Behavioral/Psychosocial

Altered Mental Status

Altered mental status (AMS) can appear suddenly and be manifested by a temporary period of unpredictable behavior that is defined as delirium. Alternatively, an AMS that gradually evolves over months or years and eventually is evidenced by loss of short-term and then long-term memory is defined as **dementia**. **Delirium** is associated with the acute onset of confusion, impaired awareness, perceptual defects that may include visual hallucinations, disorientation to place and time, and loss of recent memory. The delirious patient is incapable of communicating reliable information, and therefore providers should contact other sources. Information that is required to assess and treat the patient's delirium includes any use of recreational, OTC , and prescription drugs, preexisting endocrine or psychiatric disorders, and any prior episodes of delirium.

Dementia may be a primary condition or may develop secondary to cerebrovascular disease, trauma, infection, cancer, autoimmune disease, and psychiatric illness. Primary dementias include Alzheimer disease and frontotemporal dementia (FTD). As many as forty percent of the patients with Parkinson's exhibit Alzheimer-like dementia. Strokes, rheumatic disorders, and infectious diseases such as HIV, neurosyphilis, meningitis, and encephalitis are also associated with the development of dementia as the diseases progress. The acute onset of chronic dementia is common in severe head trauma and trauma with anoxia. Treatment is focused on patient safety and the use of antipsychotic medications according to the 2016 American Psychiatric Association guidelines.

Delirium

A patient whose attention, level of consciousness, and cognition has been disturbed and appears to be having difficulty focusing and maintaining their attention on the task at hand or what is being communicated to them may be experiencing **delirium**. Delirium is somewhat common in a hospital patient who is critically ill, has been removed from their normal environment and routine, and is dealing with potential adverse side effects of medications. Delirium, unlike dementia, is reversible in most cases.

Medications that have a high risk for the development of delirium in the patient taking them include opioids, psychoactive drugs, and anticholinergics. There are many conditions that may cause delirium, such as infections, dehydration, dementia, stroke, and traumatic brain injury, among many others.

Treatment of delirium depends on the underlying cause. If it is the adverse side effect of a medication, adjustment of the dose or cessation of its administration may be in order. A dose of lorazepam, a type of benzodiazepine, may be helpful in relieving delirium when alcohol withdrawal is the primary cause.

Dementia

Dementia is a general term used to describe a state of general cognitive decline. Although Alzheimer's disease accounts for up to 80 percent of all cases of dementia in the United States, the remaining two million cases may result from any one of several additional causes. The destruction of cortical tissue resulting from a stroke, or more commonly from multiple small strokes, often results in altered cognitive and physical function, while repetitive head injuries over an extended period also potentially result in permanent damage, limiting normal brain activity. Less common causes of dementia include infection of the brain by prions (abnormal protein fragments) as in Creutzfeldt-Jakob disease or the human immunodeficiency virus (HIV) as in AIDS, deposition of Lewy bodies in the cerebral cortex as in Parkinson's disease, and reversible conditions such as vitamin B-12 deficiency and altered function of the thyroid gland. The onset and progression of the disease relate to the underlying cause and associated patient comorbidities.

Alzheimer's Disease

Alzheimer's disease is a chronic progressive form of dementia with an insidious onset that is caused by the abnormal accumulation of amyloid-β plaque in the brain. The accumulation of this plaque eventually interferes with neural functioning, and is responsible for the progressive manifestations of the disease. Although the exact etiology is unknown, environmental toxins, vascular alterations due to hemorrhagic or embolic events, infections, and genetic factors have all been proposed as the triggering mechanism for the plaque formation. The progression of the disease and the associated manifestations are specific to the individual; however, in all individuals, there is measurable decline over time in cognitive functioning, including short-term and long-term memory, behavior and mood, and the ability to perform activities of daily living (ADLs).

The diagnosis is based on the patient's presenting history and manifestations, imaging studies of the brain, protein analysis of the cerebrospinal fluid (CSF), and cognitive assessment with measures such as the Mini-Mental State Exam. Current treatments are only supportive, although cholinesterase inhibitors and N Methyl D aspartate receptor antagonists may slow the progression of the manifestations for a limited period if administered early in the course of the disease. All patients will suffer an eventual decline in all aspects of cognitive functioning, with the average survival rate dependent on the presence of comorbidities and the level of care and support available to the patient.

Experiencing a fall with or without a resulting fracture, somatic illnesses, and caregiver strain are the most common reasons for health care visits in this population. The nursing care of the patient with Alzheimer's disease in the progressive care facilities must focus on patient safety because the usual chaotic environment of the department is disorienting to the confused patient. Safeguards against increased confusion and wandering, which is a common behavior in this patient population, should be implemented. In addition, the entire family unit should be assessed by the interdisciplinary health team to identify any alterations of family process or additional resources that are required for adequate patient care after discharge.

Agitation

Agitation is a heightened emotional state where an individual demonstrates distress through increased physical activity or verbal communication. Agitation can be brought on by a multitude of psychological and medical factors, whether preexisting or not. Agitated patients are common in many working medical environments. Therefore, knowing how to identify and treat agitation is paramount. Nervousness and anxiety are common signs of agitation in patients. When a critically ill patient demonstrates unusually high agitation, it may indicate signs of mental disturbance.

A recommended agitation scale is the **Behavioral Activity Rating Scale** (BARS). It's straightforward in its utilization, only requiring observation. Patients are scored on a scale of 1-7.

1. There is difficulty waking the patient.
2. The patient is sleeping but responds to stimuli.
3. The patient is asleep or sedated.
4. The patient shows no signs of increased activity.
5. The patient reciprocates communication and is exhibiting an increase in activity.
6. The patient is unrestrained but exhibits heightened activity.
7. The patient is restrained due to prior acts of violence and aggression.

Agitation can occur due to an untreated medical disorder, change in health, withdrawal from medication, intoxication, and much more. It's crucial to understand the cause of a patient's agitation, as it makes it easier to treat and resolve it. For example, if a patient's agitation is caused by a disturbance in their mental health, their current treatment plan should be evaluated for adjustments.

If pharmacological agents are necessary for the treatment of agitation, one of the following three classes will likely be used. **First-generation antipsychotics**, such as Haldol, work by inhibiting dopamine transmission to the brain, which has a calming effect on the patient. Second-generation antipsychotics, formally called **atypical antipsychotics**, are serotonin-dopamine antagonists, and are less likely than first-generation antipsychotics to cause extrapyramidal motor control issues. Benzodiazepines act on GABA receptors to reduce anxiety, relax muscles, produce a sedative effect, and can be used as an anticonvulsant. A last resort for a severely agitated patient is the use of physical restraints which require a physician order and must meet strict hospital protocols.

Disruptive Behaviors, Aggression, Violence

Progressive care nurses may encounter patients who exhibit disruptive behaviors, aggression, and violence. Patients may be situationally upset, or may have an underlying behavioral or mood disorder. For example, people with **antisocial personality disorders** (ASPD) show no signs of empathy. They have no awareness of how others perceive them, how to interact with others, or how to anticipate their feelings or reactions. To people without empathy, the feelings and emotions of others are not a factor in decision-making, which can lead a spectrum of behaviors that range from social awkwardness to acts of cruelty and negligence. Antisocial actions are what cause many people with antisocial behaviors to break the law or hurt others. There may be a disregard for the truth in pursuit of entertainment or personal gain, usually as a kind of manipulation. Lack of empathy makes it difficult for those with ASPD to contemplate why moral standards constructed for other people are applicable to them. Those with ASPD often lie repeatedly and consistently for personal satisfaction alone.

ASPD involves aggression that stems from poor impulse control, also known as **reactive aggression**. People diagnosed with ASPD have a predisposition to hostile intention bias. Individuals are more likely to anticipate and expect the worst from others, making them more prone to reactive outbreaks of aggression. Unlike reactive aggression, **instrumental aggression** involves an individual leveraging their aggression as a tool.

A study in 2009 found that people with ASPD have very strong rapid-response impulsivity but the same level of impulse control as non-sufferers when it came to future planning. There is a strong need to be independent, to resist being controlled by others, who are usually held in contempt. There is a willingness to use untamed aggression to back up the need for control or independence. The antisocial personality usually presents in a friendly, sociable manner, but that friendliness is always accompanied by a baseline position of detachment. There is a total lack of investment in the comfort of others, a complete focus on their own feelings and complete lack of remorse. It is very common that the person with ASPD is not the one who seeks help; often friends, families, or intimate partners attempt to get a diagnosis.

If the patient is officially diagnosed, they may be prescribed cognitive-behavioral therapy, mood stabilizers, and antidepressants. ASPD often comes with accompanying diagnoses of substance abuse disorder, borderline personality disorder, narcissistic personality disorder, and conduct disorder.

When patients are acting violently or aggressively (whether due to ASPQ or otherwise), they may require the use of restraints. **Restraints** can be defined as anything that is used, done, or said to intentionally limits a person's ability to move freely. Restraints, when applied properly, cannot be easily removed or controlled by the person. In addition to physical form, restraints can also be emotional, chemical, or environmental. Use of restraints is very controversial due to the ethical issue of personal freedom. These are a temporary solution to a problem and must always be used as a last resort. Restraints are used to limit a patient's movement to prevent injury to themselves or others, and they always require a physician's order.

Types of restraints include:

- Physical: vests, wrist restraints, straps, or anything that confines the body
- Emotional: verbal cues or emotions used to coerce the patient to act a certain way
- Environmental: side rails, locked doors, closed windows, locked beds
- Chemical: any medication used to restrict a patient's movement

The medical doctor or practitioner is responsible for ordering the use of restraints. Nurses and caregivers are responsible for applying restraints safely and for the management of a patient with a restraint. After an order is given, the physician must visit the patient within twenty-four hours of placing the order to assess its further necessity.

Other methods must be tried before restraints. They include:

- Talking with the patient about being cooperative
- Using distractions such as television, music, knitting, and folding towels or cloths
- Placing the patient within view of a caregiver, such as near the main desk
- Having someone sit with the patient
- Moving the patient to a quiet area
- Ensuring that the patient's bathroom needs are being met
- Ensuring personal items are within reach

Each facility will have a specific protocol that must be followed for restraint use. Circumstances under which restraints are used include:

- Signs of patient aggression toward self, staff, or other patients
- Interference with important medical devices, such as an IV or a catheter
- Patient movements that are potentially harmful to their health, or may cause further injury
- Potential for a patient to interfere with a procedure

The following guidelines should be used whenever applying restraints:

- Always follow the facility's restraint policy.
- Obtain an order from a physician or medical practitioner unless it is an emergency situation.
- Obtain consent from the patient or from next of kin if the patient is not capable of understanding.
- Explain to the patient what is going to happen, even if the patient is unable to understand due to confusion or dementia.
- Always monitor the patient per facility policy—check the positioning of the restraint every thirty minutes and remove every two hours for range of motion. Remember to reposition the patient and offer toileting every two hours.
- Explain the need for restraints and how long the restraints will be used.

Vests have holes for the arms and the opening crosses in the back. The straps will be secured on either side of the bed or chair, depending on the patient's location. Tie it in a quick-release knot to a lower part of the bed that does not move. Make sure that two fingers fit underneath the vest on the patient's chest so that it is not too tight.

Wrist or ankle restraints are cloths that wrap around each wrist or ankle. They have a strap that is tied to a lower, immovable part of the bed or chair. Tie it in a quick-release knot. Ensure the restraints aren't too tight and that the patient's arms or legs aren't in an awkward position. Usually a pillow will be placed under the arms and/or the knees and heels.

If restraints aren't used correctly or are used for the wrong reasons, the patient's family can take legal action against the facility. A patient in restraints becomes completely vulnerable and may feel helpless. They are at a greater risk of sexual abuse, elder abuse, psychological abuse, or violence from other patients.

Possible injuries from restraints can include:

- Broken bones
- Bruises
- Falls
- Skin tears or pressure sores
- Depression or fear due to lack of freedom
- Death from strangulation

Psychological Disorders

Anxiety Disorders

Anxiety and panic attacks are characterized by extreme, sudden, and often unpredictable feelings of paralyzing fear, nervousness, and discomfort. These situations are often debilitating for the individual experiencing them, with some reporting symptoms such as chest pain, the inability to breathe, and feeling a sense of impending death. Other common symptoms include overwhelming dizziness, nausea, sweating, trembling, accelerated heart rate, and feelings of "checking out" from reality. For a true medical diagnosis, four or more of these symptoms must be present. Typically, these episodes can last anywhere from 10 minutes to over an hour. Individuals who experience an anxiety or panic attack for the first time may be unfamiliar with the event, and it can warrant a trip to the healthcare facility. Consequently, it is important for nurses to know how to address these situations to help the patient to receive proper, adequate, and cost-efficient treatment in the future. It is important to show support and compassion toward the patient's feelings, even if the patient's fears seem irrational.

For recurrent anxiety and panic attacks, medication and/or psychotherapy is often needed to support the patient's quality of life. Selective serotonin reuptake inhibitors (SSRIs) are often prescribed to help manage anxiety symptoms. Brand names include Prozac®, Zoloft®, Paxil®, and Lexapro®.

Depression

Depression is characterized by feelings of lethargy; hopelessness; an inability to derive pleasure from once pleasurable activities; problems with sleep, eating, and substances; and/or sexual dysfunction that lasts longer than two weeks. It can be caused by genetics, an imbalance of neurochemicals, or situational contexts. Depression often presents differently in men, women, children, and older adults. Men tend to exhibit increased anger and irritability, while women tend to feel sad, worthless, and guilty. Women tend to internalize symptoms and experience depression at a higher rate and frequency than men due to unique societal issues, hormonal changes, and other factors. Children present symptoms of depression through isolation, anxiety, or acting out. Older adults are more prone to hide symptoms of depression, attribute the feelings to another health problem, or be taken less seriously than other age demographics. It should be noted that these are generalizations and not hard rules.

Depression is usually managed through psychotherapy and sometimes medication. Common medications to treat depression include SSRIs, similar to those used to treat anxiety. Depression can also be treated with serotonin and norepinephrine reuptake inhibitors, such as the brand names Cymbalta® and Effexor®. When these options don't work, tricyclic antidepressants may be prescribed. It is uncertain how tricyclic antidepressants work, and they tend to have more intense side effects, so they are usually not prescribed unless other options have been exhausted. Even with medication, some periods of depression can become so intense and unmanageable that they place the individual in a crisis or suicidal mode. In this context, emergency services are usually needed. It is important to show the depressed patient reassurance, comfort, and support, including directly asking the patient what would help comfort and support him or her during this time. Noting verbal and nonverbal communication will help determine if the patient is at risk for suicide and how severe that risk might be.

Bipolar Disorder

Bipolar disorder is characterized by extremes in mood, energy, and functioning. The individual tends to experience manic periods, marked by highly energetic, almost frenzied behaviors and excitable moods, as well as depressive periods, marked by lethargy, sadness, and isolation. Clinically, manic periods must last at least a week and depressive periods at least two weeks for an individual to be diagnosed with bipolar disorder. Bipolar is a brain disorder that may be caused by physiological distinctions in the brain or genetics. It is often treated with mood-stabilizing medications in conjunction with psychotherapy. Common medications to manage symptoms of bipolar disorder include lithium and brand names such as Depakote®.

Due to the nature of the disorder, the extremes experienced by an individual with bipolar disorder can result in a trip to the emergency department or other acute care facility. Individuals experiencing a manic period are at risk of engaging in impulsive behaviors such as drug abuse, violence, unsafe sexual encounters, and following through with suicidal thoughts. Individuals experiencing a depressive period are also at risk of having suicidal thoughts or tendencies due to a marked increase in feelings of hopelessness. Individuals with bipolar disorder can also experience periods of psychosis and have delusions or hallucinations. Nurses should be prepared to show sympathy and compassion while still being firm and direct with the patient. Patient behavior will likely be unpredictable, especially if he or she is in a manic phase. Nurses may need to use these interactions to deduce the risk factors a patient has for bipolar disorder so they can deliver effective treatment.

Substance Abuse

Substance abuse is defined, most simply, as extreme use of a drug. Abuse occurs for many reasons, such as mental health instability, inability to cope with everyday life stressors, the loss of a loved one, or enjoyment of the euphoric state that the overindulgence in a substance causes. Abused substances create some type of intoxication that alters decision-making, awareness, attentiveness, or physical impulses.

Substance abuse results in tolerance, withdrawal, and compulsive drug-taking behavior. **Tolerance** occurs when increased amounts of the substance are needed to achieve the desired effects. **Withdrawal** manifests as physiological and substance-specific cognitive symptoms (e.g., cold sweats, shivering, nausea, vomiting, paranoia, hallucinations). Withdrawal not only happens when an individual stops abusing the substance, but also occurs when he or she attempts to reduce the amount taken in an effort to stop using altogether.

Alcohol Withdrawal

Withdrawal syndrome, also known as **discontinuation syndrome**, commonly manifests as anxiety, irritability, insomnia, and decreased attention span. It is defined as the occurrence of a substance-specific condition that follows the termination of, or decline in, the consumption of a psychoactive element that the individual habitually abused.

Signs and symptoms of withdrawal syndrome, as well as management and treatment, are predicated upon the type of substance that was discontinued. The progressive care nurse must collect a comprehensive history and physical to determine the type of drug, amount and duration used, time of last ingestion, reason for the current cessation, alternative therapies used to manage withdrawal symptoms, and baseline vital signs. He or she must also remove unnecessary items from the environment, provide a quiet and calm atmosphere with minimal stimuli, maintain patient orientation (to person, place, and time), ensure patient safety by implementing seizure precautions, initiate security devices if necessary and as prescribed (verbal or written order by physician) to prevent the individual from harming himself/herself and others, and administer medications, as advised, to lessen withdrawal symptoms.

Physical dependence on alcohol is a biological need for alcohol in order to avoid physical withdrawal symptoms, which include anxiety, erratic pulse rate, tremors, seizures, and hallucinations. In its most serious form, withdrawal combined with malnourishment can lead to a potentially fatal condition known as **delirium tremens** (DTs), which is a psychotic disorder that involves tremors, disorientation, and hallucinations.

An interesting facet of the delirium tremens presentation is the interruption of normal vestibular function. The patient will think the floor is moving, the room is rotating, and the walls are falling down.

A classic symptom of a patient in alcohol withdrawal is tremoring of the hands. Patients in withdrawal are prone to self-injury because of ataxia. **Ataxia** means difficulty controlling body movements.

IV benzodiazepines, such as diazepam, are helpful in treating delirium tremens. Other medications used to treat withdrawal may include phenytoin to treat and prevent seizure activity, and IV thiamine to prevent Wernicke-Korsakoff syndrome, which includes Wernicke's encephalopathy and Korsakoff's psychosis.

Patients presenting with mild alcohol withdrawal may be treated on an outpatient basis, provided that no comorbidities require the individual to be admitted as an inpatient. Moderate or severe alcohol withdrawal, along with the presence of DTs, requires hospitalization and possible ICU admission. This is because the mortality rate from severe alcohol withdrawal with DTs has been as extreme as 20 percent if left untreated. Sedatives are the chief medications for treatment of alcohol withdrawal syndrome because they are cross-tolerant drugs that modulate GABA (Gamma-Aminobutyric Acid) function. GABA receptors are the major inhibitory neurotransmitter receptors in the brain. These drugs commonly consist of benzodiazepines and barbiturates.

Chronic Alcohol Abuse

Some individuals feel the need to have a drink to relax and calm down, as it is a central nervous system (CNS) depressant, which tends to soothe individuals and lower inhibitions. However, it also slurs speech and impairs muscle control, coordination, and reflex time. Alcohol abuse can cause cirrhosis of the liver; liver, esophagus, and stomach cancers; heart enlargement; chronic inflammation of the pancreas; vitamin deficiencies; certain anemias; and brain damage.

Chronic Tobacco Abuse

People abuse tobacco either in cigarette, cigar, pipe, or snuff form. People report many reasons for tobacco use, including a calming effect, suppression of appetite, and relief of depression. The primary addictive component in tobacco is nicotine, but tobacco smoke also contains about seven hundred carcinogens (cancer-causing agents) that may result in lung and throat cancers as well as heart disease, emphysema, peptic ulcer disease, and stroke. Withdrawal indicators include insomnia, irritability, overwhelming nicotine craving, anxiety, and depression.

Marijuana

Marijuana is considered the most frequently abused illicit drug in the United States. General effects of marijuana use include pleasure, relaxation, and weakened dexterity and memory. The active addictive ingredient in marijuana is tetrahydrocannabinol (THC). It is normally smoked (but can be eaten), and its smoke has more carcinogens than that of tobacco. The individual withdrawing from marijuana will experience increased irritability and anxiety.

Cocaine

Cocaine is a stimulant that is also known as coke, snow, or rock. It can be smoked, injected, snorted, or swallowed. Reported effects include pleasure, enhanced alertness, and increased energy. Both temporary and prolonged use have been known to contribute to damage to the brain, heart, lungs, and kidneys. Withdrawal symptoms include severe depression and reduced energy.

Heroin

Heroin is also known as smack and horse, and its use continues to increase. Effects of heroin abuse include pleasure, slower respirations, and drowsiness. Overdose and/or overuse of heroin can cause respiratory depression, resulting in death. Use of heroin as an injectable substance can lead to other complications such as heart valve damage, tetanus, botulism, hepatitis B, or human immunodeficiency virus (HIV)/AIDS infection from sharing dirty needles. Withdrawal is usually intense and presents as vomiting, abdominal cramps, diarrhea, confusion, body aches, and diaphoresis.

Methamphetamines

Methamphetamine is also known as meth, crank, and crystal, and its use continues to increase, especially in the West and Midwest regions of the United States. Methamphetamine is categorized as a stimulant that produces such effects as pleasure, increased alertness, and decreased appetite. Similar to cocaine, it can be snorted, smoked, or injected, and it can be taken orally as well. Like cocaine, it shares many of the same detrimental effects, such as myocardial infarction, hypertension, and stroke. Other prolonged usage effects include paranoia, hallucinations, damage to and loss of dentition, and heart damage. Withdrawal symptoms involve depression, abdominal cramps, and increased appetite.

Nursing interventions for the individual addicted to tobacco, alcohol, and other drugs centers around the prevention of relapse, and treatment depends on the individual and the substance that is abused. Behavioral treatment assists with recognition of abuse triggers, habits, and drug cravings, as well as providing the tactics to help one cope with these issues. A physician may prescribe nicotine patches for the tobacco abuser and methadone or Suboxone to manage withdrawal symptoms and certain drug yearnings.

Drug-Seeking Behavior

When a patient becomes dependent on a substance that causes a disruption in their relationships and physical health, it is called a **substance dependence disorder**. There are several different substances that may cause addiction including alcohol, tobacco, opioids, hallucinogens, stimulants such as cocaine and amphetamines, and sedatives/hypnotics/anxiolytics such as lorazepam. The patient begins to seek these drugs obsessively, always chasing after the next high. These drug-seeking behaviors, including manipulation, lying, and doing whatever it takes to get the substance, destroy relationships and the patient's ability to function normally.

Practice Quiz

1. A progressive care nurse is educating a patient regarding a flu shot before his discharge. He states he had one two years ago. While educating a patient on the importance of the flu vaccine, the nurse advises that the patient get the flu vaccine administered how often?

   a. Once per lifetime
   b. Every six months
   c. Annually
   d. Every two years

2. The nurse is admitting a patient fresh out of the surgical suite following repair of multiple tears and lacerations after being stabbed several times during a gang fight. The nurse knows that which of the following signs signals an improvement in the patient's condition?

   a. Rise in heart rate
   b. Stabilization of blood pressure
   c. Development of fever
   d. Low urine output

3. A patient tells the nurse that his pain is in his abdomen, just below the rib cage and to the right of his stomach. The nurse knows that the patient has reported which component of pain assessment?

   a. Location
   b. Exacerbation
   c. Alleviation
   d. Aggravation

4. What amount of blood loss is considered life-threatening and will throw a patient into hypovolemic shock?

   a. 1/8
   b. 1/7
   c. 1/5
   d. 1/10

5. Which of the following interventions will NOT help prevent a pressure ulcer from occurring in a bedridden patient?

   a. Turning the patient every two hours
   b. Encouraging early mobility
   c. Removing the pillows from the bed
   d. Ensuring proper nutrition

See answers on the next page.

Answer Explanations

1. C: The flu vaccine should be administered every year at the beginning of the flu season. Every year a strain of flu is identified as being the likely culprit for cases of the flu for that year and used in the vaccines, thus everyone six months and older should get their flu shot each and every year. The other answers are invalid.

2. B: Stabilizing the patient's blood pressure is an excellent sign that their condition is improving. Fever, oliguria, and tachycardia are all signs of deterioration and may point toward complications such as shock, bleeding, and/or infection, and need further investigation.

3. A: The patient has reported the location of his pain. Alleviation refers to an action that makes the pain better. Aggravation refers to an action that makes the pain worse. Exacerbation is a particularly intense flare-up of a chronic pain issue.

4. C: Losing 1/5 or twenty percent of one's blood volume will throw a person into hypovolemic shock and is considered life threatening. Organ failure with profound hypotension will likely follow; fluid resuscitation and blood transfusions will be needed as soon as possible.

5. C: Removing the pillows from the bed is not the best option, as these are used to support the patient's limbs and reduce pressure to bony prominences. All the other interventions, including encouraging early mobility, proper nutrition, and turning and repositioning the patient every two hours will help prevent the development of pressure ulcers.

Professional Caring and Ethical Practice

Advocacy

Advocacy

Advocacy is the promotion of the common good, especially as it applies to at-risk populations. It involves speaking out in support of policies and decisions that affect the lives of individuals who do not otherwise have a voice. Nurses meet this standard of practice by actively participating in the politics of healthcare accessibility and delivery because they are educationally and professionally prepared to evaluate and comment on the needs of patients at the local, state, and national level. This participation requires an understanding of the legislative process, the ability to negotiate with public officials, and a willingness to provide expert testimony in support of policy decisions. The advocacy role of nurses addresses the needs of the individual patient as well as the needs of all individuals in the society, and the members of the nursing profession.

In clinical practice, nurses represent the patient's interests by active participation in the development of the plan of care and subsequent care decisions. Advocacy, in this sense, is related to patient autonomy and the patient's right to informed consent and self-determination. Nurses provide the appropriate information, assess the patient's comprehension of the implications of the care decisions, and act as the patient advocates by supporting the patient's decisions. Patient advocacy for acutely ill patients requires the nurse to represent the patient's decisions even though those decisions may be opposed to those of the healthcare providers and family members.

Nurses understand the complex care requirements of patients with multiple comorbidities and are often called upon to intercede on a patient's behalf to facilitate the delivery of adequate and appropriate care in both the acute care setting and the primary care environment. In addition, nurses understand the care needs of the greater community and serve as advocates for the provision of preventative interventions and policies that affect public health. Nurses advocate for increased resources to address the needs of specific community populations, including school-age children. In this way, nurses practice **beneficence**, defined as doing good for another individual, including acting as an advocate, supporting the individual's autonomy, and working to ensure justice. Related to beneficence is the concept of **nonmaleficence**, which means non-harming, or inflicting the least harm possible to reach a beneficial outcome.

Professionally, nurses advocate for policies that support and promote the practice of all nurses with regard to access to education, role identity, workplace conditions, and compensation. The responsibility for professional advocacy requires nurses to provide leadership in the development of the professional nursing role in all practice settings that may include acute care facilities, colleges and universities, or community agencies. Leadership roles in acute care settings involve participation in professional practice and shared governance committees, providing support for basic nursing education by facilitating clinical and preceptorship experiences, and mentoring novice graduate nurses to the professional nursing role. In the academic setting, nurses work to ensure the diversity of the student population by participating in the governance structure of the institution, conducting and publishing research that supports the positive impact of professional nursing care on patient outcomes, and serving as an advocate to individual nursing students to promote their academic success. In the community, nurses assist other nurse-providers to collaborate with government officials to meet the needs that are specific to that location.

The role requirements for advocacy require nurses to maintain clinical expertise through continuing education (formal and informal), to actively follow and comment on legislative initiatives that affect at-risk populations, and to model the professional nursing role in practice.

Moral Agency

The nurse must function as a moral agent. This means that the nurse must be morally accountable and responsible for personal judgment and actions. Moral integrity is doing what is true to your values without compromising them. Nurses often act and conduct their responsibilities as they feel morally correct. **Moral agency** is defined as the ability to identify right and wrong actions based on widely accepted moral criteria. The performance of nurses as moral agents is dependent on life experiences, advanced education, and clinical experience in healthcare agencies. Moral agency can often cause cognitive dissonance in nurses as some decisions go against their training and beliefs. However, as nurses undertake more responsibilities, they need to be able to address ethical dilemmas without deemphasizing care.

The role of moral agent requires nurses to have a strong sense of self and a clear understanding of the definition of right and wrong; however, nurses must also be aware that these perceptions of right and wrong will be challenged every day. In reality, nurses who act as the moral agents and are accountable for right and wrong decisions commonly encounter situations where the correct and moral action related to the patient's right to self-determination is opposed to the right and moral action with respect to competent patient care.

Caring Practices

Models of Caring

There are several models that were created to define the art and science of nursing, which is different from the practice of medicine, even though nurses expertly use assessment, diagnosing, planning, intervention, and evaluation to provide holistic care for all patients. Caring is the most commonly identified characteristic of nursing care and it is the central concept of most nursing models. One such framework is the **6 C's of Caring** model that was proposed to define the unique characteristics of nursing practice that distinguish nursing from the remaining patient care disciplines. These personal attributes shape the skilled nursing practice of nurses.

In the 6 C's of Caring model, **compassion** is defined as being in a state of empathy with another individual, especially with regard to pain and suffering. **Competence** requires the active pursuit of knowledge and it is demonstrated by nurses' performance in each domain of learning, including the psychomotor, cognitive, and affective domains. The **conscience** directs nurses' moral and ethical decisions and prompts a response to instances of injustice. **Confidence** is a direct reflection of nurses' trust in their own ability to provide appropriate care for all assigned patients. Confidence is gained through formal and informal education, clinical experience, and life experience. It is evident in all aspects of the nurses' professional practice, including the clinical environment and the community. **Commitment** is the pursuit of excellence in all areas of professional nursing practice, including direct patient care, promotion of the profession, personal enrichment through education, mentoring of novice nurses, and support of public health initiatives at all levels of government. **Comportment** refers to all aspects of nurses' professional behavior in the clinical setting and the community.

While the 6 C's model is used to define nursing as a caring profession, the **Synergy Model** proposes a novel paradigm for nursing that considers patients' specific needs as the driving force in health care. Nursing is viewed as a coordinated, competence-based response to such needs rather than as a series of tasks that may or may not satisfy them. The model is based on the following assumptions: the patient is viewed holistically with attention to the mind, body, and spirit dimensions; the patient, the family, and the community all contribute context to the nurse–patient relationship; characteristics of either the patient or the nurse cannot be viewed in isolation because they are interrelated; and the goal of nursing is the return of the patient to the optimal level of wellness as defined by the patient. Death is considered an acceptable outcome of care to all nurses, but to different degrees according to their experience level. Novice, or level 1 nurses, understand that the patient's death is a possibility, yet they do not comprehend that the death is inevitable or acceptable. Experienced, or level 2 nurses, know from interacting with the patient and family, and from expert assessment of the patient's progress, that death may be an acceptable outcome. Expert, or level 3 nurses, recognize death as an acceptable outcome, and demonstrate skills in managing end-of-life care. They create care plans to manage patient death in the best way possible, to the benefit of the patient and the family.

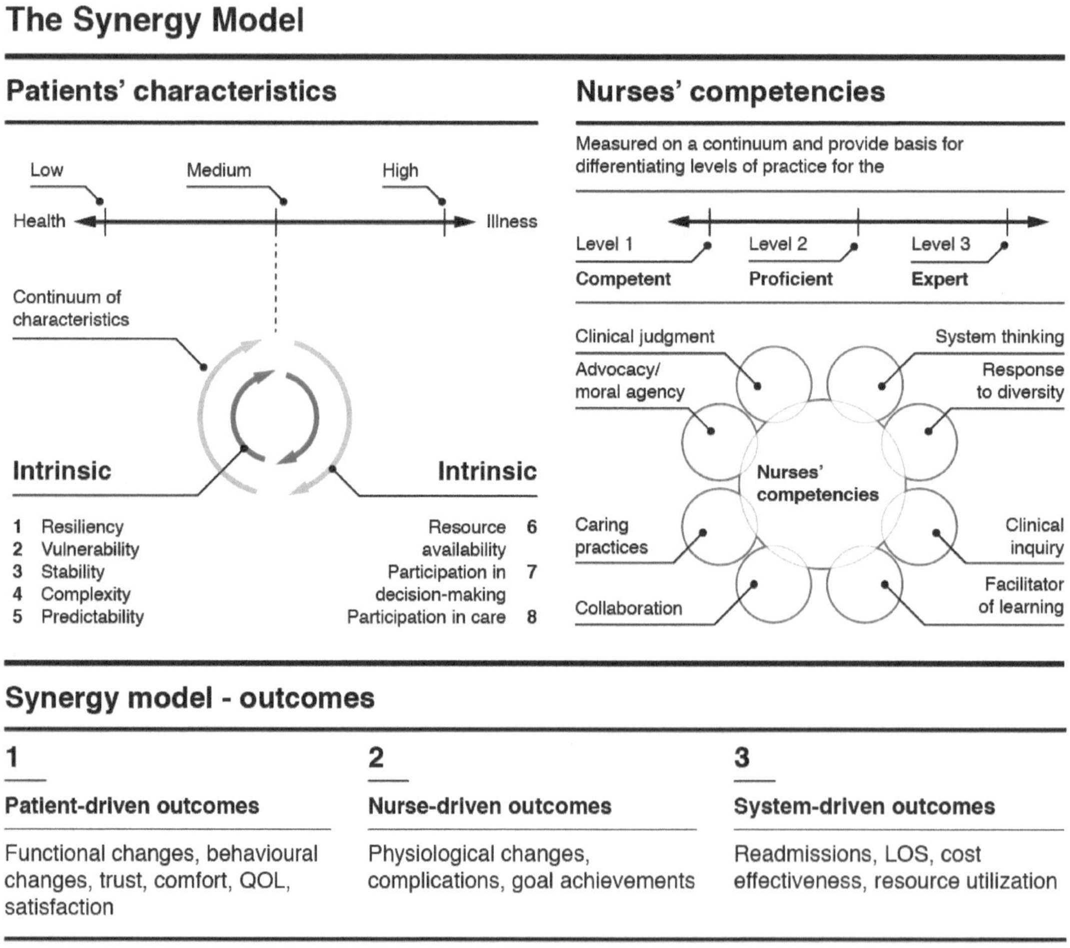

Caring practices are identified as one of the eight nursing competencies in the Synergy Model. Nurses establish and maintain a therapeutic patient-care environment, based on consideration of the needs of the patient and the family, that promotes healing and minimizes discomfort and stress. The model identifies vigilance and engagement as essential elements of the caring practices. **Vigilance** as a caring skill is viewed on a continuum according to the ability of nurses to recognize and respond to patient needs. Novice nurses are capable of responding to usual and predictable changes in the patient's condition; however, responding to more subtle cues requires an increased level of clinical competence, and preventing any potential hazards requires even greater nursing skill. **Engagement** in the nurse–patient relationship refers to the degree to which nurses commit to the nurse–patient relationship. Researchers note that favorable patient outcomes are associated with the degree of caregiver engagement; however, there is also evidence that the incidence of burnout in experienced nurses is related to the degree of their engagement in patient care. The third attribute of the caring practices is **responsiveness**, which means that the reaction of the patient's family, the healthcare institution, and the nursing staff will all have an effect on the patient's progress.

Ethical Dilemmas

Healthcare providers routinely face situations with patients where they must analyze various moral and ethical considerations. In acute settings, where quick judgment and action is necessary to care and where patients are often not fully sound in body or mind, ethical dilemmas can arise without much time to process resolutions.

The AACN Certification Corporation adheres to an established **Code of Ethics**, which states moral and ethical guidelines that nurses should incorporate into their practice. Above all else, nurses have the responsibility to do no harm while advocating for, promoting good health outcomes for, minimizing injury to, and protecting the overall health and functioning of their patients. It is important to consider the patient holistically when applying these values, such as considering what the patient may view as a good quality of life, what family values the patient holds, other family members that may be affected (such as a spouse or children), legal considerations, and logistical considerations (such as how much time and medical resources are available). When patients are unable to make decisions autonomously, or even to indicate consent to treatment (as can be common in emergency cases), nurses should act from these responsibilities to make wise and compassionate decisions on the patients' behalf.

Dilemmas that can arise for nursing staff include situations where the patient may have cultural or personal beliefs that prevent lifesaving treatment. For example, a female patient may not want to be treated by any male staff, or a patient that needs a blood transfusion may not accept this procedure due to religious beliefs. In cases where the patient is able to directly communicate their wishes, the nurse may need to defer to the patient's wishes in order to preserve the patient's autonomy. This may mean providing alternative means of care (such as finding available female medical providers to assist with the female patient that does not want to be treated by male staff). It may mean withholding treatment that the patient refuses. If the patient's life is in question and rapid medical action is necessary to save the patient's life, nursing staff may need to intervene even if it is against the patient's wishes. Ethical considerations like these will vary by case and patient, and will depend on the severity of the case, the medical and personal history of the patient, and the judgment of the nurse in question. In all cases, it is ideal if the nurse and patient are able to communicate openly with each other about the case and potential medical options, and hope that the resolution is able to be for the greatest good.

Response to Diversity

Characteristics of diversity include, but are not limited to, ethnicity, race, gender, religious preference, age, lifestyle, and values. According to the Synergy Model, patient needs and characteristics must be "linked" to nursing competencies to achieve maximum health. Nurses are aware that unmet cultural or diversity needs and preferences can adversely affect patient outcomes in much the same way that somatic illness affects outcomes; therefore, cultural sensitivity is an essential nurse competency. The development of cultural sensitivity and demonstrated appreciation of diversity by nurses is also viewed as a continuum in the Synergy Model. Novice nurses, who are learning to negotiate the institutional environment, may assess the patient's preferences but often continue to provide care that is consistent with their own belief system. As competent nurses gain life and clinical experience, they actively question patients to learn about and accommodate the traditions and customs of a diverse population, while helping the patient and family to understand the culture of the institution. Expert nurses are able to anticipate the needs of the patient and family by integrating cultural differences into the plan of care whenever possible. All of these nursing interventions work to alleviate the stress related to the acute care environment.

Research indicates that diversity in the workplace strengthens the workgroup by allowing consideration of multiple worldviews and a better understanding of the patient population served by the institution. Multiple viewpoints can also be an advantage in conflict resolution, especially when the conflict is related to diversity issues. The Synergy Model suggests that nurses become more sensitive to diversity issues with experience and that this sensitivity is applicable to the work environment as well as direct patient care. Attention to diversity issues also, however, requires institutional support for resource allocation and management. Depending on the specific needs of the patient population, services such as foreign language interpreters, appropriate food service, counseling services, and accommodation for religious observances must be considered. To optimize patient care, expert nurses assess the needs of the patient and family, and provide access to the appropriate institutional resources.

The most significant threat to success in this process is **ethnocentrism**, which means that group members are unable to consider views that are contrary to their own beliefs. Alternative definitions in the literature view ethnocentrism as possessing false assumptions about another culture, which assumes that ethnocentric behavior is based on incorrect or incomplete information about other traditions and practices. Attention to diversity issues requires that providers proceed on the assumption that ethnocentrism is a universal human characteristic that must be addressed by the provision of appropriate information and instruction. In addition to understanding their own cultural views, nurses must be aware that many patients have preconceived views of "westerners" and our cultural norms, which may or may not be accurate, but can potentially affect the nurse–patient relationship. The resolution of ethnocentrism in a caring relationship requires acknowledgment of its existence and education as to the meaning of the traditions and practices.

Cultural Considerations

Patients will come from all backgrounds and cultures, and medical providers should be aware of the different cultural needs that may present themselves in a healthcare setting. **Culture** can encompass anything from a person's geographical location, race, ethnicity, age, socioeconomic status, and religious beliefs that influence the behaviors, traditions, and rituals that he or she chooses to engage in each day. It is important to note that cultural considerations will present themselves daily. Some patients may be unable to speak English and will need interpretive services. Some patients may request that only same-sex providers treat them. Some patients may need to keep culturally valuable adornments in place that could interfere with treatment (i.e., a metal symbol on a patient that needs magnetic resonance imaging, a procedure where metal poses an extreme danger). Respecting and attending to different cultural needs will provide the patient with a better healthcare experience, lead to increased patient satisfaction, and impact overall health outcomes (as patients will be more likely to seek out care if they feel comfortable doing so).

Medical providers can show that they consider cultural differences by kindly and compassionately asking patients to share cultural viewpoints, to share aspects of the medical system and services that make them comfortable or uncomfortable, and to continuously create rapport that allows the patient to feel comfortable in voicing their concerns. Medical providers should be mindful of any preconceived notions that they hold of certain cultures, and if possible, actively work to dispel these. Medical providers should also be mindful to not make presumptions, even if those presumptions come from an intention to be empathetic. For example, a patient who looks to be of Asian descent may have been born and raised in the United States and not identify well with any part of Asian culture. Finally, many healthcare organizations offer internal trainings that cover cultural considerations and cultural diversity. For staff that feel their knowledge and experience is limited in this aspect, these trainings can provide an avenue for personal and professional growth.

Having a diverse staff can be extremely beneficial when servicing a patient demographic that encompasses many cultures. Having a medical provider who is able to relate directly with a patient's culture can make the patient feel more comfortable and open. Additionally, a diverse staff can overcome common obstacles such as language barriers or lack of patient education. In this regard, healthcare organizations and nursing leadership should work to actively recruit a diverse workforce.

Multicultural, Spiritual, and Religious Factors That May Affect the Client's Health Status

Multiculturalism is an integral aspect of culture in the United States, which comprises people from many countries and cultures, often speaking different languages. When it comes to nursing care, each client will come from a different cultural and religious background. This can lead to many challenges, such as language barriers, or more subtle but complex differences. Both the client and the nurse will have their own cultural and religious biases and beliefs that will influence the way they look at treatment.

One aspect of multiculturalism is that cultures can be **individualistic** or **collectivist**, which will play a part in how the client views health and healthcare. In individualistic societies, decisions are made by the individual and things like privacy and independence are valued. On the other hand, in a collectivist society, decisions related to health may be a community responsibility, and the assumption will be that the whole family will be involved in a client's treatment. This may not only involve the family but also the spiritual or religious community as well. While upholding ethical guidelines around confidentiality and privacy, a progressive care nurse must also respect the culture that the client comes from and involve the community as much or as little as the client desires.

There are many things that are affected by spiritual, religious, and cultural beliefs. First, it is beneficial to describe the difference between spirituality and religion. Spirituality is a client's belief in the operation of a higher self and/or higher components of the universe. A spiritual client may not profess a certain religion, but may engage in practices such as yoga or meditation. On the other hand, religion is a profession of belief in a God(s) or divine being and a belief in a higher order that controls the universe. Religious clients often identify by the title of the doctrine they subscribed to.

Consequently, it is important for the progressive care nurse to be aware of differing practices such as cupping, candling, acupuncture, refusal to accept blood transfusions, and dietary restrictions that could be confused with abuse or neglect when compared against traditional Western American culture. Traditional medicines of the client's culture or medical practices of that culture may be preferred over what doctors recommend. Moreover, there are gender roles that may affect the nature of the relationship with the client and the services provided. For example, there may be a gender preference with a doctor or the client may opt out of medical care altogether when in the presence of an opposite-sex provider. Different cultures also have different views of doctors: some are held in such high esteem that they will never be questioned, even if a client is confused or in disagreement. In addition, the client's view of death and what happens after death may play a large role in decisions that are made and will be particularly significant in palliative and hospice care.

Being culturally competent is a necessity for every nurse. **Cultural competency** refers to the ability to understand, accept, and respect a client's culture and religion, while recognizing one's own cultural and religious biases. Nurses cannot assume that every client will share the same cultural and ideological beliefs, but must view every single client as different and coming from a unique cultural background. One obvious aspect of cultural competence is to ensure that there are no language or communication barriers, and if needed, that a translator or another nurse is available. It is also important for the nurse to understand, recognize, and support the client's specific cultural and religious beliefs. This is done by asking questions and learning everything possible about their culture. Diversity should not be feared or avoided, but embraced and affirmed by the progressive care nurse. Educate and inform the client about treatment options while acknowledging and respecting their beliefs, if they are different.

Facilitation of Learning

Facilitation of learning refers to the process of assessing the learning needs of the patient and family, the nursing staff, and caregivers in the community, and creating, implementing, and evaluating formal and informal educational programs to address those needs. Novice nurses often view patient care and patient education as separate entities; however, experienced nurses are able to integrate the patient's educational needs into the plan of care. Nurses are aware that the patient often requires continued reinforcement of the educational plan after discharge, which necessitates coordination with home care services.

As facilitators of learning, nurses may be involved in a large-scale effort to educate all patients over 65 admitted to the nursing unit about the need for both Prevnar 13 and Pneumovax 23 to prevent pneumonia. In contrast, nurses may provide one-on-one instruction for a patient recently diagnosed with diabetes. The first step of any teaching-learning initiative is the assessment of the learning needs of the participants. Specific needs that will influence the design and content of the educational offering include the language preference and reading level of the participants. In addition, nurses must consider the effect of certain patient characteristics identified in the Synergy Model on the patient's capacity to process information. Diminished resiliency or stability, and extreme complexity, must be considered in the development of the educational plan. Nurses are also responsible for creating a "bridge" between teaching-learning in the acute care setting and the home environment. A detailed discharge plan, close coordination with outpatient providers, and follow-up phone calls to the patient may be used to reinforce the patient's knowledge of the plan of care.

Successful learning plans for staff members and colleagues also consider the motivation of the participants to engage in the process. Successful facilitators include a variety of teaching strategies to develop the content and evaluate learning, in order to address adult learning needs and preferences such as preferred language and reading level. Research indicates that when adults do not have a vested interest in the outcomes of the teaching/learning process, they may not participate as active learners.

The remaining element of successful facilitation of learning to be considered is the availability and quality of learning resources. There is evidence that individuals with different learning styles respond differently to various learning devices. For instance, visual learners may be attracted to digital tools such as the iPad that can create interactive educational plans, which include self-study options for the patient. The minimum requirements for successful facilitation of learning include the skilled staff to develop the educational materials, paper, a copy machine, and staff to interact with the patient in the learning session.

Barriers to the facilitation of learning must be anticipated and accommodated. Changes in the patient's condition commonly require reduction in the time spent in each learning session due to fatigue. Cognitive impairment can impede comprehension and retention of the information and will require appropriate teaching aids. The learning abilities of the patient's family members must also be assessed. Adequate instruction time might be the greatest barrier. Learning needs are assessed and discharge planning is begun on the day of admission, however, shortened inpatient stays require evaluation of the patient's comprehension of the plan of care.

Lifelong Learning

Since the medical and healthcare fields are always rapidly changing due to technological advances, new research, organizational and governmental regulations, and through continuous process improvements in healthcare delivery, nurses can expect to continue their education throughout the course of their careers. Consequently, the ability to learn new topics will be a necessary skill in order to remain a competent practitioner. Lifelong learning and continuing education are associated with improved patient outcomes, job satisfaction, personal validation and achievement, and obtaining skills that were not taught or available at the time that the nurse was enrolled in a formal education program. The most crucial association with lifelong learning activities is the improvement in quality of care. Incompetent or unaware nursing staff means a great deal of risk for the patient. By constantly striving to improve their knowledge and practical skills, nurses decrease the chance that they will be held liable for negligence or malpractice, and they are taking tangible actions to adhere to the ethical tenets of the healthcare profession.

While avenues to continue professional development in the nursing field may be formal (such as obtaining extra relevant degrees or certifications, publishing research, or enrolling in trainings offered by the nurse's workplace), many opportunities require intrinsic motivation, such as taking personal initiative to keep abreast of current relevant literature, consulting with mentors, or experiencing different responsibilities within the field. However, even with these varied opportunities and with the multitude of personal and professional benefits that engaging in lifelong learning activities bring, there are still some barriers for nurses. These include obstacles like disinterest, lack of time on the job or outside of the job to participate in activities, an inability to balance work and life needs with job demands, and lack of financial resources (to pay for educational activities and/or to take the time off to participate in them). In this regard, it is helpful for leadership and subordinate employees to work together to overcome these barriers.

Nurses who are in positions of leadership can help push for organizational support for development activities, and promote a culture of top-down change and support. In the events that development activities are free or hosted by the nurse's workplace, it is imperative that the nurse realizes this is a valuable opportunity and take the time to attend and fully engage in the experience. This shows that such activities are in demand and valued, and is likely to make affordable and accessible professional development activities part of the workplace culture.

Research

Nursing research is a crucial component of evidence-based practice (EBP), high quality healthcare delivery, and positive patient outcomes. Effective nursing research creates and compiles bodies of knowledge relating to all clinical and non-clinical aspects of nursing. Nurses who play a role in nursing research are typically advanced-level, senior practitioners who have the necessary experience to contribute further to existing bodies of nursing knowledge through personal expertise, the ability to run or be involved in conducting research trials, and in accurately collecting and analyzing data. Nurse researchers typically have advanced educational degrees, such as a master's or doctorate degree, and may work in specialized fields as a nurse practitioner. However, as entry-level nurses spend more time and gain more exposure to different aspects of the field, they should keep in mind that a nurse researcher is a highly skilled and rewarding career path that is critical to the development and advancement of the nursing field. High quality nursing research shapes the scope of clinical education for entry-level and experienced nurses; influences healthcare policy at the local, state, and federal levels; and enhances standard operating procedures within a healthcare organization. Together, these allow for organizations to deliver the highest level of care to patients who need them at the lowest costs.

Nurses who choose to pursue research as a career can expect to become involved in different aspects of research design and the research process. Nurse researchers will need to pass training modules that review the legalities and ethics of working with human populations in research, which is a different avenue than treating patients for disease or injury. Nurse researchers can expect to learn how to write research proposals, which serves as a large component of applying for funding, in addition to becoming familiar with seeking out viable funding sources. Depending on the end goal of the study, nurse researchers may learn how to design objective study trials, collect data through laboratory work or through sample surveys, conduct and interpret statistical data analysis, and write conclusive discussions about their findings.

Upon completion, nurse researchers can expect to be involved in the publication process, where a formal manuscript detailing the design and findings of the research study are submitted to scholarly journals. Journals often require extensive revisions and editing, so nurses should be prepared to follow up with their manuscripts. Most research projects include collaboration with doctorate-level researchers from other disciplines who share a vested interest in the topic or have skills to contribute to the project. For example, health research teams often include a biostatistician whose primary contribution is to compile, analyze, and interpret collected data. Entry-level nurses, interns, or students may choose to assist with simpler, but necessary, tasks such as survey administration or data entry. Recruiting individuals to help with these sorts of tasks can provide a great support to the research team.

The National League for Nursing (NLN) is an organization in the United States that promotes research activities through networking, support, guidelines, and funding. The NLN publishes research priorities every four years. Current priorities include further investigating evidence-based practices, promoting research exposure to student learners in order to set the foundation for health promotion and disease prevention, and evaluating best practices relating to end-of-life and other life transitional care for both patients and their families. The NLN's website, www.nln.org, is an excellent resource for current nurses to find continuing education opportunities and explore research tools to support and enhance their career paths.

Evidence-Based Practice

Evidence-based practice (EBP) is a research-driven and facts-based methodology that allows healthcare providers to make scientifically supported, reliable, and validated decisions in delivering care. EBP takes into account rigorously tested, peer-reviewed, and published research relating to the case, the knowledge and experience of the healthcare provider, and clinical guidelines established by reputable governing bodies. This framework allows healthcare providers to reach case resolutions that result in positive patient outcomes in the most efficient manner, therefore allowing the organization to provide the best care using the least resources.

There are seven steps to successfully utilizing EBP as a methodology in the nursing field. First, the work culture should be one of a "spirit of inquiry." This culture allows staff to ask questions to promote continuous improvement and positive process change to workflow, clinical routines, and non-clinical duties. Second, the **PICOT framework** should be utilized when searching for an effective intervention, or working with a specific interest, in a case. The PICOT framework encourages nurses to develop a specific, measurable, goal-oriented research question that accounts for the patient population and demographics (P) involved in the case, the proposed intervention or issue of interest (I), a relevant comparison (C) group in which a defined outcomes (O) has been positive, and the amount of time (T) needed to implement the intervention or address the issue. Once this question has been developed, staff can move onto the third step, which is to research. In this step, staff will explore reputable sources of literature (such as peer-reviewed scholarly journals, interviews with subject matter experts, or widely accepted textbooks) to find studies and narratives with evidence that supports a resolution for their question.

Once all research has been compiled, it must be thoroughly analyzed. This is the fourth step. This step ensures that the staff is using unbiased research with stringent methodology, statistically significant outcomes, reliable and valid research designs, and that all information collected is actually applicable to their patient. (For example, if a certain treatment worked with statistical significance in a longitudinal study of pediatric patients with a large sample size, and all other influencing variables were controlled for, this treatment may not necessarily work in a middle-aged adult. Therefore, though the research collected is scientifically backed and evidence-based for a pediatric population, it does not support EBP for an older population.) The fifth step is to integrate the evidence to create a treatment or intervention plan for the patient. The sixth step is to monitor the implementation of the treatment or intervention and evaluate whether it was associated with positive health outcomes in the patient. Finally, practitioners have a moral obligation to share the results with colleagues at the organization and across the field, so that it may be best utilized (or not) for other patients.

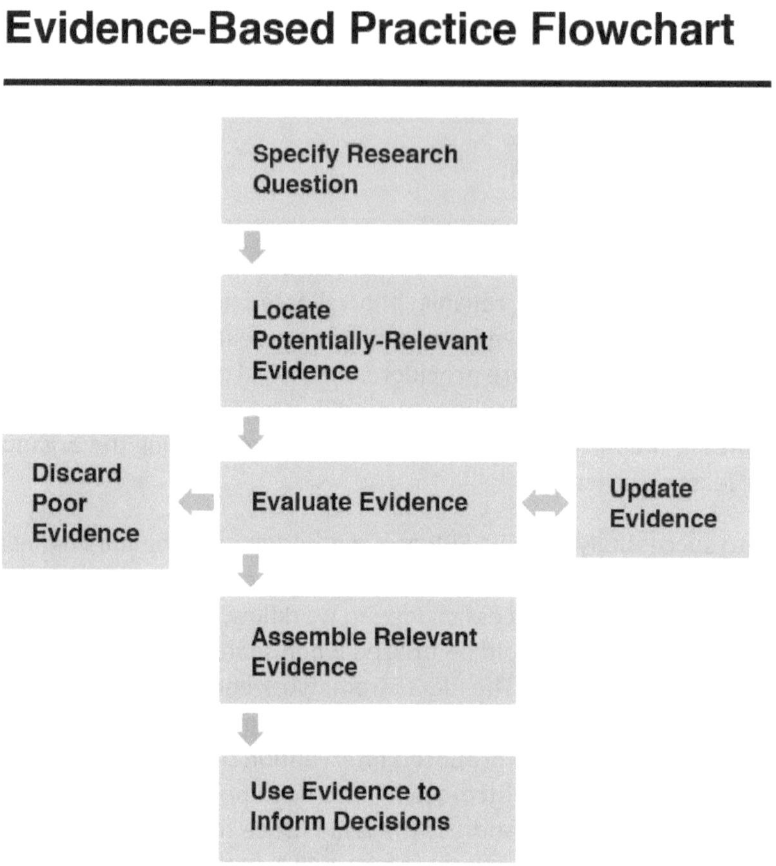

Collaboration

Collaboration occurs when interested parties work together to achieve a mutual goal. According to the Synergy Model, nurses collaborate with the patient, family, and other providers to satisfy the patient's healthcare needs. Several attributes of the process have been identified, including goal setting, problem-solving, and communicating and decision-making, which serve as an indication of the skills required of the individuals involved in the collaborative process. Some of the benefits of collaboration include improved patient outcomes, decreased healthcare costs, decreased length of stay, improved patient and nurse satisfaction, and improved teamwork. Collaboration related to patient care has been widely studied and is considered as both a process and an outcome, which occurs when no single individual is able to solve a stakeholder (patient) problem. Collaboration as a process is defined as a synthesis of diverse opinions and skills that is employed to solve complex problems. As an outcome, collaboration is defined as a complex solution to a problem that requires the expertise of more than one individual. This view of collaboration characterizes the process as a series of actions by more than one individual, which creates a solution to a complex problem.

Initially, all members of the collaborative team must identify their own biases and acknowledge the effect of these mental models on the decision-making process. In addition, members must also be aware that the complexity of the problem will be matched by the complexity of the mental models of the collaborative team members, which will influence the decision-making process. It is also essential for team members to recognize the elements of diversity in the group. For instance, while stereotyping is obviously to be avoided, there are gender differences that should be considered. Research indicates that men tend to be more task oriented, and women tend to be more relationship oriented in the problem-solving process; this means that consideration of both points of view is necessary for genuine collaboration.

Another requisite skill of the collaborative team is the development and usage of conflict resolution skills, which are required to counteract this common barrier to effective collaboration. Team members are required to separate the task from the emotions that are inherent in the discussion. Effective collaboration also requires that members of the team display a cooperative effort that works to create a win–win situation, while recognizing that collaboration is a series of activities that require time and patience for satisfactory completion.

Common barriers to effective collaboration include conflicting professional opinions, ineffective communication related to the conflict, and incomplete assessment of the required elements of the care plan. Research indicates that physicians tend to stress "cure" related activities while nurses tend to encourage "care" related activities, which means that some resolution of these differences is required for effective communication. Although the Synergy Model defines collaboration as a necessary part of the process that matches the patient's needs with the appropriate nursing competencies, it is also possible that the end product of the collaborative process may be the best possible solution for the patient and at the same time be totally unacceptable to the patient. Collaborative team members should also be aware that while successful collaboration improves patient outcomes, research indicates that genuine collaborative efforts are rarely noted in patient care, often because the group is unable to integrate the diverse mental models of the group members. This means the initial first steps of the process mentioned previously are essential to the success of the collaborative process.

Systems Thinking

Systems thinking is defined as a link between individuals and their environment. For nurses, this refers to their ability to understand the influence of the healthcare environment on patient outcomes. Systems thinking is identified as the goal of all of the **Quality and Safety Education for Nurses** (QSEN) competencies, which are acquired by nurses on a continuum that ranges from the care of the individual patient to the care of the entire patient population. The QSEN competencies were originally identified to improve patient outcomes in response to extensive research that identified a significant difference between the care of patients and the improvement in patient outcomes resulting from that care. The nursing competencies include patient-centered care, evidence-based practice, teamwork and collaboration, safety, quality and improvement, and informatics. Successful interventions associated with each of these criteria for professional nursing practice require the ability to apply the systems thinking approach to care.

Competency related to systems thinking requires appropriate education and clinical experience, and is also identified as one of the nursing competencies in the Synergy Model. In that model, novice nurses view the patient and family as isolated in the nursing unit rather than being influenced by the healthcare system, while experienced nurses are able to integrate all of the resources in the healthcare system to improve patient outcomes. Several of the learning activities designed to improve nurses' ability to acquire systems thinking include creation of a grid (see Figure 4) that identifies the nursing competencies across the continuum from isolated, individual care to the level of care associated with systems thinking. There are assessment models that apply this exercise to specialty care units such as emergency care, long-term care, and outpatient care, which identify specific systems needed for these areas.

Other exercises include tracking unit statistics for the QSEN competencies followed by the creation, implementation, and evaluation of a plan that applies systems thinking to address that competency. All of these activities assist nurses to integrate patients' needs with all available resources in order to improve outcomes. Root cause analysis can also be used as a learning exercise for systems theory because this process, which is commonly used to investigate errors, looks at all elements of an institution's relationship with the error. Case studies and reflection are also recommended as useful learning aids for systems thinking. In addition, there are valid assessment instruments that can be used to assess systems thinking skills acquired through these learning activities.

The influence of systems thinking on patient outcomes is widely recognized, and most acute care institutions and nursing programs report that educational opportunities to provide nurses with the appropriate skills are offered; however, research indicates that there has been little progress toward the goal of systems thinking by all professional nurses since the initiation of the QSEN competencies more than 15 years ago. This lack of progress applies to both physicians and nurses, according to the available research related to physician education. Professional nurses are responsible for accessing all available resources to support their ability to employ systems thinking in the care of patients and in their role as preceptors for novice nurses. The ultimate benefit of systems thinking, related to the QSEN competencies, is improved patient safety, while the ultimate benefit of systems thinking in professional nursing practice is improved patient outcomes.

Clinical Inquiry

Clinical inquiry is an ongoing process that evaluates and challenges clinical practice in order to propose the needed change. Clinical inquiry has several components or attributes, including critical thinking, clinical reasoning, clinical judgment, critical reasoning and judgment, and creative thinking. The process is viewed as the critical structure for the establishment of evidenced based practice and quality improvement efforts. In the Synergy Model, professional nurses employ clinical inquiry to innovate and facilitate interventions that are appropriate to patient care needs. Clinical inquiry is a rigorous process that requires attention to the rules of nursing research, such as attention to sample size, and a correct match among the data, the study design, and the statistical measures. When used to implement evidence-based practice, clinical inquiry can result in replacing an outdated, even counterproductive nursing intervention with an intervention that effectively addresses the needs of the patient. Nurses who are involved in this form of clinical inquiry are viewed as evaluators and innovators in the Synergy Model. Matching patient needs with nursing competencies means that professional nurses are responsible for challenging all nursing interventions to be sure that they represent current best practice standards. As innovators, nurses are in the best position to research, implement, and evaluate alternative care practices.

Nurses acquire clinical inquiry skills on a continuum that is based on education and clinical experience. As is the case with the other nursing competencies included in the Synergy Model, this progressive development is consistent with Benner's novice to expert model that views the development of nursing expertise as a progressive process that requires ongoing education and clinical experience. Novice nurses are able to implement clinical innovations developed by others, to identify their own learning needs, and to enlist the aid of other nurses to identify critical needs of the patient. Experienced nurses are able to question the adequacy of interventions and to begin to challenge the "we have always done it this way" philosophy that is the most common rationale for many nursing interventions. They are also able to assess the utility of alternative interventions. The Synergy Model views the practice of expert nurses as the point at which clinical inquiry and clinical reasoning become inseparable elements of clinical practice. Expert nurses are able to predict changes in the patient's condition that require revision of the plan of care, and are also able to develop and implement alternative approaches to address those changes.

Public funds are the most common source of research funding, which means that researchers are obligated to design studies that provide valid results that are applicable to some form of patient care and to disseminate the results appropriately. Common barriers to nursing research efforts include inadequate funding, limited access to appropriate patient populations, and lack of institutional support for research initiatives. The rapid expansion of new knowledge from multiple sources can also inhibit the assimilation and application of new care interventions by expert nurses. In addition, the final step of the clinical inquiry process, knowledge translation or dissemination, may be the most important step. **Knowledge translation** refers to the complex process of synthesizing the research findings, disseminating those findings to others, and integrating the findings into clinical practice. Barriers to this process include lack of rigor in the original research design with respect to sample size, data interpretation, and the applicability of the research findings. The failure of nursing researchers to access all possible modes of the dissemination of study results has also been identified as a significant barrier to the application of new interventions. All of these system-wide and individual barriers potentially limit the use of innovative patient care interventions.

Practice Quiz

1. Which of the following is cited as the MOST common source of funding for nursing research?
    a. Pharmaceutical companies
    b. Public funds
    c. Non-profit organizations
    d. Private institutions

2. The clinical practice of expert nurses reflects all of the nursing competencies identified in the Synergy Model. Which of the following ethical principles is the overall principle guiding nurses' actions?
    a. Beneficence
    b. Advocacy
    c. Autonomy
    d. Justice

3. Which of the following statements is consistent with the concept of moral agency?
    a. The patient's decisions will always be honored.
    b. Nurses assume accountability for their decisions.
    c. Institutions rarely act as moral agents.
    d. Advocacy and moral agency are interchangeable concepts.

4. Which of the following choices represents the learning sequence of a nurse from novice to expert with regard to caring practices?
    a. The nurse anticipates the needs of the patient in the community, acknowledges death as a potential outcome, and responds to subtle changes in the patient's condition.
    b. The nurse facilitates solutions to patient and family concerns related to death and dying, modifies caring practices to the individual patient, and maintains a safe physical environment.
    c. The nurse bases care on standards and protocols, views death as an acceptable outcome, and anticipates and avoids patient problems.
    d. The nurse recognizes the patient as a unique being, facilitates the care of the patient across the caring continuum, and focuses on the patient's customary needs.

5. Which of the following choices is most consistent with nurses' responsibilities associated with advocacy?
    a. Notifying the nursing supervisor of any conflict to assure resolution of the patient issue.
    b. Considering the patient's point of view and being prepared to support and explain the point of view as needed.
    c. Providing comprehensive documentation of the patient's care in the EHR.
    d. Understanding all relevant laws associated with the nursing care of the patient.

See answers on the next page.

Answer Explanations

1. B: Research indicates that public funds are the most common source of funding, which means that researchers are obligated to design studies that provide valid results that are applicable to some form of patient care and to disseminate the results appropriately. The remaining sources also provide funding; however, public funds are noted to be the common source.

2. A: Beneficence is defined as doing good for another individual, which would include acting as an advocate, supporting the individual's autonomy, and working to ensure justice.

3. B: When nurses act as moral agents they are required to also assume responsibility for their decisions. The patient's opinions will be identified and accommodated whenever possible; however, there may be conflict between the patient's opinions and the recommended plan of care. The institution may act as the moral agent for patients without any social support. The difference between moral agency and advocacy is the element of accountability. Moral agents are required to take responsibility for their decisions.

4. C: Novice nurses base their care on standards and protocols, experienced nurses view death as an acceptable outcome, and expert nurses anticipate and avoid patient problems. The remaining choices identify nurses, caring practices in random order. Choice *A*: Expert nurses anticipate the needs of the patient in the community, novice nurses acknowledge death as a potential outcome, experienced nurses respond to subtle changes in the patient's condition. Choice *B*: Expert nurses facilitate solutions to patient and family concerns related to death and dying, experienced nurses modify caring practices for the individual patient, and novice nurses maintain a safe physical environment. Choice *D*: Experienced nurses recognize the patient as a unique being, expert nurses facilitate the care of the patient across the caring continuum, and novice nurses focus on the patient's customary needs.

5. B: Sharing, supporting, and explaining the patient's point of view are activities that are consistent with advocacy. The remaining choices contribute to good professional practice but are not specifically related to the concept of advocacy.

PCCN Practice Test #1

Clinical Judgment

Cardiovascular

1. A STEMI in which the full thickness of the heart wall has been damaged results in which of the following ECG changes?
   a. T-wave inversion
   b. ST-segment elevation
   c. QT prolongation
   d. U-wave elevation

2. What is one way a woman may present differently than a man when experiencing a heart attack?
   a. Symptoms beginning days to weeks before actual attack
   b. Profuse sweating
   c. Crushing chest pain
   d. Elevated serological markers

3. What other condition may mimic the symptoms of a heart attack?
   a. Cirrhosis of the liver
   b. Kidney failure
   c. Acid reflux
   d. Pneumonia

4. What serological marker indicates that cardiac muscle tissue has been damaged and cell contents are being released into the bloodstream?
   a. Creatinine
   b. BUN
   c. CK-MB
   d. Troponin

5. Which of the following statements about the cardiac catheterization procedure is true?
   a. The brachial artery is a common access site.
   b. The thin tube threaded into the patient's heart has a camera called a scope on the end for visualization of heart structures.
   c. Angioplasty and stent placement are commonly performed to open occluded coronary vessels.
   d. The patient is put under general anesthesia for the procedure.

6. Which of the following patients is NOT at increased risk for the development of an embolism?
   a. A 24-year-old with a broken femur
   b. An 85-year-old female with a history of a stroke
   c. A 62-year-old male with first-degree heart block
   d. A 19-year-old female two weeks postpartum

7. The nurse is receiving reports at the beginning of the shift. One of the patients has been admitted to the hospital and is awaiting transfer to the ICU with an admitting diagnosis of obstructive shock. Which of the following findings are characteristic of obstructive shock?
   a. Jugular vein distention, peripheral edema, and pulmonary congestion
   b. Decreased urine output, increased BUN, and increased creatinine
   c. Chest pain, fatigue, and lightheadedness
   d. Problems with coordination, blurred vision, and partial paralysis

8. Which of the following would NOT indicate arterial insufficiency?
   a. Cyanosis of lower extremities
   b. Loss of hair in legs
   c. Sores that will not heal
   d. Pooling of blood and edema

9. What is the most common cause of edema caused by venous insufficiency?
   a. Deep vein thrombosis (DVT)
   b. Obesity
   c. Pregnancy
   d. Old age

10. What test is often used to determine if a patient has peripheral arterial disease?
   a. Echocardiography
   b. CT scan of the leg
   c. Electrocardiogram
   d. Ankle-brachial BP index

11. The progressive care nurse understands that which of the following is the most concerning symptom associated with peripheral vascular disease (PVD)?
   a. Faint peripheral pulses
   b. Restricted mobility
   c. Critical limb ischemia
   d. Pale feet when elevated

12. What risk does high blood pressure pose in the postoperative period following an endarterectomy?
   a. Bleeding
   b. Infection
   c. Pulmonary edema
   d. Stroke

13. What type of drug therapy coupled with antithrombotic therapy is often used post-endarterectomy?
   a. Antiplatelet
   b. Beta-blocker
   c. Angiotensin-converting enzyme
   d. Angiotensin II receptor blockers

14. What is the main concern faced when using an artificial graft to bypass an occluded artery in the fem-pop bypass procedure?
   a. Localized infection
   b. Narrowing leading to reocclusion
   c. Lower extremity edema
   d. Tissue rejection

15. Which type of drug class is often used to reduce preload in cardiogenic pulmonary edema?
   a. Beta-blockers such as metoprolol
   b. Calcium channel blockers such as verapamil
   c. Narcotics such as morphine
   d. Diuretics such as furosemide

16. A patient has had three separate blood pressure readings of 138/88, 132/80, and 135/89, respectively. The progressive care nurse anticipates the patient to be categorized by the physician as which of the following?
   a. Prehypertensive
   b. Normal
   c. Stage 1 hypertension
   d. Stage 2 hypertension

17. What differentiating factor would let a nurse know that a lower extremity ulcer is arterial rather than venous?
   a. Color of wound
   b. Culture taken from wound
   c. Depth of wound
   d. Measurement of wound

18. Which of the following is NOT a usual sign that a patient is in shock?
   a. Increased urine output
   b. Distant heart sounds
   c. Bluish tinted skin
   d. Faint and rapid pulse

19. If dopamine does not do an adequate job of maintaining blood pressure in a patient experiencing cardiogenic shock, which potent vasoconstrictor will be considered to raise the blood pressure?
   a. Dobutamine
   b. Norepinephrine
   c. Milrinone
   d. Nitroglycerin

20. The progressive care nurse is caring for a patient with congestive heart failure and is reviewing their medications with them during medication teaching. The patient expresses concern about their potassium level after recalling an issue with low potassium when prescribed a diuretic in the past. Which medication does the nurse explain is a potassium-sparing diuretic during this teaching?
   a. Lasix® (furosemide)
   b. Demadex® (torsemide)
   c. Aldactone® (spironolactone)
   d. Microzide® (hydrochlorothiazide)

21. Which item in the family history assessment performed by the progressive care nurse is a red flag for hypertrophic cardiomyopathy and should be investigated further?
   a. Heart disease of the father
   b. Diabetes mellitus of the mother
   c. Sudden death of a grandmother
   d. Stroke of a grandfather

22. What is the most common and deadly heart rhythm detected in patients experiencing cardiac arrest?
   a. Atrial fibrillation
   b. Ventricular tachycardia
   c. Ventricular fibrillation
   d. Supraventricular tachycardia

23. According to the Frank-Starling law of the heart, a patient with heart failure will respond to an increase in preload in which of the following ways?
   a. Increased contractility
   b. Decreased cardiac output
   c. Change in rhythm
   d. Increased heart rate

24. Which of the following is a commonly used anticoagulant that works by blocking the body's ability to adhere platelets together?
   a. Paxil
   b. Coumadin
   c. Heparin
   d. Aspirin

25. What myocardial conduction defect is hereditary, may result in syncope or sudden death, and often occurs in healthy adults or children?
   a. Third-degree heart block
   b. First-degree heart block
   c. Bundle branch block
   d. Long QT syndrome

26. Which of the following is NOT a congenital heart defect found in the tetralogy of Fallot?
   a. Pulmonary valve stenosis
   b. Ventricular septal defect
   c. Atrial septal defect
   d. Hypertrophic right ventricle

27. Which of the following lifestyle modifications would address the major cause of most aortic aneurysms?
   a. Low-fat diet
   b. Smoking cessation
   c. Exercise program
   d. Meditation

28. A 44-year-old male patient calls the progressive care nurse to the room, complaining of chest pain and shortness of breath. Examination by the nurse reveals distended neck veins and muffled heart sounds. The patient's blood pressure is 80/55 mmHg. The nurse should suspect which of the following?
   a. Cardiac tamponade
   b. Abdominal aortic aneurysm (AAA)
   c. Cardiopulmonary arrest
   d. Cardiogenic shock

29. The nurse is caring for a patient with an acute exacerbation of congestive heart failure (CHF). Which clinical manifestation should be most concerning to the nurse?
   a. An oxygenation level of 92 percent
   b. Dyspnea on exertion
   c. New onset of peripheral edema
   d. Elevated BNP levels

30. A patient recently admitted to the floor as a direct admit from her cardiologist office begins complaining of new onset chest pain, 10/10 to left chest and shoulder. The patient is diaphoretic, and vital signs reveal patient's heart rate is 64 bpm, BP is 132/78 mmHg, respiratory rate is 20, and oxygen saturation is 98% on room air. Which of the following actions should the nurse anticipate as part of the patient's care?

I. IV administration of magnesium sulfate
II. IV administration of morphine sulfate
III. IV administration of nitroglycerin
IV. IV administration of acetaminophen

   a. I and II only
   b. I, III, and IV only
   c. II and III only
   d. II, III, and IV only

31. Which of the following statements made by the patient would cause the nurse to suspect an abdominal aortic aneurysm (AAA)?
   a. "I have indigestion when I lie down."
   b. "I often have a pulsating sensation in my abdomen."
   c. "I get fatigued and short of breath on exertion."
   d. "I have extreme pain radiating down my left arm."

32. A patient is admitted with a diagnosis of heart failure. Which assessment finding supports the diagnosis of left-sided heart failure?
   a. Pitting edema
   b. Ascites
   c. Fatigue
   d. Tachycardia

33. A patient with primary hypertension is being treated with medications to reduce blood volume and lower systemic vascular resistance. Which of the following medication combinations should the progressive care nurse anticipate for the patient?
   a. A diuretic and a calcium channel blocker (CCB)
   b. A diuretic and an angiotensin-converting enzyme (ACE) inhibitor
   c. An angiotensin II receptor blocker (ARB) and morphine
   d. A diuretic and a beta-blocker

34. Which of the following is a contraindication for thrombolytic therapy?
   a. Current anticoagulant therapy
   b. Over age 75
   c. Severe hepatic disease
   d. INR of 3.5

Pulmonary

1. All EXCEPT which of the following help define acute respiratory distress syndrome (ARDS)?
   a. Timing
   b. Origin of edema
   c. Pulmonary artery wedge pressure
   d. Severity of hypoxemia

2. An 18-year-old female on your unit is complaining of worsening wheezing, shortness of breath, and a cough over the past twelve hours. She has a history of asthma and has been using her albuterol metered-dose inhaler (MDI) frequently for the last two hours. She's given supplemental oxygen, both albuterol and ipratropium (Combivent®) via nebulizer, and methylprednisolone IV in quick succession. Shortly afterwards, she complains of anxiety, develops hand tremors, and her pulse increases from 80 to 120 beats per minute (bpm). Which treatment is most likely responsible for her anxiety, tremors, and tachycardia?
   a. Supplemental oxygen
   b. Albuterol
   c. Ipratropium
   d. Methylprednisolone

3. A 65-year-old ex-smoker presents with a complaint of increasing shortness of breath over the past 24 hours. He has a medical history of chronic obstructive pulmonary disease (COPD). He is administered supplemental oxygen, albuterol via nebulizer, methylprednisolone IV, and a dose of azithromycin IV. Which of these therapies has been clinically proven to decrease the risk of treatment failure and death?
   a. Supplemental oxygen
   b. Albuterol
   c. Methylprednisolone
   d. Azithromycin

4. All EXCEPT which of the following are components of Virchow's triad?
   a. Heart disease
   b. Hypercoagulability
   c. Endothelial injury/dysfunction
   d. Hemodynamic changes such as stasis or turbulence

5. A 66-year-old female with type 2 diabetes mellitus presents with a nonproductive cough, nasal congestion, wheezing, and occasional shortness of breath for the last ten days. She reports that her symptoms are worse at night. A chest x-ray, complete blood count (CBC), and comprehensive metabolic panel (CMP) are all unremarkable, except for an elevated blood glucose level of 150 mg/dL. What is the most appropriate course of management?
   a. Bronchoscopy with bronchoalveolar lavage (BAL)
   b. Sputum gram stain and culture
   c. Arterial blood gas (ABG) analysis
   d. Doxycycline 100 mg BID for seven days

6. Which of the following is an indication for the placement of a vena cava filter to prevent pulmonary embolism (PE)?
   a. Pregnancy
   b. Documented recurrent PE
   c. Active smoking history
   d. Age less than 65 years

7. Which of the following medications administered during status asthmaticus targets the systemic inflammation being experienced by the patient?
   a. Inhaled bronchodilators
   b. Subcutaneous epinephrine
   c. Nebulized albuterol
   d. Oral corticosteroids

8. Which of the following surgeries performed by a cardiothoracic surgeon removes a section of an airway leading to the lung, sewing together the top and bottom of the section removed?
   a. Pneumonectomy
   b. Lobectomy
   c. Sleeve resection
   d. Wedge resection

9. Which category of pulmonary embolism entails impairment of right ventricular function as well as severe hypotension?
   a. Small
   b. Submassive
   c. Massive
   d. Grand

10. In an attempt to diagnose a PE in a patient with renal failure, which type of scan will likely be performed?
   a. Transesophageal echocardiography
   b. CT scan with contrast
   c. MRI of the thoracic cage
   d. V/Q scan

11. What flow rate should the nurse set for the nasal cannula of a patient with chronic obstructive pulmonary disease (COPD)?
   a. 1 L/min
   b. 3 L/min
   c. 5 L/min
   d. 7 L/min

12. Patients on the cusp of respiratory failure may exhibit which of the following early signs and symptoms?
   a. Decreased respiratory rate
   b. Unconsciousness
   c. Cyanosis
   d. Agitation

13. Which of the following is not an example of a drug that may cause respiratory failure in higher doses or in sensitive patients?
   a. Morphine
   b. Hydrocodone
   c. Naloxone
   d. Alprazolam

14. What is the most common bacterial cause of pneumonias in patients?
   a. *Streptococcus pneumoniae*
   b. *Klebsiella pneumoniae*
   c. *Chlamydophila pneumoniae*
   d. *Mycoplasma pneumoniae*

15. Which category of pneumonia is more likely to occur in a patient who is undergoing chemotherapy for a metastatic lung cancer?
   a. Community-acquired
   b. Hospital-acquired
   c. Immunocompromised
   d. Healthcare-associated

16. Which of the following is a common symptom of COPD?
   a. Dry cough
   b. Morning headache
   c. Narrow chest
   d. Weight gain

17. Which of the following actions by a patient with COPD creates its own positive end-expiratory pressure?
   a. Tripod posing
   b. Wide open-mouth breathing
   c. Pursed-lip breathing
   d. Frequent coughing

18. The nurse is caring for a patient with OSA who is prescribed CPAP therapy. Which of the following statements by the patient indicates an understanding of the purpose of CPAP therapy?
   a. "The CPAP machine will help me fall asleep faster."
   b. "CPAP therapy will cure my sleep apnea completely."
   c. "The CPAP machine will keep my airway open while I sleep."
   d. "CPAP therapy will help me breathe in more oxygen during the night."

19. The nurse is caring for a patient with COPD who is prescribed tiotropium bromide (Spiriva). Which of the following statements by the patient indicates an understanding of the medication's action?
   a. "Spiriva will relax the muscles in my airways and help me breathe easier."
   b. "Spiriva will decrease the inflammation in my lungs and prevent exacerbations."
   c. "Spiriva will thin the mucus in my airways and make it easier to cough up."
   d. "Spiriva will stimulate the production of natural surfactant in my lungs."

20. The nurse is caring for a patient who presents with a pneumothorax. Upon assessment, the nurse notes that the patient has no evidence of a rib fracture or associated lung disease. Which type of pneumothorax should the nurse suspect in this patient?
   a. Tension pneumothorax
   b. Spontaneous pneumothorax
   c. Traumatic pneumothorax
   d. Iatrogenic pneumothorax

21. The nurse is providing education to a patient with a history of PE who is prescribed Warfarin and asks about consuming foods high in vitamin K. Which of the following statements by the nurse is the most appropriate response?
   a. "It is important to avoid foods high in vitamin K because they can interfere with the effectiveness of Warfarin."
   b. "You should consume foods with vitamin K consistently to maintain a balanced diet while on Warfarin."
   c. "It is important to maintain a consistent intake of vitamin K to avoid sudden changes in Warfarin's effectiveness."
   d. "You should completely eliminate foods high in vitamin K from your diet to ensure the optimal effects of Warfarin."

Endocrine/Hematology/Neurology/Gastrointestinal/Renal

1. A patient who has been NPO (nothing by mouth) all morning for a cardiac catheterization complains of nausea and "just not feeling right." The nurse notices that he is sweating. What condition should the nurse suspect and investigate right away?
    a. Hypochondria
    b. Hypoglycemia
    c. Hypotension
    d. Hypothyroidism

2. A decreased amount of vasopressin in the body will likely produce which of the following conditions?
    a. SIADH
    b. Diabetes type I
    c. Diabetes insipidus
    d. Diabetes type II

3. Which of the following metabolic components involved in diabetic ketoacidosis is responsible for the "fruity" smell that a person with DKA gives off when they breathe?
    a. Alanine
    b. Triglycerides
    c. Acetone
    d. Glycerol

4. High blood sugar stimulates the kidneys to do which of the following?
    a. Produce less urine
    b. Concentrate the urine
    c. Retain more sodium
    d. Produce more urine

5. Which body system will exhibit the most obvious effects of a state of hyperosmolar hyperglycemic nonketotic syndrome (HHNK)?
    a. Neurologic
    b. Cardiac
    c. Endocrine
    d. Pulmonary

6. A progressive care nurse is caring for a patient who is being evaluated for a small-bowel obstruction. The nurse understands that which of the following assessment findings is consistent with this condition?
    a. pH 7.32, PCO_2 38, HCO_3 20
    b. Serum osmolality 285 mosm/kg
    c. Serum sodium 128 mmol/L
    d. Lower abdominal distention

7. A progressive care nurse is preparing a discharge plan for a patient with risk factors for acute pancreatitis. Which of the following information should be included in this plan?
   a. Endoscopic retrograde cholangiopancreatography (ERCP) imaging is required to confirm the diagnosis.
   b. Ultrasonography is the most useful imaging study when significant abdominal distention is present.
   c. Current research confirms the efficacy of rectal administration of indomethacin to reduce the incidence of pancreatitis due to the ERCP procedure.
   d. There is no scientific rationale to explain why some individuals with chronic ETOH abuse develop acute pancreatitis while others do not develop pancreatitis.

8. The nurse is caring for a patient with manifestations of peptic ulcer disease. Which of the following statements is correct?
   a. Stomach pain begins 20 to 30 minutes after eating.
   b. The condition is associated with an increased risk of malignancy.
   c. Endoscopy is used to establish hemostasis.
   d. Chronic NSAID use is the most common etiology.

9. Which of the following is a commonly used anticoagulant that works by blocking the body's ability to adhere platelets together?
   a. Paxil
   b. Coumadin
   c. Heparin
   d. Aspirin

10. Which of the following is a commonly used anticoagulant that works by preventing the activation of thrombin?
   a. Paxil
   b. Warfarin
   c. Heparin
   d. Aspirin

11. Which of the following statements is true?
   a. As fluid levels decrease, electrolyte levels increase.
   b. As fluid levels increase, electrolyte levels increase.
   c. As fluid levels osmose, electrolyte levels diffuse.
   d. As fluid levels homogenize, electrolyte levels dissipate.

12. Which of the following statements about diabetes is correct?
   a. Type 2 diabetes mellitus is diagnosed based on the pancreas's inability to produce insulin.
   b. Gestational diabetes mellitus is diagnosed based on the mother's inability to produce glucose.
   c. Type 3 diabetes mellitus is diagnosed based on the pancreas's inability to produce insulin.
   d. Type 1 diabetes mellitus is diagnosed based on the pancreas's inability to produce insulin.

13. Patients with type 2 diabetes can manage their symptoms with which of the following?
    a. An insulin pump and finger prick testing strips
    b. Steroid injections and stevia sugar substitutes
    c. A regular yoga practice
    d. Lifestyle changes and metformin

14. Which of the following statements is correct?
    a. The sodium-potassium pump is responsible for membrane potential.
    b. The calcium-phosphorus balance is responsible for membrane potential.
    c. The sodium chloride molecule is responsible for hormone production.
    d. The magnesium channel is responsible for regular waste excretion.

15. Diabetic ketoacidosis is an acute complication that occurs primarily in patients who have which of the following?
    a. Type 1 diabetes
    b. Type 2 diabetes
    c. Gestational diabetes
    d. A primarily ketogenic diet

16. Immunocompromised patients should do which of the following?

I. Always practice extraordinary personal hygiene and handwashing habits.
II. Avoid eating moldy cheeses, such as blue cheese.
III. Only drink bottled water.
IV. Ask for help with caring for pets and taking out trash.

    a. I and IV only
    b. I, II, and III
    c. I, II, and IV
    d. All of the above

17. Stage 5 of chronic kidney disease usually requires which of the following to manage the condition?
    a. Steroid and antidiuretic hormone injections
    b. Dialysis or a kidney transplant
    c. A full-time home health aide
    d. Hospice services

18. A progressive care nurse is caring for a patient who had a seizure today for the first time. The patient said that she noticed a strange odor just prior to "not feeling well." Vital signs are BP 120/74, HR 76, and an oral temperature 97.8°F. The patient has no complaints of pain and no recent history of viral or bacterial illness. A friend witnessed that seizure and stated that the muscular movement lasted about 30 seconds. The patient was incontinent during the seizure but did not suffer any injuries. The patient recovered without any further manifestations of seizure activity. The nurse understands that which of the following interventions is most appropriate for this patient?
    a. Obtain laboratory analysis of recreational drug use.
    b. Institute oral therapy of AEDs.
    c. Prepare the patient for an immediate lumbar puncture for CSF analysis.
    d. Obtain an EEG and an MRI.

19. The progressive care nurse is caring for a patient with an emerging ischemic stroke. The nurse should prepare to administer which of the following fibrinolytic agents?

a. Urokinase
b. Streptokinase
c. Alteplase
d. Tenecteplase

20. Which of the following solutions is used to correct the hyponatremia associated with syndrome of inappropriate antidiuretic hormone?

a. Normal saline
b. Hypertonic saline
c. Hypotonic saline
d. Lactated ringer's solution

21. Which of the following anemia categories, in which heme and globin do not synthesize appropriately, does thalassemia fall into?

a. Thrombocytic
b. Macrocytic
c. Normocytic
d. Microcytic

22. Where should nurses assess for pallor in a patient with dark skin who is suspected to be anemic?

a. Forearms
b. Cheeks
c. Conjunctiva
d. Scalp

24. Which of the following are true regarding encephalopathy?

I. It is complication of a primary problem.
II. It is brain damage.
III. It is an altered mental state.
IV. It is caused by a lack of oxygen to the brain.

a. I, II, and III
b. I, II, and IV
c. II, III, and IV
d. All of the above

25. The nurse is caring for a patient with acute kidney injury who is prescribed erythropoietin. The nurse understands that this medication is used for what purpose?

a. To stimulate red blood cell production
b. To increase urine output
c. To combat infection
d. To suppress the immune system

Musculoskeletal/Multisystem/Psychosocial

1. The progressive care nurse is admitting a new 72-year-old male patient to the unit. As she works through her assessment, the nurse recognizes that which of the following is NOT a risk factor for falls for this patient in this environment?
    a. Using a cane to walk
    b. Inadequate lighting in a room
    c. Muscle weakness
    d. Slower reflexes

2. While working with a patient who is three days post-op from a coronary artery bypass graft (CABG), the progressive care nurse notices that the patient looks pale and feels cold while ambulating in their room. What action does the nurse take first to prevent a fall?
    a. Assist the patient back to bed.
    b. Encourage the patient to eat a snack.
    c. Increase the flow rate on the patient's nasal cannula.
    d. Assess the patient's vital signs.

3. Which of the following options correctly names the type of common medication used to treat anxiety and depression?
    a. Antipsychotics
    b. Selective serotonin reuptake inhibitors (SSRIs)
    c. Dopamine reuptake inhibitors
    d. Homeopathic options

4. What is one evidence-based reason that some microbial bacteria have become resistant to antibiotics?
    a. Patients who are prescribed antibiotics and fail to finish the dosage
    b. Climate change
    c. The presence of genetically modified organisms in the food system
    d. Overly sterile hospital environments

5. A nurse is about to enter the room of an acutely ill patient in droplet isolation. Which personal protective equipment (PPE) should the nurse don first?
    a. Gloves
    b. Mask
    c. Gown
    d. Goggles

6. The nursing staff are preparing to admit an acutely ill patient to the unit. In the report from the ER, the patient was described as displaying aggressive behavior. What is the first thing that the nursing team should do to prevent harm to patients and staff by a patient with a strong history of aggressive behavior?
    a. Seclude the patient.
    b. Establish trust and rapport.
    c. Administer a sedative by mouth.
    d. Use 4-point restraints.

7. While assessing a patient who takes amitriptyline, which symptom supports the nurse's concern that the patient may be developing tardive dyskinesia?

a. Tongue thrusting
b. Headache
c. Blurred vision
d. Fever

8. Which of the following is the best antibiotic treatment for pneumonia caused by community-associated methicillin-resistant Staphylococcus aureus (CA-MRSA)?

a. Azithromycin
b. Doxycycline
c. Vancomycin
d. Levofloxacin

9. A 55-year-old male presents with a cough producing rust-colored sputum, a fever (102° F), and shortness of breath. A complete blood count (CBC) reveals an elevated white blood cell count with predominant neutrophils. A chest x-ray reveals consolidation of the left, lower lobe of the lung. Blood cultures reveal gram-positive diplococci. What is the most likely cause of this patient's pneumonia?

a. *Haemophilus influenzae*
b. *Moraxella catarrhalis*
c. *Streptococcus pneumoniae*
d. *Staphylococcus aureus*

10. An acutely ill patient with broken ribs after a trauma is being given IV and PO pain medications. What additional medication does the nurse expect to see ordered at this time to combat a common side effect of this drug class?

a. Dolophine® (methadone)
b. Biaxin® (clarithromycin)
c. Tegretol® (carbamazepine)
d. Colace® (docusate sodium)

11. Which supplement does the nurse plan to administer to the patient struggling with alcohol withdrawal upon admission to the unit?

a. Niacin
b. Thiamine
c. Riboflavin
d. Folate

12. During a level of consciousness assessment, the nurse finds no articulated verbal response with limited moaning, accompanied by arousal only after vigorous stimulation. How should the nurse document these findings?

a. "The patient is lethargic."
b. "The patient is obtunded."
c. "The patient is stuporous."
d. "The patient is comatose."

13. The nurse is educating a patient regarding assistive devices and answers a question regarding the proper length of a cane. Which response by the nurse correctly answers this question?

a. "Canes should be the length that feels most comfortable for each individual."
b. "The length of the cane should support the elbow to be only slightly flexed."
c. "It is best for the cane to be the length that encourages full flexion of the elbow."
d. "A properly fitted cane allows you to lean forward with full extension of the elbow during ambulation."

14. The nurse has just admitted a patient to her unit with signs and symptoms of septic shock. The patient was discharged from the medical-surgical floor last week after being treated for pneumonia. What findings support a septic shock diagnosis?

I. Metabolic acidosis
II. Respiratory alkalosis
III. Narrowing pulse pressure
IV. Increased cardiac output

a. I only
b. I and II
c. I and III
d. I, II, III, and IV

15. A forty-nine-year-old patient experiencing severe alcohol withdrawal exhibits vestibular disturbance by reporting which of the following symptoms?

a. "I have a terrible headache."
b. "The room seems like it's spinning!"
c. "My hands won't stop shaking!"
d. "I feel like I'm going to throw up."

16. A patient with a terminal cancer diagnosis is placed in hospice care. Which of the following is the title of the person who will make his healthcare decisions when he becomes incapacitated?

a. Hospice nurse
b. Healthcare power of attorney
c. Caregiver
d. Legal guardian

17. When assessing a patient's wound, the nurse knows that reddening, malodor, and pus discharge are signs of what?

a. Healing
b. Surgery
c. Trauma
d. Infection

18. The nurse taking care of a patient with an MRSA infection knows that multidrug-resistant organisms arise from which of the following causes?
   a. Overuse of antivirals
   b. Underuse of antivirals
   c. Underuse of antibiotics
   d. Overuse of antibiotics

19. Which of the following words describes delirium and differentiates it from dementia?
   a. Slow onset
   b. Irreversible
   c. Chronic
   d. Transient

20. A new graduate nurse is discussing symptoms of alcohol withdrawal with her preceptor. Which of the following could the nurse list to indicate an understanding of the symptoms of alcohol withdrawal?
   a. Tachycardia
   b. Hypotension
   c. Bradycardia
   d. Paralysis

Professional Caring and Ethical Practice

1. PCCN practice is based on the principles of ethical behavior. Which of the following correctly identifies the moral principle that may require knowledge of the legislative process?
   a. Fidelity
   b. Autonomy
   c. Advocacy
   d. Beneficence

2. Nurses are responsible for which of the following elements of informed consent?
   a. Identification of alternatives to the planned procedure
   b. Description of associated risks and benefits
   c. Explanation of the planned procedure or diagnostic test
   d. Assessment of the patient's understanding of the information that is provided

3. Which of the following correctly identifies a critical distinction between the two concepts of advocacy and moral agency?
   a. Advocacy is legally binding.
   b. Moral agency requires accountability for right and wrong decisions.
   c. Advocacy is implied in the paternalistic view of patient care.
   d. Moral agency only refers to support for at-risk populations.

4. Which of the following ethical principles is most closely related to advocacy?
   a. Distributive justice
   b. Beneficence
   c. Nonmaleficence
   d. Fidelity

5. Which of the following word pairs identifies the six Cs of caring practices that are most closely associated with caring for acutely ill patients?
   a. Compassion and curiosity
   b. Confidence and collaboration
   c. Conscience and creativity
   d. Commitment and competence

6. The PCCN who is employed in the Cardiac Care Unit is reassigned to the Neonatal Intensive Care Unit for the evening. The PCCN refuses the assignment based on a lack of experience caring for newborn infants. This action is based on which of the following ethical principles?
   a. Advocacy
   b. Nonmaleficence
   c. Autonomy
   d. Fidelity

7. The Synergy Model proposes a novel paradigm of nursing. Which of the following statements correctly identifies a characteristic of nursing practice in this model?
   a. Resiliency
   b. Creativity
   c. Collaboration
   d. Complexity

8. A progressive care nurse is caring for a patient who had a colectomy two days ago. While assisting the patient back to bed, the nurse notes that the patient's heart rate and respiratory rate are slightly elevated, and the patient states, "I can feel my pulse." The nurse assesses the patient for additional signs of heart failure. This intervention is an example of which of the following caring practices according to the Synergy Model?
   a. Engagement by a novice nurse
   b. Vigilance by an experienced nurse
   c. An expected response to predictable changes by the novice nurse
   d. Collaboration by an experienced nurse

9. At which level of the caring practices continuum identified in the Synergy Model is death initially viewed as an acceptable patient outcome?
   a. Level 1
   b. Level 2
   c. Level 3
   d. Death is considered as an acceptable outcome at all levels of caring practice.

10. How does the institution support diversity?
   a. Requiring all employees to speak a second language
   b. Providing mandatory cultural sensitivity training for all managers
   c. Offering alternative food services
   d. Providing alternative solutions to all patient requests

11. A novice nurse is caring for a patient who requires a blood transfusion. The patient, however, has refused the transfusion due to a religious objection to the therapy. The nurse says, "I don't understand why the patient's sister can't donate the blood. No one should object to receiving blood from a family member when you need it." Which of the following statements correctly identifies the critical issue in this situation?

a. The nurse is displaying an ethnocentric attitude that dismisses the patient's religious practices as irrelevant to the need for the therapy.
b. The nurse thinks that the patient is concerned about contracting an infectious disease from the donated blood.
c. The nurse thinks that the patient doesn't understand the necessity of the blood transfusion.
d. The nurse believes that blood donation from family members is safe.

12. A nurse is preparing a teaching plan for a patient with the following characteristics: moderately impaired resiliency, stability, and complexity. Which of the following teaching-learning approaches is most appropriate for this patient?

a. Provide a one-hour teaching-learning session twice a day for the next two days.
b. Provide the patient with written information from a nursing journal.
c. Leave the instruction for the outpatient care provider.
d. Meet with the patient for 15–20 minutes to assess their ability to participate.

13. According to the Synergy Model, which of the following choices is associated with the patient's vulnerability?

a. The patient is financially stable.
b. The patient smoked cigarettes for thirty years prior to quitting five years ago.
c. The patient is married.
d. The patient actively participates in decisions related to the plan of care.

14. A nurse is developing a plan of care for a patient population that is culturally diverse. Which of the following statements correctly identifies the appropriate nursing actions?

a. The nurse follows the standard protocol for the predominant culture of the community.
b. The nurse focuses on the cultural needs of the largest group in the population.
c. The nurse Identifies and acknowledges their own biases and addresses the needs of the patient.
d. The nurse meets the needs of the group according to their own values and beliefs.

15. Which of the following statements is consistent with the major premise of the Synergy Model?

a. Family participation in patient care improves outcomes.
b. The model is based on the condition of patients and the function of the nursing staff.
c. The model only relates to critical care environments.
d. Synergy is said to exist when the environment and nursing competencies are consistent with the needs of the patient and the patient's family.

16. According to the literature, which of the following interventions would most likely be chosen by a physician in a collaborative group?

a. Initiating a Social Service referral to address caregiver strain
b. Fitting the patient with a brace to treat the effects of foot drop
c. Providing the patient's wife with the names of local Parkinson's support groups
d. Facilitating the family's request for spiritual care

17. Which of the following nursing interventions would be an example of systems thinking?
   a. Ensuring that the patients who are being discharged have all of their prescriptions
   b. Organizing a teaching/learning session for patients and families on the nursing unit related to the importance of handwashing
   c. Soliciting performance evaluations from colleagues
   d. Participating in the agency implementation of the electronic health record

18. Which of the following statements is consistent with the basic assumption of the QSEN competencies?
   a. The use of systems thinking by all providers will narrow the differences between the care that is delivered and the rate of positive outcomes.
   b. Systems thinking is the goal of all nursing competencies.
   c. Successful application of all QSEN nursing competencies will improve patient safety.
   d. The ability to use systems thinking is dictated by the nurse's level of basic nursing education.

19. Which of the following learning exercises related to systems thinking potentially provides the most comprehensive view of the institution?
   a. Root cause analysis
   b. Competency grids
   c. Process diagrams
   d. Case studies

20. Which of the following choices is identified as a significant barrier to the applicability of research to practice by the individual nurse?
   a. The rapid expansion of new knowledge reported from multiple sources
   b. Inadequate funding sources
   c. Lack of motivation
   d. Insufficient knowledge

21. Which of the following statements is consistent with the description of clinical inquiry in the Synergy Model?
   a. Novice nurses begin to compare and contrast alternative solutions to patient problems.
   b. Changes in clinical practice result from clinical experience and the application of research findings.
   c. Clinical inquiry is critical to the care of the vulnerable patient.
   d. The model identifies clinical inquiry as identical to clinical reasoning.

22. A progressive care nurse is caring for a patient with the following entries in the EHR: 1) patient admitted with fever of unknown origin and atypical abdominal pain for three days; 2) patient has requested DNR status; however, the patient's son has voiced objections to that order; and 3) patient demonstrates lab evidence of chronic renal failure. According to the Synergy Model, which of the following statements is consistent with this information?
   a. The patient demonstrates high stability.
   b. The patient's history is consistent with multiple resources.
   c. The patient's condition indicates low vulnerability.
   d. The patient's status is highly complex.

23. Which of the following nursing interventions is most consistent with the competencies of caring practices, advocacy, and moral agency?
    a. Developing cultural awareness of care team members
    b. Mentoring novice nurses in the use of research findings
    c. Facilitating the patient's transition from one level of care to another on the health continuum
    d. Refining educational programs for patients and families

24. According to the Synergy Model, at what level of nursing competence do the nursing competencies of clinical inquiry and clinical reasoning become inseparable in the research process?
    a. The experienced nurse
    b. The novice nurse
    c. The expert nurse
    d. All levels of competency

25. Which of the following has NOT been identified as a barrier to the application of nursing research findings to clinical practice?
    a. Inadequate funding
    b. Insufficient translation
    c. Lack of qualified nursing staff
    d. Limited patient populations

Answer Explanations #1

Clinical Judgment

Cardiovascular

1. B: An ST-segment elevation is the classic ECG reading that indicates a STEMI, in which the full thickness of the heart wall has been damaged, leading to the significant ECG changes. T-wave inversion can be linked to a number of cardiac disorders, both benign and life-threatening, but in the case of heart attacks, it is linked to NSTEMIs. The QT-segment prolongation is part of a condition in which the patient experiences irregular, chaotic heart rhythms from time to time and is not associated with an active myocardial infarction. The U-wave is sometimes too small to be observed on a normal ECG. It follows the T-wave and is not significant in showing heart wall damage, although it can become elevated in hypokalemia.

2. A: A woman may have flulike symptoms, anxiety, or jaw or back pain days to weeks before the actual cardiac event. These symptoms may be overlooked and the correct diagnosis missed if the clinician is unaware of gender differences. The other three symptoms listed are classic, well-known symptoms of a myocardial infarction.

3. C: Acid reflux, along with anxiety or panic attacks, may mimic the chest pain experienced during a heart attack. The proximity of the upper sphincters of the stomach involved in acid reflux to the heart muscle are the cause of the confusion. The patient's presentation, history, and physical along with lab testing and assessment will aid in correct diagnosis. While liver cirrhosis, kidney failure, and pneumonia all involve organs close to the heart, they do not mimic the symptoms of a heart attack.

4. D: Troponin is a muscle cell protein that is released when cardiac tissue is broken down during an ischemic event. Elevated levels of troponin in the bloodstream indicate cardiac muscle damage. Creatinine and BUN are waste products of the body, and higher levels of these in the bloodstream indicate kidney failure or damage, not heart damage. CK-MB is a cardiac enzyme, not muscle cell content. Therefore, it is slightly different, but could also indicate cardiac damage.

5. C: Angioplasty and stent placement often occur during routine cardiac catheterization to open up occluded blood vessels. There is no camera or scope; instead, dye is shot through the catheter and x-ray images are obtained to visualize structures. The femoral artery is the most commonly accessed blood vessel for left heart catheterization versus the brachial artery, which can be used but is not as common. The patient is not put to sleep, but rather given medicine to help them relax while keeping them awake.

6. C: A first-degree heart block is NOT a direct risk factor for the development of an embolus. Women during pregnancy and in the postpartum period, individuals with a history of a previous stroke, and patients with fractures that involve long bones are all at risk for the development of an embolus.

7. A: Jugular vein distention, peripheral edema, and pulmonary congestion are characteristics of blood volume backing up due to an obstruction. Decreased urine output, increased BUN, and increased creatinine are signs of renal failure. Chest pain, fatigue, and lightheadedness are signs of an MI. Problems with coordination, blurred vision, and paralysis are symptomatic of a stroke.

8. D: The pooling of blood and edematous swelling are signs of a venous insufficiency rather than an arterial one. Remember, arteries bring oxygen, so when there is a lack of oxygen, tissues cannot get oxygen, thus causing cyanosis and hair loss, and sores or wounds cannot heal. When venous blood is not returning to the heart, pooling and edema occur.

9. A: DVT is the most common cause of edema caused by venous insufficiency. The other three factors are also causes, but not as common as DVT.

10. D: An ankle-brachial BP index is commonly used to diagnose peripheral arterial disease by comparing the blood pressures of the two sites, thus assessing blood flow. An echocardiogram is a sonographic test used to visualize the structures of the heart, such as in heart failure. A computed tomography (CT) scan would not be useful for visualizing arterial structures of the extremities, or at least it is not commonly used. An electrocardiogram is used to measure and track electrical activity of heart muscle.

11. C: Critical limb ischemia (CLI) is the most concerning symptom of PVD. It is indicative of decreased circulation even at rest. Faint peripheral pulses may be a finding associated with PVD, but are not the most concerning symptom. Restricted mobility may be a sequela to PVD, but it is also not the most concerning. Feet that become pale when elevated are a symptom of PVD, but this is not the most concerning symptom.

12. D: A stroke is a potential complication of hypertension in a patient post-endarterectomy. The nurse must carefully monitor and treat high blood pressure should it occur. Bleeding would be marked by low blood pressure. Infection is a noncardiac issue; thus, it is unrelated to blood pressure in this instance. Pulmonary edema can occur as a result of heart failure and is not pertinent to the monitoring for high blood pressure.

13. A: Antiplatelet therapy, commonly aspirin, is coupled with antithrombotic therapy in the postoperative period following endarterectomy to prevent clotting of blood caused by platelet aggregation, thus reoccluding the blood vessels just operated on. Beta-blockers, ACE inhibitors, and ARBs are not commonly paired with antithrombotics; rather, they target blood pressure issues and heart failure.

14. B: When using an artificial graft, rather than a patient's own vessel, to graft in between the femoral and popliteal arteries in the leg, narrowing and reocclusion are a concern. This is a known complication of these types of grafts. Infection is always a risk but nonspecific to this instance. Edema is associated with venous occlusion and insufficiency. Tissue graft rejection is another nonspecific possibility.

15. D: Diuretics such as furosemide (Lasix®) will help reduce preload in the patient experiencing cardiogenic pulmonary edema. Metoprolol and other beta-blockers are used in heart failure to slow the beating of the heart. Calcium channel blockers, such as verapamil, are used for heart dysrhythmias such as atrial fibrillation and in some cases of heart failure, improving the heart's ability to pump. Narcotics such as morphine are sometimes used to reduce anxiety and oxygen hunger in acute cases of pulmonary edema.

16. A: Prehypertension is defined as systolic pressures ranging between 120 and 139 mmHg or diastolic pressures between 80 and 89 mmHg. Normal blood pressure is less than 120/80 mmHg. Stage 1 hypertension ranges from 140 to 159 mmHg systolic or 90 to 99 mmHg diastolic. Stage 2 hypertension is greater than or equal to 160 mmHg systolic or greater than or equal to 100 mmHg diastolic.

17. C: The depth of the wound is the biggest clue as to whether the ulcer arose out of an arterial insufficiency or a venous insufficiency. Arterial ulcers are usually nonhealing and deep, eventually exposing tendons and bones if left untreated. The color of the ulcer may vary across a spectrum, regardless of the type. Cultures from the wound only tell what types of infectious agents have entered the ulcerative tissue. The size of the wound is irrelevant.

18. A: A patient in shock will usually exhibit oliguria, in which urine output has dramatically decreased or stopped altogether, signaling a shutting down of the kidneys due to lack of perfusion from the heart. Other signs of decreased perfusion as seen in a shock state are distant heart sounds, cyanosis, and faint and rapid pulse.

19. B: Norepinephrine is a potent vasoconstrictor that may be used if dopamine is inadequate in maintaining normal blood pressure in a patient experiencing cardiogenic shock. Dobutamine is an option but is used for systemic vasodilation with stronger beta effects than the others mentioned here. Milrinone causes vasodilation and positive inotropic effects. Nitroglycerin is a potent vasodilator that would lower blood pressure rather than raise it.

20. C: Aldactone® (spironolactone), Choice *C,* is a potassium-sparing diuretic and supports the patient's concern regarding their potassium level at this time. This medication does not encourage the excretion of potassium via urine. Lasix® (furosemide) and Demadex® (torsemide) are loop diuretics and Microzide® (hydrochlorothiazide) is a thiazide diuretic. These medications do not specifically target conserving potassium in the body to address the patient's concern arising from their history. Therefore, Choices *A, B,* and *D* are incorrect.

21. C: The sudden death of a grandmother needs to be probed for if a cause was determined. If she passed away suddenly because of hypertrophic cardiomyopathy that had been previously undiagnosed before autopsy, the patient should be screened for this condition as well, as it often may be asymptomatic until syncope or sudden death occurs. The other three conditions listed are of value, but do not point toward hypertrophic cardiomyopathy specifically.

22. C: Ventricular fibrillation is the most common rhythm detected when a patient goes into cardiac arrest. This is because the fibrillation of the ventricles produces inadequate heart contraction to pump the blood to the vital organs. Without oxygen, the patient "falls out," becoming unconscious and unresponsive. Patients in ventricular fibrillation need immediate cardiopulmonary resuscitation—most importantly, defibrillation. The other rhythms mentioned—atrial fibrillation, ventricular tachycardia, and supraventricular tachycardia—may present serious complications for the patient and must be treated, but are not the most common cause of cardiac arrest.

23. B: A patient with heart failure will not be able to respond to increased preload as a normal, healthy patient would, resulting in decreased cardiac output. Contractility is not increased as well as in a healthy heart. Changes in rhythm and rate are not significant as far as patients with heart failure and their response to preload.

24. D: Aspirin works by inhibiting platelet aggregation to prevent clot formation. Paxil® is used to treat anxiety and depression. Coumadin® (warfarin) works by blocking Vitamin K dependent clotting factors. Heparin enhances the effect of antithrombin III to inhibit thrombin activation.

25. D: Long QT syndrome is a rare, hereditary condition found many times in healthy children and adults that may be asymptomatic until a syncopal episode or even sudden death occurs. First- and third-degree heart block occurs when there are conduction problems between the atria and ventricles, resulting in "missed" heartbeats. Bundle branch block occurs when there is an interruption in the electrical impulse across the ventricles of the heart.

26. C: An atrial septal defect is not part of the tetralogy of Fallot. The tetralogy of Fallot includes a ventricular septal defect, an aorta arising from both ventricles (an atrial septal defect), and hypertrophy of the overworked right ventricle due to pulmonary valve stenosis.

27. B: Cigarette smoking is a major cause of atherosclerosis, the most common cause of aortic aneurysm. Following a low-fat diet would help with dyslipidemia, which may be a contributor to atherosclerosis, but it is not as important as stopping smoking, which causes the inflammatory, toxic effects that produce atherosclerosis. Exercise is helpful in coping with stress effectively, as is meditation, but not specific to atherosclerosis that causes aortic aneurysms.

28. A: Beck's triad of muffled heart sounds, distended neck veins, and hypotension are cardinal signs of cardiac tamponade. Chest pain and back pain are the most common presenting symptoms with the AAA. Heart function, breathing, and consciousness are not evident in cardiopulmonary arrest. Cardiogenic shock includes ashen, cyanotic, or mottled extremities; distant heart sounds; and rapid and faint peripheral pulses.

29. C: New onset of peripheral edema may be signaling decompensation by the right side of the heart and progressive heart failure. Oxygenation levels for CHF patients are generally lower but tolerated well. Ninety-two percent is an acceptable oxygen saturation level for this patient. Dyspnea upon exertion is not an unusual finding during a CHF exacerbation. Elevated BNP levels, although abnormal, are anticipated with CHF.

30. C: Morphine is part of most cardiac protocols given for cardiac pain relief when patients have an unacceptable pain level, while nitroglycerine is a vasodilator that reduces preload in the presence of chest pain. Magnesium sulfate is administered for the Torsade de pointes dysrhythmia and is not part of general chest pain protocol. With a pain level 10/10 and diaphoresis, acetaminophen would not be an appropriate pain management choice.

31. B: An abdominal aneurysm may present or be found on examination as a pulsating mass in the abdomen. Indigestion when lying down is associated with gastrointestinal reflux disease (GERD) and is not indicative of an AAA. Fatigue and shortness of breath on exertion may be indicative of coronary artery or pulmonary disease. It is not directly associated with an AAA. Pain radiating down the left arm is a classic sign of a myocardial infarction (MI).

32. D: Symptoms of left-sided heart failure are tachycardia, shortness of breath, and the expectoration of frothy pink sputum. Pitting edema is symptomatic of right-sided heart failure and increased venous pressure that backs up into the tissues, causing edema. Ascites is a result of diffuse congestion in the liver caused by the increased venous pressure that characterizes right-sided heart failure. Fatigue is a generalized symptom not associated with the diagnosis of either right- or left-sided heart failure.

33. B: The diuretic reduces blood volume, and the ACE inhibitor reduces SVR by interfering with the RAAS. An ARB reduces systemic vascular resistance, but morphine is used to treat pain. The diuretic reduces blood volume, but a beta-blocker increases myocardial contractility. The diuretic reduces blood volume, but a CCB works by increasing myocardial contractility.

34. **D:** An INR of 3.5 is elevated and will cause bleeding complications if thrombolytic therapy is initiated before the INR returns to the normal level of less than or equal to 1.1.

Pulmonary

1. **C:** Acute respiratory distress syndrome (ARDS) is defined by the timing, a chest x-ray, the origin of the edema, and the severity of hypoxemia. In terms of timing, the onset of symptoms in ARDS is within one week of the inciting incident. A chest x-ray should reveal bilateral lung infiltrates not explained by consolidation, atelectasis, or effusions. The edema origin is not explained by heart failure or fluid overload, and the severity of hypoxemia is based on the PaO_2/FiO_2 ratio while on 5 cm of continuous positive airway pressure (CPAP).

2. **B:** The scenario depicts an episode of status asthmaticus. Common pharmacological agents used to treat this condition include albuterol (short-acting Beta-2 agonist), ipratropium (anticholinergic), and methylprednisolone (corticosteroid). Her new symptoms (anxiety, tremors, and tachycardia) are all common side effects which can be attributed to albuterol. Anticholinergics can induce side effects such as dry mouth, blurred vision, and constipation. Corticosteroids (if used for longer than two weeks) can have side effects such as weight gain, osteoporosis, thinning of skin, cataracts, easy bruising, and diabetes. She should be switched to the short-acting Beta-2 agonist levalbuterol because it's as effective as albuterol but without the alarming side effects.

3. **D:** This scenario depicts a moderate to severe acute exacerbation of COPD. Azithromycin is a macrolide antibiotic. In clinical trials, the use of antibiotics in individuals with a moderate to severe exacerbation of COPD diminishes the risk of treatment failure and death. Oxygen and albuterol target dyspnea. In clinical trials, the administration of oral corticosteroids fairly early in the midst of a COPD exacerbation decreased the need for hospitalization.

4. **A:** Virchow's triad identifies factors that contribute to the thrombotic process associated with deep venous thrombosis (DVT) and pulmonary embolism (PE). The triad consists of hypercoagulability, endothelial injury/dysfunction, and hemodynamic changes such as stasis and turbulence. Heart disease is a risk factor for DVT and PE, but it is not part of Virchow's triad.

5. **D:** This scenario depicts a case of acute bronchitis. The most common causes of acute bronchitis are respiratory viruses (such as influenza A and B), respiratory syncytial virus (RSV), parainfluenza, adenovirus, rhinovirus, and coronavirus. Acute bronchitis should not be routinely treated with antibiotics, but there are exceptions to this rule. It's reasonable to use antibiotics if an existing medical condition poses a risk of serious complications. Antibiotic treatment of acute bronchitis is also reasonable in individuals older than 65 years of age with a hospitalization in the past year, those being currently treated with a steroid, and those diagnosed with congestive heart failure or diabetes.

6. **B:** Vena cava filters are also known as inferior vena cava (IVC) filters or Greenfield filters. They are used to prevent a pulmonary embolism (PE). Indications for the placement of a vena cava filter include:

- An absolute contraindication to anticoagulants
- Survival after a massive PE and a high probability that a recurrent PE will be fatal
- Documented recurrent PE

7. **D:** The big hint here is the route of administration: Oral corticosteroids will pass through the gastrointestinal tract, where they will be absorbed into the systemic circulation in the small intestine,

affecting the body system as a whole. Inhaled and nebulized drugs such as bronchodilators and albuterol will directly affect the inflamed airways of status asthmaticus, thus not affecting systemic inflammation. The same goes for epinephrine administered subcutaneously. Its action will primarily be targeting the airways, with bronchodilation being the desired effect.

8. C: Sleeve resection is a thoracic surgery in which an affected part of the airway is removed, with the top and bottom sections being sewn together. This action is similar to cutting a stain off a sleeve and reattaching the top and bottom sections of the sleeve back together—hence, the name "sleeve resection." Pneumonectomy is the removal of an entire lung. Lobectomy is the removal of a lobe. Wedge resection refers to removing a part of an affected lobe.

9. C: A massive pulmonary embolism impairs right ventricular function as well as causing marked hypotension. Small does not affect the right ventricular function or blood pressure. Submassive affects the right ventricle without hypotension. Grand is not a category of a PE.

10. D: A patient who is in renal failure with a suspected PE will likely undergo V/Q scanning, in which ventilation and perfusion of the lungs are visualized. Transesophageal echocardiography is used for visualizing the back of the heart and is not appropriate in this scenario. CT scanning with contrast is contraindicated, as the patient with renal failure cannot tolerate the dye, which is primarily metabolized by the kidney. MRI is not a usual scan for a PE.

11. A: Choice *A* is an appropriate flow rate for the nurse to set for the nasal cannula. Patients with chronic obstructive pulmonary disease (COPD) require oxygen at low flow rates to maintain the hypoxic stimulus to breathe. Choices *B*, *C*, and *D* are too high for a patient with COPD because these rates would suppress their stimulus to breathe.

12. D: An early sign of respiratory distress is agitation, along with confusion and oxygen hunger. Later signs of respiratory distress occur when the patient has become fatigued because of the respiratory effort they have put forth. These signs include decreased respiratory rate, unconsciousness, and cyanosis.

13. C: Naloxone, or Narcan, is the antidote for respiratory depression caused by an opioid overdose. Morphine and hydrocodone are examples of opioids that might cause respiratory failure if overdose occurs. Alprazolam is an example of a benzodiazepine, a known cause of respiratory failure if overdosed.

14. A: *Streptococcus pneumoniae* is the most common cause of bacterial pneumonia. The other three organisms listed are also bacterial and may cause pneumonia but are not as common as *S. pneumoniae.*

15. C: Immunocompromised pneumonia occurs in patients whose immune systems have been weakened. It may occur in patients who have an HIV infection or are undergoing chemotherapy or radiation regimens. Community-acquired pneumonia occurs in persons who had little to no contact with medical facilities prior to the infection. Hospital-acquired pneumonias occur in patients who have been hospitalized and as a result of immobilization. Health care–associated pneumonias occur in patients in long-term facilities or some other health care facility besides a hospital.

16. B: A morning headache is a common symptom of COPD. The cough associated with COPD is usually productive. A barrel chest, not a narrowed chest, is common due to hyperinflation of the lungs. Patients with COPD will often experience weight loss and muscle wasting because of the disease.

17. C: Pursed-lip breathing, breathing through a small, straw-like opening of the mouth, creates positive end-expiratory pressure (PEEP) for the patient with compromised lung function, as is the case with COPD patients. Tripod breathing is common in COPD patients but does not increase PEEP; rather, it creates more space for lung volume when they are having trouble breathing. Wide open-mouth breathing is not helpful for increasing PEEP. Frequent coughing is caused by the body's constant mucociliary response to try and clear mucus from inflamed airways.

18. C: CPAP therapy is used in the management of OSA to provide a constant positive pressure in the airway, preventing collapse and maintaining patency during sleep. It does not directly affect falling asleep, Choice *A*, or cure sleep apnea completely, Choice *B*. CPAP therapy does not increase the oxygen content of the air breathed in, Choice *D*, but it helps to maintain the airway and prevent interruptions in breathing.

19. A: Spiriva is an anticholinergic bronchodilator that helps to relax the smooth muscles in the airways, resulting in bronchodilation and improved airflow. It does not directly decrease inflammation, Choice *B*; thin mucus, Choice *C*; or stimulate surfactant production, Choice *D*.

20. B: Spontaneous pneumothorax occurs without any obvious cause or traumatic event. It is more common in individuals without any underlying lung disease and is frequently seen in tall, thin individuals. Choice *A* occurs when air enters the pleural space and cannot escape, leading to increasing pressure and compression of the heart and lungs. Choice *C* occurs as a result of trauma or injury to the chest, such as a rib fracture. Choice *D* is caused by a medical intervention or procedure, such as a lung biopsy or insertion of a central venous catheter.

21. C: Vitamin K plays a role in the body's natural clotting process, and Warfarin works by inhibiting the synthesis of certain clotting factors dependent on vitamin K. Maintaining a consistent intake of vitamin K helps maintain the desired therapeutic effect of Warfarin without unnecessary restrictions. Choice *A* is incorrect because it suggests avoiding vitamin K–rich foods altogether, which is not necessary for most patients on Warfarin. Although Choice *B* recognizes the importance of a balanced diet, it does not highlight the important fact that vitamin K may alter Warfarin's effectiveness; therefore, it is incorrect. Choice *D* is not necessary and may lead to nutritional imbalances.

Endocrine/Hematology/Neurology/Gastrointestinal/Renal

1. B: The nurse should suspect hypoglycemia based on the circumstances and symptoms being experienced by the patient. Hypoglycemia may occur when a patient receiving insulin therapy, as may be the case here if the patient is diabetic, has been NPO for a procedure. Fasting in addition to insulin therapy if not carefully monitored and tweaked will likely cause hypoglycemia. Sweating, nausea, and malaise are all hypoglycemic symptoms. A blood sugar reading should be immediately obtained to determine if hypoglycemia is the cause and, if so, treated with oral glucagon. Hypochondria is always possible but should be a diagnosis made by a psychiatrist. Hypotension is a less likely option given the circumstances, though not completely improbable. Hypothyroidism is unlikely and not a condition that the nurse would be able to independently diagnose without proper lab work and clinical workup.

2. C: Diabetes insipidus is caused by a decreased amount of vasopressin secreted by the pituitary gland in the body. This decrease will cause massive diuresis, leading to dehydration and hypovolemia. SIADH is the opposite situation in which vasopressin is overly released, also called antidiuretic hormone, and fluid is retained, leading to hyponatremia. Diabetes type I and diabetes type II, the two types of diabetes mellitus, share the name diabetes but are slightly different. Diabetes describes a condition in which polyuria occurs, and in the case of diabetes mellitus (mellitus is Latin for "sweetened with honey," describing the sweetness of urine in diabetes mellitus), it is because of hyperglycemia that the polyuria occurs.

3. C: Acetone, a ketoacid produced during the breakdown of fatty acids during diabetic ketoacidosis, is expelled through respiration, thus giving a person in DKA a "fruity" smell to the breath. Glycerol and alanine are byproducts of fat and muscle breakdown as alternative energy sources convert to glucose. Triglycerides are broken down into free fatty acids as another alternative to glucose as energy for metabolism in the body.

4. D: Massive urine production, or polyuria, is the result of a hyperglycemic state in the body and a hallmark sign of any diabetic condition. Urine is not concentrated, but rather diluted. Sodium, potassium, and other electrolyte imbalances may occur as a result of polyuria but are not a direct effect of hyperglycemia.

5. A: The most obvious effects of the super-concentrated blood that are characteristic of HHNK will appear neurologically. Confusion, seizures, coma, stroke-like syndromes, dizziness, and drowsiness are all neurological symptoms that appear in HHNK. The other systems of the body, such as cardiac, endocrine, and pulmonary may be affected but are not directly associated with the usual symptomology of HHNK.

6. C: Small-bowel obstruction is associated with severe fluid and electrolyte losses. The normal serum sodium level is 135 to 145 mEq/L; therefore, Choice *C* is indicative of deficient serum sodium and severe alterations in fluid balance. Small-bowel obstruction is manifested by metabolic alkalosis due to the loss of acids with vomiting. Choice *A* is consistent with metabolic acidosis, not alkalosis, and is therefore incorrect. As noted, small-bowel obstruction is associated with fluid volume deficits; however, the reported serum osmolality of 285 mOsm/kg is within the normal range for serum osmolality (275–295 mOsm/kg); therefore, Choice *B* is incorrect. Abdominal distention in large-bowel obstruction most commonly occurs in the lower abdomen, while abdominal distention in the small bowel most commonly occurs in the epigastric or upper abdominal area; therefore, Choice *D* is incorrect.

7. D: Chronic alcohol abuse and biliary tract dysfunction are the most frequent causes of acute pancreatitis; however, there are no identified criteria that explain why some individuals will experience pancreatitis while others do not. Acute pancreatitis is most often diagnosed by the presenting history and physical examination. ECRP is only indicated in patients with acute pancreatitis and concomitant biliary disease; therefore, Choice *A* is incorrect. Ultrasonography is generally less useful than CT imaging for pancreatitis, and its efficacy is significantly decreased in the presence of abdominal distention, which distorts the images; therefore, Choice *B* is incorrect. Although rectal indomethacin is used commonly to treat acute pancreatitis resulting from ERCP imaging, controversy remains regarding the efficacy of the therapy; therefore, Choice *C* is incorrect.

8. C: Endoscopy is used to diagnose the condition and to cauterize hemorrhagic sites. The treatment algorithm for peptic ulcer disease recommends surgical intervention if two endoscopic attempts at hemostasis are unsuccessful. The pain related to peptic ulcer disease does not begin until the ingested food has reached the duodenum; therefore, the pain does not begin for two to three hours after a meal, while the onset of pain with gastric ulcers is twenty to thirty minutes after a meal. Choice *A* is incorrect. Gastric ulcers are associated with an increased incidence of malignancy, not peptic ulcers; therefore,

Choice *B* is incorrect. NSAID use is a commonly associated cause of peptic ulcer disease. However, even excluding patients who use NSAIDs, more than sixty percent of the cases of peptic ulcer disease are related to H. pylori infection; therefore, Choice *D* is incorrect.

9. D: Aspirin works by inhibiting platelet aggregation to prevent clot formation. Paxil® is used to treat anxiety and depression. Coumadin® (warfarin) works by blocking Vitamin K dependent clotting factors. Heparin enhances the effect of antithrombin III to inhibit thrombin activation.

10. C: Heparin works by enhancing the effect of antithrombin III which prevents the activation of thrombin and thus prevents fibrinogen from being converted to fibrin. It is important to note that heparin does not get rid of pre-existing clots, it helps prevent clot expansion and formation of new clots. Paxil® is used to treat anxiety and depression. Coumadin® (warfarin) works by blocking Vitamin K dependent clotting factors. Aspirin works on platelet aggregation.

11. A: Since electrolytes need to be suspended in a certain amount of liquid to move optimally and carry out their intended function, fluid level in the body is important. As fluid levels increase beyond a state of fluid-electrolyte balance, electrolyte levels will decrease, since there is too much fluid present. If fluid levels are too low, such as in a state of dehydration, there will be too many electrolytes per unit of fluid, which also prevents the electrolytes from carrying out their intended function.

12. D: Patients with type 1 diabetes cannot produce enough or any insulin and are required to manually administer it into their system. This answer option is the only one that has an appropriate, logical pairing; therefore, it is the correct statement.

13. D: Patients with type 2 diabetes cannot use the insulin their body produces to break down food into glucose. They can manage their symptoms with lifestyle changes, such as losing weight, diet, and exercise. They can also use the drug metformin, which helps regulate their blood glucose levels.

14. A: The sodium-potassium pump is a balance maintained between sodium on the inside of a cell and potassium in the blood outside of the cell. Maintaining this balance creates membrane potential across the cell. The other pairings listed in the statements do not make sense.

15. A: Patients with type 1 diabetes are prone to diabetic ketoacidosis due to the absence of adequate insulin in their blood. This absence makes it more likely for the body to use fatty acids for energy rather than carbohydrates, and without insulin, this can lead to excessive ketones in the blood. Excessive ketones lead to an acidic blood environment.

16. C: Immunocompromised patients need to minimize their contact with potentially infectious or illness-causing agents as much as possible, since even mild illnesses can be life-threatening to them. All the practices listed are recommended for patients who have a compromised immune system with the exception of only drinking bottled water. While clean water and clean drinking vessels should always be used, water does not need to necessarily be bottled.

17. B: Stage 5 chronic kidney disease is the last stage of progression for this condition. By this time, it is serious enough to require constant dialysis (a process that filters the blood for the kidneys) or a kidney transplant because the kidneys have failed.

18. D: The appropriate response to an initial unprovoked seizure episode—one that is not related to a specific cause such as head trauma—is to identify any abnormal electrical activity of the brain with an

EEG and any anatomical lesions in the brain with MRI. There is no indication of substance use in the patient's history, which means that this assessment would not be a priority for this patient at this point; therefore, Choice *A* is incorrect. General guidelines indicate that AED therapy should be delayed until a second unprovoked seizure episode occurs and after the initial EEG and MRI studies are completed; therefore, Choice *B* is incorrect. The patient's history does not support the possibility of infection as the precipitating event for this seizure activity, which means performing the invasive lumbar puncture would not be indicated; therefore, Choice *C* is incorrect.

19. C: Alteplase is the single fibrinolytic agent approved for the treatment of ischemic stroke because it is associated with fewer adverse effects than the remaining agents. Streptokinase and tenecteplase have been used effectively to treat patients with acute myocardial infarction; however, in patients with ischemic stroke, streptokinase has been associated with an increased risk of intracranial hemorrhage and death. Current evidence for the efficacy and safety of urokinase and tenecteplase does not support their use for the treatment of ischemic stroke. Therefore, Choices *A, B*, and *D* are incorrect.

20. B: Hypertonic saline, in which the sodium is more concentrated, is often used to correct the dilutional hyponatremia of SIADH. Normal saline has a 0.9% concentration of sodium, which is the same as circulating blood and thus will not be helpful in correcting hyponatremia. Hypotonic saline, in which there is less than 0.9% concentration of sodium, will also not be helpful in restoring normal sodium levels to the blood. Lactated ringer's solution is not a fluid used for the purpose of restoring normal sodium levels.

21. D: Thalassemia is considered a microcytic anemia, in which heme and globin do not synthesize appropriately and oxygen-carrying capacity is compromised. Normocytic anemias are those that include normally-sized red blood cells that are deficient in number. Aplastic anemia is an example of a normocytic anemia. Macrocytic anemias are defined as red blood cells that are quite large in shape, leading to abnormalities in oxygen-carrying ability and oxygen delivery. Thrombocytic refers to a platelet, a different component of the blood, and is thus irrelevant in this scenario.

22. C: A person with dark skin tones who is suspected to be anemic will show pallor in the conjunctiva of the eyes along with the palms of the hands, bottoms of feet, buccal mucosa, and lips. Forearms, scalp, and cheeks will not show pallor, per se, but may show a gray, ashy hue if they are truly anemic.

24. A: Encephalopathy is a general term that means brain disease, damage, or malfunction, with the major symptom being an altered mental state. It is not always caused by a lack of oxygen to the brain; that is anoxic encephalopathy. However, there are other possible causes. For example, hepatic encephalopathy is caused by liver disease. Encephalopathy is often considered a complication of a primary problem.

25. A: Patients with acute kidney injury may experience anemia as the kidneys are unable to produce enough erythropoietin, a hormone that stimulates red blood cell production. To help with the anemia, erythropoietin can be given to help produce more red blood cells. Choices *B, C,* and *D* are all incorrect. Diuretics are used to increase urine output, antibiotics are used to treat infection, and immunosuppressants are used to suppress the immune system.

Musculoskeletal/Multisystem/Psychosocial

1. A: Use of a cane is not a risk factor for falls in the elderly. A cane would actually benefit a person by giving them extra stability when walking. Poor lighting is a risk factor because it could cause someone to stumble over items on the floor or cause an imbalance by bumping into unseen furniture. Muscle weakness and slower reflexes are also risk factors for falls in the elderly.

2. A: The most immediate action the nurse should take after noticing that the patient looks pale and feels cold is to assist the patient back to bed to prevent a fall. Afterward, the nurse can assess the patient's nutrition and hemodynamic status, Choices *B*, *C*, and *D*.

3. B: Selective serotonin reuptake inhibitors (SSRIs) are a class of drugs that can treat both anxiety and depression symptoms. Therefore, brand names of this drug, such as Prozac®, Zoloft®, and Lexapro®, may be prescribed to individuals who are suffering from anxiety, depression, or a combination of both.

4. A: There is a documented tendency for patients who are prescribed antibiotics to stop taking the dosage once their symptoms subside. However, stopping a prescription antibiotic before the dose is completed does not kill all of the harmful bacteria. The bacteria that remain evolve to become resistant to the antibiotic, and the medicine is no longer effective. Other reasons for resistance include over-prescription for medical cases that do not necessarily require antibiotics.

5. C: The first piece of personal protective equipment the nurse should don is a gown, Choice *C,* per guidelines from the CDC. Choice *A*, gloves, are donned next, followed by Choice *B*, mask, and ultimately, Choice *D*, goggles, are donned last. The nurse must follow this sequence to ensure protection against infection transmission.

6. B: When working with a patient who has a strong history of aggressive behavior, the nursing team should start the therapeutic relationship by establishing trust and rapport. The team should strive to maintain a proactive approach to support and anticipate patient needs. The use of medication, Choice *C*; restraints, Choice *D*; and seclusion, Choice *A*, while potential interventions for care, should not happen first or without warrant by the current episode.

7. A: Tardive dyskinesia, a serious side effect of antipsychotic medication, produces many involuntary movements including tongue thrusting. Tardive dyskinesia is an involuntary neurologic movement disorder with persistent effect. Headache, Choice *B*; blurred vision, Choice *C*; and fever, Choice *D*, are not symptoms of tardive dyskinesia.

8. C: Community-associated, methicillin-resistant Staphylococcus aureus (CA-MRSA) is notoriously resistant to most antibiotics, except vancomycin and linezolid, with linezolid quickly becoming the agent of choice for the treatment of CA-MRSA pneumonia.

9. C: This scenario depicts a case of community-acquired pneumonia (CAP), specifically pneumococcal pneumonia. The most common cause of CAP is *Streptococcus pneumoniae*, or pneumococcus. It's a gram-positive bacterium, usually occurring in pairs (diplococci). The other bacteria (*Haemophilus influenzae, Moraxella catarrhalis*, and *Staphylococcus aureus*) are less common causes of CAP.

10. D: Colace® (docusate sodium), Choice *D*, can be prescribed alongside opiates to ease constipation, a common side effect of this drug class. Choice *A* represents a medication that is prescribed for opioid addiction and would not be prescribed at the time of opioid prescription for symptom management. Choice *B* and Choice *C* are both contraindicated for use while taking opiates and should be avoided at this time.

11. B: Thiamine, Choice *B,* represents a supplement given to a patient struggling with alcohol withdrawal, typically during the first few days of their inpatient hospitalization. Thiamine is often deficient in the patient experiencing frequent and excessive alcohol consumption. Choices *A*, *C*, and *D*, while important B vitamins, do not directly correlate with the patient's treatment needs at this time and therefore are not routinely administered as part of the treatment plan for alcohol withdrawal.

12. C: Choice *C* identifies a stuporous patient exhibiting no articulated verbal response with limited moaning, accompanied by arousal only after vigorous stimulation. Lethargic, Choice *A,* describes a patient who appears drowsy and arouses with gentle stimulation. Obtunded, Choice *B,* describes a patient who responds to repeated external stimulation to maintain attention. A patient that is comatose, Choice *D,* indicates they have no discernible response to stimulation. The levels of consciousness proceed with increasing severity from confused, to lethargic, to obtunded, to stuporous, and finally to comatose.

13. B: Choice *B* represents the correct way to measure and use a cane. The length of the cane should ensure that the patient is able to slightly flex the elbow to allow for proper body mechanics and safety. Choice *A* is subjective and should be avoided. Choice *C* should be avoided, as full flexion does not represent properly supported posture or ambulation. Choice *D* must be avoided because full extension of the arm with a forward lean is unsafe and does not support a steady gait.

14. B: During septic shock, metabolic acidosis and respiratory alkalosis are expected findings, along with a symptom presentation of shortness of breath, temperature changes, confusion, and diaphoresis. Thus, *I* and *II* are correct. *III* is incorrect, as the patient would likely experience a widening pulse pressure, not one that is narrowing. *IV* is incorrect, as the patient would display a decreased cardiac output.

15. B: All the symptoms reported by the patient are part of severe alcohol withdrawal; however, reporting that the room is spinning points towards vestibular disturbance. Patients experiencing vestibular disturbance will feel that the room is rotating, the walls are falling, and the floor is moving. The GI symptoms, headache, and tremors relate to different systems affected by the alcohol withdrawal.

16. B: Healthcare power of attorney is the legal term for the person appointed by the patient to make their healthcare decisions should they become incapacitated. This may be a caregiver, but not necessarily. The hospice nurse does not make the decisions but rather follows the doctor's orders and gives council to the patient and their family. A legal guardian may also be appointed to be the healthcare power of attorney, but not necessarily.

17. D: An infected wound will become reddened, inflamed, and discharge pus. A surgical wound should be clean with approximated boundaries. A trauma wound may be irregularly shaped and large. A healing wound develops scabbing and possibly scar tissue but should not appear as the wound described.

18. D: Overuse of antibiotics is what led to the mutation and uprising of drug-resistant organisms such as MRSA, VRE, and CRE. These types of "superbugs" are resistant to antibiotic treatments that used to work against them such as methicillin, amoxicillin, penicillin, and oxacillin. Stronger, broader antibiotic treatments must be used for longer periods of time to kill off drug-resistant organisms that cause infections.

19. D: Delirium is transient, reversible, and usually has an acute onset with an illness. Dementia, on the other hand, is a slow-developing, irreversible, and chronic condition often accompanied by another chronic diagnosis such as Parkinson's or Alzheimer's. Dementia may be slowed, but never fully reversed. Delirium usually can be treated and reversed by treating the underlying cause.

20. A: When a person abruptly stops drinking alcohol after prolonged excessive use, they develop alcohol withdrawal. It is a serious condition that presents with tachycardia, hypertension, tremors, sweating, and potential seizures. Choices *B, C,* and *D* are all incorrect because they are not symptoms of alcohol withdrawal.

Professional Caring and Ethical Practice

1. C: Advocacy involves supporting appropriate programs and actions for marginalized or at-risk populations. At the community level, the role of advocate for the PCCN may require knowledge of the legislative process to bring about change. In direct patient care, the PCCN will be the advocate for the patient by providing the information necessary for informed choices and supporting those choices in the development of the plan of care. Fidelity refers to trust. Autonomy refers to the right of self-determination. Beneficence refers to acting in the best interest of other individuals in society.

2. D: While the physician is legally responsible for satisfying all elements of informed consent, nurses are ethically responsible for assessing the patient's ability to process and understand the implications of informed consent. Nurses protect the patient's autonomy by raising these questions and concerns. The remaining elements of informed consent are required of the physician, rather than the nurses.

3. B: Moral agency refers to decision-making that includes accountability for right and wrong decisions by the moral agent. Advocacy is an ethical principle that is not legally enforced. However, many argue that paternalism is contrary to advocacy because of the assumption that the "system" knows what is best for the patient without concern for the patient's wishes. Moral agency is not restricted to a specific population; however, the PCCN will assess the ability of all patients to make informed decisions.

4. A: Distributive justice refers to the allocation of scarce resources while advocacy is support for policies that protect at-risk populations. The PCCN understands that scarce resource allocation may be sub-standard in certain populations. In nursing, nonmaleficence refers to the act of inflicting the least amount of harm possible in order to reach a favorable result. Fidelity refers to faithfulness but does not specifically address resources or the patient population.

5. D: The PCCN demonstrates professional competence as a result of a commitment to lifelong learning that is required for expert care of acutely ill patients. The remaining pairs each contain only a single element of the six elements of caring, compassion, confidence, and conscience.

6. B: The nurse is attempting to prevent possible harm that may occur as a result of lack of preparation for this specialty care assignment. The issue in this example is accepting or rejecting an assignment in the absence of adequate educational preparation. Although the infants in the NICU are an at-risk population, the nurse's actions are focused on unsafe care for the next eight hours as opposed to long-term solutions for staffing problems. The nurse is not promoting individual free will or the free will of the infants. As previously stated, the issue in this example is unsafe staffing, and while trust or fidelity might be an element of the PCCN's refusal to float to NICU, the most significant reason for the refusal is nonmaleficence.

7. C: In the Synergy Model, optimum patient care is achieved when the nurse facilitates communication and collaboration with the interdisciplinary team. The nurse possesses the clinical competence to anticipate the needs of the patient and respond appropriately by accessing the required system resources. Resiliency refers to the patient's potential for improved functional status. Creativity is not a characteristic of nursing care identified in the Synergy Model. The complexity of the patient's care needs is assessed according to the number of body systems that are involved.

8. B: Vigilance refers to the ability of the nurse to recognize and respond to changes in the patient's condition. According to the Synergy Model, vigilance as a caring practice is a learned behavior that evolves with clinical experience, which means that the novice nurse will identify predictable alterations in the patient's condition, while the experienced nurse will identify and respond to more subtle changes. The most experienced nurse is capable of intervening to prevent some adverse events. Engagement refers to committing to the patient care relationship, rather than responding to changes in the patient's condition. The changes noted in the patient's condition are early, subtle indications of heart failure. The novice nurse would initially associate the changes with the surgical procedure, while the experienced nurse would assess the patient for heart failure. Although collaboration with other providers may have been an outcome of the nurse's assessment, the initial care was an independent action.

9. B: The nurse at the second level of clinical practice continuum understands that the patient's death may be an acceptable outcome based on the knowledge accumulated through engagement with the patient and family and expert assessment of the patient's progress. The level 1 nurse understands that the patient may possibly die, but the nurse does not comprehend that the death is inevitable or acceptable. According to the Synergy Model, experienced nurses possess skills in managing end-of-life care, which benefits both the patient and the family. This special caring practice not only acknowledges death as an acceptable outcome but consists of a plan of care to achieve that outcome in the best way possible. According to the model, death is initially viewed as an acceptable outcome at the second level of caring practices.

10. C: The institution can support diversity by providing resources that satisfy cultural practices such as dietary rules. Institutions also may provide interpreters, information sessions for employees, and accommodations for religious observances. Under normal circumstances, requiring employees to speak a second language would severely limit the pool of eligible employees and would not be an effective strategy. Educational programs should be provided for all employees and should not be limited to supervisory staff. Offering alternative solutions to all requests for accommodation could be viewed as paternalistic and culturally insensitive. The institution is required to consider ways to satisfy all reasonable patient requests.

11. A: The novice nurse is comparing her own beliefs to the patient's beliefs and lacks the knowledge to understand the patient's point of view. This is the definition of ethnocentrism, which can adversely affect the nurse–patient relationship. The remaining observations could potentially affect the patient's refusal of the therapy, however, the patient's refusal in this example is clearly related to the religious objection.

12. D: The information indicates that the patient may be relatively stable, yet it is necessary to assess their ability to participate in the lesson for more than 15–20 minutes due to fatigue. Teaching-learning sessions of one hour or more will most likely be unproductive for this patient because of the limitations from fatigue. Teaching-learning sessions of one hour or more will most likely be unproductive for the patient with the identified Synergy Model score due to the limitations imposed by their multiple morbidities and moderately impaired resiliency. Literature from a nursing journal may or may not be appropriate to the patient's learning needs, however, simply providing printed information without additional instruction or discussion does not allow for assessment of the patient's comprehension of the information. The nurse caring for a patient in the acute care environment is responsible for assessing the patient's learning and initiating the necessary instruction. The teaching plan and the patient's progress will be reported to the community provider; however, the process should be started by the inpatient nursing staff.

13. B: According to the model, vulnerability refers to the presence of any stressor, actual or potential, that could adversely affect the patient's health. A history of smoking increases the patient's vulnerability to additional health alterations. Socioeconomic status and being married are related to resource availability, which refers to the availability of financial and emotional resources that are necessary to support the patient's recovery. The patient's active participation in the plan of care is considered to have a positive effect on care outcomes.

14. C: Nurses must acknowledge their own biases and recognize that those biases will affect their ability to provide culturally sensitive care. Standard protocols related to cultural beliefs and practices are an imperfect solution to the problem of culturally sensitive care because they are not individualized to the specific patient. Meeting the needs of the largest group in a population generally means that the cultural needs of the minority groups within the population are not met. As previously stated, culturally competent care results when caregivers first consider their own biases and the possible effect of those beliefs on patient care. If nurses base their care only on their own beliefs, the patient's beliefs and practices will be ignored.

15. D: The major premise of the Synergy Model states that synergy—optimum health—can only be achieved when agency resources and nursing competencies are congruent with the patient's needs. Family participation in the patient's care may improve outcomes, however, the synergy is related to the patient–nurse–healthcare agency triad.

16. B: The literature indicates that physicians are most likely to opt for the "cure" rather than the "care," which means that they choose interventions that provide an action or treatment that will address the patient's problems. In contrast, nurses intervene to address relationship issues. According to this view, the physician would choose to apply a brace to treat the patient's condition, while the nurse would be more likely to address affective domain issues such as stress, social support, and spiritual needs.

17. D: Participating in an agency-wide project is an example of systems thinking because it extends the focus of nurses beyond the care of an individual patient. The remaining interventions are examples of progressive systems thinking. The novice nurse is concerned with the meds for the individual patient; the nurse with more experience will be providing teaching-learning sessions in the nursing unit, rather than the entire institution, and soliciting performance evaluations from colleagues as well as supervisors.

18. C: The QSEN competencies were originally identified to improve patient safety in response to research that indicated that nearly 100,000 people died each year as a result of provider errors. The QSEN competencies refer to nursing activities and are often used as the basis for undergraduate nursing curricula. Systems thinking is the process by which nurses meet the competencies, and attainment of this ability is an incremental process based on nurses' continuing education and clinical experiences. Although systems thinking is associated with the QSEN competencies, and the use of systems thinking has improved patient outcomes, the basic assumption of the QSEN competencies was improved patient safety as a result of expert nursing care.

19. A: Root cause analysis is a structured examination of an incident or procedure that is focused on identifying the point at which an error occurred. The process is based on a comprehensive review of all parts of the organizational structure, which would support nurses' understanding of the systems thinking. Competency grids, process diagrams, and case studies are strategies that measure nursing competence related to the QSEN patient safety criteria.

20. A: Attention to the rapid expansion of knowledge that is reported from multiple sources requires significant amounts of time that may limit the ability of the individual nurse to assimilate the results into practice. Inadequate funding is a barrier to the initiation of a nursing research project. Insufficient motivation and knowledge are personal characteristics that may influence the process; however, the rapid expansion of knowledge has been identified as the most significant barrier.

21. C: The Synergy model identifies clinical inquiry as a nursing competency that develops as a result of clinical experience and enables nurses to apply research findings to clinical practice. Novice nurses in the model are able to identify changes in the patient's condition, but do not have the skill to identify alternative interventions. Nursing competencies that are identified as critical to the care of vulnerable patients include advocacy, moral agency, collaboration, and systems thinking. Clinical reasoning is not discussed in the Synergy Model; however, clinical judgment is identified as an essential element of the clinical inquiry competency of expert nurses.

22. D: The patient has evidence of high complexity due the unknown nature of their diagnosis, altered family dynamics, and evidence of chronic renal failure. Complexity is related to the number of systems that are affected by the patient's health issues. This demonstrates alterations in at least three systems; therefore, the complexity is rated as high. The remaining choices are positive indicators. Stability refers to the patient's response to therapy; high stability is associated with a low risk of death, which is not consistent with this patient's chronic renal failure and other unknown conditions. Resources refers to family support and financial resources, and this patient's family is at odds with the care decisions; therefore, the patient is lacking strong social support. Vulnerability refers to the patient's potential of being affected by various stressors. The patient is vulnerable due to chronic illness and alterations in the family dynamic.

23. C: Facilitating a patient's transition from one point on the health continuum to another requires caring practices in addition to advocacy and moral agency. Moral agency may be employed to ensure that the patient's wishes are considered, especially those wishes associated with end-of-life concerns. Developing cultural awareness is an example of a response to diversity, and the remaining two choices refer to the facilitation of learning.

24. C: The Synergy Model identifies expert nursing practice as the level of nursing competency in which clinical reasoning becomes an integrated element in the process of clinical inquiry. According to the model, prior to that point, nurses are capable of performing at some level of clinical inquiry and may be able to use clinical reasoning in patient care, but the total integration of the two does not occur until the expert level of nursing practice.

25. B: Insufficient translation is not a common barrier to the application of nursing research in clinical practice. Common barriers include inadequate funding, limited access to appropriate patient populations, lack of institutional support for research initiatives, and the rapid expansion of new knowledge from multiple sources.

PCCN Practice Test #2

Clinical Judgement

Cardiovascular

1. The nurse is caring for a patient who was admitted to the progressive care unit yesterday after arriving at the emergency department with signs and symptoms of a myocardial infarction (MI). The nurse is reviewing the patient's chart and notes that on arrival, the patient's electrocardiogram (ECG) showed ST-segment elevation. Which of the following statements best describes the key pathophysiological difference between ST elevation myocardial infarction (STEMI) and non-STEMI (NSTEMI)?

   a. STEMI is associated with complete occlusion of a coronary artery, whereas NSTEMI is associated with partial occlusion.
   b. NSTEMI is more severe and has a higher mortality rate than STEMI.
   c. STEMI is characterized by elevated troponin levels, and NSTEMI is not.
   d. STEMI involves ST-segment elevation on the ECG, and NSTEMI does not.

2. The nurse is caring for a 72-year-old patient with a history of hypertension, hyperlipidemia, and atrial fibrillation (AFib) who was admitted to the progressive care unit after presenting to the emergency department with chest pain, shortness of breath, and diaphoresis. The patient was diagnosed with NSTEMI, and the use of fibrinolytic therapy was considered. The nurse questions why fibrinolytic therapy was considered based on the patient's presentation. Which of the following statements best explains why fibrinolytics would NOT be indicated for this patient?

   a. Fibrinolytics are contraindicated in patients with a history of AFib.
   b. Fibrinolytics are not effective in patients with elevated troponin levels.
   c. Fibrinolytics are primarily used for patients with STEMI.
   d. Fibrinolytics increase the risk of hemorrhagic complications in patients with NSTEMI.

3. The nurse is caring for a 73-year-old patient with a history of diabetes mellitus and hyperlipidemia who was admitted to the progressive care unit after presenting to the emergency department with complaints of nausea, lightheadedness, and mild indigestion. Upon further testing, the patient was diagnosed with STEMI, and the primary nurse is curious about the patient's atypical presentation of an MI. In which of the following patient populations is a silent MI more likely to occur?

   a. Patients with a history of gastrointestinal disorders
   b. Patients with a history of diabetes mellitus
   c. Patients with a history of thyroid disorders
   d. Patients with a history of asthma

4. The nurse is caring for a 58-year-old postoperative patient following a diagnosis of STEMI two days ago. Which of the following surgical procedures did this patient most likely have?

   a. Coronary artery bypass graft (CABG) surgery
   b. Aortic valve replacement
   c. Carotid endarterectomy
   d. Percutaneous coronary intervention (PCI)

5. A 58-year-old patient with a history of hypertension is admitted to the progressive care unit after presenting to the emergency department with chest pain and shortness of breath. The patient was diagnosed with a right-sided MI, and the nurse is wondering why nitroglycerin administration was not initiated in the emergency department. Which of the following reasons best explains why nitroglycerin is contraindicated in patients with a right-sided MI?

a. Nitroglycerin may cause an increase in cardiac workload.
b. Nitroglycerin may interfere with the effects of other cardiac medications.
c. Nitroglycerin may lead to excessive vasodilation and a decrease in preload.
d. Nitroglycerin may cause a paradoxical increase in blood pressure.

6. A 68-year-old patient with a history of hypertension, hyperlipidemia, and smoking is admitted to the progressive care unit after presenting to the emergency department with chest pain and shortness of breath. The patient's ECG on arrival showed no significant ST-segment changes. Which of the following pathophysiological differences is most helpful in differentiating between NSTEMI and unstable angina?

a. Degree of coronary artery blockage
b. Presence of myocardial cell death
c. Location of the affected coronary artery
d. Severity of chest pain

7. The nurse is caring for a 55-year-old patient who was diagnosed with unstable angina after presenting to the emergency department with intermittent chest pain that occurs at rest and is not relieved by nitroglycerin. Which of the following risks should the nurse recognize as most closely associated with unstable angina?

a. Increased risk of sudden cardiac death
b. Higher likelihood of developing heart failure
c. Increased risk of developing AFib
d. Increased risk of progression to MI

8. A 62-year-old patient is admitted with fever, fatigue, and new-onset heart murmur. After further diagnostic tests, the patient is diagnosed with infective endocarditis. Which of the following pathogens should the nurse recognize as the most common culprit of infective endocarditis?

a. *Staphylococcus aureus*
b. *Clostridium difficile*
c. *Pseudomonas aeruginosa*
d. *Streptococcus pneumoniae*

9. The nurse is caring for a patient diagnosed with pericarditis. Which of the following symptoms is a typical clinical manifestation of this condition?

a. Pulsus paradoxus
b. Chest pain that improves when leaning forward
c. Peripheral edema
d. Wheezing

10. A 58-year-old patient with a history of hypertension presents with severe, sudden-onset chest pain that radiates to the back. The doctor suspects a dissecting aortic aneurysm. Which diagnostic test is most commonly used to confirm this diagnosis?
   a. Echocardiogram
   b. Chest x-ray
   c. CT scan
   d. ECG

11. The nurse is caring for a patient who is postoperative day one following an abdominal aortic aneurysm (AAA) repair. Which of the following assessment findings would be of most concern to the nurse?
   a. Absent bowel sounds
   b. Mild incisional pain
   c. Decreased sensation and movement in the legs
   d. Urine output of 50 mL/hr

12. The nurse is caring for a patient who is on the first postoperative day following CABG surgery. Which of the following complications is the nurse most likely to encounter during the immediate postoperative period?
   a. Hypotension
   b. Thrombocytopenia
   c. AFib
   d. Transient ischemic attack

13. The nurse is providing care to a patient who has been recently discharged from the ICU following cardiac surgery. The patient asks the nurse about the long-term care and lifestyle modifications needed for optimal recovery. Which of the following responses by the nurse is most appropriate?
   a. "You should avoid any physical activity or exercise for at least six months."
   b. "It is important to strictly adhere to a low-sodium diet and limit fluid intake."
   c. "Gradually resume your normal activities and follow a structured cardiac rehabilitation program."
   d. "You can stop taking all your prescribed medications once you feel better."

14. The nurse is caring for a patient who suddenly presents with hypotension, muffled heart sounds, and jugular venous distension. The nurse suspects cardiac tamponade. Which of the following is another clinical sign of this condition?
   a. Normal pulse pressure
   b. Pulsus paradoxus
   c. Widened pulse pressure
   d. Positive Homan's sign

15. The nurse is caring for a patient diagnosed with cardiac tamponade. What is the definitive treatment for this condition?
   a. Administration of vasopressors
   b. Cardiac catheterization
   c. Pericardiocentesis
   d. Cardiopulmonary resuscitation (CPR)

16. The nurse is preparing a patient for a diagnostic cardiac catheterization. Which of the following instructions should the nurse give the patient before the procedure?
   a. The patient will be put under general anesthesia.
   b. The patient should fast for 24 hours before the procedure.
   c. The patient might feel a warm sensation when the dye is injected.
   d. The patient will need to stay in the hospital for a week following the procedure.

17. A patient is recovering from an interventional cardiac catheterization in which a stent was placed in a coronary artery. Which medication would the nurse expect to administer post-procedure to this patient?
   a. Antiplatelet agent
   b. Beta-blocker
   c. Calcium channel blocker
   d. Diuretic

18. The nurse is caring for a 79-year-old patient who presents with severe shortness of breath, hypotension, and crackles in the lower lobes bilaterally. The patient's cardiac index is low, and the physician suspects cardiogenic shock. Which of the following conditions in the patient's medical history might have contributed to this diagnosis?
   a. Chronic obstructive pulmonary disease (COPD)
   b. Acute myocardial infarction (AMI)
   c. Pneumonia
   d. Asthma

19. A 65-year-old patient who recently suffered a severe MI is now showing signs of cardiogenic shock, including hypotension and tachycardia. The doctor has prescribed dobutamine. What is the primary reason for administering this medication?
   a. To improve renal perfusion
   b. To reduce preload and afterload
   c. To increase myocardial oxygen demand
   d. To increase cardiac output

20. The nurse is caring for a 40-year-old patient diagnosed with dilated cardiomyopathy. The patient asks why they experience breathlessness during mild exertion. What is the best explanation for this?
   a. The heart is unable to pump blood efficiently, leading to fluid buildup in the lungs.
   b. There is a decrease in the oxygen-carrying capacity of the blood.
   c. The respiratory muscles are weakened due to the disease process.
   d. There is an obstruction to the outflow of blood from the heart.

21. The nurse is caring for a 55-year-old patient with a history of hypertrophic cardiomyopathy (HCM). The patient has no history of hypertension or other cardiovascular diseases. The nurse recognizes that one potential risk associated with HCM is sudden cardiac death. Which of the following is a typical finding in HCM that could lead to this outcome?
   a. Myocardial ischemia due to narrowed coronary arteries
   b. Disorganized myocardial architecture and abnormal diastolic function
   c. Reduced cardiac output due to ventricular dilation
   d. Severe mitral valve regurgitation, leading to heart failure

22. The nurse is caring for a 62-year-old patient who suddenly complains of palpitations. The ECG reveals AFib with a rapid ventricular response. The nurse knows that immediate medical intervention is critical to prevent which of the following complications?
  a. MI
  b. Stroke
  c. Angina
  d. Hypertension

23. The nurse is caring for a patient diagnosed with AFib. Which medication would the nurse anticipate administering to this patient to help manage the arrhythmia?
  a. Hydrochlorothiazide
  b. Metoprolol
  c. Digoxin
  d. Warfarin

24. A nurse is providing discharge education to a 65-year-old patient diagnosed with chronic heart failure. The nurse emphasizes the importance of recognizing the signs of an acute exacerbation. Which of the following signs should the nurse include in the discussion?
  a. Decreased urination
  b. Weight loss
  c. Increased shortness of breath, particularly at night
  d. Decreased swelling in lower extremities

25. The nurse is caring for a 72-year-old patient with acute heart failure. The patient's blood pressure is 90/60 mm Hg, heart rate is 110 BPM, and oxygen saturation is 88%. Which of the following interventions should be the nurse's first priority?
  a. Start supplemental oxygen.
  b. Administer diuretics as ordered.
  c. Administer a beta-blocker.
  d. Increase IV fluids.

26. A 50-year-old male patient in the progressive care unit with a history of uncontrolled hypertension is observed to be restless and anxious. His blood pressure readings over the past 24 hours have ranged from 185/95 mm Hg to 210/110 mm Hg. The patient reports a severe headache and has been complaining of blurred vision. Recognizing these signs and symptoms, the nurse understands that the patient may be experiencing which of the following conditions?
  a. Hypertensive urgency
  b. Hypertensive emergency
  c. Acute heart failure
  d. Acute stroke

27. The nurse is caring for a 62-year-old patient with a history of type 2 diabetes and uncontrolled hypertension. The patient has been prescribed a regimen of hydrochlorothiazide and lisinopril. What is the primary reason these medications were chosen for this patient?
  a. To reduce the risk of kidney damage associated with diabetes and hypertension
  b. To improve blood glucose control
  c. To treat potential cardiac arrhythmias
  d. To decrease the patient's risk of developing atherosclerosis

28. A 68-year-old patient with a history of uncontrolled hypertension is admitted to the progressive care unit following an episode of chest pain at home. On admission, the patient's blood pressure is recorded at 220/120 mm Hg. Despite the administration of IV antihypertensives, the patient's blood pressure remains significantly elevated and is accompanied by worsening dyspnea and chest discomfort. The nurse should prepare for which of the following potential complications in this patient?

a. MI
b. Cardiac arrest
c. Pulmonary embolism (PE)
d. Acute renal failure

29. The nurse is caring for a 59-year-old female patient with a severe headache, confusion, and blurred vision. Her blood pressure is 230/115 mm Hg, and IV nitroprusside is initiated. The nurse should closely monitor for which of the following when administering this medication?

a. Hyperkalemia
b. Hypotension
c. Bradycardia
d. Hyperglycemia

30. The nurse is caring for a 64-year-old patient who underwent a minimally invasive mitral valve repair 48 hours ago. The patient complains of shortness of breath and appears increasingly anxious. Their vitals show a heart rate of 115 BPM and blood pressure of 90/68 mm Hg. What should the nurse suspect as the most likely cause of these symptoms?

a. PE
b. Pericardial effusion
c. Deep vein thrombosis (DVT)
d. Postoperative infection

31. A 56-year-old patient on postoperative day two following a minimally invasive direct coronary artery bypass (MIDCAB) complains of localized chest pain and shortness of breath. On examination, the nurse notes reduced breath sounds on the left side and dullness to percussion. What does the nurse suspect based on these findings?

a. MI
b. Atelectasis
c. Pneumothorax
d. Pleural effusion

32. The nurse is caring for a 70-year-old female patient who has a history of rheumatic fever during her childhood. She now reports a history of fatigue and shortness of breath on exertion. An echocardiogram reveals stenosis and regurgitation of the mitral valve. These findings are most consistent with which of the following conditions?

a. Mitral valve prolapse
b. Aortic stenosis
c. Mitral valve disease
d. Tricuspid regurgitation

33. A 75-year-old male patient has a history of aortic stenosis and is in the progressive care unit following a transcatheter aortic valve replacement (TAVR) procedure. Which of the following postoperative complications should the nurse be vigilant for in this patient?

a. Acute kidney injury
b. Pericardial effusion
c. Aortic dissection
d. Stroke

34. A 67-year-old patient presents with intermittent claudication, particularly when walking upstairs or uphill. The patient reports a smoking history of 40 pack-years and has a documented history of poorly controlled hypertension and hyperlipidemia. The nurse recognizes these as risk factors for which of the following conditions?

a. DVT
b. Peripheral artery disease (PAD)
c. AAA
d. Varicose veins

Pulmonary

1. A 62-year-old patient is admitted to the progressive care unit with acute respiratory distress syndrome (ARDS). The nurse understands that which of the following is a characteristic feature of ARDS?

a. Rapid onset of wheezing and dyspnea
b. Elevated carbon dioxide levels and respiratory acidosis
c. Diffuse alveolar damage and impaired gas exchange
d. Hyperinflation of the lungs and increased residual volume

2. A 40-year-old patient is admitted to the progressive care unit with severe asthma exacerbation. Which of the following medications should the nurse anticipate administering as a first-line treatment?

a. Corticosteroids
b. Long-acting beta-agonists
c. Anticholinergic agents
d. Short-acting beta-agonists

3. The nurse is assessing a patient with COPD. Which of the following pulse oximetry reading ranges would the nurse anticipate for this patient?

a. 85%–90%
b. 88%–92%
c. 92%–95%
d. 95%–98%

4. A 65-year-old patient is scheduled to undergo a video-assisted thoracic surgery (VATS) for the resection of a lung nodule. The nurse is providing preoperative education to the patient. Which of the following statements made by the patient indicates understanding of the surgical procedure?

a. "I will have a large incision made in my chest for the surgery."
b. "The surgeon will use a scope and small incisions to perform the surgery."
c. "I will be placed on a heart-lung machine during the surgery."
d. "The surgery will involve the removal of the entire lung."

5. A 50-year-old patient with known obstructive sleep apnea (OSA) is admitted to the progressive care unit for overnight monitoring. The nurse understands that the primary goal of treatment for OSA is which of the following?
   a. To promote weight loss
   b. To maintain a regular sleep schedule
   c. To provide CPAP therapy
   d. To administer sedative medications at bedtime

6. A 68-year-old patient is admitted to the progressive care unit with a large pleural effusion. The nurse recognizes that which of the following interventions is a priority in managing this condition?
   a. Administering diuretic medications
   b. Performing thoracentesis
   c. Providing supplemental oxygen therapy
   d. Initiating antibiotic therapy

7. A 55-year-old patient with COPD and respiratory failure has been receiving mechanical ventilation for the past week. The health-care team decides to initiate a weaning trial to assess the patient's readiness for extubation. During the weaning trial, the patient exhibits increased work of breathing, decreased oxygen saturation, and increased respiratory rate. The nurse recognizes that these findings suggest which of the following?
   a. Respiratory distress and the need for continued mechanical ventilation
   b. Successful weaning from mechanical ventilation
   c. Normal physiological response during the weaning process
   d. Ineffective breathing pattern due to anxiety

8. A 45-year-old patient is diagnosed with pulmonary hypertension. Which of the following best describes the underlying pathophysiology of this condition?
   a. Dilated and weakened pulmonary arteries, leading to decreased blood flow
   b. Inflammation and infection of the pulmonary vasculature, causing narrowing and occlusion
   c. Impaired gas exchange in the alveoli, leading to reduced oxygen uptake
   d. Increased pulmonary vascular resistance due to vasoconstriction and remodeling of pulmonary arterioles

9. A 45-year-old patient is admitted to the progressive care unit following a traumatic brain injury. The patient has a decreased level of consciousness and requires close monitoring. The nurse recognizes that a decreased level of consciousness can lead to respiratory depression due to which of the following mechanisms?
   a. Increased stimulation of the respiratory centers in the brain stem
   b. Activation of the sympathetic nervous system, causing bronchodilation
   c. Depressed responsiveness of the respiratory centers in the brain stem
   d. Increased production of surfactant in the alveoli

10. The nurse is caring for a 62-year-old patient with COPD who was admitted for acute respiratory failure. The nurse understands that acute respiratory failure is characterized by which of the following?
   a. Severe hypoxemia with normal or low carbon dioxide levels
   b. Severe hypoxemia with elevated carbon dioxide levels
   c. Mild hypoxemia with normal or low carbon dioxide levels
   d. Mild hypoxemia with elevated carbon dioxide levels

11. The nurse is caring for a 65-year-old patient who has been diagnosed with pneumonia. Which of the following is an appropriate nursing intervention to promote effective airway clearance in this patient?
   a. Administering nebulized bronchodilators
   b. Assisting with incentive spirometry
   c. Providing chest physiotherapy
   d. Performing endotracheal suctioning

12. A 55-year-old male patient with a history of pneumonia presents with a persistent cough, shortness of breath, chest pain, and a high-grade fever. On physical examination, decreased breath sounds are auscultated on the affected side, and there is dullness to percussion. A chest x-ray reveals fluid collection with the presence of pus in the pleural space. Which of the following diagnoses should the nurse anticipate?
   a. Pneumothorax
   b. Hemothorax
   c. Empyema
   d. Pleural effusion

13. A 55-year-old patient is admitted to the progressive care unit with a diagnosis of severe ARDS. The nurse understands that which of the following interventions is a key component in the management of ARDS?
   a. Administering corticosteroids
   b. Implementing lung-protective ventilation strategies
   c. Providing high-flow oxygen therapy
   d. Administering diuretic medications

14. The nurse is assessing a patient for risk factors associated with PE. Which of the following factors should the nurse consider as a potential risk factor for PE in this patient?
   a. Older than 65 years of age
   b. History of DVT
   c. COPD
   d. Body mass index (BMI) of 22 kg/m^2

15. The nurse is performing a respiratory assessment and notes decreased breath sounds, asymmetrical chest expansion, and tracheal deviation to the unaffected side. The nurse recognizes these findings as suggestive of which of the following pleural space complications?
   a. Pneumothorax
   b. Hemothorax
   c. Pleural effusion
   d. Chylothorax

16. The nurse is caring for a 60-year-old patient with a history of pulmonary hypertension who has been admitted with worsening dyspnea on exertion and fatigue. The nurse understands that which of the following is a characteristic finding in pulmonary hypertension?
   a. Elevated pulmonary artery wedge pressure (PAWP)
   b. Decreased pulmonary vascular resistance
   c. Right ventricular hypertrophy
   d. Increased left ventricular ejection fraction

17. A 68-year-old patient with a history of chronic pain is admitted to the progressive care unit. The nurse notes the patient's respiratory rate is six breaths per minute and the patient is difficult to arouse. The nurse suspects respiratory depression. Which of the following actions should the nurse prioritize?

a. Administering naloxone
b. Assisting with endotracheal intubation
c. Providing supplemental oxygen
d. Assessing the patient's level of consciousness

18. The nurse is caring for a 55-year-old patient who is suspected of having the flu. The patient presented with symptoms of fever, body aches, cough, and fatigue. The patient also mentions receiving the flu vaccine last year and asks the nurse why they still got the flu. Which of the following statements is the most appropriate response by the nurse?

a. "The flu vaccine is 100% effective in preventing the flu, so it's unusual that you still got infected."
b. "The flu vaccine is not 100% effective, so it's possible that you were still able to contract the virus."
c. "It's possible that you were exposed to a different strain of the flu virus that wasn't covered by last year's vaccine."
d. "It takes a couple of weeks for the flu vaccine to provide full protection, so you may have been exposed before it took effect."

19. The nurse is providing education to a patient with asthma who has been prescribed corticosteroids in the form of an inhaler. Which of the following statements by the patient indicates understanding of the importance of rinsing the mouth after inhaler use?

a. "Rinsing my mouth after using the inhaler will help improve the absorption of the medication."
b. "Rinsing my mouth will prevent the corticosteroid from reaching my lungs effectively."
c. "Rinsing my mouth will help decrease the side effects of the corticosteroid on my throat."
d. "Rinsing my mouth can reduce the risk of developing oral thrush from the corticosteroid."

20. A 58-year-old patient is admitted to the progressive care unit following a pneumonectomy for lung cancer. The nurse is assessing the patient and notes absent breath sounds on the right side, tracheal deviation to the right, and decreased chest expansion on the right side. The nurse recognizes these findings as suggestive of which of the following complications?

a. Pneumothorax
b. Hemothorax
c. Atelectasis
d. Empyema

21. The nurse is caring for a patient with a respiratory condition who is experiencing impaired gas exchange and respiratory distress. Which of the following characteristics would indicate acute respiratory failure rather than chronic respiratory failure?

a. Gradual onset of symptoms
b. History of long-term oxygen therapy (LTOT)
c. Normal arterial blood gas (ABG) values
d. Severe hypoxemia and hypercapnia

Endocrine/Hematology/Neurology/Gastrointestinal/Renal

1. Which of the following is a clinical manifestation of diabetes mellitus?
   a. Hematuria
   b. Polyuria
   c. Oliguria
   d. Hemoptysis

2. Which of the following urinalysis findings would indicate that a patient may be experiencing diabetic ketoacidosis?
   a. Positive nitrites
   b. Positive leukocytes
   c. Positive bilirubin
   d. Positive ketones

3. Hyperglycemia can potentially lead to what issue for patients with diabetes?
   a. Retinal detachment
   b. Secondary infections
   c. Dysphagia
   d. Hyperactivity

4. The nurse is caring for a patient who presents with dizziness, tachycardia, and diaphoresis. The patient's blood sugar is 50mg/dL. What action should the nurse take?
   a. Have the patient sit down and take deep breaths.
   b. Have the patient eat a fast-acting carbohydrate.
   c. Administer insulin.
   d. Do not administer anything per mouth.

5. Which of the following findings would the nurse expect to find in a patient diagnosed with diabetic ketoacidosis?
   a. Hyperventilation
   b. Oliguria
   c. Hypoglycemia
   d. Hypoventilation

6. The nurse is caring for a pediatric patient with sickle cell anemia who is currently going through a sickle cell crisis. He is experiencing pain in his hands and feet and appears short of breath and tired. What is the primary intervention the nurse should take in caring for her patient experiencing a sickle cell crisis?
   a. Apply ice packs to areas of pain.
   b. Administer both oral and intravenous fluids.
   c. Encourage the patient to exercise for thirty minutes.
   d. Administer intravenous immunoglobulin (IVIG) to boost the immune system.

7. A patient presents with jaundice, dark urine, and fatigue—characteristic signs of hemolytic anemia. What laboratory value would explain the cause of the patient's clinical manifestations?

a. Elevated sodium levels
b. Increased red blood cell levels
c. Decreased white blood cell levels
d. Elevated bilirubin levels

8. Which of the following clinical manifestations are indicative of iron-deficiency anemia?

a. An inflamed and sore tongue
b. Hyperactivity
c. Bradycardia
d. Fingernail clubbing

9. A nursing student is learning about different types of anemia. Which of the following statements would indicate an understanding of the cause of aplastic anemia?

a. "Aplastic anemia is caused by the bone marrow not producing enough red and white blood cells and platelets."
b. "Aplastic anemia is caused by physical trauma."
c. "Aplastic anemia is caused by low iron levels due to diet."
d. "Aplastic anemia is caused by an inherited defected gene that causes red blood cells to have a sickled shape."

10. What laboratory test is used to monitor the effectiveness of a patient receiving Coumadin (warfarin) therapy?

a. Platelet count
b. Hemoglobin count
c. Prothrombin time (PT)
d. Activated partial thromboplastin time (aPTT)

11. Which of the following is a complication of liver failure?

a. Hepatic encephalopathy
b. Glomerulonephritis
c. Hepatitis B
d. Fatty liver disease

12. A nurse in the neurology unit is caring for a patient with a history of seizures. While taking the patient's vital signs, she notices that the patient is having a focal aware seizure. What manifestations would the nurse see for this type of seizure?

a. Muscle jerking and rigidity
b. Loss of consciousness
c. Automatisms
d. Sphincter relaxation

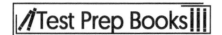

13. A patient states that he has a severe headache along with nausea. He is currently admitted to the neurology unit status post hemorrhagic stroke. The nurse knows that she should assess for which of the following potential complications because of the patient's symptoms?
   a. Aphasia
   b. Hemiplegia
   c. Seizures
   d. Increased intracranial pressure

14. Which of the following statements by the new graduate nurse indicates an understanding of how to manage a patient having a tonic-clonic seizure?
   a. "I will put a spoon in the patient's mouth to hold their tongue down and prevent them from choking."
   b. "I will hold the patient down so that he does not injure himself during the seizure."
   c. "I will time the seizure for emergency medical services."
   d. "I will perform mouth-to-mouth breathing to assist the patient in maintaining oxygenation."

15. All of the following are precursors to ischemic stroke EXCEPT:
   a. Diabetes
   b. Hypolipidemia
   c. Smoking
   d. Hypertension

16. Which of the following diagnostic tests can help diagnose a patient with gastrointestinal reflux disease (GERD)?
   a. A routine complete blood count (CBC)
   b. An upper endoscopy
   c. An abdominal ultrasound
   d. A fasting glucose test

17. Which of the following clinical manifestations indicates a possible lower GI bleed?
   a. Hematochezia
   b. Hematemesis
   c. Melena
   d. Diarrhea

18. The nurse is caring for a patient with an upper GI bleed. Which of the following would be the nurse's priority and initial intervention?
   a. Draw blood for complete blood count (CBC).
   b. Administer IV fluids.
   c. Administer oral proton pump inhibitors (PPIs).
   d. Provide the patient with an immediate blood transfusion.

19. Which of the following is a common precursor to *Clostridium difficile* (*C. diff*) infection?
   a. Illicit drug use
   b. GERD
   c. Poor handwashing
   d. Antibiotic use

20. A patient is receiving discharge teaching from his nurse after having a laparoscopic gastric banding surgery. Which of the following statements by the patient indicates an understanding of his diet during the recovery period?

a. "I am able to eat solid foods after seventy-two hours."
b. "I am allowed to have carbonated beverages to help settle my stomach."
c. "I should only eat clear broths for two to four weeks."
d. "I can resume my regular diet as soon as I feel better."

21. Which of the following is a precursor to acute kidney injury?

a. Having a solitary kidney
b. A diagnosis of sepsis
c. Excessive intake of sugary drinks
d. Age less than sixty-five years

22. The dialysis nurse is caring for a patient with chronic kidney disease. Which of the following should the nurse consider when caring for a patient receiving hemodialysis?

a. Monitoring the patient's respiratory status
b. Providing the patient with high potassium, sodium, and phosphoric-containing foods
c. Monitoring the patient's blood pressure
d. Encouraging the patient to consider a kidney transplant

23. The nurse is reviewing recent blood work drawn on a patient. She sees that the patient's potassium level is 7.0 mEq/L. Which of the following clinical manifestations would the nurse expect her patient to present with?

a. Cardiac arrhythmia
b. Hyperreflexia
c. Nausea and vomiting
d. Mental status changes

24. A patient with end-stage renal disease is receiving discharge education from the nurse. Which of the following statements by the patient indicates an understanding of following a low-phosphorus diet?

a. "For breakfast I should try to eat oatmeal or bran."
b. "Drinking milk daily will help strengthen my bones on this diet."
c. "Incorporating white rice is okay for this diet."
d. "I should eat more beans and lentils to help my digestive system."

25. Which of the following interventions should the nurse implement when caring for a patient with acute kidney injury?

a. Obtain daily weights.
b. Administer intravenous spironolactone.
c. Encourage increased fluids.
d. Administer cyclosporine by mouth.

Musculoskeletal/Multisystem/Psychosocial

1. The nurse in the orthopedic unit is caring for an elderly patient with a hip fracture who is currently bedridden. Which of the following interventions should the nurse implement for this patient?
    a. Assist the patient in performing range of motion exercises.
    b. Apply compression stockings to the patient's lower extremities.
    c. Administer pain medication as needed.
    d. Turn and reposition the patient every two hours.

2. The nurse hears one of her patients yelling from their room. Upon entry, she notices that the patient has taken a fall. Which of the following interventions should the nurse take first?
    a. Notify the physician.
    b. Put the patient on fall precautions.
    c. Check for injuries.
    d. Assess the patient's level of consciousness.

3. An elderly man presents in the emergency department with complaints of difficulty walking and feeling unsteady when walking. He reports that he is afraid that he is going to fall and has a few near falls this month. The nurse assesses the patient and notes that the patient has a stooped posture and shuffling gait. Which of the following gait disorders does the nurse suspect the patient may have?
    a. Myasthenia Gravis
    b. Parkinson's Disease
    c. Multiple Sclerosis
    d. Duchenne Muscular Dystrophy

4. Which of the following interventions should the nurse implement to promote comfort and relaxation during the end of life?
    a. Administer pain medication as needed.
    b. Encourage the patient to eat their regular diet.
    c. Limit visitors and keep the room dark to reduce stimulation.
    d. Help the patient participate in daily physical activity.

5. Which of the following patients has the highest risk of developing a catheter-associated urinary tract infection (CAUTI)?
    a. An eighty-year-old male who recently underwent orthopedic surgery for a broken leg and has a catheter in place
    b. A fifty-year-old woman with urinary incontinence who has a catheter in place
    c. A thirty-year-old male with a history of recurrent urinary tract infections who has a catheter in place
    d. A fifty-five-year-old female with a history of hypotension who has a catheter in place

6. Which of the following actions should the nurse take to prevent central-line associated bloodstream infection (CLABSI) when caring for a patient with a peripherally inserted central catheter (PICC)?
    a. Change the dressing every twenty-four hours.
    b. Use the same infusion tubing for all medications.
    c. Perform hand hygiene before and after handling the line.
    d. Use a clean technique during dressing changes.

7. What is the most effective intervention to prevent a surgical site infection (SSI)?
   a. Administering prophylactic antibiotics prior to surgery
   b. Maintaining a sterile technique during surgery
   c. Performing hand hygiene before and after patient contact
   d. Drawing a complete blood count on the patient prior to surgery

8. Which of the following medications would be administered to a patient with an influenza infection?
   a. Amoxicillin
   b. Fluconazole
   c. Tamiflu
   d. Doxorubicin

9. When caring for a patient with Methicillin-resistant Staphylococcus aureus (MRSA), what type of precautions should the nurse implement?
   a. Airborne precautions
   b. Standard precautions
   c. Droplet precautions
   d. Contact precautions

10. The nurse is preparing to administer gabapentin to her patient that suffers from chronic pain due to arthritis. What should the nurse monitor in this patient after administering gabapentin?
   a. Hyperactivity
   b. Sedation
   c. Tachycardia
   d. Constipation

11. Which of the following adverse effects should the nurse prioritize when monitoring a patient receiving opioid analgesics for a broken tibia?
   a. Constipation
   b. Respiratory depression
   c. Nausea
   d. Sedation

12. The family member of a patient receiving palliative care tells the nurse that the patient is losing a lot of weight and has very low energy. Which of the following responses is most appropriate by the nurse?
   a. "We don't usually intervene at this stage as this is part of the dying process."
   b. "Let's assess their nutritional status and identify any contributing factors."
   c. "We should encourage the patient to eat more to maintain weight."
   d. "I will start intravenous fluids to help maintain the client's weight."

13. The nurse is performing rounds on her patients and notices that one of them is experiencing altered mental status. Which of the following interventions should the nurse implement?
   a. Assess the patient's vital signs.
   b. Administer Narcan to the patient.
   c. Provide a snack for the patient.
   d. Administer Haldol to the patient.

14. A nurse is caring for a patient with a history of alcohol abuse who has been diagnosed with acute pancreatitis. Upon assessment of the patient, the nurse notes that they are disoriented and confused and that their level of consciousness is fluctuating. Which of the following is most likely the cause of the patient's delirium?

a. Medication side effects
b. Infection from pancreatitis
c. Hypoxia
d. Alcohol withdrawal

15. Which of the following is a risk factor for potentially developing dementia?

a. Frequent infections
b. Increasing age
c. Being male
d. Hypotension

16. The nurse enters the patient's room to obtain vital signs. Upon their interaction, the patient becomes increasingly agitated and aggressive. Which of the following interventions should the nurse implement?

a. Quietly leave the patient's room and return when they are calm.
b. Offer a diversional activity using a calm tone.
c. Administer Haldol to the patient.
d. Let the patient know that this behavior is not tolerated.

17. A patient experiencing anxiety may receive which of the following medications?

a. Risperidone
b. Lorazepam
c. Carvedilol
d. Diphenhydramine

18. A nurse is taking care of a college-age student who has recently started taking an antidepressant. Which of the following side effects should the nurse monitor for?

a. Fever
b. Rash
c. Hallucinations
d. Suicidal ideation

19. A nurse is caring for a patient with alcohol withdrawal who is prescribed lorazepam for their withdrawal symptoms. This medication is most effective when administered in which way?

a. Once daily at night
b. Every six to eight hours as needed
c. Every two to four hours scheduled
d. A one-time dose at the start of withdrawal symptoms

20. Which of the following conditions is a result of chronic alcohol abuse?

a. Liver disease
b. Infectious diseases
c. Hormonal imbalances
d. Genetic disorders

Professional Caring and Ethical Practice

1. A nurse is preparing to discharge an elderly patient after their hospital stay. The patient tells the nurse that they are worried about managing their medications on their own at home. Which of the following actions should the nurse take?
   a. Provide the patient with written instructions for their medications.
   b. Coordinate a home health nurse to visit the patient after their discharge.
   c. Discuss the patient's concerns with the healthcare team to develop a plan of care.
   d. Ask one of the patient's family members to take control of medications for the patient at home.

2. The oncoming nurse is taking care of a patient on intravenous antibiotics. When she checks the medication bag and compares it to the order in the patient's EMAR, she notices that the dose is incorrect. Which of the following actions would be appropriate for the nurse to take?
   a. Administer an additional bag of antibiotics to compensate for the incorrect dose.
   b. Notify the healthcare provider and pharmacy of the error.
   c. Allow the current antibiotic to finish infusing and redraw a complete blood count (CBC).
   d. Inform the patient and their family about the medication error.

3. The nurse is caring for a patient who is non-English speaking and is having a difficult time communicating with the healthcare team. Which action should the nurse take as an advocate for this patient?
   a. Ask another nurse who speaks the patient's language to help with communication.
   b. Have a family member of the patient come in to translate.
   c. Use a translation app to speak with the patient.
   d. Document the communication difficulties in the patient's chart.

4. The nurse is caring for a patient that has recently had a stroke. The patient is having difficulties with communication. Which of the following actions by the nurse would be an example of caring practice?
   a. Use nonverbal communication to show empathy and support.
   b. Restrict visitors to prevent excessive stimulation.
   c. Speak to the patient in a slow and loud voice.
   d. Pretend that the patient is speaking normally.

5. A patient with a terminal illness discloses to their nurse that they would like to transfer to hospice care. Which of the following actions by the nurse is the most appropriate and an example of compassionate care?
   a. Withhold all medical interventions and focus on comfort measures only.
   b. Avoid discussing the patient's prognosis and continue care per the provider's orders.
   c. Provide emotional support to the patient.
   d. Meet with the healthcare team and the patient to create a palliative care plan.

6. A pediatric patient is feeling anxious about their upcoming surgery. Which of the following actions by the nurse indicates caring and compassionate care?
   a. Decrease the child's involvement in their healthcare decision-making to decrease anxiety.
   b. Explain to the child that they do not have anything to worry about and that it will be okay.
   c. Listen to the child's concerns and provide age-appropriate explanations.
   d. Utilize diversion techniques to decrease the child's anxiety.

7. The nurse is caring for a patient who identifies as transgender. Which of the following interventions is the most appropriate?

a. Avoid using pronouns when addressing the patient.
b. Use gender-neutral terms when addressing the patient.
c. Use the patient's chosen name and pronouns.
d. Encourage the patient to speak with their provider regarding transitioning.

8. What is the most appropriate nursing intervention for a patient who speaks a different language?

a. Use a professional interpreter.
b. Use a family member to interpret as they know the patient best.
c. Speak slowly and loudly to help the patient understand.
d. Provide the patient with written instructions in their language.

9. Which of the following is an example of providing culturally competent care for a patient of Asian descent?

a. Use a professional interpreter for all communication.
b. Maintain eye contact to make them feel comfortable.
c. Reassure the patient that their health care team will make the best decisions for them.
d. Encourage the patient's family members to participate in the patient's care and decision-making.

10. Which of the following should the nurse prioritize when providing education about breastfeeding to expectant parents?

a. The use of pre-recorded video demonstration
b. The use of practice dolls
c. The use of written step-by-step instructions
d. The use of verbal discussion

11. The nurse is providing an educational session on asthma triggers and management for individuals with asthma. Which of the following actions by the nurses will help facilitate learning the best?

a. Present a PowerPoint lecture.
b. Show a video on asthma management.
c. Encourage people in the group to share their personal asthma triggers and experiences.
d. Hand out pamphlets on asthma triggers and pamphlets.

12. The nurse is holding an informational group for parents about childhood immunizations. Which of the following teaching methods would be the most effective to facilitate learning for the parents?

a. Hand out copies of the childhood immunization schedule.
b. Have a group discussion on common immunization concerns and misconceptions.
c. Show an informational video on the importance of childhood immunizations.
d. Teach parents how to administer the immunizations.

13. Which of the following would be the most appropriate action the nurse could take to help facilitate learning for a patient that has just received a colostomy?

a. Provide diagrams and written instructions on how to apply the appliance.
b. Show a video on colostomy care to the patient.
c. Demonstrate colostomy care to the patient and allow them to practice on a mannequin.
d. Have the patient participate in a colostomy support group.

14. The nurse is caring for a diabetic patient on insulin therapy. She notes that the patient's blood glucose levels have been elevated despite receiving scheduled insulin. The nurse should collaborate with which healthcare professional?

a. Endocrinologist
b. Gastroenterologist
c. Dietician
d. Urologist

15. The nurse works in a community health clinic. Which of the following actions by the nurse aims to improve healthcare services to underserved communities?

a. Implement a COVID-19 vaccination program for the clinic's staff.
b. Provide health education sessions for clinic patients.
c. Hang informational posters in the clinic.
d. Collaborate with local religious organizations to organize health fairs.

16. Who should the nurse collaborate with for a patient that has complex wounds that require specialized care?

a. Wound-ostomy nurse
b. Patient care assistant
c. Primary care provider
d. Dietician

17. The nurse is caring for a patient with a chronic illness who sees healthcare professionals across several specialties. Which of the following actions by the nurse is an example of interdisciplinary collaboration?

a. Notifying the patient's primary care provider of the patient's health history
b. Sharing the patient's test results with all involved healthcare professionals
c. Helping schedule follow-up appointments for the patient with several specialists
d. Keeping the patient's medical information private

18. The hospital where the nurse works has been experiencing an increase in patient readmissions. How can the nurse become involved in addressing this issue?

a. Provide detailed written discharge instructions for patients.
b. Create an improved, standardized discharge education process with the interdisciplinary team.
c. Conduct a root cause analysis on reasons for readmission.
d. Reiterate the importance of medication adherence to the patients.

19. The nurse is part of the quality improvement team at their hospital. Which of the following actions by the nurse demonstrates systems thinking?

a. Identify underlying factors that are contributing to errors.
b. Collect data on individual staff members' performance.
c. Implement new protocols to reduce errors.
d. Determine which staff members are responsible for errors.

20. How can the nurse apply systems thinking when caring for a patient who has a chronic illness?

a. Identifying all the physical systems involved in the patient's chronic illness
b. Focusing on the patient's psychosocial needs
c. Implementing disease-specific interventions for the patient

d. Coordinating with several healthcare providers and specialists for their treatment plan

21. The nurse is running a root cause analysis of a medication error that occurred at the hospital. Which of the following actions by the nurse indicates the use of systems thinking for this cause analysis?
   a. Monitor the nurse that made the error during their shift.
   b. Identify and address all the factors that contributed to the medication error.
   c. Implement a double-check system for medication administration.
   d. Notify the nurse manager.

22. A patient has developed an unexpected complication after having a surgical procedure. Which action should the nurse take to best help the patient?
   a. Discuss the complication with the surgeon.
   b. Conduct a literature review to gather evidence-based information on the surgery and its complications.
   c. Document the complication in the patient's medical records.
   d. Notify the charge nurse of the complication.

23. The nurse is caring for a patient who has had an adverse reaction to a medication. Which of the following actions by the nurse is an example of clinical inquiry?
   a. Research potential causes and interventions for the adverse reaction.
   b. Document the adverse reaction in the patient's medical record.
   c. Notify the adverse reaction to the patient's healthcare provider.
   d. Reference medication administration guidelines for further information.

24. Which of the following research articles should the nurse utilize to conduct a literature review?
   a. Qualitative studies
   b. Expert opinions
   c. Case studies
   d. Randomized control trials

25. The nurse is responsible for implementing new evidence-based practices at the hospital. Which of the following actions by the nurse is most important in implementing these practices at the hospital?
   a. Hanging posters on evidence-based practices in the break room
   b. Testing the evidence-based practices first and collecting data on their effectiveness
   c. Collaborating with the healthcare team and staff to share evidence-based practices that will be implemented
   d. Providing handouts to the staff on the new practices

Answer Explanations #2

Clinical Judgement

Cardiovascular

1. A: The key pathophysiological difference between STEMI and NSTEMI is the extent of coronary artery occlusion. STEMI occurs when a coronary artery is completely blocked, leading to more extensive myocardial damage. In contrast, NSTEMI results from partial occlusion of a coronary artery, leading to a smaller area of myocardial damage. Both STEMI and NSTEMI are associated with elevated troponin levels, and STEMI is typically more severe than NSTEMI; therefore, Choices *B* and *C* are incorrect. Although Choice *D* is a true statement, it describes an ECG manifestation rather than the underlying pathophysiology; therefore, it is also incorrect.

2. C: Fibrinolytic therapy, also known as thrombolytic therapy, is primarily used for patients with STEMI, which is characterized by complete occlusion of a coronary artery. In these cases, fibrinolytics help dissolve the clot and restore blood flow to the affected myocardial tissue. NSTEMI, on the other hand, is associated with partial occlusion of a coronary artery, and the use of fibrinolytics is not indicated for this condition. Instead, treatment focuses on antiplatelet therapy, anticoagulation, and possible PCI to reduce the risk of further ischemia and myocardial damage. Choices *A*, *B*, and *D* are incorrect because they do not accurately describe the primary reason for not using fibrinolytics in NSTEMI cases.

3. B: Silent MIs refer to cases in which the patient does not experience the typical chest pain or other classic symptoms of a heart attack. Instead, they may present with atypical symptoms or no symptoms at all. This phenomenon is more common in patients with diabetes mellitus due to diabetic neuropathy, which can affect the nerves responsible for transmitting pain signals. In addition, older adults and men may also be at a higher risk. Choices *A*, *C*, and *D* are not specifically associated with an increased likelihood of experiencing a silent MI.

4. D: PCI is the most appropriate and preferred surgical intervention for a patient diagnosed with STEMI. PCI, also known as angioplasty with stenting, is a minimally invasive procedure used to open the blocked coronary artery and restore blood flow to the affected myocardial tissue. Choice *A* may be considered in select cases of STEMI with complex coronary anatomy or when PCI is not feasible, but it is not the first-line treatment. Choices *B* and *C* are not relevant to the management of STEMI because they address different cardiovascular issues.

5. C: Nitroglycerin is contraindicated in patients with a right-sided MI because it may lead to excessive vasodilation and a decrease in preload, which can worsen right ventricular function. The right ventricle is already compromised in a right-sided MI, and reducing preload with nitroglycerin can further impair its function, leading to significant hypotension and a worsening clinical condition. Choices *A*, *B*, and *D* do not accurately describe the reason for nitroglycerin contraindication in right-sided MIs.

6. B: The presence of myocardial cell death is the most helpful pathophysiological difference in differentiating between NSTEMI and unstable angina. In NSTEMI, myocardial cell death occurs due to partial occlusion of the coronary artery, leading to elevated troponin levels. In contrast, unstable angina does not involve myocardial cell death, and troponin levels remain normal. Choices *A*, *C*, and *D* are not specific enough to differentiate between NSTEMI and unstable angina because these factors can vary between individuals and do not provide a clear distinction between the two conditions.

7. D: Unstable angina is associated with an increased risk of progression to MI. This is due to the fact that unstable angina typically results from a partially occluded coronary artery, which can progress to myocardial ischemia and MI. Choices *A*, *B*, and *C* are not as closely associated with unstable angina.

8. A: *Staphylococcus aureus* is the most common cause of infective endocarditis. *Clostridium difficile*, Choice *B*; *Pseudomonas aeruginosa*, Choice *C*; and *Streptococcus pneumoniae*, Choice *D*, are not typically associated with infective endocarditis. *Clostridium difficile* is a bacterium that causes gastrointestinal infections, *Pseudomonas aeruginosa* is commonly associated with nosocomial infections, and *Streptococcus pneumoniae* is more commonly associated with pneumonia and meningitis.

9. B: Pericarditis primarily presents with chest pain that improves when leaning forward. Pulsus paradoxus, Choice *A*, is associated with cardiac tamponade; peripheral edema, Choice *C*, is a common symptom of heart failure; and wheezing, Choice *D*, is more indicative of respiratory conditions such as asthma and COPD.

10. C: CT scan is the preferred method for diagnosing an aortic dissection due to its accuracy and rapid results. An echocardiogram, Choice *A*, may be used if a CT scan isn't available, but its sensitivity is less. A chest x-ray, Choice *B*, may appear normal in cases in which the aortic dissection is small or localized or if the dissection is limited to the descending aorta; therefore, it is not a reliable diagnostic method. Furthermore, in the early stages of an aortic dissection or shortly after symptom onset, there may not have been sufficient time for significant changes or complications to manifest on a chest x-ray. An ECG, Choice *D*, is typically used to rule out an MI, which can mimic an aortic dissection, but is not the correct diagnostic test for this condition.

11. C: Postoperative patients, particularly those who have undergone an AAA repair, are at risk for ischemia due to the clamp and unclamp procedure during surgery. Decreased sensation and movement in the legs could suggest spinal cord ischemia, which is a serious complication. Absent bowel sounds, Choice *A*, could indicate paralytic ileus, which is common after surgery and typically resolves on its own. Mild incisional pain, Choice *B*, is expected after surgery and can be managed with appropriate pain medication. A urine output of 50 mL/hr, Choice *D*, is within the normal range and does not raise immediate concern.

12. C: After CABG surgery, the nurse is most likely to encounter AFib because it is a common postoperative cardiac arrhythmia. Hypotension, Choice *A*, can occur but is generally well-managed with fluid and medication adjustments. Thrombocytopenia, Choice *B*, can occur due to heparin administration or platelet consumption during cardiopulmonary bypass, but it is not as frequently observed as AFib. Transient ischemic attack, Choice *D*, is not common in the immediate postoperative period of CABG surgery.

13. C: After cardiac surgery, it is important for the patient to gradually resume their normal activities and participate in a structured cardiac rehabilitation program. Complete avoidance of physical activity or exercise, Choice *A*, is not recommended after cardiac surgery because gradual and supervised activity helps in regaining strength and overall recovery. Although a low-sodium diet and fluid restriction, Choice *B*, may be necessary for some patients depending on their specific condition, it is not the only focus of long-term care and lifestyle modifications. Stopping prescribed medications, Choice *D*, without medical advice is not advisable because these medications are often essential for long-term management and prevention of complications.

14. B: The patient's presentation of hypotension, muffled heart sounds, and jugular venous distension are consistent with cardiac tamponade. However, to further confirm the diagnosis, the nurse should assess for pulsus paradoxus, which is a classic finding in cardiac tamponade. Pulsus paradoxus is caused by the exaggerated decrease in blood pressure during inspiration due to the impaired cardiac filling caused by the pericardial effusion. Cardiac tamponade is also characterized by a narrowed pulse pressure due to compromised ventricular filling, making Choices *A* and *C* incorrect. A positive Homan's sign, Choice *D*, is unrelated to cardiac tamponade and is associated with DVT.

15. C: Pericardiocentesis is the definitive treatment for cardiac tamponade. In this procedure, a needle or catheter is inserted into the pericardial sac to drain the accumulated fluid, relieving the pressure on the heart. Administration of vasopressors, Choice *A*, may temporarily increase blood pressure, but it does not address the underlying issue of fluid accumulation around the heart. Cardiac catheterization, Choice *B*, is a diagnostic procedure that may provide information about the underlying cause of cardiac tamponade, but it is not the definitive treatment. CPR, Choice *D*, is a life-saving procedure performed during cardiac arrest and is not specific to treating cardiac tamponade.

16. C: Before a diagnostic cardiac catheterization, the patient should be informed that they might feel a warm sensation when the dye is injected. This is because a contrast dye is used during the procedure to visualize the coronary arteries. Although the patient may receive sedation or local anesthesia for the procedure, general anesthesia, Choice *A*, is not typically required for a diagnostic cardiac catheterization. Fasting for 24 hours, Choice *B*, is not necessary for this procedure, and it is important to clarify the specific fasting instructions with the patient based on the hospital's protocol. Choice *D* is incorrect because patients are typically discharged the same day following a cardiac catheterization unless the patient has underlying conditions that would require additional monitoring.

17. A: Interventional cardiac catheterization involves both diagnostic aspects and therapeutic procedures (e.g., angioplasty, stenting) to treat blockages or structural abnormalities that are found during the procedure. In this scenario, the nurse would expect to administer an antiplatelet agent after coronary artery stent placement to prevent the formation of blood clots. Antiplatelet medications, such as aspirin or P2Y12 inhibitors (e.g., clopidogrel), are commonly prescribed in this setting to reduce the risk of stent thrombosis and subsequent cardiovascular events. Beta-blockers, Choice *B*, are commonly used for the management of hypertension, arrhythmias, and certain heart conditions, but they are not directly related to the post-procedural care of coronary artery stent placement. Similarly, calcium channel blockers, Choice *C*, are often used for blood pressure control and the management of certain cardiac conditions, but they are not specifically indicated for post-stent placement care. Diuretics, Choice *D*, may be used for the management of fluid overload in some cardiac conditions, but they are not directly related to stent placement.

18. B: AMI can significantly compromise the pumping ability of the heart, leading to cardiogenic shock, a state in which the heart fails to supply enough blood to the organs. COPD, Choice *A*; pneumonia, Choice *C*; and asthma, Choice *D*, can cause shortness of breath, but they do not typically result in cardiogenic shock.

19. D: The primary reason for administering dobutamine in this situation is to increase cardiac output. Dobutamine is a positive inotrope that enhances the force of the heart's contractions, leading to an improved pumping capacity and subsequently increasing cardiac output. In the context of cardiogenic shock, in which the heart's ability to supply adequate blood flow to the organs is compromised, increasing cardiac output is crucial for improving tissue perfusion and supporting vital organ function. Improving renal perfusion, Choice *A,* may be an indirect effect of increasing cardiac output because better cardiac function can enhance blood flow to the kidneys. However, the primary goal of administering dobutamine is to enhance cardiac output rather than directly targeting renal perfusion. Reducing preload and afterload, Choice *B*, is typically accomplished using other medication classes, such as diuretics (for reducing preload) and vasodilators (for reducing afterload), which work by different mechanisms than dobutamine. Increasing myocardial oxygen demand, Choice *C,* is not a desirable effect in the context of a compromised heart because it could potentially worsen ischemia and further damage cardiac tissue.

20. A: Dilated cardiomyopathy is characterized by the enlargement and weakening of the left ventricle, the primary pumping chamber of the heart, leading to a reduced ability to effectively pump blood. This can lead to fluid buildup in the lungs, causing shortness of breath, especially during exertion. Decreased oxygen-carrying capacity, Choice *B;* weakening of respiratory muscles, Choice *C*; and outflow obstruction, Choice *D*, are not the primary reasons for breathlessness in dilated cardiomyopathy.

21. B: HCM is characterized by the abnormal thickening of the heart muscle, which can lead to disorganization of myocardial architecture and abnormal diastolic function. This abnormal structure and function can disrupt the heart's normal electrical pathways and cause life-threatening arrhythmias, leading to sudden cardiac death. Myocardial ischemia, Choice *A*; reduced cardiac output due to ventricular dilation, Choice *C*; and severe mitral valve regurgitation, Choice *D*, can occur in various heart conditions, but they are not typical findings in HCM.

22. B: Patients with AFib have a disrupted atrial rhythm, which can lead to the pooling and clotting of blood in the atria. If a clot dislodges and travels to the brain, it can cause a stroke. Although AFib can exacerbate underlying heart disease and potentially increase the risk for MI, Choice *A*; angina, Choice *C*; or hypertension, Choice *D*, these complications are less immediate and less directly related to AFib than stroke.

23. B: In the management of AFib, metoprolol is commonly used as a medication to help control the heart rate. AFib is characterized by irregular and often rapid heart rhythms, and beta-blockers such as metoprolol are effective in slowing down the heart rate. Hydrochlorothiazide, Choice *A*, is a diuretic primarily used for managing hypertension and reducing fluid volume. Digoxin, Choice *C*, is a medication that can be used to control heart rate, but it is generally reserved for specific cases. Warfarin, Choice *D*, is an anticoagulant medication used to prevent blood clot formation in patients with AFib to reduce the risk of stroke. However, the primary focus in this question is on medication for heart rate control, making metoprolol the most appropriate choice.

24. C: Exacerbations of chronic heart failure are often characterized by increased shortness of breath, especially when lying down (orthopnea or paroxysmal nocturnal dyspnea), due to fluid accumulation in the lungs. Although decreased urination, Choice *A*, may occur due to reduced renal perfusion, it is not a primary sign of an acute exacerbation. Weight loss, Choice *B*, and decreased swelling in lower extremities, Choice *D*, are typically signs of improved, not worsening, heart failure.

25. A: When a patient with acute heart failure presents with hypoxia (indicated by the low oxygen saturation), the first intervention should be to improve oxygenation. Diuretics, Choice *B,* could help decrease fluid overload but should only be administered after ensuring adequate oxygenation. Administering a beta-blocker, Choice *C,* is not appropriate in ADHF and could exacerbate the condition. Increasing IV fluids, Choice *D,* would typically worsen heart failure.

26. B: This patient's significantly elevated blood pressure in combination with their signs/symptoms suggests a hypertensive emergency, which requires immediate blood pressure reduction. Hypertensive urgency, Choice *A*, is characterized by significantly elevated blood pressure without signs of organ damage. Acute heart failure, Choice *C*, and acute stroke, Choice *D*, could be potential complications of a hypertensive emergency but do not fully explain this patient's symptoms and findings.

27. A: Hydrochlorothiazide is a diuretic that reduces blood pressure by helping the body eliminate excess sodium and water, and lisinopril is an ACE inhibitor that also lowers blood pressure and can have a specific protective effect on the kidneys in patients with diabetes. Improving blood glucose control, Choice *B,* is not the main action of these medications. Treating potential cardiac arrhythmias, Choice *C*, and decreasing the risk of developing atherosclerosis, Choice *D*, are also not the primary reasons for choosing these particular medications.

28. A: This patient's uncontrolled hypertension, coupled with chest pain and worsening dyspnea, is highly suggestive of MI, especially because the symptoms have persisted despite attempts to lower the blood pressure. Although cardiac arrest, Choice *B,* could be a potential outcome if the MI is not treated, it's not an immediate complication. PE, Choice *C,* typically presents with sudden-onset chest pain and dyspnea but is less likely given the patient's history and the absence of other common risk factors. Acute renal failure, Choice *D,* could be a potential complication of uncontrolled hypertension over time, but it would not explain the patient's acute chest pain.

29. B: Nitroprusside is a potent vasodilator used in hypertensive emergencies to rapidly decrease blood pressure. When administering nitroprusside, the nurse should closely monitor for hypotension as a potential side effect. The medication's primary action is to reduce blood pressure, and excessive lowering of blood pressure can lead to inadequate perfusion to vital organs. Choices *A*, *C*, and *D* are not the priority for the nurse to monitor when administering nitroprusside.

30. B: After a cardiac procedure, such as a minimally invasive mitral valve repair, one potential complication is the development of pericardial effusion, which refers to the accumulation of fluid in the pericardial sac surrounding the heart. In this case, the patient's symptoms of shortness of breath, tachycardia, and hypotension, along with the recent cardiac procedure, raise suspicion for pericardial effusion. The accumulation of fluid puts pressure on the heart, leading to compromised cardiac function and subsequent symptoms. Although other conditions such as PE, Choice *A*, can cause similar symptoms, the timeline and nature of the procedure make pericardial effusion more likely. DVT, Choice *C*, typically presents with localized leg pain or swelling and is less likely to cause these specific symptoms. Postoperative infection, Choice *D*, may present with additional signs, such as fever or localized redness, swelling, or discharge, which are not mentioned in this scenario.

31. D: The patient's symptoms and physical examination findings (localized chest pain, shortness of breath, reduced breath sounds, and dullness to percussion) are most consistent with a pleural effusion, or fluid accumulation in the pleural space. An MI, Choice *A*, would typically present with more severe chest pain and systemic symptoms. Atelectasis, Choice *B*, could cause similar symptoms but is less likely given the lack of common risk factors (such as recent surgery or immobility). A pneumothorax, Choice *C*, would typically present with sudden-onset dyspnea and potentially severe chest pain and would be less likely to cause dullness to percussion.

32. C: This patient's history of rheumatic fever, along with symptoms of fatigue and shortness of breath on exertion and echocardiographic findings of mitral stenosis and regurgitation, is most consistent with rheumatic heart disease affecting the mitral valve. Mitral valve prolapse, Choice *A*, is typically asymptomatic and would not explain the patient's symptoms. Aortic stenosis, Choice *B,* would not explain the findings on the echocardiogram. Tricuspid regurgitation, Choice *D,* would also not explain the echocardiogram findings, which are specific to the mitral valve.

33. D: TAVR is a minimally invasive procedure to replace the aortic valve, but it carries a risk of causing a stroke due to the potential for dislodging aortic plaque or valve tissue that can embolize to the brain. Acute kidney injury, Choice *A*, could occur due to contrast-induced nephropathy if contrast was used during the procedure, but it's not as directly related to the procedure as stroke. Pericardial effusion, Choice *B,* and aortic dissection, Choice *C,* are not common complications of TAVR.

34. B: In a patient with a history of hypertension, hyperlipidemia, and smoking, the symptoms of intermittent claudication (pain when walking that is relieved by rest) are classic for PAD. DVT, Choice *A,* would typically present with leg pain and swelling, not intermittent claudication. AAA, Choice *C,* and varicose veins, Choice *D,* are not directly associated with the symptoms described.

Pulmonary

1. C: Diffuse alveolar damage and impaired gas exchange are characteristic features of ARDS. The condition is characterized by widespread inflammation and injury to the alveoli, leading to impaired oxygenation and ventilation. Choice *A* may occur in conditions such as asthma, but it is not specific to ARDS. Choice *B* is more commonly associated with respiratory failure rather than ARDS. Choice *D* is characteristic of obstructive lung diseases such as COPD, not ARDS.

2. D: Short-acting beta-agonists are the first-line treatment for bronchodilation in acute asthma exacerbations. They provide rapid relief of bronchospasm by stimulating beta-2 adrenergic receptors in the airways. Choices *A*, *B*, and *C* may also be used in the management of asthma, but they are not the initial bronchodilator therapy. Corticosteroids help reduce airway inflammation and are commonly used in combination with short-acting beta-agonists. Long-acting beta-agonists and anticholinergic agents have a longer onset of action and are typically used for maintenance therapy in asthma.

3. B: For a patient with COPD, the nurse would anticipate a pulse oximetry reading range of 88%–92%. This range takes into account the impaired gas exchange and reduced oxygen saturation often seen in COPD. Choice *A* would indicate lower oxygen levels and potential hypoxemia. Although Choices *C* and *D* would be considered within the normal range, these higher levels are less likely to be seen in patients with COPD due to their underlying respiratory condition.

4. B: VATS is a type of minimally invasive thoracic surgery that involves the use of a scope and small incisions to perform the procedure. This technique allows for a less invasive approach than traditional open surgery. Choice *A* is incorrect because minimally invasive surgery does not involve a large incision. Choice *C* is incorrect because the use of a heart-lung machine, or cardiopulmonary bypass, is not typically required for thoracic procedures and is more commonly used in open-heart surgeries in which the heart itself needs to be temporarily bypassed. Choice *D* is incorrect because minimally invasive thoracic surgery typically involves the removal of a portion of the lung rather than the entire lung, which is also indicated in the question.

5. C: The primary goal of treatment for OSA is to provide CPAP therapy. CPAP helps keep the airway open during sleep by delivering a constant flow of pressurized air. It prevents airway collapse and maintains adequate oxygenation. Although Choices *A* and *B* may be beneficial in managing OSA, they are not the primary goals of treatment. Choice *D* is contraindicated in OSA because it can further relax the upper airway muscles and worsen the obstruction.

6. B: Performing thoracentesis is a priority intervention in managing a large pleural effusion. Thoracentesis involves the insertion of a needle or catheter into the pleural space to drain the fluid. It helps relieve symptoms such as dyspnea and improves lung function. Choice *A* may be considered if the effusion is due to CHF, but the primary intervention is to remove the accumulated fluid. Choice *C* may be beneficial in improving oxygenation, but it does not address the underlying issue of fluid accumulation. Choice *D* would be indicated if the pleural effusion is associated with infection, but it also does not address the underlying issue.

7. A: The patient's increased work of breathing, decreased oxygen saturation, and increased respiratory rate during the weaning trial indicate respiratory distress and the need for continued mechanical ventilation. These findings suggest that the patient is not yet ready to be extubated and requires ongoing support from the ventilator. Successful weaning from mechanical ventilation is characterized by stable vital signs, improved gas exchange, and minimal or no signs of respiratory distress. Choices *B* and *C* are incorrect because the patient's symptoms do not suggest a successful weaning or normal physiological response. Choice *D* is incorrect because the patient's respiratory distress is likely related to the physiological challenges of weaning rather than anxiety.

8. D: Pulmonary hypertension is characterized by increased pulmonary vascular resistance due to vasoconstriction and remodeling of pulmonary arterioles. These changes in the pulmonary vasculature result in elevated pressure within the pulmonary arteries, leading to right ventricular hypertrophy and eventual right heart failure. Choices *A*, *B*, and *C* do not accurately describe the pathophysiology of pulmonary hypertension.

9. C: A decreased level of consciousness can lead to respiratory depression due to the depressed responsiveness of the respiratory centers in the brain stem. The brain stem contains the respiratory centers responsible for regulating breathing. When the level of consciousness is reduced, such as in cases of head injury or sedation, the brain stem's ability to respond to changes in oxygen and carbon dioxide levels may be impaired, resulting in decreased respiratory drive and subsequent respiratory depression. Choice *A* is incorrect because increased stimulation of the respiratory centers in the brain stem would typically lead to increased respiratory drive, not depression. Choice *B* is unrelated to the respiratory centers and pertains to sympathetic nervous system activity. Choice *D* is incorrect because surfactant production is not directly influenced by the level of consciousness.

10. B: Acute respiratory failure is characterized by severe hypoxemia (low oxygen levels) and hypercapnia (elevated carbon dioxide levels). It typically occurs in patients with underlying lung diseases such as COPD, in which impaired gas exchange leads to inadequate oxygenation and retention of carbon dioxide. Choices *A*, *C*, and *D* are incorrect because they do not reflect the characteristic features of acute respiratory failure.

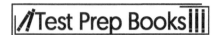

11. C: Providing chest physiotherapy is an appropriate nursing intervention to promote effective airway clearance in a patient with pneumonia. Chest physiotherapy involves various techniques, such as percussion, vibration, and postural drainage, to help mobilize and remove secretions from the lungs. Choice *A* is primarily used to relieve bronchospasm in conditions such as asthma and COPD. Choice *B* helps to improve lung volumes and prevent atelectasis but may not be sufficient for airway clearance in pneumonia. Choice *D* is an invasive procedure reserved for patients with a compromised airway or excessive secretions.

12. C: In this case, the patient's symptoms and physical examination findings are consistent with empyema. Choice *A* refers to the accumulation of air in the pleural space, leading to lung collapse, which does not align with the patient's presentation. Choice *B* involves the presence of blood in the pleural space, which is not indicated in this patient. Choice *D* also involves fluid in the pleural space, but it does not necessarily involve the presence of pus.

13. B: Implementing lung-protective ventilation strategies is a key component in the management of severe ARDS. Lung-protective ventilation involves using lower tidal volumes, maintaining PEEP, and avoiding high plateau pressures to minimize ventilator-induced lung injury. Choice *A* is not recommended as a routine therapy for ARDS. Choice *C* may be used to support oxygenation, but it does not address the underlying lung injury. Choice *D* may be considered in certain situations, such as fluid overload, but it is not a primary intervention for ARDS management.

14. B: A history of DVT is a significant risk factor for the development of PE. DVT occurs when a blood clot forms in the deep veins, typically in the legs. If this clot dislodges and travels to the pulmonary arteries, it can cause a PE. Patients with a history of DVT are at an increased risk of developing a PE. Choice *A* is a general risk factor for various health conditions but not specifically for a PE. Choice *C* is a respiratory condition that can lead to other pulmonary complications, but it is not a direct risk factor for a PE. Choice *D* falls within the normal range and is not a specific risk factor for a PE.

15. A: The findings of decreased breath sounds, asymmetrical chest expansion, and tracheal deviation to the unaffected side are suggestive of a pneumothorax. A pneumothorax occurs when air accumulates in the pleural cavity, leading to lung collapse and the associated clinical manifestations. Choices *B*, *C*, and *D* do not accurately describe this patient's symptoms.

16. C: Right ventricular hypertrophy is a characteristic finding in pulmonary hypertension. Pulmonary hypertension is characterized by elevated pressure in the pulmonary arteries, leading to increased workload on the right ventricle and subsequent hypertrophy. Choice *A* is a characteristic of left-sided heart failure. Choice *B* is incorrect because pulmonary hypertension is associated with increased pulmonary vascular resistance, not decreased resistance. Choice *D* is indicative of improved systolic function of the left ventricle and is not typically seen in pulmonary hypertension.

17. B: Assisting with endotracheal intubation is the priority action for a patient with severe respiratory depression. Endotracheal intubation provides a secure airway and allows for mechanical ventilation to support adequate oxygenation and ventilation. Choice *A* is not appropriate in this scenario because there is no indication or suspicion of opioid-induced respiratory depression. Choice *C* may help improve oxygenation temporarily but does not address the underlying respiratory depression. Choice *D* is important but should not delay the initiation of interventions to secure the airway and support ventilation.

18. C: The most appropriate response by the nurse is to explain that it is possible the patient was exposed to a different strain of the flu virus that wasn't covered by last year's vaccine. Influenza viruses can change and mutate over time, resulting in new strains that may not be fully protected by previous vaccinations. Choice *A* is incorrect because the flu vaccine is not 100% effective in preventing the flu. Choice *B* is incorrect because it wrongly implies that contracting the virus despite the vaccine is a common occurrence, which can lead to misunderstanding and reduced vaccine compliance. Choice *D* is incorrect because it does not address the possibility of exposure to a different strain of the virus and focuses on the timing of vaccine effectiveness, which is not relevant in this case.

19. D: Corticosteroids can increase the risk of developing oral thrush, a fungal infection in the mouth, because they can disrupt the natural balance of microorganisms. Rinsing the mouth with water after inhaler use helps to remove any residual medication and reduce the risk of oral thrush. Choice *A* is incorrect because rinsing the mouth does not affect the absorption of the medication in the lungs. Choice *B* is incorrect because rinsing the mouth does not prevent the corticosteroid from reaching the lungs effectively. Choice *C* is incorrect because rinsing the mouth primarily helps reduce the risk of developing oral side effects rather than decreasing throat-related side effects.

20. C: The findings of absent breath sounds on the right side, tracheal deviation to the right, and decreased chest expansion on the right side are suggestive of atelectasis, which is a common complication after pneumonectomy. Atelectasis refers to the collapse or closure of lung tissue, leading to reduced ventilation and decreased breath sounds. Choices *A*, *B*, and *D* do not accurately describe this patient's presentation.

21. D: Severe hypoxemia and hypercapnia would indicate acute respiratory failure rather than chronic respiratory failure. Acute respiratory failure is characterized by a sudden and severe impairment of gas exchange, resulting in low levels of oxygen (hypoxemia) and high levels of carbon dioxide (hypercapnia) in the blood. Choices *A* and *B* are more associated with chronic respiratory failure. Choice *C* is incorrect; normal ABG values would not be expected in either acute or chronic respiratory failure because both conditions result in abnormal gas exchange, leading to altered ABG values.

Endocrine/Hematology/Neurology/Gastrointestinal/Renal

1. B: Diabetes mellitus is a set of disorders that result in increased blood sugar levels in the body (hyperglycemia), also known as glucose. Glucose provides energy for the body, especially for our muscles, tissues, and the brain. When there is too much glucose in the blood, or hyperglycemia, there can be several symptoms that develop. The most common clinical manifestations of diabetes mellitus can be categorized as the "three Ps" or "the three polys"—polyuria, polydipsia, and polyphagia. These terms represent large increases in urination, thirst, and appetite. Choice *A* is incorrect as hematuria, or blood in the urine, is not typically associated with diabetes mellitus. Hematuria is typically seen with kidney disease, injury, or infection. Choice *C* is also incorrect as oliguria, or low urine output, occurs in patients with kidney disease or injury. Oliguria may also occur when a person is dehydrated or as a side effect of medications. Hemoptysis, or coughing up blood, is not a clinical manifestation of diabetes mellitus. It is typically caused by several different types of pulmonary conditions such as pneumonia, tuberculosis, or pulmonary embolism. This makes Choice *D* incorrect.

2. D: Diabetic ketoacidosis occurs in diabetic patients that cannot produce enough insulin and do not have control of their blood sugars. Since there is not enough glucose available for cellular use, the body breaks down fats in an attempt to get energy from another source. When the liver breaks down fat, the metabolic byproduct is ketone bodies which can be seen in the urine and blood. Positive nitrites and leukocytes in the urine are an indication of a possible urinary tract infection—not diabetic ketoacidosis—making Choices *A* and *B* incorrect. Positive bilirubin in the urine can indicate a possible liver condition, making Choice *C* incorrect.

3. B: Hyperglycemia, or increased blood sugar, is known to decrease the effectiveness of the body's immune system. As a result, patients with uncontrolled hyperglycemia are prone to secondary infections. Although hyperglycemia can affect the nerves of the eyes and cause blurred vision, there is no direct correlation between hyperglycemia and retinal detachment, making Choice *A* incorrect. Dysphagia, or difficulty swallowing, is not caused by hyperglycemia. Dysphagia is caused by damage to the nervous system or oral and esophageal cancers; therefore, Choice *C* is incorrect. Hyperglycemia can lead to severe fatigue, not hyperactivity, making Choice *D* also incorrect.

4. B: This patient is experiencing hypoglycemia, or low blood sugar. Hypoglycemia can become serious or even life-threatening, leading to possible coma or death if untreated. The most important action the nurse can take for a patient experiencing hypoglycemia is to administer 15mg of a fast-acting carbohydrate such as candy, fruit juice, or soda. The nurse should recheck the patient's blood sugar in fifteen minutes and should see improvement. Having the patient sit down and take deep breaths may be beneficial if they are feeling anxious, but it is not the primary step in managing hypoglycemia, making Choice *A* incorrect. It would not be appropriate to administer insulin to an individual who is experiencing hypoglycemia because insulin lowers blood sugar, making Choice *C* incorrect. This would not be safe for an individual already experiencing low blood sugar. Choice *D* is incorrect because the nurse should administer a fast-acting carbohydrate per mouth if the person is alert. If unconscious and hypoglycemic, the nurse can administer IM glucagon.

5. A: When a person has diabetic ketoacidosis, their blood becomes acidic. In an effort to compensate for the strongly acidic environment, the respiratory system will eliminate excess carbon dioxide through rapid and shallow respirations known as Kussmaul respirations. Oliguria, or low urine output, does not occur in patients with diabetic ketoacidosis. In fact, they experience polyuria, or increased urine output. This is because the kidneys will excrete any excess glucose in the body. This pulls fluid with it and leads to increased urination, making Choice *B* incorrect. Patients with diabetic ketoacidosis experience blood sugars at or above 300mg/dL, an indication of hyperglycemia. This makes Choice *C* incorrect. As mentioned above, patients with diabetic ketoacidosis experience hyperventilation in the form of Kussmaul respirations, not hypoventilation, making Choice *D* also incorrect.

6. B: Sickle cell disease is an inherited blood disorder characterized by red blood cells that have a sickle shape. The sickle shape causes less oxygen to be carried. Not only this, but the sickled red blood cells can clump together and block blood vessels. This can lead to a sickle cell crisis, causing severe pain, swelling in the extremities, and anemia. Providing adequate hydration can help slow or prevent the sickled cells from clumping together, allowing for blood to flow easier which leads to decreased pain and improved oxygenation. Applying ice packs to areas of pain should never be done for patients with sickle cell as they decrease circulation and lead to worsening pain, making Choice *A* incorrect. Warm packs are recommended as an alternative. Although exercise is important—especially for those with sickle cell to help prevent clumping of red blood cells—increased physical activity during a crisis can actually cause more pain due to the lack of oxygen being carried in the blood, making Choice *C* incorrect. Choice *D* is incorrect as sickle cell anemia is not related to immune function. Administering intravenous immunoglobulin would not be indicated for this patient; rather, intravenous immunoglobulin is used for autoimmune and infectious diseases such as Kawasaki disease and lymphocytic lymphoma.

7. D: Hemolytic anemia is caused by the destruction of red blood cells (RBCs). There are several potential factors that can cause RBCs to become destroyed or hemolyzed. Some of these include infections, medications, toxins, physical trauma, and inherited disorders. As red blood cells are destroyed, the yellow pigment known as bilirubin is produced. Elevated levels of bilirubin can lead to jaundice—the yellowing of the skin and sclera—dark urine, and even fatigue. This makes Choice *A* incorrect as elevated sodium levels are not related to hemolytic anemia, and clinical manifestations of elevated sodium levels include excessive thirst, oliguria, muscle twitching, and even seizures. Choice *B* is incorrect because increased red blood cell levels do not have a direct correlation with increased levels of bilirubin, only the destruction of red blood cells. Choice *C* is also incorrect as white blood cells do not have a direct correlation with bilirubin.

8. A: Iron deficiency anemia is a type of anemia typically caused by a low intake of iron in one's diet. Symptoms of iron-deficiency anemia include an inflamed and sore tongue, fatigue, brittle and spoon-shaped nails, dizziness, weakness, and cold hands or feet. Low iron levels cause the tongue to become reddened and painful because there is a lack of oxygen being received in the area. Choice *B* is incorrect as low iron levels would lead to increased fatigue and weakness due to the decreased oxygenation occurring in the body. Choice *C* is also incorrect as iron deficiency may cause increased heart rate, or tachycardia, due to the body attempting to compensate for low oxygen levels in the blood. Choice *D* is also incorrect because fingernail clubbing is a clinical manifestation of chronic obstructive pulmonary disorders. As mentioned above, iron-deficiency anemia leads to brittle and spoon-shaped nails due to malnutrition.

9. A: By definition, aplastic anemia is when the body stops producing (or doesn't produce enough) blood cells, including red and white blood cells and platelets. The bone marrow, where these cells are produced, is usually damaged by factors such as autoimmune disorders, radiation, and chemotherapy. Choice *B* is incorrect because physical trauma is a precursor to hemolytic anemia. Choice *C* is incorrect as low iron levels due to poor diet can cause iron-deficiency anemia. Choice *D* is also incorrect because this statement indicates the cause of sickle-cell anemia.

10. C: Coumadin, also known as warfarin, is an anticoagulant medication that prevents blood clots. Its mechanism of action is through interference with the synthesis of vitamin K-dependent clotting factors, which are important factors needed for blood to clot. Coumadin can be prescribed to prevent or even treat conditions including deep vein thrombosis or pulmonary embolism. Prothrombin time (PT) is the laboratory test used to measure how long it takes for blood to clot. Even though platelets are important in the clotting process, it does not indicate the effectiveness of Coumadin therapy. Instead, it is better at assessing the risk or possibility of bleeding or clotting disorders, making Choice *A* incorrect. Choice *B* is also incorrect because Coumadin does not have any effect on hemoglobin, or red blood cell count. Activated partial thromboplastin time (aPTT) is a test that can monitor the effectiveness of heparin therapy, another type of anticoagulant medication, making Choice *D* incorrect.

11. A: Liver failure has several causes ranging from autoimmune disorders to toxins or viruses. In chronic and severe liver failure, there is an increased risk for hepatic encephalopathy, a neurological disorder that is usually temporary. It is characterized by four stages, beginning with mild confusion and agitation and eventually leading up to a coma. Treatment includes the administration of lactulose and antibiotics. Glomerulonephritis is characterized by damage to the filtering mechanisms of the kidneys, usually caused by an immune response. It affects an entirely different organ; therefore, Choice *B* is incorrect. Hepatitis B is a liver infection that can potentially lead to liver failure, making Choice *C* incorrect.

Hepatitis B is not a complication of liver failure. Fatty liver disease can also lead to liver damage, especially in severe cases, but it is not a complication of liver failure itself. This makes Choice *D* incorrect.

12. C: Focal seizures are a type of seizure that occurs in one localized area in the brain. Manifestations of the seizure depend on where in the brain the seizure is occurring. Typically, common clinical manifestations include changes in senses and automatisms. Automatisms are repetitive movements such as lip-smacking or chewing. Choices *A, B,* and *D* are incorrect as these are clinical manifestations of tonic-clonic seizures.

13. D: Nausea and severe headache are signs of increased intracranial pressure (ICP) in patients diagnosed with hemorrhagic stroke. Increased ICP can lead to life-threatening complications including brain herniation and even death. Although aphasia, hemiplegia, and seizures are also potential complications of a patient who has had a hemorrhagic stroke, they are not related to the symptoms the patient described. This makes Choices *A, B,* and *C* incorrect.

14. C: When a person is having a seizure, it is important to time the length of the seizure as seizures extending beyond five minutes or more will typically need medication to stop. It is not recommended to put anything in a person's mouth who is having a seizure because this can cause choking, making Choice *A* incorrect. When a person is having a seizure, their movements and body should not be held down. This can cause more injuries and make the person aggressive or agitated because of possible confusion. This makes Choice *B* incorrect. Providing mouth-to-mouth breathing for a patient during a seizure is not recommended because the person's chest will stiffen during the seizure. When the seizure stops, the person should resume breathing normally, making Choice *D* incorrect.

15. B: Ischemic stroke is a stroke caused by a disruption of blood and oxygen flow to the brain, typically caused by a blood clot or narrowed vessel. Diabetes, smoking, and hypertension all increase the risk for ischemic strokes because they can contribute to blood clots and stenosis of arteries. Hypolipidemia is not a precursor to stroke, but hyperlipidemia is, making Choice *B* correct for this question. Hyperlipidemia, also known as high cholesterol, can lead to fatty plaque buildup in vessels, which also contributes to potential blood clots and vessel narrowing or stenosis.

16. B: GERD is a disease where the stomach contents, specifically stomach acid, regurgitates upwards from the stomach into the esophagus. This can cause symptoms such as heartburn, difficulty swallowing, and abdominal or chest pain. One way doctors diagnose GERD is through an upper gastrointestinal endoscopy, where a scope is placed into the patient's esophagus and the beginning of the stomach to identify any physical signs of irritation that can indicate GERD. A complete blood count cannot diagnose GERD, making Choice *A* incorrect. Even though GERD may cause lower blood counts, there are a multitude of things that can cause low blood counts, making this test inconclusive. An abdominal ultrasound helps identify things like kidney stones or tumors that may cause abdominal pain, making Choice *C* incorrect. Choice *D* is also incorrect as fasting glucose tests are tests used to help diagnose and manage diabetes, not GERD.

17. A: A lower GI bleed is typically caused by hemorrhoids or anal fissures, diverticulosis, colon polyps, and even cancers of the colon or anus. Because the bleeding is in the lower portion of the GI tract, the blood typically presents as frank red blood with the passage of stools, known as hematochezia. Choices *B* and *C* are incorrect because they are associated with an upper GI bleed. Hematemesis is the vomiting of blood, especially vomit that appears "coffee-ground-like." Melena is dark and tarry stools that may appear black in color. Choice *D* is also incorrect as diarrhea can have several causes and does not directly indicate the potential for a lower GI bleed.

18. B: An upper GI bleed is typically caused by esophagitis or gastritis, esophageal varices, or even cancer. It typically presents as a melena or hematemesis, and sometimes both. Melena is a dark and tarry stool, and hematemesis is vomiting coffee ground-like substances. Due to the increased fluid loss, it is essential that fluids are replaced to maintain blood pressure to support continuous perfusion to the patient's vital organs. Although drawing blood for a CBC, administering proton pump inhibitors, and providing the patient with a blood transfusion may also be done for a patient with a GI bleed, the nurse's first intervention is making sure that the patient is normovolemic, or has enough blood volume. This makes Choices *A, C,* and *D* incorrect.

19. D: A *Clostridium difficile* (*C. diff*) infection is an infection of the gastrointestinal system caused by the *Clostridium difficile* bacteria. It leads to frequent diarrhea, abdominal cramping, dehydration, and nausea. The most common cause of *C. diff* is antibiotic use, especially for an extended period of time. Treatment of *C. diff* includes antibiotics such as vancomycin. Choice *A* is incorrect as illicit drug use does not directly correlate to the development of a *C. diff* infection. GERD may cause similar symptoms to *C. diff* but having GERD does not lead to the development of *C. diff*, making Choice *B* incorrect. Poor handwashing can spread *C. diff* but doesn't necessarily lead to its development, making Choice *C* incorrect.

20. C: Gastric banding surgery is a type of bariatric surgery that separates the stomach into two different pouches to help restrict food intake for those who suffer from obesity. It is a reversible surgery. It is important for the nurse to educate the patient on following a liquid or puree-only diet for the first two to four weeks to help the stomach heal and reduce complications. Clear broths are an example of what the patient may eat during these first few weeks. Choice *A* is incorrect as any solid food eaten too prematurely can cause irritation and discomfort to the stomach, increasing the risk for complications. Choice *B* is also incorrect because carbonated beverages can cause additional discomfort and irritation. Not only this, but carbonated beverages will not provide the adequate nutrition needed to recover. Returning to the patient's regular diet as soon as he or she feels better is not recommended, making Choice *D* incorrect. Resuming a regular diet too soon may cause complications.

21. B: Acute kidney injury (AKI) is characterized by a sudden decrease in renal function or kidney failure. It typically has a short onset of a few hours or days. There are several risk factors that may lead to AKI, but one of the primary precursors is severe infection or sepsis. Sepsis can affect the cardiovascular system, causing reduced blood flow throughout the body. If the kidneys do not receive enough blood and oxygen, the kidney tissue becomes injured, leading to several other complications. Having a solitary kidney does not predispose a person to acute kidney injury, unless that solitary kidney has been affected detrimentally, making Choice *A* incorrect. While an excessive intake of sugary drinks may irritate the bladder and cause an increased risk of a urinary tract infection, consuming sugary drinks does not directly correlate with acute kidney injury, making Choice *C* incorrect. Choice *D* is incorrect because an older age, especially over sixty-five years, is a risk factor for AKI, not younger.

22. C: Hemodialysis is used for patients with chronic kidney disease that may not be able to receive a kidney transplant. The kidneys of these patients are unable to filter waste through their kidneys. In hemodialysis, blood is removed from the patient, filtered through what is called a dialysis membrane, and returned to the patient. Due to the large amount of blood that is out of the body at one time, it is important to make sure that blood pressures are assessed throughout the dialysis process to ensure that the patient does not experience hypotension or disequilibrium syndrome. Although monitoring respiratory status may be important in other areas of nursing, it is not a priority in dialysis care, making Choice *A* incorrect. Patients who are undergoing dialysis should avoid foods with high potassium, sodium, and phosphor levels because dialysis alters the electrolyte levels within the blood. High levels of these electrolytes can potentially become dangerous, making Choice *B* incorrect. Choice *D* is also incorrect because kidney transplants may not be an option for many patients—the nurse should not discuss this with the patient at this time.

23. A: A normal potassium level ranges from 3.5-5.3 mEq/L. A value of 7.0 mEq/L indicates hyperkalemia, which can present as muscle weakness, and, most commonly, cardiac arrhythmia. Choice *B* is incorrect as hyperreflexia is a clinical manifestation of hypocalcemia, or calcium levels below 8.5 mEq/dL. Choice *C* is incorrect as nausea and vomiting commonly present in patients with hyponatremia, or sodium levels less than 135 mEq/dL. Mental status changes are common in patients experiencing hypernatremia, or sodium levels greater than 145 mEq/dL which makes Choice *D* also incorrect.

24. C: Patients with chronic kidney disease and end-stage renal disease are unable to remove phosphorus, sodium, and potassium through their kidneys. These patients should avoid high phosphorus, sodium, and potassium diets. High levels of phosphorus can cause the weakening of the bones, as phosphorus binds to calcium and removes it from the body. White rice is a low-phosphorus food and is okay for the patient with end-stage renal disease to eat. Choices *A, B,* and *D* are all incorrect because these foods are high in phosphorus.

25. A: Patients with acute kidney injury are prone to retaining fluid because their kidneys are unable to filter effectively. The nurse needs to obtain daily weights at the same time every day with the patient wearing the same clothing to determine if the patient is retaining fluid. Administering intravenous spironolactone is inappropriate because spironolactone, although a diuretic, spares potassium. This can cause complications in patients with acute kidney injury who already are unable to filter electrolytes, making Choice *B* incorrect. Encouraging increased fluids is also inappropriate because the patient may be on a fluid restriction since they are prone to retaining fluid, making Choice *C* incorrect. Choice *D* is also incorrect because cyclosporine is an immunosuppressive drug that is not used in acute kidney injury. Cyclosporine is a nephrotoxic drug, which can cause damage to the kidneys.

Musculoskeletal/Multisystem/Psychosocial

1. D: A bedridden and immobile patient is at risk of developing pressure ulcers. For this reason, the nurse should turn and reposition the patient every two hours to alleviate the pressure on the patient's bony prominences since they are unable to reposition themselves. Although assisting the patient to perform range of motion exercises is helpful, it is not the primary intervention, making Choice *A* incorrect. Choice *B* is incorrect because compression stockings are not necessary in this case unless the patient is at a higher risk for deep vein thrombosis. Administering pain medication is also important but not the primary intervention for this immobile patient making Choice *C* incorrect. It is far more important to ensure that the patient does not develop pressure sores because that can lead to further complications such as infections.

2. D: When a patient falls, the first action the nurse should take is to assess their level of consciousness to help determine the patient's neurological status and potential injuries. If the patient is unconscious, they may have sustained a head injury that may need immediate attention. Choices *A, B,* and *C* are all appropriate interventions, but they are not the first intervention the nurse should take in this case, making them incorrect.

3. B: The patient's symptoms and clinical manifestations align with that of Parkinson's Disease. Parkinson's Disease is a neurodegenerative disorder that alters movement. These patients have a stooped posture and shuffling gait but also have difficulty initiating movements and stopping them. These patients also experience tremors and postural instability, putting them at increased risk for falls. Choice *A* is incorrect as Myasthenia Gravis is an autoimmune disorder that affects the signaling between nerve cells and muscles. This condition leads to muscle weakness and fatigue, ptosis, and difficulty chewing or smiling. Choice *C* is also incorrect because Multiple Sclerosis is an autoimmune disease that affects the central nervous system, leading to disruptions in nerve function. Common symptoms include numbness and tingling in the limbs and face, blurred or double vision, weakness, and fatigue. Choice *D* is also incorrect as Duchenne Muscular Dystrophy is a genetic disorder that affects the muscles and begins to appear in boys between ages two and five. Symptoms of this disorder include toe walking, enlarged calf muscles, weakness, and muscle wasting.

4. A: One of the most important parts of end-of-life care is pain control to ensure comfort. The appropriate intervention for this patient is to administer pain medication as needed. Choices *B, C,* and *D* are all incorrect. Encouraging the patient to eat their regular diet may cause discomfort since the body is naturally shutting down, so this should be avoided. When patients no longer want to eat or drink, they may eat ice chips to help with any dryness or oral discomfort. The dying process is emotional; therefore, preventing visitors from being with the patient may cause additional stress which goes against maintaining comfort for the dying patient. Since the body is naturally shutting down, the patient is not expected to participate in physical activity, and they may not have enough energy to do so. Making them do so would be inappropriate at this stage.

5. C: Patients with a history of recurrent urinary tract infections have a higher risk of developing CAUTI due to the presence of bacteria that congregates in the urinary tract. Although those who have urinary incontinence also have a higher risk for CAUTI, having a history of recurrent urinary tract infections is a stronger risk factor for the development of CAUTI, making Choice *B* incorrect. Choices *A* and *D* are both incorrect because neither a broken leg nor hypotension necessarily leads to an increased risk for CAUTI.

6. C: It is important to perform hand hygiene before and after handling the PICC because handwashing is the most effective way to prevent the spread of germs. Choice *A* is incorrect as changing the dressing every twenty-four hours is unnecessary and may cause an even further risk of infection. Dressings should be changed every five to seven days, or when they are visibly soiled. Choice *B* is incorrect because using the same infusion tubing for all medications increases the risk of contamination – infusion tubing can be used for up to three days as long as it is the same medication. Choice *D* is incorrect as a sterile technique should be used during dressing changes.

7. A: The most effective intervention to prevent a surgical site infection (SSI) in a patient is to administer prophylactic antibiotics before surgery. Choices *B* and *C* are also appropriate interventions, but they are not the most effective. Choice *D*, drawing labs prior to surgery, may be necessary to determine patient stability, but this intervention does not directly prevent SSI.

8. C: Patients with the influenza virus may be given Tamiflu, an antiviral, which can help improve and treat symptoms. It should be administered within forty-eight hours of symptom onset to have the best efficacy. Amoxicillin would not be administered because it is an antibiotic that is solely used to treat bacterial infections, making Choice *A* incorrect. Choice *B* is also incorrect because fluconazole is an antifungal medication that is used to treat fungal infections. Doxorubicin would not be administered to a patient with influenza either, as this drug is a chemotherapy drug used to slow the growth of cancer cells, making Choice *D* incorrect.

9. D: MRSA is an antibiotic-resistant bacteria that is spread through physical contact. Contact precautions include a gown and gloves. Choices *A, B,* and *C* are all incorrect because MRSA is not an airborne disease and is not spread through droplets. Contact precautions are more effective in preventing the spread of MRSA than standard precautions.

10. B: Gabapentin is an anticonvulsant and nerve pain medication that is used frequently for patients who have chronic pain. Some of the major side effects include fatigue, dizziness, nausea, vomiting, and diarrhea. The nurse should make sure that the patient is not heavily sedated to the point of danger because if the patient attempts to ambulate, they may fall and become injured. Choice *A* is incorrect because gabapentin does not cause hyperactivity but instead fatigue and tiredness. Choices *C* and *D* are also incorrect because gabapentin is known to cause bradycardia and diarrhea, not tachycardia or constipation.

11. B: Opioid analgesics cause several side effects including constipation, respiratory depression, nausea, and sedation among many others. The most important adverse effect the nurse should monitor for is respiratory depression, as opioids depress the central nervous system. The nurse should monitor respiratory rate, pattern, and depth as well as oxygen saturation levels. If severe respiratory depression occurs, it can become fatal. Choices *A, C,* and *D* are all incorrect because they are not the priority adverse effects the nurse should monitor when administering opioid analgesics.

12. B: The most appropriate response from the nurse is to discuss reviewing the patient's nutritional status and any contributing factors to their weight loss, which can include nausea or difficulty swallowing. It would be counterintuitive and unsafe to have a patient eat solids if they are having difficulty swallowing. Choice *A* is incorrect as the nurse should collaborate with the multidisciplinary team to determine a plan of care for nutrition, energy levels, and quality of life during the dying process. However, it is true that at the end stages of life, patients become weaker and do not have an interest in consuming food compared to previously. Choice *C* is also incorrect because having a patient eat at the end of the dying process may cause additional discomfort and decrease the quality of life. Choice *D* is also incorrect because the additional fluids administered may cause edema and discomfort for the patient, again decreasing the quality of life.

13. A: Having an altered mental status can be an indicator of a medical emergency. Therefore, the nurse should assess vital signs to help identify physiological changes and determine appropriate interventions for the patient. Choice *B* is incorrect as Narcan is an opioid antagonist used for opioid overdoses. Although opioid overdose may cause an altered level of consciousness, it is not the only symptom. Patients also present with bradypnea, small pupils, and blue skin due to decreased circulation. Choice *C* is also incorrect. Trying to get the patient to eat something with an altered level of consciousness can cause an increased risk for aspiration since they may not be able to swallow safely. Choice *D* is incorrect as well because Haldol is an antipsychotic, which is usually administered to reduce aggression and agitation in people experiencing psychosis.

14. D: The most likely cause for the patient's delirium is their alcohol withdrawal since being admitted into the hospital. Common symptoms of alcohol withdrawal include tremors, anxiety, sweating, increased heart rate, delirium, and, in severe cases, seizures. Although Choices *A, B,* and *C* can all potentially cause delirium, they are not the most likely cause in this situation.

15. B: The biggest risk factor for the development of dementia is increasing age. In fact, once over sixty-five years of age, a person's risk for developing dementia doubles every five years. Frequent infections are not considered a risk factor for dementia, making Choice *A* incorrect. Choices *C* and *D* are also incorrect because research has shown that being female and having hypertension may increase an individual's risk of developing dementia, not being male or having hypotension.

16. B: For patients experiencing aggression and agitation, it is best to divert their attention while maintaining a calm tone to prevent escalation of the situation. Choice *A* is incorrect because leaving their room may cause increased frustration. Administering Haldol, an antipsychotic drug, to the patient is unwarranted in this situation. Haldol is typically used in psychiatric emergencies for people experiencing psychosis, making Choice *C* incorrect. Choice *D* is also incorrect as this statement may escalate their behavior.

17. B: Lorazepam is a drug from the benzodiazepine medication class that is prescribed to treat anxiety and panic disorders. Choices *A, C,* and *D* are all incorrect as they are not anti-anxiety medications. Risperidone is an antipsychotic medication. Carvedilol is a cardiac medication for arrhythmias and hypertension. Diphenhydramine is an antihistamine used for allergic reactions.

18. D: Suicidal thoughts or ideation is a potential side effect of many antidepressants, specifically in the beginning stages of treatment. Research has shown that the risk for suicidal ideation is higher in people less than twenty-five years old who have just recently started antidepressant therapy. The nurse should monitor for this side effect for this patient because of their age. Fever, rash, and hallucinations are not side effects of antidepressants, making Choices *A, B,* and *C* incorrect.

19. C: Patients diagnosed with alcohol withdrawal present with insomnia, anxiety, tremors, and other symptoms. The amount of time that symptoms last depends on the severity of the person's alcohol dependence and other factors such as co-occurring conditions. Generally, it can last for several days or weeks. Benzodiazepines such as lorazepam are widely used for patients with alcohol withdrawal because this class of drugs works on the same neuroreceptor that alcohol binds to within the brain. Benzodiazepines help calm down the overactive nervous system that occurs during alcohol withdrawal and can help with the symptoms. It is best taken every two to four hours around the clock because this allows for a steady blood level, lessening the recurrence of withdrawal symptoms. Giving the medication once daily or only once at the onset of symptoms is insufficient, making Choices *A* and *D* incorrect. Choice *B* is also incorrect because only administering the medication as needed causes blood levels to alter and allows for the recurrence of withdrawal symptoms.

20. A: Excessive, long-term drinking of alcohol can cause inflammation, scarring, and cirrhosis of the liver. These can potentially lead to liver disease, liver failure, and even death. Although alcohol abuse can weaken the immune system, causing individuals who abuse alcohol to be more susceptible to infections, alcohol abuse does not directly cause infectious diseases, making Choice *B* incorrect. Choice *C* is also incorrect because alcohol abuse does not directly cause hormonal imbalances, but it can affect the functioning of the endocrine system. This may lead to hormonal imbalances as a secondary effect. Choice *D* is also incorrect because alcohol abuse can certainly exacerbate symptoms of genetic disorders, but they do not necessarily cause these disorders.

Professional Caring and Ethical Practice

1. C: Since the patient is expressing concerns about life at home after discharge, the nurse must advocate for the patient and coordinate with their healthcare team to create a plan of care that addresses the patient's concerns and promotes their safety and health well after discharge. If the nurse discharges the patient without addressing their concerns, it can potentially harm the patient and violate ethical principles. Although providing written instructions for the patient on when to take their medications and what they are for may be helpful, it is not the best choice to address their concerns, making Choice *A* incorrect. Coordinating a home health nurse to visit the patient after discharge may be helpful, but before this the healthcare team needs to determine the needs of the patient, making Choice *B* incorrect. Choice *D* is also incorrect as the nurse should not pass the responsibility onto the family of the patient.

2. B: The nurse should take action to address the medication error and prevent harm to the patient. By notifying the healthcare provider and the pharmacy of the error, the situation can be fixed promptly. Administering an additional bag of antibiotics to compensate for the incorrect dose would not be ethical and may cause more harm to the patient, making Choice *A* incorrect. Allowing the current antibiotic to finish infusing and redrawing blood tests is also not appropriate. Depending on the dose the patient receives, this could cause additional harm, making Choice *C* incorrect. Not only this, but the nurse cannot administer an additional bag unless prescribed by the healthcare provider. Informing the patient and their family about the medication error is an important action, but it is not the first action the nurse should take to prevent further harm to the patient, making Choice *D* incorrect also.

3. A: The nurse should facilitate effective communication between the patient and the healthcare team. The nurse can coordinate with another nurse on their unit who speaks the patient's language to assist in communication or utilize interpreter services within the hospital. Choice *B* is incorrect as having a family member may be helpful, but there could be difficulty explaining medical terms if the family member doesn't understand themselves. Using a translation app is a possibility, but it can cause miscommunication because sometimes words and phrases are not translated correctly, making Choice *C* incorrect. Documenting the communication difficulties in the patient's chart has no effect on facilitating effective communication between the patient and the healthcare team, making Choice *D* incorrect.

4. A: Patients who have difficulties with communication may exhibit frustration. The nurse should show empathy and support through nonverbal communication which can include therapeutic touch, smile, or nodding for reassurance. Choice *B* is incorrect as restricting visitors reduces the patient's social support and can cause unnecessary distress. Choice *C* is also incorrect because even though the patient has communication difficulties, they do not have hearing difficulties; therefore, the nurse should not change how she speaks to the patient because they still understand what she is saying. Choice *D* is also incorrect since pretending like the patient is speaking normally and failing to acknowledge the difficulty can cause even more distress to the patient.

5. D: Respecting a patient's preferences and goals is an important part of compassionate care, especially for those who have been diagnosed with a terminal illness. The nurse should collaborate with the patient's healthcare team as well as the patient to create a palliative care plan that supports the patient's goals. This allows the promotion of dignity and comfort during the dying process. Choice *A* is incorrect as the nurse would not solely make this decision. It is a decision that is made by the patient and healthcare team together. Choice *B* is also incorrect as this ignores the patient's ultimate wishes.

Providing emotional support to the patient is certainly helpful, especially during the dying process, but it is not the only or most important action that can be taken, making Choice *C* incorrect.

6. C: The nurse should acknowledge the child's feelings and address their concerns to provide caring and compassionate care. By explaining things in a way that the child can understand, their anxiety may decrease. Choice *A* is incorrect as this may cause increased anxiety since the child might not have any idea of what is going on. Choice *B* is also incorrect as this doesn't represent compassionate and therapeutic care—it does not address the child's concerns. Choice *D*, utilizing diversion techniques, may be helpful to decrease the child's anxiety temporarily, but it will not address the root cause of their anxiety regarding the surgery.

7. C: The nurse should use the patient's chosen name and pronouns to respectfully address them. Choice *A* is incorrect as avoiding using pronouns can make the nurse-patient interaction awkward and nontherapeutic, causing unnecessary stress for the patient. Choice *B* is also incorrect as this may be dismissive of the patient's gender identity. Choice *D* is also incorrect because this does not assist the current interaction with the patient.

8. A: Using a professional interpreter is important to provide safe and effective care for the patient. The professional interpreter is trained in medical terminology to help explain medical conditions. Using a family member to interpret is not the best choice as they can be biased and may withhold information if they do not want the patient to know everything that is happening medically. Not only this, but family members may not fully understand medical terminology. This makes Choice *B* incorrect. Choice *C* is incorrect because this will not help the patient's understanding. Choice *D* is also incorrect as they may not be able to read or write in their own language, and they also may not understand medical terminology.

9. D: In Asian cultures, family plays an important part in decision-making, especially when it comes to health. Allowing the patient's family members to participate in the patient's care and decision-making is the most culturally competent option as it will make the patient feel more comfortable with the care that they receive. Using a professional interpreter for communication may be helpful if the patient speaks another language, but this was not stated in the question, making Choice *A* incorrect. Choice *B* is incorrect as Asian culture views prolonged eye contact as rude and disrespectful. Choice *C* is incorrect also as the patient's health care team would not make the decisions for the patient. The patient is involved in the decision-making process of their care.

10. B: The most effective method to educate families and facilitate learning is utilizing practice dolls and mannequins. This allows those who are learning to gain hands-on experience so they can be comfortable on their own. Although playing a pre-recorded video demonstration may be helpful, it is not the best choice because it does not allow the expectant parents to have hands-on practice, making Choice *A* incorrect. Providing written step-by-step instructions may be helpful as a reference, but it isn't the most effective way to facilitate learning, making Choice *C* incorrect. This is also true for Choice *D*, making it also incorrect.

11. C: Having the group participate in a discussion regarding their personal asthma triggers and experiences will help enhance the education based on the group's experiences. Although Choices *A, B,* and *D* may be helpful, discussing personal experiences may be more beneficial overall to understanding how asthma triggers can be managed.

12. B: There are a lot of concerns and misconceptions related to childhood immunizations. Having a group discussion will allow the nurse to answer questions and debunk misconceptions so parents can leave the informational group with better knowledge. Choice *A* would not be helpful as parents do not need to know the immunizations needed for their children; this is something that their primary care provider will monitor. The role of the parents is to bring their children for routine well-child and immunization visits. Choice *C* is also incorrect as this may not answer the parents' concerns. An informational video may be helpful to incorporate within the group, but it shouldn't be the only component. Choice *D* is incorrect since parents are not allowed to administer immunizations.

13. D: Although all of the options may be useful in helping the patient feel more comfortable with their colostomy, having the patient participate in a colostomy support group will help the patient learn more than just how to apply and remove the colostomy appliance. The patient can learn the struggles of other people with colostomies, and how they manage them in their daily lives. Choices *A, B,* and *C* should be implemented to help the patient understand how to care for their ostomy, but having the support group will provide a different level of support and insight for the patient.

14. A: An endocrinologist specializes in the management of hormonal disorders, including diabetes, and should be consulted to create an improved treatment plan for the patient. A gastroenterologist is a doctor that specializes in disorders of the gastrointestinal tract. They would not be consulted for this patient, making Choice *B* incorrect. Although consulting a dietician may be helpful as a part of the treatment plan for this patient, it is not the best choice in this case, making Choice *C* incorrect. Choice *D* is also incorrect because a urologist specializes in disorders that affect the urinary tract, which is unrelated to the pathophysiology of diabetes.

15. D: This option can help with outreach to underserved communities since the fairs will be held outside of the clinic. Choice *A* does not have any benefit to the underserved communities making this choice incorrect. Choice *B* is also incorrect as this only benefits the clinic's patients and not underserved communities that may not receive regular healthcare. Choice *C* is incorrect as this also does not provide appropriate outreach to individuals outside of the clinic.

16. A: Collaborating with a wound care specialist, such as a wound-ostomy nurse, can allow for appropriate wound care that will increase the likelihood of positive outcomes for the patient. The nurse may collaborate with the patient care assistant to help during wound dressing procedures but would not solely collaborate with them making Choice *B* incorrect. Although notifying the primary care provider may be important to keep them up to date with the patient's health, a wound specialist would be the best to collaborate with making Choice *C* incorrect. Nutrition is very helpful with wound healing, so consulting and working with a dietician may be helpful; however, since the wound is more complex, wound care should be managed first, making Choice *D* incorrect.

17. B: Interdisciplinary collaboration requires open and timely communication between healthcare providers. The nurse should share pertinent test results with the members of the patient's healthcare team so that their care plan is well-rounded. Choice *A* is incorrect as the primary care provider would already have a record of the patient's health history. Choice *C* is incorrect as simply making appointments with the patient's specialists does not constitute collaboration. Choice *D* is also incorrect because keeping the patient's medical information private and excluding their healthcare team from this information would not lead to any benefit for the patient.

18. C: The nurse should conduct a root cause analysis to determine the reasons for increased readmission rates prior to taking any interventions. This will then allow the nurse to collaborate with other healthcare professionals to decrease readmission rates. Choice *A* is helpful but does not address the root cause. Choice *B* is also helpful, but this cannot be done until the root cause is addressed. Choice *D* is also incorrect as the nurse does not know whether the cause of readmissions is due to medication compliance. However, this is an important idea to discuss during discharge teaching.

19. A: By identifying the underlying factors that are contributing to errors, the nurse is taking a systems approach. This action allows the nurse to determine weaknesses and how to improve them. Collecting data on the performance of individual staff members does not account for factors that may be causing them to have such performances, making Choice *B* incorrect. Choice *C* is also incorrect since the nurse needs to understand the root cause of errors prior to implementing new protocols. Protocols should be tailored to the cause. Choice *D* is also incorrect as this doesn't solve why the errors are occurring.

20. D: Systems thinking involves utilizing several interconnected components to provide a holistic approach to a patient's care. This includes considering their social, psychological, and physical needs, not just the physical needs of the patient. The nurse should coordinate with several healthcare professionals who can help the patient meet their various needs. Choice *A* is incorrect since limiting the identification to only physical systems and issues is not holistic. Choice *B* is incorrect as this also only focuses on one aspect of their treatment plan. Although implementing disease-specific interventions for the patient may be helpful, these interventions fail to acknowledge the psychological and social factors that the patient experiences. This makes Choice *C* incorrect.

21. B: Systems thinking involves understanding the multiple factors that contribute to an event. The nurse should consider all of the potential factors that contributed to the medication error as part of her root cause analysis. Choice *A* is incorrect since focusing on the nurse who made the error does not provide further explanation as to why it happened or how it can be prevented. Choice *C* is incorrect as this should already be in place and is part of the rights of medication administration. The nurse manager should already be aware of the event, making Choice *D* incorrect.

22. B: Since the complication is unexpected, the nurse should reference literature to gather evidence-based information on the surgery and potential adverse effects. This can help her collaborate with the interdisciplinary team to create an effective plan of care for the patient. Discussing the complication with the surgeon should certainly occur, but it is not the best option to help the patient, especially if the surgeon is unaware of this type of complication. This makes Choice *A* incorrect. The complication should be documented in the patient's medical record, but it is not the best choice the nurse can make to help the patient, making Choice *C* incorrect. The charge nurse should also be notified of the complication, but this is not the best choice the nurse can make to help the patient, making Choice *D* incorrect.

23. A: The nurse should research and gather evidence to better understand the adverse reaction, its possible causes, and ways to prevent and manage it. This is an example of clinical inquiry. Documenting the adverse reaction in the patient's medical record is important but is not an example of clinical inquiry, making Choice *B* incorrect. Notifying the healthcare provider of the reaction is necessary but also is not an example of clinical inquiry, making Choice *C* incorrect. Choice *D* is incorrect since this would only provide information about how to administer the medication and would not provide answers on what caused the adverse reaction and how to prevent or manage it.

24. D: Randomized control trials are the best piece of evidence to use when evaluating the effectiveness of interventions or treatments. Since participants are randomly assigned to different interventions or control groups, determining cause-and-effect relationships between interventions and outcomes is more accurate than other types of research. Qualitative studies are not the best primary source of evidence since they have a potential for bias and have limited generalizability, making Choice *A* incorrect. Choice *B* is also incorrect as this does not provide evidence-based findings and may also have a potential for bias. Choice *C* is incorrect as these findings aren't generalizable to larger populations since they may not be widely representative of such populations.

25. C: When implementing new evidence-based practices, it is important to educate the staff on what the practice is, why it is being implemented, and how to follow it. This will allow for a more seamless transition into practice. Choice *A* is incorrect as simply hanging posters about the new practices in the break room has little to no effect on applying them to clinical practice. Most staff members may overlook them and not pay attention. Choice *B* is incorrect because these practices have already been proven to have positive outcomes. They do not need to be tested by the nurse individually prior to implementation. Choice *D* is also incorrect as the staff members need hands-on education about these practices with explanations.

PCCN Practice Test #3

To keep the size of this book manageable, save paper, and provide a digital test-taking experience, the 3rd practice test can be found online. Scan the QR code or go to this link to access it:

testprepbooks.com/bonus/pccn

SCAN ME

The first time you access the tests, you will need to register as a "new user" and verify your email address.

If you have any issues, please email support@testprepbooks.com.

Dear PCCN Test Taker,

Thank you for purchasing this study guide for your PCCN exam. We hope that we exceeded your expectations.

Our goal in creating this study guide was to cover all of the topics that you will see on the test. We also strove to make our practice questions as similar as possible to what you will encounter on test day. With that being said, if you found something that you feel was not up to your standards, please send us an email and let us know.

We have study guides in a wide variety of fields. If you're interested in one, try searching for it on Amazon or send us an email.

Thanks Again and Happy Testing!
Product Development Team
info@studyguideteam.com

FREE Test Taking Tips Video/DVD Offer

To better serve you, we created videos covering test taking tips that we want to give you for FREE. **These videos cover world-class tips that will help you succeed on your test.**

We just ask that you send us feedback about this product. Please let us know what you thought about it—whether good, bad, or indifferent.

To get your **FREE videos**, you can use the QR code below or email freevideos@studyguideteam.com with “Free Videos” in the subject line and the following information in the body of the email:

a. The title of your product

b. Your product rating on a scale of 1-5, with 5 being the highest

c. Your feedback about the product

If you have any questions or concerns, please don’t hesitate to contact us at info@studyguideteam.com.

Thank you!

SCAN HERE

Made in United States
Troutdale, OR
01/27/2024

17199363R00151